NARRATIVE
SOCIOLOGY

NARRATIVE SOCIOLOGY

EDITED BY

Leslie Irvine, Jennifer L. Pierce,
and Robert Zussman

Vanderbilt University Press
Nashville

Library of Congress Cataloging-in-Publication Data
Names: Irvine, Leslie J., 1958- editor. | Pierce, Jennifer L., 1958- editor.
   | Zussman, Robert, editor.
Title: Narrative sociology / edited by Leslie J. Irvine, Jennifer L. Pierce,
   Robert Zussman.
Description: Nashville : Vanderbilt University Press, 2019. | Includes
   bibliographical references.
Identifiers: LCCN 2018047487 | ISBN 9780826522450 (paperback)
Subjects: LCSH: Sociology. | BISAC: SOCIAL SCIENCE / Sociology / General.
Classification: LCC HM585 .N37 2019 | DDC 301—dc23 LC record available at https://
lccn.loc.gov/2018047487

ISBN 978-0-8265-2245-0 (paperback)

CONTENTS

INTRODUCTION

"Narrative sociology" is not a recognized subfield in sociology in the sense that social stratification or the sociology of the family or social movements is a subfield. There is no journal of narrative sociology, no American Sociological Association section, not even a collection of sociologists who swap secret handshakes. At most, narrative is a general approach to sociology. This approach is characterized by the convictions that people make meanings, that meaning is organized in sequences (which is to say that meaning is made through stories), and that these meanings have consequences at both individual and collective levels. But even such a basic statement requires qualification. At least a few sociologists advocate for "narrative positivism," a notion that sequence matters even in the absence of meaning. There is also a deep divide between those who treat narrative as a form of causal explanation and those who treat narrative as something to be explained.

These qualifications notwithstanding, narrative analysis is a powerful presence within sociology (and the social sciences more generally). Since the 1980s, the number of books and articles in sociology that take narrative seriously, whether methodologically or substantively, has exploded. Nearly half a million articles related to narrative appeared in sociology journals from 1980–2010 compared to just over ten thousand in the previous thirty years. Joined to related developments in anthropology, sociolinguistics, political science, and critical legal studies, these developments have amounted to nothing less than a "narrative turn." Sociologists who have followed this turn have developed new approaches to long-standing questions—where identities come from and how they influence social action; how inequalities are maintained and reproduced; why some social movements are able to gain political traction when others don't; and how authority and power become institutionalized—while upsetting longstanding answers to questions about culture, self-interest, and instrumental rationality.

Within substantive areas, narrative has an uneven presence. Perhaps most notably, narrative has been critical to the various subfields of sociology that deal with the social construction of categories (gender, race, sexuality, disability studies, and the sociology of deviance). Indeed, wherever everyday meaning-making is at issue, narrative has been fundamental, as in the sociology of knowledge, the sociology of the self, and the sociology of medicine, especially that part of the sociology of medicine that deals with the experience of illness. Narrative has also been critical to those fields that deal with the collective (as well as the individual) creation of meaning, as in the study of social movements and, to a lesser degree, organizations more generally. As a causal approach, narrative has been critical to historical and comparative sociology. Curiously, given the parallels between narrative sociology and literary criticism, narrative has not been particularly important in most versions of the sociology of culture. (The study of collective memory is an important exception.) Neither has narrative been deployed much in the sociology of education, economic sociology, the sociology of religion, or demography. This does not mean, however, that there cannot be narrative approaches to these subfields; to the contrary, it means there is an opportunity to innovate.

Collectively, our interest in narrative stems from its contribution to meaning. We are particularly interested in how narrative creates selves and gives meaning to lives. Moreover, we find narrative sociologically relevant because stories that can seem individual and singular are not. They are always connected to some kind of social group, cultural trope, genre, historical event, and so on. Narratives are at once individual and social. Further, stories tied to institutions and social collectivities can be incredibly powerful. Thus, we see narratives as meaning-making, but also as fundamentally sociological. The three of us have individually studied, taught, and written about narrative for over two decades. Although our interests have taken us in different directions, our discussions have long suggested the presence of theories, approaches, and works that we consider essential to the field. It is time, then, to make the narrative approach explicit.

We do not imagine this volume as a simple summary. Rather, we imagine it as an intervention, an effort to create and define a field that does not yet quite exist. We do not shy away from the task of creating a new canon, of defining classics, of delineating a range of effective research methods, of identifying exemplars of narrative analysis, of setting the boundaries for a field in the making. It is time for a volume that makes connections among ideas (and among sociologists), that brings together theoretical, methodological, and substantive statements about narrative, and that brings together material on identity and social movements and inequality written by scholars who are often only vaguely aware of one another's work.

Themes of the Book

This book has three parts. Part I addresses general issues, such as the definition of narrative and the "narrative turn" in sociology, the distinction between those who approach narrative as explanation and those who understand narrative as an object of inquiry, and the sociological work narratives do in constructing meanings, selves, social groups, institutions, and collective resistance. Part II provides several examples of what we call "sociological narrative forms," that is, a particular way of writing sociological knowledge and structuring the text. Part III examines the work narratives can do sociologically in varied institutional contexts. Here we focus on both narratives "from above," that is, narratives that are imposed on individuals and groups by culture, institutions, and influential figures, and narratives "from below," or narratives that individuals produce in resisting the authority of culture, institutions, and powerful figures.

PART I

Varieties of Narrative

Part IA

What Is Narrative?

In everyday usage, "narrative" has come to refer to many forms of speech—from ways of framing arguments to almost any strand of interpretation. We have no deep objections to this broad use of the term, but in this book we mean something more specific. In this, we follow the lead of literary scholars and linguists (Barthes 1977; Labov 1972). For them, narrative takes the form of a story with an identifiable beginning, middle, and end—a classic formulation that dates to Aristotle's *Poetics*. In narrative, sequence matters. As historian Hayden White puts it, "narrativizing" life experience means "imposing upon it the form of a story" (1980: 7). However, stories are more than sequences. They also have a point of view. (We are using the terms *story* and *narrative* interchangeably here.)[1] Stories also have narrators. To belabor the obvious, stories do not exist apart from someone (or some*ones*) who tells them. These narrators take many forms—collective or individual, engaged or dispassionate, consensual or conflictual. Stories need not take chronological form (although they often do), but they always involve the organization of events in some relationship to one another. Thus, the narrator does not describe a single event nor every imaginable event, but rather selects those deemed most relevant to a point of view while deleting others. This is the selective dimension of narrative. Most importantly, narrative links events through a plot that gives the events meaning. Plots may involve, among other things, intention, fate, or a moral lesson. Plot distinguishes narrative from other written or spoken forms, such as a chronicle (a mere list of events), an argument (more abstract), or a description (often lacking a distinctive point of view). Without the plot, events would be meaningless occurrences with no apparent relationship or significance; there would be no story.

This definition of narrative, though not shared by all social scientists, has influenced their varied uses of the term. Psychologist Donald Polkinghorne, for instance, describes narrative as "the primary form by which human experience is made meaningful" and narrative meaning as "a cognitive process that organizes human experiences into temporally meaningful episodes" (1988: 1). Sociologist Arthur Frank understands narrative in simpler terms as "one thing happens in consequence of another" (2010: 25). Laurel Richardson (1990) recognizes the literary dimensions of narrative and argues that it is one of two modes of thought in sociology, the other being the logico-scientific (see also Bruner 1986). In her view, sociology privileges the logico-scientific mode and suppresses the narrative mode in an effort to distinguish itself from literature. She rejects this simplistic dichotomy, arguing that *all* forms of writing, including the logico-scientific, use literary devices (see also Maines 1993).

Whatever definition of narrative sociologists may use, they make a common distinction in their approach to studying narrative. Narrative can be a way of doing sociology as a means of exposition and explanation, or narrative can represent something to be explained. Polkinghorne characterizes these as the *process* of making a story, in the first case, and the *results* of that process, in the second (1988:13). In the first approach, sociologists may adopt a narrative style in their writing and use that narrative to explain why a specific event occurred. This approach has a long history in sociology (see Maines 1993). For example, in *The Challenger Launch Decision*, Diane Vaughan writes an organizational narrative that details the repeated, collective failures in decision-making at NASA that led up to the *Challenger* disaster (Vaughan, this volume). In *On the Run*, Alice Goffman begins with a narrative of the assault of one of the young men in her study, which we include here in Part II. Goffman's brief narrative establishes the major issues explored throughout her book. In *Sidewalk*, Mitchell Duneier (1999) uses narrative to immerse readers in the daily routines of the book vendors in Greenwich Village.

In the second approach, sociologists investigate different kinds of narratives and the uses they can have in different contexts. One frequent use involves constructing both individual and collective identities. For example, Arthur Frank (this volume) examines different "voices" of illness, or the different narratives through which seriously ill people characterize their experiences. Leslie Irvine (1999) analyzes how members of the twelve-step group Codependents Anonymous use the discourse of codependency to formulate different narratives of the self. Thomas DeGloma (2014) explores the common logic through which people produce unique narratives of "awakenings," or radical transformations of consciousness, perception, or orientation to life. Scott Harris (2006) examines how couples assemble the "raw materials" of their experiences into stories, and portrays equality and inequality as "situated narrative accomplishments" (p. 45). Similarly, Ken Plummer (1995) describes what he terms "sexual stories," including stories of "coming out," and analyzes how they have operated politically to break cultural silences about taboo topics. And, in a notable example, Francesca Polletta (1998) argues that narratives of "spontaneous" resistance helped form the collective identities that drove the civil rights movement.

A variant of this tradition—still stressing the uses of narrative although in a different way—derives very broadly from the work of Michel Foucault and emphasizes the uses of narrative as a form of social control or domination rather than identity formation. This sense of narrative runs through many critiques of psychoanalysis and confession, both religious and criminal (Illouz 2008; Hepworth and Turner 1982). Joseph Davis (2005), for example, shows how collective stories of victimization shape individual narratives of sexual abuse.

Clearly, sociology offers abundant examples of both traditions of narrative analysis. In this first section of the volume, we have included a selection of work that illustrates what makes narrative distinctive from other types of sociological analysis. The interdisciplinarity of the selections highlights what narrative sociology shares with the humanities and other social sciences. As Wolf Lepenies (1988) explains, sociology occupies a disciplinary space between the "two cultures" of the arts and the sciences.[2] To an even greater degree, *narrative* sociology manifests both the aesthetic interests of the former and the epistemological concerns of the latter. The readings we include here acknowledge that aesthetic impulses from work in other disciplines inform narrative sociology. As Jaber Gubrium and James Holstein point out, "the narrative landscape is exceptionally broad, and its borders have been porous enough to make for extensive cross-fertilization" (2009: vii).

In "Sociology Before and After the Narrative Turn," Francesca Polletta and colleagues outline both the major themes in narrative sociology and its general weaknesses. Polletta et al. argue that, as sociologists drew on narrative frameworks in response to the logico-scientific methods discussed above, some traded insight into "individual meaning-making" for the ability to analyze power, inequality, and social change. Fortunately, this focus has shifted, and the later sections in Part III show how narrative can operate as a form of social control or a vehicle for social transformation.

The next reading, cited earlier, is Hayden White's 1980 article, "The Value of Narrativity in the Representation of Reality," reprinted here in its entirety. White, known for his literary analyses of historical writing, is a key figure in history's "narrative turn" of the 1970s and 1980s. He argues that the historian's task involves more than just listing events in chronological order, and he exposes the assumptions of this particular strategy of presenting history.[3] Yet, he also argues that a narrative strategy of translating knowing into telling has an agenda, too. In particular, putting events into a story endows them with "significance that they do *not* possess as a mere sequence" (his emphasis). Often, this significance is a moral one, originating in the social system that provides the context for the story.

We also include Laurel Richardson's 1988 article, "The Collective Story: Postmodernism and the Writing of Sociology." Richardson, too, discusses the disciplinary space between science and literature out of which narrative sociology emerged. She describes her struggle to navigate the entangled issues of "guiding metaphor" and "narrative voice" in her work. The guiding metaphor—portraying Native Americans, for example, as resisting colonialism or as assimilating to "civilization"— shapes the story being told. The voice of the teller, typically the voice of authority, stands above or at least apart from the experience of the story. Untangling this knot led Richardson to position herself as telling a "collective story," allowing people to speak for themselves while also speaking "of and for them, as a sociological analyst."

This section of the book concludes with an excerpt from *Telling Stories: The Use of Personal Narratives in the Social Sciences and History*. It also addresses the tensions of the "two cultures." Authors Mary Jo Maynes, Jennifer L. Pierce, and Barbara Laslett discuss what distinguishes narrative sociology from more positivist social scientific ways of knowing. The excerpt reprinted here, which comes from the introduction of the book, focuses on the features of personal narratives, first-person accounts of individual lives over time and within social context. As the authors argue, "the stories people tell about their lives are never simply individual, but are told in historically specific times and settings and draw on the rules and models in circulation that govern how story elements link together in narrative logics." In this light, personal narratives can operate analytically to bridge the individual and the social.

Notes

1. Some scholars treat these terms interchangeably, while others distinguish story from narrative and use story only when referring to fictional compositions; cf. Polkinghorne 1988.
2. Lepenies draws the phrase from a 1956 article by C. P. Snow, which appeared in the *New Statesman*, the weekly political and literary journal founded by Sidney and Beatrice Webb.
3. White's essay has been criticized for its purportedly Eurocentric view of annals and chronicles as "lower" forms, compared to fully narrative histories (e.g., Waldman 1981), and for its assumption that narrative and moralizing are necessarily linked (e.g., Mink 1981).

References

Barthes, Roland. 1977. "Introduction to the Structural Analysis of Narrative." In *Music, Image, Text*. Translated by Stephen Heath. New York: Fontana Press.

Davis, Joseph E. 2005. *Accounts of Innocence: Sexual Abuse, Trauma, and the Self*. Chicago: University of Chicago Press.

DeGloma, Thomas. 2014. *Seeing the Light: The Social Logic of Personal Discovery*. Chicago: University of Chicago Press.

Duneier, Mitchell. 1999. *Sidewalk*. New York: Farrar, Straus and Giroux.

Gubrium, Jaber F., and James A. Holstein. 2009. *Analyzing Narrative Reality*. Thousand Oaks CA: SAGE Publications.

Harris, Scott R. 2006. *The Meanings of Marital Equality*. Albany NY: The State University of New York Press.

Hepworth, Mike, and Bryan S. Turner. 1982. *Confession: Studies in Deviance and Religion*. London, Boston: Routledge & Kegan Paul.

Illouz, Eva. 2008. *Saving the Modern Soul: Therapy, Emotions, and the Culture of Self-Help*. Berkeley: University of California Press.

Irvine, Leslie. 1999. *Codependent Forevermore: The Invention of Self in a Twelve Step Group*. Chicago: University of Chicago Press.

Labov, William. 1972. *Language in the Inner City: Studies in Black English Vernacular*. Philadelphia: University of Pennsylvania Press.

Lepenies, Wolf. 1988. *Between Literature and Science: The Rise of Sociology*. Cambridge UK: Cambridge University Press.

Mink, Louis O. 1981. "Everyman His or Her Own Annalist." *Critical Inquiry* 7(4): 777–83.

Plummer, Ken. 1995. *Telling Sexual Stories: Power, Change, and Social Worlds*. London: Routledge.

Polletta, Francesca, 1998. "'It Was Like a Fever . . .': Narrative and Identity in Social Protest." *Social Problems* 45(2): 137–59.

Polletta, Francesca, Pang Ching Bobby Chen, Beth Gharrity Gardner, and Alice Motes. 2011. *Annual Review of Sociology* 37: 109–30

Waldman, Marilyn Robinson. 1981. "'The Otherwise Unnoteworthy Year 711': A Reply to Hayden White." *Critical Inquiry* 7(4): 784–92.

Further Reading

Bruner, Jerome. 1986. *Actual Minds, Possible Worlds*. Cambridge MA: Harvard University Press.

Maines, David R. 1993. "Narrative's Moment and Sociology's Phenomena: Toward a Narrative Sociology." *Sociological Quarterly* 34(1): 17–38.

Richardson, Laurel. 1990. "Narrative and Sociology." *Journal of Contemporary Ethnography* 19(1): 116–35.

1
_____

THE SOCIOLOGY OF STORYTELLING

Francesca Polletta, Pang Ching Bobby Chen,
Beth Gharrity Gardner, and Alice Motes

Sociology Before and After the Narrative Turn

Sociological work on narrative before the 1980s was largely divided into symbolic interactionist studies of how people gave accounts to avert threats to their self-image and status (Scott & Lyman 1968, see work reviewed in Orbuch 1997) and ethnomethodological studies of how people used stories in conversation to maintain interactional order (see work reviewed in Goodwin & Heritage 1990).

The concerns animating the wave of theorizing about narrative that emerged in the 1980s were different. Led by philosophers and, especially, psychologists critical of reigning behaviorist frameworks, scholars emphasized the centrality of narrative to cognition (Bruner 1986, Polkinghorne 1988), self (MacIntyre 1981, McAdams 1993), and community (MacIntyre 1981, Carr 1986). Stories were not just things people told, they were things that people lived (Ricoeur 1984, Polkinghorne 1988, McAdams 1993). The stories that people told offered insight into the ways they fashioned identities from available cultural materials. The same was true of collective identities. The stories told by groups, communities, and nations created bonds of belonging and identity (MacIntyre 1981, Carr 1986). Groups without coherent stories were

Excerpted from Francesca Polletta, Pang Ching Bobby Chen, Beth Gharrity Gardner, and Alice Motes, "The Sociology of Storytelling," *Annual Review of Sociology* 37 (2011): 109–30. Reproduced and modified with permission of *Annual Review of Sociology*, Volume © by Annual Reviews, *www.annualreviews.org*.

vulnerable to fragmentation; those with them were capable of acting collectively (Carr 1986).

A second theme animating the new scholarship on narrative also asserted the sensemaking role of stories, but in expert knowledge rather than everyday life. Scholars showed that what passed as universal categories, neutral standards, scientific facts, and objective progress were actually stories: moralizing accounts whose claim to truth rested on their verisimilitude rather than their veracity (in history, White 1980; in science, Latour & Woolgar 1986, Gusfield 1976; in law, Bell 1987, Williams 1987, Delgado 1989). To determinedly tell those suppressed stories, for its part, would expose the unstated reference points of ostensible universals. It would make clear the particularity of the experiences that were masked by the authorial voice. Storytelling here was conceived as an explicitly normative project, a way of subverting the discursive bulwarks of disciplinary authority (Ewick & Silbey 1995).

All three themes—stories as central to self and collectivity, stories as the basis for disciplinary authority, and stories as a critical and even liberatory discursive form—were prominent in the sociological work on narrative that began to appear in the late 1980s. In one stream of work, sociologists analyzed people's stories to shed light on motivations for their actions that might not be apparent even to the people themselves. For example, the stories that interviewees told about their partner's infidelity revealed more about their emotional response to divorce than the objective fact of having experienced infidelity (Riessman 1990). Women who recounted their domestic abuse as a "dark romance" in which violence was the price one paid for love were likely to tolerate that abuse (Wood 2001). Men who recounted the violent crimes they had committed as a minor part of a heroic struggle in which they took their mistreatment by the system "like a man" were probably more likely to commit crimes again (Presser 2008; see also Ewick & Silbey 1998 on the meanings people made of law, Morrill et al. 2000 on conflict in high school, Hollander 2002 on experiences of sexual assault, and Frank 1995 on illness). Sociologists of class and ethnic identity formation argued that resonant stories created collective interests and actions that one simply could not predict from people's structural location (Steinmetz 1992, Somers 1994, Cornell 2000).

In a more methodological vein, sociologists exposed the narrative tropes on which sociological empiricism depended (Richardson 1990, Maines 1993, Somers 1994, Brown 1998). The solution was not to try to excise such tropes from sociological inquiry. Most narrative sociologists rejected the idea of an objective reality that could be tapped by non-narrative methods (some historical sociologists, by contrast, argued that objective reality—and in particular, the contingent and multicausal character of historical developments—could be captured by narrative methods [see Abell 2004 for a review]). Rather, the task was to tell stories that were self-conscious about their partiality and recognized the researcher's own role in the interactions she was studying [and to recognize, too, that the author could never fully know her own role (cf. Clough 1992)]. Narrative sociological approaches overlapped with autoethnography (Bochner & Ellis 1992) and modes of qualitative inquiry that privileged empathy, authenticity, and an openness of meaning as alternatives to positivist truth (Denzin 1997).

These streams of theory and research generated sociological work that was novel and compelling. However, scholars' view of narrative primarily as a tool for individual meaning-making, along with their reliance on interview material, necessarily put to the side sociological questions about power, solidarity, inequality, and social change. For example, the centrality of story to identity and action was more asserted than demonstrated. Certainly sociologists were more attuned than scholars in other fields to the idea that narratives were constraining as well as enabling (Riessman 1990, Wood 2001, Presser 2008). But they were not able to say much about the sources of narrative constraints, other than to attribute them to culture broadly understood. Nor did they say how those constraints operated and whether they were always accepted by cultural subjects or were sometimes negotiated or contested.

A second problem associated with the narrative turn was a tendency to assume that narrative played the same role in group life as in individual life. At the very least, the notion of a sense-making collectivity should have been problematic. But it underpinned claims that groups required shared stories, that incoherent stories weakened solidarity, and that communities with strong collective narratives were better able to withstand setbacks than those without such narratives. Again, sociologists who treated class and ethnic identities as narratively fashioned recognized constraint as well as agency (Somers 1994, Kane 2000), drawing attention, for example, to the fact that ethnic stories were often imposed rather than collectively self-fashioned (Cornell 2000, Cornell & Hartmann 2007). But they failed to broach a very different set of possibilities: that stronger narratives might be those that were less coherent rather than more coherent, or that groups might be better off with multiple, even inconsistent, narratives that somehow seemed to hang together, or that the possession of a fortifying group narrative might be a consequence of a group's strength rather than the cause of it.

Similarly, claims for the liberatory capacity of storytelling were plausible but incomplete. If disadvantaged groups' stories were marginalized in mainstream discourse, the argument ran, then to tell those stories necessarily challenged the norms of disciplinary authority. Moreover, stories' capacity to elicit empathy across chasms of difference might gain a hearing for claims that would be otherwise ignored. But this perspective assumed that all people's stories were heard the same way. An alternative possibility was that storytelling, like other discursive forms, was embedded in hierarchies of cultural authority that shaped the credibility of particular stories. Furthermore, these hierarchies might well intersect with other hierarchies, based on race, class, gender, and so on. Completely aside from their content, then, stories might be persuasive when told by some groups and seen as unconvincing when told by others. They might ratify preexisting inequalities even as they sought to challenge them.

Literature Cited

Abell P. 2004. Narrative explanation: An alternative to variable centered explanation? *Annu. Rev. Sociol.* 30:287–310

Bell D. 1987. *And We Are Not Saved: The Elusive Quest for Racial Justice.* New York: Basic Books

Bochner A, Ellis C. 1992. Personal narrative as a social approach in interpersonal communication. *Commun. Theory* 2:165–72

Brown RH. 1998. *Toward a Democratic Science: Scientific Narration and Civic Communication.* New Haven, CT: Yale Univ. Press

Bruner J. 1986. *Actual Minds, Possible Worlds.* Cambridge, MA: Harvard Univ. Press

Carr D. 1986. Narrative and the real world: An argument for continuity. *Hist. Theory* 25(2):117–31

Clough PT. 1992. *The End(s) of Ethnography: From Realism to Social Criticism.* Newbury Park, CA: Sage

Cornell S. 2000. That's the story of our life. In *We Are a People: Narrative and Multiplicity in Constructing Ethnic Identity,* ed. P Spickard, WJ Burroughs, pp. 41–53. Philadelphia, PA: Temple Univ. Press

Cornell S, Hartmann D. 2007. *Ethnicity and Race: Making Identities in a Changing World.* Thousand Oaks, CA: Pine Forge Press. 2nd ed.

Delgado R. 1989. Storytelling for oppositionists and others: A plea for narrative. *Mich. Law Rev.* 87:2411–41

Denzin N. 1997. *Interpretive Ethnography: Ethnographic Practices for the 21st Century.* London: Sage

Ewick P, Silbey S. 1995. Subversive stories and hegemonic tales: Toward a sociology of narrative. *Law Soc. Rev.* 29:197–226

Ewick P, Silbey S. 1998. *The Common Place of Law: Stories from Everyday Life.* Chicago: Univ. Chicago Press

Frank AW. 1995. *The Wounded Storyteller: Body, Illness, and Ethics.* Chicago: Univ. Chicago Press

Goodwin C, Heritage J. 1990. Conversation analysis. *Annu. Rev. Anthropol.* 19:283–307

Gusfield J. 1976. The literary rhetoric of science: Comedy and pathos in drinking driver research. *Am. Sociol. Rev.* 41(1):16–34

Hollander JA. 2002. Resisting vulnerability: The social reconstruction of gender in interaction. *Soc. Probl.* 49(4):474–96

Kane A. 2000. Narratives of nationalism: Constructing Irish national identity during the Land War, 1879–1882. *Natl. Identities* 2:245–64

Latour B, Woolgar S. 1986. *Laboratory Life: The Construction of Scientific Facts*. Princeton, NJ: Princeton Univ. Press

MacIntyre A. 1981. *After Virtue: A Study in Moral Theory*. Durham, NC: Duke Univ. Press

Maines D. 1993. Narrative's moment and sociology's phenomena: Toward a narrative sociology. *Sociol. Q.* 34:17–38

McAdams D. 1993. *Stories We Live By: Personal Myths and the Making of the Self.* New York: William Morrow

Morrill C, Adelman M, Yalda C, Musheno M, Bejarano C. 2000. Telling tales in school: Youth culture and conflict narratives. *Law Soc. Rev.* 34:521–66

Orbuch TL. 1997. People's accounts count: The sociology of accounts. *Annu. Rev. Sociol.* 23:455–78

Polkinghorne D. 1988. *Narrative Knowing and the Human Sciences*. Albany: State Univ. N.Y. Press

Presser L. 2008. *Been a Heavy Life: Stories of Violent Men*. Urbana-Champaign: Univ. Ill. Press

Richardson L. 1990. Narrative and sociology. *J. Contemp. Ethnogr.* 19:115–25

Ricoeur P. 1984. *Time and Narrative*. Chicago: Univ. Chicago Press

Riessman C. 1990. *Divorce Talk: Women and Men Make Sense of Personal Relationships*. New Brunswick, NJ: Rutgers Univ. Press

Scott MB, Lyman SM. 1968. Accounts. *Am. Sociol. Rev.* 33:46–62

Somers M. 1994. The narrative constitution of identity: A relational and network approach. *Theor. Soc.* 23:605–49

Steinmetz G. 1992. Reflections on the role of social narratives in working-class formation: Narrative theory and the social sciences. *Soc. Sci. Hist.* 16:489–515

White H. 1980. The value of narrativity in the representation of reality. *Crit. Inq.* 7:5–27

Williams P. 1987. Alchemical notes: Reconstructing ideals from deconstructed rights. *Harvard Civ. Rights–Civ. Lib. Law Rev.* 22:401–34

Wood JT. 2001. The normalization of violence in heterosexual romantic relationships: Women's narratives of love and violence. *J. Soc. Pers. Relat.* 18:239–61

2

THE VALUE OF NARRATIVITY IN THE REPRESENTATION OF REALITY

Hayden White

To raise the question of the nature of narrative is to invite reflection on the very nature of culture and, possibly, even on the nature of humanity itself. So natural is the impulse to narrate, so inevitable is the form of narrative for any report of the way things really happened, that narrativity could appear problematical only in a culture in which it was absent—absent or, as in some domains of contemporary Western intellectual and artistic culture, programmatically refused. As a panglobal fact of culture, narrative and narration are less problems than simply data. As the late (and already profoundly missed) Roland Barthes remarked, narrative "is simply there like life itself . . . international, transhistorical, transcultural."[1] Far from being a problem, then, narrative might well be considered a solution to a problem of general human concern, namely, the problem of how to translate *knowing* into *telling*,[2] the problem of fashioning human experience into a form assimilable to structures of meaning that are generally human rather than culture-specific. We may not be able fully to comprehend specific thought patterns of another culture, but we have relatively less difficulty *understanding* a story coming from another culture, however exotic that culture may appear to us. As Barthes says, "narrative . . . is *translatable* without fundamental damage" in a way that a lyric poem or a philosophical discourse is not.

This suggests that far from being one code among many that a culture may utilize for endowing experience with meaning, narrative is a metacode,

Source: *Critical Inquiry*, Vol. 7, No. 1, On Narrative (Autumn, 1980), pp. 5–27
Published by: The University of Chicago Press

a human universal on the basis of which transcultural messages about the nature of a shared reality can be transmitted. Arising, as Barthes says, between our experience of the world and our efforts to describe that experience in language, narrative "ceaselessly substitutes meaning for the straightforward copy of the events recounted." And it would follow, on this view, that the absence of narrative capacity or a refusal of narrative indicates an absence or refusal of meaning itself.

But what *kind* of meaning is absent or refused? The fortunes of narrative in the history of historical writing give us some insight into this question. Historians do not *have* to report their truths about the real world in narrative form; they may choose other, non-narrative, even anti-narrative, modes of representation, such as the meditation, the anatomy, or the epitome. Tocqueville, Burckhardt, Huizinga, and Braudel,[3] to mention only the most notable masters of modern historiography, refused narrative in certain of their historiographical works, presumably on the assumption that the meaning of the events with which they wished to deal did not lend itself to representation in the narrative mode. They refused to tell a story about the past, or, rather, they did not tell a story with well-marked beginning, middle, and end phases; they did not impose upon the processes that interested them the *form* that we normally associate with storytelling. While they certainly *narrated* their accounts of the reality that they perceived, or thought they perceived, to exist within or behind the evidence they had examined, they did not *narrativize* that reality, did not impose upon it the form of a story. And their example permits us to distinguish between a historical discourse that narrates, on the one side, and a discourse that narrativizes, on the other; between a discourse that openly adopts a perspective that looks out on the world and reports it and a discourse that feigns to make the world speak itself and speak itself *as a story.*

The idea that narrative should be considered less as a *form* of representation than as a *manner of speaking* about events, whether real or imaginary, has been recently elaborated within a discussion of the relationship between "discourse" and "narrative" that has arisen in the wake of structuralism and is associated with the work of Jakobson, Benveniste, Genette, Todorov, and Barthes. Here narrative is regarded as a manner of speaking characterized, as Genette expresses it, "by a certain number of exclusions and restrictive conditions" that the more "open" form of discourse does not impose upon the speaker. According to Genette,

> Benveniste shows that certain grammatical forms like the pronoun
> "I" (and its implicit reference "thou"), the pronominal "indicators"
> (certain demonstrative pronouns), the adverbial indicators (like

"here," "now," "yesterday," "today," "tomorrow," etc.) and, at least in French, certain verb tenses like the present, the present perfect, and the future, find themselves limited to discourse, while narrative in the strictest sense is distinguished by the exclusive use of the third person and of such forms as the preterit and the pluperfect.[4]

This distinction between discourse and narrative is, of course, based solely on an analysis of the grammatical features of two modes of discourse in which the "objectivity" of the one and the "subjectivity" of the other are definable primarily by a "linguistic order of criteria." The subjectivity of the discourse is given by the presence, explicit or implicit, of an "ego" who can be defined "only as the person who maintains the discourse." By contrast, "the objectivity of narrative is defined by the absence of all reference to the narrator." In the *narrativizing* discourse, then, we can say, with Benveniste, "Truly there is no longer a 'narrator.' The events are chronologically recorded as they appear on the horizon of the story. Here no one speaks. The events seem to tell themselves."[5]

What is involved in the production of a discourse in which "events seem to tell themselves," especially when it is a matter of events that are explicitly identified as "real" rather than "imaginary," as in the case of historical representations?[6] In a discourse having to do with manifestly imaginary events, which are the "contents" of fictional discourses, the question poses few problems. For why should not imaginary events be represented as "speaking themselves"? Why should not, in the domain of the imaginary, even the stones themselves speak—like Memnon's column when touched by the rays of the sun? But *real* events should not speak, should not tell themselves. Real events should simply be; they can perfectly well serve as the *referents* of a discourse, can be spoken about, but they should not pose as the *tellers* of a narrative. The lateness of the invention of historical discourse in human history and the difficulty of sustaining it in times of cultural breakdown (as in the early Middle Ages) suggest the *artificiality* of the notion that *real* events could "speak themselves" or be represented as "telling their own story." Such a fiction would have posed no problems before the distinction between real and imaginary events was imposed upon the storyteller; storytelling becomes a problem only *after* two orders of events dispose themselves before him as possible components of his stories and his storytelling is compelled to exfoliate under the injunction to keep the two orders unmixed in his discourse. What we call "mythic" narrative is under no obligation to keep the two orders of events distinct from one another. Narrative becomes a *problem* only when we wish to give to *real* events the *form* of story. It is because real events do not offer themselves as stories that their narrativization is so difficult.

What is involved, then, in that finding of the "true story," that discovery of the "real story" within or behind the events that come to us in the chaotic form of "historical records"? What wish is enacted, what desire is gratified, by the fantasy that *real* events are properly represented when they can be shown to display the formal coherency of a story? In the enigma of this wish, this desire, we catch a glimpse of the cultural function of narrativizing discourse in general, an intimation of the psychological impulse behind the apparently universal need not only to narrate but to give to events an aspect of narrativity.

Historiography is an especially good ground on which to consider the nature of narration and narrativity because it is here that our desire for the imaginary, the possible, must contest with the imperatives of the real, the actual. If we view narration and narrativity as the instruments by which the conflicting claims of the imaginary and the real are mediated, arbitrated, or resolved in a discourse, we begin to comprehend both the appeal of narrative and the grounds for refusing it. If putatively real events are represented in a non-narrative form, what kind of reality is it that offers itself, or is conceived to offer itself, to perception? What would a non-narrative representation of historical reality look like?

Fortunately, we have examples aplenty of representations of historical reality which are non-narrative in form. Indeed, the official wisdom of the modern historiographical establishment has it that there are three basic kinds of historical representation, the imperfect "historicality" of two of which is evidenced in their failure to attain to full narrativity of the events of which they treat. These three kinds are: the annals, the chronicle, and the history proper.[7] Needless to say, it is not narrativity alone which permits the distinction among the three kinds, for it is not enough that an account of events, even of past events, even of past real events, display all of the features of narrativity in order for it to count as a proper history. In addition, professional opinion has it, the account must manifest a proper concern for the judicious handling of evidence, and it must honor the chronological order of the original occurrence of the events of which it treats as a baseline that must not be transgressed in classifying any given event as either a cause or an effect. But by common consent, it is not enough that a historical account deal in real, rather than merely imaginary, events; and it is not enough that the account in its order of discourse represent events according to the chronological sequence in which they originally occurred. The events must be not only registered within the chronological framework of their original occurrence but narrated as well, that is to say, revealed as possessing a structure, an order of meaning, which they do *not* possess as mere sequence.

The annals form, needless to say, completely lacks this narrative component, consisting only of a list of events ordered in chronological sequence. The chronicle, by contrast, often seems to wish to tell a story, aspires to narrativity, but typically fails to achieve it. More specifically, the chronicle usually is marked by a failure to achieve narrative *closure*. It does not so much conclude as simply terminate. It starts out to tell a story but breaks off *in medias res*, in the chronicler's own present; it leaves things unresolved or, rather, leaves them unresolved in a story-like way. While annals represent historical reality *as if* real events did not display the form of story, the chronicle represents it *as if* real events appeared to human consciousness in the form of *unfinished* stories.

Official wisdom has it that however objective a historian might be in his reporting of events, however judicious in his assessment of evidence, however punctilious in his dating of *res gestae*, his account remains something less than a proper history when he has failed to give to reality the form of a story. Where there is no narrative, Croce said, there is no history,[8] and Peter Gay, writing from a perspective that is directly opposed to the relativism of Croce, puts it just as starkly: "Historical narration without analysis is trivial, historical analysis without narration is incomplete."[9] Gay's formulation calls up the Kantian bias of the demand for narration in historical representation, for it suggests, to paraphrase Kant, that historical narratives without analysis are empty, while historical analyses without narrative are blind. So, we may ask, what kind of insight does narrative give into the nature of real events? What kind of blindness with respect to reality does narrativity dispel?

In what follows I will treat the annals and chronicle forms of historical representation not as the "imperfect" histories they are conventionally conceived to be but rather as particular products of possible conceptions of historical reality, conceptions that are alternatives to, rather than failed anticipations of, the fully realized historical discourse that the modern history form is supposed to embody. This procedure will throw light on the problems of both historiography and narration alike and will illuminate what I conceive to be the purely conventional nature of the relationship between them. What will be revealed, I think, is that the very distinction between real and imaginary events, basic to modern discussions of both history and fiction, presupposes a notion of reality in which "the true" is identified with "the real" only insofar as it can be shown to possess the character of narrativity.

When we moderns look at an example of a medieval annals, we cannot but be struck by the apparent naiveté of the annalist; and we are inclined to ascribe this naiveté to the annalist's apparent refusal, inability, or unwillingness to transform the set of events ordered vertically as a file of annual markers into the elements of a linear/horizontal process. In other words, we are likely to be put off by the annalist's apparent failure to see that historical events dispose themselves to the percipient eye as "stories" *waiting to be told*, waiting to be narrated. But surely a genuinely historical interest would require that we ask not how or why the annalist failed to write a "narrative" but rather what kind of notion of reality led him to represent in the *annals form* what, after all, he took to be real events. If we could answer this question, we might be able to understand why, in our own time and cultural condition, we could conceive of narrativity itself as a problem.

Volume one of the *Monumenta Germaniae Historica*, series *Scriptores*, contains the text of the *Annals of Saint Gall*, a list of events that occurred in Gaul during the eighth, ninth, and tenth centuries of our era.[10] Although this text is "referential" and contains a representation of temporality,[11] it possesses none of the attributes that we normally think of as a story: no central subject, no well-marked beginning, middle, and end, no peripeteia, and no identifiable narrative voice. In what are, for us, the theoretically most interesting segments of the text, there is no suggestion of any necessary connection between one event and another. Thus, for the period 709–734, we have the following entries:

> 709. Hard winter. Duke Gottfried died. 710. Hard year and deficient in crops. 711.
>
> 712. Flood everywhere.
>
> 713.
>
> 714. Pippin, Mayor of the Palace, died. 715. 716. 717.
>
> 718. Charles devastated the Saxon with great destruction. 719.
>
> 720. Charles fought against the Saxons.
>
> 721. Theudo drove the Saracens out of Aquitaine. 722. Great crops.
>
> 723.
>
> 724.
>
> 725. Saracens came for the first time. 726.
>
> 727.
>
> 728.
>
> 729.
>
> 730.
>
> 731. Blessed Bede, the presbyter, died.

732. Charles fought against the Saracens at Poitiers on Saturday.

733.

734.

This list immediately locates us in a culture hovering on the brink of dissolution, a society of radical scarcity, a world of human groups threatened by death, devastation, flood, and famine. All of the events are extreme, and the implicit criterion for their selection is their liminal nature. Basic needs— food, security from external enemies, political and military leadership— and the threat of their failing to be provided are the subjects of concern; but the connection between basic needs and the conditions for their possible satisfaction is not explicitly commented on. *Why* "Charles fought against the Saxons" remains as unexplained as *why* one year yielded "great crops" and another produced "flood[s] everywhere." Social events are apparently as incomprehensible as natural events. They seem to have the same order of importance or unimportance. They seem merely to have *occurred*, and their importance seems to be indistinguishable from the fact that they were recorded. In fact, it seems that their importance consists of nothing other than the fact that they were recorded.

And recorded *by whom*, we have no idea; nor any idea of *when* they were recorded. The entry for 725 ("Saracens came for the first time") suggests that this event at least was recorded *after* the Saracens had come *a second time* and sets up what we might consider to be a genuine narrativist expectation; but the coming of the Saracens and their repulsion is not the subject of this account. Charles' fight "against the Saracens at Poitiers on Saturday" is recorded, but the outcome of the battle is not told. And that "Saturday" is disturbing because the month and day of the battle are not given. There are too many loose ends—no plot in the offing; and this is frustrating, if not disturbing, to the modern reader's story expectations as well as his desire for specific information.

We note further that this account is not really inaugurated. It simply begins with the "title" (if it is a title) *Anni domini*, which stands at the head of two columns, one of dates, the other of events. Visually, at least, this title links the file of dates in the left-hand column with the file of events in the right-hand column in a promise of signification which we might be inclined to take for "mythical" were it not for the fact that "*Anni domini*" refers us both to a cosmological story given in Scripture and to a calendrical convention which historians in the West today still use to mark the units of their histories. We should not too quickly refer the meaning of the text to the mythic framework which it invokes by designating the "years" as being "of the Lord"; for these years have a regularity which the Christian mythos, with its clear hypotactic ordering of the events which make it up (Creation, Fall, Incarnation, Resurrection, Second Coming), does not possess. The regularity of the calendar signals the "realism" of the account, its intention to deal in real rather than imaginary events. The calendar locates events not in the time of eternity, not in *kairotic* time, but in chronological time, in time as it is *humanly* experienced. This time has no high points or low points; it is, we might say, paratactical and endless. It has no gaps. The list of times is full, even if the list of events is not.

Finally, the annals does not *conclude*; it simply terminates. The last entries are the following:

> 1045. 1046. 1047. 1048. 1049. 1050. 1051. 1052.
> 1053. 1054. 1055.
> 1056. The Emperor Henry died; and his son Henry succeeded to the rule.
> 1057. 1058. 1059. 1060. 1061. 1062. 1063. 1064.
> 1065. 1066. 1067. 1068. 1069. 1070. 1071. 1072.

The continuation of the list of years at the end of the account does, to be sure, suggest a continuation of the series ad infinitum or, rather, until the Second Coming. But there is no story conclusion. How could there be, since there is no central subject *about which* a story could be told?

Nonetheless, there must be a story since there is surely a plot—if by "plot" we mean a structure of relationships by which the events contained in the account are endowed with a meaning by being identified as parts of an integrated whole. By the plot of this story, however, I do not mean the myth of the Fall and Redemption (of the just parts of humankind) contained in the Bible; rather, I am referring to the list of dates given in the left-hand file of the text which confers coherence and fullness on the events by registering them under *the years in which they occurred*. To put it another way, the list of dates can be seen as the signifieds of which the events given in the right-hand column are the signifiers. The "meaning" of the events is their registration in this kind of list. This is why, I presume, the annalist would have felt little of the anxiety which the modern scholar feels when confronted with what appear to be "gaps," "discontinuities," and lack of causal connections between the events recorded in the text. The modern scholar seeks fullness and continuity in an order of events; the annalist has both in the sequence of the years. Which is the more "realistic" expectation?

Recall that we are dealing neither with oneiric nor infantile discourse. It may even be a mistake to call it "discourse" at all, but it has something discursive about it. The text summons up a "substance," operates in the domain of memory rather than of dream or fantasy, and unfolds under the sign of "the real" rather than that of the "imaginary." In fact, it seems eminently rational and, on the face of it, rather prudent in both its manifest desire to record only those events about which there could be little doubt as to their occurrence and its resolve not to interpellate facts on speculative grounds or to advance arguments about how the events are really connected to one another.

Modern commentators have remarked on the fact that the annalist recorded the Battle of Poitiers of 732 but failed to note the Battle of Tours which occurred in the same year and which, as every schoolboy knows, was one of "the ten great battles of world history." But even if the annalist had known of Tours, what principle or rule of meaning would have required him to record it? It is only from *our* knowledge of the *subsequent* history of Western Europe that we can presume to rank events in terms of their world historical significance, and even then that significance is less "world historical" than simply Western European, representing a tendency of modern historians to rank events in the record hierarchically from within a perspective that is culture-specific, not universal at all.

It is this need or impulse to rank events with respect to their significance for the culture or group that is writing its own history that makes a narrative representation of real events possible. It is surely much more "universalistic" simply to record events as they come to notice. And at the minimal level on which the annals unfolds, what gets put into the account is of much greater theoretical importance for the understanding of the nature of narrative than what gets left out. But this does raise the question of the function in this text of the recording of those years in which "nothing happened." For in fact every narrative, however seemingly "full," is constructed on the basis of a set of events which *might have been included but were left out*; and this is as true of imaginary as it is of realistic narratives. This consideration permits us to ask what kind of notion of reality authorizes construction of a narrative account of reality in which continuity rather than discontinuity governs the articulation of the discourse.

If we grant that this discourse unfolds under a sign of a desire for the real, as we must do in order to justify the inclusion of the annals form among the types of historical representation, we must conclude that it is a product of an image of reality in which *the social system*, which alone could provide the diacritical markers for ranking the importance of events, is only minimally present to the consciousness of the writer or, rather, is present as a factor in the composition of the discourse only by virtue of its absence. Everywhere it is the forces of disorder, natural and human, the forces of violence and destruction, which occupy the forefront of attention. The account deals in *qualities* rather than *agents*, figuring forth a world in which things *happen to* people rather than one in which people *do* things. It is the hardness of the winter of 709, the hardness of the year 710 and the deficiency of the crops of that year, the flooding of the waters in 712, and the imminent presence of death which recur with a frequency and regularity that are lacking in the representation of acts of human agency. Reality for this annalist wears the face of adjectives which override the capacity of the nouns they modify to resist their determinacy. Charles does manage to devastate the Saxons, to fight against them, and Theudo even manages to drive the Saracens out of Aquitaine. But these actions appear to belong to the same order of existence as the natural events which bring either "great crops" or "deficient" harvests and are as seemingly incomprehensible.

The absence of a principle for assigning importance or significance to events is signaled above all in the gaps in the list of events in the right-hand file, for example in the year 711 in which, so it seems, nothing happened. The overabundance of the waters noted for the year 712 is preceded and followed by years in which also "nothing happened." This puts one in mind of Hegel's remark that periods of human happiness and security are blank pages in history. But the presence of these blank years in the annalist's account permits us to perceive, by way of contrast, the extent to which narrative strains to produce the effect of having filled in all the gaps, to put an image of continuity, coherency, and meaning in place of the fantasies of emptiness, need, and frustrated desire that inhabit our nightmares about the destructive power of time. In fact, the annalist's account calls up a world in which need is everywhere present, in which scarcity is the rule of existence, and in which all of the possible agencies of satisfaction are lacking, absent, or exist under imminent threat of death.

The notion of possible gratification is, however, implicit in the list of dates that make up the left-hand column. The fullness of this list attests to the fullness of time or at least to the fullness of the "years of the Lord." There is no scarcity of years; they descend regularly from their origin, the year of the Incarnation, and roll relentlessly on to their potential end, the Last Judgment. What is lacking in the list of events to give it a similar regularity and fullness is a notion of a social center by which both to locate them with respect to one another and to charge them with ethical or moral significance. It is the absence of any consciousness of a *social* center that prohibits the annalist from ranking the events which he treats as elements of a historical field of occurrence. And it is the absence of such a center that precludes or undercuts any impulse he might have had to work up his discourse into the form of a narrative. Without such a center, Charles' campaigns against the Saxons remain simply "fights," the invasion of the Saracens simply a "coming," and the fact that the Battle of Poitiers was fought on a Saturday as important as the fact that the battle was even fought at all.

All this suggests to me that Hegel was right when he opined that a genuinely historical account had to display not only a certain form, that is, the narrative, but also a certain content, namely, a political-social order. In his introduction to his *Lectures on the Philosophy of History*, Hegel wrote:

> In our language the term *History* unites the objective with the
> subjective side, and denotes quite as much the *historia rerum
> gestarum*, as the *res gestae* themselves; on the other hand it
> comprehends not less what has *happened*, than the *narration* of what
> has happened. This union of the two meanings we must regard as
> of a higher order than mere outward accident; we must suppose
> historical narrations to have appeared contemporaneously with
> historical deeds and events. It is an internal vital principle common
> to both that produces them synchronously. Family memorials,
> patriarchal traditions, have an interest confined to the family and
> the clan. The *uniform course of events* [my italics] which such a
> condition implies, is no subject of serious remembrance; though
> distinct transactions or turns of fortune, may rouse Mnemosyne
> to form conceptions of them—in the same way as love and the
> religious emotions provoke imagination to give shape to a previously
> formless impulse. But it is the State which first presents subject-
> matter that is not only *adapted* to the prose of History, but involves
> the production of such history in the very progress of its own
> being.[12]

Hegel goes on to distinguish between the kind of "profound sentiments," such as "love" and "religious intuition and its conceptions," and "that outward existence of a political constitution which is enshrined in . . . rational laws and customs [which] is an *imperfect* Present; and cannot be thoroughly understood without a knowledge of the past." This is why, he concludes, there are periods which, although filled with "revolutions, nomadic wanderings, and the strangest mutations," are destitute of any "*objective* history." And their destitution of an objective history is a function of the fact that they could produce "no *subjective* history, no annals. We need not suppose," he remarks, "that the records of such periods have accidentally perished; rather, because they were not possible, do we find them wanting." And he insists that "only in a State cognizant of Laws, can distinct transactions take place, accompanied by such a clear consciousness of them as supplies the ability and suggests the necessity of an enduring record" (p. 61). When, in short, it is a matter of providing a *narrative* of real events, we must suppose that a subject of the sort that would provide the impulse to record its activities must exist.

Hegel insists that the proper subject of such a record is the state, but the state is to him an abstraction. The reality which lends itself to narrative representation is the *conflict* between desire, on the one side, and the law, on the other. Where there is no rule of law, there can be neither a subject nor the kind of event which lends itself to narrative representation. This proposition could not be empirically verified or falsified, to be sure; it rather enables a presupposition or hypothesis which permits us to imagine how both "historicity" and "narrativity" are possible. It also authorizes us to consider the proposition that neither is possible without some notion of the legal subject which can serve as the agent, agency, and subject of historical narrative in all of its manifestations, from the annals through the chronicle to the historical discourse as we know it in its modern realizations and failures.

The question of the law, legality, or legitimacy does not arise in those parts of the *Annals of Saint Gall* which we have been considering; at least, the question of *human* law does not arise. There is no suggestion that the "coming" of the Saracens represents a transgression of any limit, that it should not have been or might have been otherwise. Since everything that happened, happened apparently in accordance with the divine will, it is sufficient simply to note its happening, to register it under the appropriate "year of the Lord" in which it occurred. The coming of the Saracens is of the same moral significance as Charles' fight against the Saxons. We have no way of knowing whether the annalist would have been impelled to flesh out his list of events and rise to the challenge of a narrative representation of those events if he had written in the consciousness of the threat to a specific social system and the possibility of anarchy against which the legal system might have been erected. But once we have been alerted to the intimate relationship that Hegel suggests exists between law, historicality, and narrativity, we cannot but be struck by the frequency with which narrativity, whether of the fictional or the factual sort, presupposes the existence of a legal system against or on behalf of which the typical agents of a narrative account militate. And this raises the suspicion that narrative in general, from the folktale to the novel, from the annals to the fully realized "history," has to do with the topics of law, legality, legitimacy, or, more generally, *authority*. And indeed, when we look at what is supposed to be the next stage in the evolution of historical representation after the annals form, that is, the chronicle, this suspicion is borne out. The more historically self-conscious the writer of any form of historiography, the more the question of the social system and the law which sustains it, the authority of this law and its justification, and threats to the law occupy his attention. If, as Hegel suggests, historicality as a distinct mode of human existence is unthinkable without the presupposition of a system of law in relation to which a specifically legal subject could be constituted, then historical self-consciousness, the kind of consciousness capable of imagining the need to represent reality as a history, is conceivable only in terms of its interest in law, legality, legitimacy, and so on.

Interest in the social system, which is nothing other than a system of human relationships governed by law, creates the possibility of conceiving the kinds of tensions, conflicts, struggles, and their various kinds of resolutions that we are accustomed to find in any representation of reality presenting itself to us as a history. Perhaps, then, the growth and development of historical consciousness which is attended by a concomitant growth and development of narrative capability (of the sort met with in the chronicle as against the annals form) has something to do with the extent to which the legal system functions as a subject of concern. If every fully realized story, however we define that familiar but conceptually elusive entity, is a kind of allegory, points to a moral, or endows events, whether real or imaginary, with a significance that they do not possess as a mere sequence, then it seems possible to conclude that every historical narrative has as its latent or manifest purpose the desire to *moralize* the events of which it treats. Where there is ambiguity or ambivalence regarding the status of the legal system, which is the form in which the subject encounters most immediately the social system in which he is enjoined to achieve a full humanity, the ground on which any closure of a story one might wish to tell about a past, whether it be a public or a private past, is lacking. And this suggests that narrativity, certainly in factual storytelling and probably in fictional storytelling as well, is intimately related to, if not a function of, the impulse to moralize reality, that is, to identify it with the social system that is the source of any morality that we can imagine.

The annalist of Saint Gall shows no concern about any system of merely human morality or law. The entry for 1056, "The Emperor Henry died; and his son Henry succeeded to the rule," contains in embryo the elements of a narrative. Indeed, it *is* a narrative, and its narrativity, in spite of the ambiguity of the connection between the first event (Henry's death) and the second (Henry's succession) suggested by the particle "and," achieves closure by its tacit invocation of the legal system: the rule of genealogical succession which the annalist takes for granted as a principle rightly governing the passing of authority from one generation to another. But this small narrative element, this "narreme," floats easily on the sea of dates which figures *succession* itself as a principle of cosmic organization. Those of us who know what was awaiting the younger Henry in his conflicts with his nobles and with the popes during the period of the investiture struggle, in which the issue of precisely *where* final authority on earth was located was fought out, may be irritated by the economy with which the annalist recorded an event so fraught with future moral and legal implications. The years 1057–72, which the annalist simply lists at the end of his record, provided more than enough "events" that pre-figured the onset of this struggle, more than enough conflict to warrant a full narrative account of its inception. But the annalist simply ignored them. He apparently felt that he had done his duty solely by listing the dates themselves. What is involved, we might ask, in this refusal to nar-rate?

To be sure, we can conclude—as Frank Kermode suggested in his remark on this text during our discussion-that the annalist of Saint Gall was just not a very good diarist; and such a commonsensical judgment is manifestly justified. But the incapacity to keep a good diary is not theoretically different from the unwillingness to do so. From the standpoint of an interest in narrative itself, a "bad" narrative can tell us more about narrativity than a good one. If it is true that the annalist of Saint Gall was an untidy or lazy narrator, we must ask what he lacked that would have made him a competent narrator. What is absent from his account which, if it had been present, would have permitted him to transform his chronology into a historical narrative?

The vertical ordering of events itself suggests that our annalist did not want in metaphoric or paradigmatic consciousness. He does not suffer from what Roman Jakobson calls "similarity disorder." Indeed, all of the events listed in the right-hand column appear to be considered as the *same kind* of event; they are all metonymies of the general condition of scarcity or overfullness of the "reality" which the annalist is recording. *Difference*, significant variation within similitude, is figured only in the left-hand column, the list of dates. Each of these functions as a metaphor of the fullness and completion of the time of the Lord. The image of orderly succession that this column calls up has no counterpart in the events, natural and human, which are listed on the right-hand side. What the annalist lacked that would have led him to make a narrative out of the set of events he recorded was a capacity to endow *events* with the same kind of "propositionality" that is implicitly present in his representation of the sequence of dates. This lack resembles what Jakobson calls "contiguity disorder," a phenomenon represented in speech by "agrammatism" and in discourse by a dissolution of "the ties of grammatical coordination and subordination" by which "word heaps" can be aggregated into meaningful sentences.[13] Our annalist was not, of course, aphasic—as his capacity to contrive meaningful sentences amply shows. But he lacked the capacity to substitute meanings for one another in chains of semantic metonymies that would transform his list of events into a discourse about the events considered as a totality evolving in time.

Now, the capacity to envision a set of events as belonging to the same order of meaning requires a metaphysical principle by which to translate difference into similarity. In other words, it requires a "subject" common to all of the *referents* of the various sentences that register events as having occurred. If such a subject exists, it is the "Lord" whose "years" are treated as manifestations of His power to cause the events which occur in them. The subject of the account, then, does not exist *in time* and could not therefore function as the subject of a narrative. Does it follow that in order for there to be a narrative, there must be some equivalent of the Lord, some sacral being endowed with the authority and power of the Lord, existing in time? If so, what could such an equivalent be?

The nature of such a being, capable of serving as the central organizing principle of meaning of a discourse that is both realistic and narrative in structure, is called up in the mode of historical representation known as the chronicle. By common consensus among historians of historical writing, the chronicle form is a "higher" form of historical conceptualization and represents a mode of historiographical representation superior to the annals form.[14] Its superiority consists, it is agreed, in its greater comprehensiveness, its organization of materials "by topics and reigns," and its greater narrative coherency. The chronicle also has a central subject, the life of an individual, town, or region, some great undertaking, such as a war or crusade, or some institution, such as a monarchy, episcopacy, or monastery. The link of the chronicle with the annals is perceived in the perseverance of the chronology as the organizing principle of the discourse, and, so we are told, this is what makes the chronicle something less than a fully realized "history." Moreover, the chronicle, like the annals but unlike the history, does not so much "conclude" as simply terminate; typically it lacks closure, that summing up of the "meaning" of the chain of events with which it deals that we normally expect from the well-made story. The chronicle typically promises closure but does not provide it— which is one of the reasons that the nineteenth-century editors of the medieval chronicles denied them the status of genuine histories.

Suppose that we look at the matter differently. Suppose that we do not grant that the chronicle is a "higher" or more sophisticated representation of reality than the annals but is merely a *different* kind of representation, marked by a desire for a kind of order and fullness in an account of reality that remains theoretically unjustified, a desire that is, until shown otherwise, purely gratuitous. What is involved in the imposition of this order and the provision of this fullness (of detail) which mark the differences between the annals and the chronicle?

I take as an example of the chronicle type of historical representation the *History of France* of Richerus of Reims, written on the eve of the year A.D. 1000 (ca. 998).[15] We have no difficulty recognizing this text as a narrative: it has a central subject ("the conflicts of the French" [1:3]); it has a proper geographical center (Gaul) and a proper social center (the archiepiscopal see of Reims, beset by a dispute over which of two claimants to the office of archbishop is the legitimate occupant of it); and it has a proper beginning in time (given in a synoptic version of the history of the world from the Incarnation down to the time and place of Richerus' own writing of his account). But the work fails as a "proper" history, at least according to the opinion of later commentators, by virtue of two considerations. First, the order of the discourse follows the order of chronology; it presents events in the order of their occurrence and cannot, therefore, offer the kind of meaning that a narratologically governed account can be said to provide. Second, and this is probably a consequence of the "annalistic" order of the discourse, the account does not so much *conclude* as simply *terminate*; it merely "breaks off" with the flight of one of the disputants for the office of archbishop and throws on the reader the burden of retrospectively reflecting on the linkages between the beginning of the account and its ending. The account comes down to the writer's own "yesterday," adds one more fact to the series which began with the Incarnation, and then simply ceases. As a result, all of the normal narratological expectations of the reader (this reader) remain unfulfilled. The work appears to be unfolding a plot but then belies its own appearance by merely stopping *in medias res*, with a cryptic notation: "Pope Gregory authorizes Arnulfus to assume provisionally the episcopal functions, while awaiting the legal decision that would either confer these upon him or withdraw the right to them" (2:133).

And yet Richerus is a self-conscious narrator. He explicitly says at the outset of his account that he proposes "especially to preserve in writing [*ad memoriam reducere scripto specialiter propositum est*]" the "wars," "troubles," and "affairs" of the French and, moreover, to write them up in a manner superior to other accounts, especially that of one Flodoard, an earlier scribe of Reims who had written an annals on which Richerus has drawn for information. Richerus notes that he has drawn freely on Flodoard's work but that he has often "put other words" in place of the original ones and "modified completely the style of the presentation [*pro aliis longe diversissimo orationis scemate disposuisse*]" (1:4). He also situates himself in a tradition of historical writing by citing such classics as Caesar, Orosius, Jerome, and Isidore as authorities for the early history of Gaul and suggests that his own personal observations gave him insight into the facts he is recounting that no one else could claim. All of this suggests a certain distance from his own discourse which is manifestly lacking in the writer of the *Annals of Saint Gall*. Richerus' discourse is a *fashioned* discourse, the narrativity of which, in comparison to that of the annalist, is a function of the self-consciousness with which this fashioning activity is entered upon.

Paradoxically, however, it is this self-conscious fashioning activity, an activity which gives to Richerus' work the aspect of a historical *narrative*, that decreases its "objectivity" as a *historical* account—or so the consensus of modern analysts of the text has it. For example, a modern editor of the text, Robert Latouche, indicts Richerus' pride in the originality of his style as the cause of his failure to write a proper history. "Ultimately," Latouche notes, "the *History* of Richer is not properly speaking [*proprement parler*] a history, but a work of rhetoric composed by a monk . . . who sought to imitate the techniques of Salluste." And he adds, "what interested him was not the material [*matière*] which he molded to fit his fancy, but the form" (1:xi).

Latouche is certainly right in his characterization of Richerus' failings *as a historian* supposedly interested in the "facts" of a certain period of history but is just as surely wrong in his suggestion that the work fails *as a history* because of the writer's interest in "form" rather than "matter." By "*matière*," of course, Latouche means the referents of the discourse, the events taken individually as objects of representation. But Richerus is interested in "the conflicts of the French [*Gallorum congressibus in volumine regerendis*]" (1:2), especially the conflict in which his patron, Gerbert, archbishop of Reims, was currently involved for control of the see. Far from being interested primarily in form rather than matter or content, Richerus was only interested in the latter; for this conflict was one in which his own future was entailed. Where *authority* lay for the direction of affairs in the see of Reims was the question which Richerus hoped to help resolve by the composition of his narrative. We can legitimately suppose that his impulse to write a narrative of this conflict was in some way connected with a desire on his part to represent (both in the sense of writing about and in the sense of acting as an agent of) an authority whose legitimacy hinged upon the establishment of "facts" that were of a specifically historical order.

Indeed, once we note the presence of the theme of *authority* in this text, we also perceive the extent to which the truth claims of the narrative and indeed the very *right* to narrate hinges upon a certain relationship to authority per se. The first authority invoked by the author is that of his patron, Gerbert; it is by his authority that the account is composed (". . . *imperii tui, pater santissime G[erbert], auctoritas seminarium dedit*" [1:2]). Then there are those "authorities" represented by the classic texts on which he draws for his construction of the early history of the French (Caesar, Orosius, Jerome, etc.). There is the "authority" of his predecessor as a historian of the see of Reims, Flodoard, an authority with whom he contests as narrator and on whose style he professes to improve. It is on his own authority that Richerus effects this improvement, by putting "other words" in place of Flodoard's and modifying "completely the style of the presentation." There is, finally, not only the authority of the Heavenly Father, who is invoked as the ultimate cause of everything that happens, but the authority of Richerus' own father (referred to throughout the manuscript as "p. m." [*pater meus*] who figures as a central subject of a segment of the work and as the witness on whose authority the account in this segment is based.

The problem of authority pervades the text written by Richerus in a way that cannot be ascribed to the text written by the annalist of Saint Gall. For the annalist, there is no need to claim the authority to narrate events since there is nothing problematical about their status as manifestations of a reality that is being contested. Since there is no "contest," there is nothing to narrativize, no need for them to "speak themselves" or be represented *as if* they could "tell their own story." It is necessary only to record them in the order that they come to notice, for since there is no contest, there is no story to tell. It is because there was a contest that there is something to narrativize for Richerus. But it is not because the contest was not resolved that the quasi narrative produced by Richerus has no closure; for the contest was in fact resolved—by the flight of Gerbert to the court of King Otto and the installation of Arnulfus as archbishop of Reims by Pope Gregory. What was lacking for a proper discursive resolution, a narrativizing resolution, was the moral principle in light of which Richerus might have judged the resolution as either just or unjust. Reality itself has judged the resolution by resolving it as it has done. To be sure, there is the suggestion that a kind of justice was provided for Gerbert by King Otto who, "having recognized Gerbert's learning and genius, installs him as bishop of Ravenna." But that justice is located at another place and is disposed by another authority, another king. The end of the discourse does not cast its light back over the events originally recorded in order to redistribute the force of a meaning that was immanent in all of the events from the beginning. There is no justice, only force; or rather only an authority that presents itself as different kinds of forces.

I wish to stress that I do not offer these reflections on the relationship between historiography and narrative as anything other than an attempt to illuminate the distinction between story elements and plot elements in the historical discourse. Common opinion has it that the plot of a narrative imposes a meaning on the events that comprise its story level by revealing at the end a structure that was immanent in the events *all along*. What I am trying to establish is the nature of this immanence in any narrative account of *real* events, the kind of events that are offered as the proper content of historical discourse. The reality of these events does not consist in the fact that they occurred but that, first of all, they were remembered and, second, that they are capable of finding a place in a chronologically ordered sequence.

In order for an account of the events to be considered a historical account, however, it is not enough that they be recorded in the order of their original occurrence. It is the fact that they *can* be recorded otherwise, in an order of narrative, that makes them at once questionable as to their authenticity and susceptible to being considered tokens of reality. In order to qualify as "historical," an event must be susceptible to at least two narrations of its occurrence. Unless at least two versions of the same set of events can be imagined, there is no reason for the historian to take upon himself the authority of giving the true account of what really happened. The authority of the historical narrative is the authority of reality itself; the historical account endows this reality with form and thereby makes it desirable, imposing upon its processes the formal coherency that only stories possess.

The history, then, belongs to the category of what might be called the "discourse of the real," as against the "discourse of the imaginary" or the "discourse of desire." The formulation is Lacanian, obviously, but I do not wish to push the Lacanian aspects of it too far. I merely wish to suggest that we can comprehend the appeal of historical discourse by recognizing the extent to which it makes the real desirable, makes the real into an object of desire, and does so by its imposition, upon events that are represented as real, of the formal coherency that stories possess. Unlike the annals, the reality that is represented in the historical narrative, in "speaking itself," speaks *to* us, summons us from afar (this "afar" is the land of forms), and displays to us a formal coherency that we ourselves lack. The historical narrative, as against the chronicle, reveals to us a world that is putatively "finished," done with, over, and yet not dissolved, not falling apart. In this world, reality wears the mask of a meaning, the completeness and fullness of which we can only *imagine*, never experience. Insofar as historical stories can be completed, can be given narrative closure, can be shown to have had a *plot* all along, they give to reality the odor of the *ideal*. This is why the plot of a historical narrative is always an embarrassment and has to be presented as "found" in the events rather than put there by narrative techniques.

The embarrassment of plot to historical narrative is reflected in the all but universal disdain with which modern historians regard the "philosophy of history," of which Hegel provides the modern paradigm. This (fourth) form of historical representation is condemned because it consists of nothing but plot; its story elements exist only as manifestations, epiphenomena, of the plot structure, in the service of which its discourse is disposed. Here reality wears a face of such regularity, order, and coherence that it leaves no room for human agency, presenting an aspect of such wholeness and completeness that it intimidates rather than invites to imaginative identification. But in the plot of the philosophy of history, the various plots of the various histories which tell us of merely regional happenings in the past are revealed for what they really are: images of that authority which summons us to participation in a moral universe that, but for its story form, would have no appeal at all.

This puts us close to a possible characterization of the demand for closure in the history, for the want of which the chronicle form is adjudged to be deficient as a narrative. The demand for closure in the historical story is a demand, I suggest, for moral meaning, a demand that sequences of real events be assessed as to their significance as elements of a *moral* drama. Has any historical narrative ever been written that was not informed not only by moral awareness but specifically by the moral authority of the narrator? It is difficult to think of any historical work produced during the nineteenth century, the classic age of historical narrative, that was not given the force of a moral judgment on the events it related.

But we do not have to prejudge the matter by looking at historical texts composed in the nineteenth century; we can perceive the operations of moral consciousness in the achievement of narrative fullness in an example of late medieval historiography, the *Cronica* of Dino Compagni, written between 1310 and 1312 and generally recognized as a proper historical narrative.[16] Dino's work not only "fills in the gaps" which might have been left in an annalistic handling of its subject matter (the struggles between the Black and White factions of the dominant Guelf party in Florence between 1280 and 1312) and organizes its story according to a well-marked ternary plot structure; it also achieves narrative fullness by explicitly invoking the idea of a social system to serve as a fixed reference point by which the How of ephemeral events can be endowed with specifically moral meaning. In this respect, the *Cronica* clearly displays the extent to which the chronicle must approach the form of an allegory, moral or anagogical as the case may be, in order to achieve *both* narrativity and historicality.

It is interesting to observe that as the chronicle form is displaced by the proper history, certain of the features of the former disappear. First of all, no explicit patron is invoked: Dino's narrative does not unfold under the authority of a specific patron, as Richerus' does; instead, Dino simply asserts his right to recount notable events (*cose notevoli*) which he has "seen and heard" on the basis of a superior capacity of foresight. "No one saw these events in their beginnings [*principi*] more certainly than I," he says. His prospective audience is not, then, a specific ideal reader, as Gerbert was for Richerus, but rather a *group* that is conceived to share his perspective on the true nature of all events: those citizens of Florence who are capable, as he puts it, of recognizing "the benefits of God, who rules and governs for all time." At the same time, he speaks to another group, the depraved citizens of Florence, those who are responsible for the "conflicts" (*discordie*) that had wracked the city for some three decades. To the former, his narrative is intended to hold out the hope of deliverance from these conflicts; to the latter, it is intended as an admonition and a threat of retribution. The chaos of the last ten years is contrasted with more "prosperous" years to come, after the emperor Henry VII has descended on Florence in order to punish a people whose "evil customs and false profits" have "corrupted and spoiled the whole world."[17] What Kermode calls "the weight of meaning" of the events recounted is "thrown forward" onto a future just beyond the immediate present, a future fraught with moral judgment and punishment for the wicked.[18]

The jeremiad with which Dino's work closes marks it as belonging to a period before which a genuine historical "objectivity," which is to say, a secularist ideology, had been established—so the commentators tell us. But it is difficult to see how the kind of narrative fullness for which Dino is praised could have been attained without the implicit invocation of the moral standard that he uses to distinguish between those real events worthy of being recorded and those unworthy of it. The events that are actually recorded in the narrative appear "real" precisely insofar as they belong to an order of moral existence, just as they derive their meaning from their placement in this order. It is because the events described conduce to the establishment of social order or fail to do so that they find a place in the narrative attesting to their reality. Only the contrast between the governance of God and the anarchy of the current social situation in Florence could justify the apocalyptical tone and narrative function of the final paragraph, with its image of the emperor who will come to chasten those "who brought evil into the world through [their] bad habits." And only a moral authority could justify the turn in the narrative which permits it to come to an *end*. Dino explicitly identifies the end of his narrative with a "turn" in the moral order of the world: "The world is beginning now to turn over once more [*Ora vi si ricomincia il mondo a rivolgere addosso*] . . . : the Emperor is coming to take you and despoil you, by land and by sea."[19]

It is this moralistic ending which keeps Dino's *Cronica* from meeting the standard of a modern, "objective" historical account. Yet it is this moralism which alone permits the work to end or, rather, to *conclude* in a way different from the way that the annals and the chronicle forms do. But on what other grounds could a narrative of real events *possibly* conclude? When it is a matter of recounting the concourse of real events, what other "ending" could a given sequence of such events have than a "moralizing" ending? What else could narrative closure consist of than the *passage* from one moral order to another? I confess that I cannot think of any other way of "concluding" an account of *real* events; for we cannot say, surely, that any sequence of real events actually comes to an end, that reality itself disappears, that events *of the order of the real* have ceased to happen. Such events could only have seemed to have ceased to happen when meaning is shifted, and shifted by narrative means, from one physical or social space to another. Where moral sensitivity is lacking, as it seems to be in an annalistic account of reality, or is only potentially present, as it appears to be in a chronicle, not only meaning but the means to track such shifts of meaning, that is, narrativity, appears to be lacking also. Where, in any account of reality, narrativity is present, we can be sure that morality or a moralizing impulse is present too. There is no other way that reality can be endowed with the kind of meaning that both displays itself in its consummation and withholds itself by its displacement to another story "waiting to be told" just beyond the confines of "the end."

What I have been working around to is the question of the *value* attached to narrativity itself, especially in representations of reality of the sort which historical discourse embodies. It may be thought that I have stacked the cards in favor of my thesis (that narrativizing discourse serves the purpose of moralizing judgments) by my use of exclusively medieval materials. And perhaps I have; but it is the modern historiographical community which has distinguished between annals, chronicle, and history forms of discourse on the basis of their attainment of narrative fullness or failure to attain it. And this same scholarly establishment has yet to account for the fact that just when, by its own account, historiography was transformed into a so-called objective discipline, it was the narrativity of the historical discourse that was celebrated as one of the signs of historiography's maturation as a science—a science of a special sort, but a science nonetheless. It is the historians themselves who have transformed narrativity from a manner of speaking into a paradigm of the form which reality itself displays to a "realistic" consciousness. It is they who have made narrativity into a value, the presence of which in a discourse having to do with real events signals at once its objectivity, its seriousness, and its realism.

I have sought to suggest that this value attached to narrativity in the representation of real events arises out of a desire to have real events display the coherence, integrity, fullness, and closure of an image of life that is and can only be imaginary. The notion that sequences of real events possess the formal attributes of the stories we tell about imaginary events could only have its origin in wishes, daydreams, reveries. Does the world really present itself to perception in the form of well-made stories, with central subjects, proper beginnings, middles, and ends, and a coherence that permits us to see "the end" in every beginning? Or does it present itself more in the forms that the annals and chronicle suggest, either as mere sequence without beginning or end or as sequences of beginnings that only terminate and never conclude? And does the world, even the social world, ever really come to us as already narrativized, already "speaking itself" from beyond the horizon of our capacity to make scientific sense of it? Or is the fiction of such a world, a world capable of speaking itself and of displaying itself as a form of a story, necessary for the establishment of that moral authority without which the notion of a specifically social reality would be unthinkable? If it were only a matter of realism in representation, one could make a pretty good case for both the annals and chronicle forms as paradigms of ways that reality offers itself to perception. Is it possible that their supposed want of objectivity, manifested in their failure to narrativize reality adequately, has nothing to do with the modes of perception which they presuppose but with their failure to represent the *moral* under the aspect of the *aesthetic?* And could we answer that question without giving a narrative account of the history of objectivity itself, an account that would already prejudice the outcome of the story we would tell in favor of the *moral* in general? Could we ever narrativize *without* moralizing?

Notes

1. Roland Barthes, "Introduction to the Structural Analysis of Narratives," *Music, Image, Text*, trans. Stephen Heath (New York, 1977), p. 79.
2. The words "narrative," "narration," "to narrate," and so on derive via the Latin *gnārus* ("knowing," "acquainted with," "expert," "skilful," and so forth) and *narrō* ("relate," "tell") from the Sanskrit root *gnâ* ("know"). The same root yields γνώριμος ("knowable," "known"): see Emile Boisacq, *Dictionnaire étymologique*

de la langue grecque (Heidelberg, 1950), under the entry for this word. My thanks to Ted Morris of Cornell, one of our great etymologists.

3. See Alexis de Tocqueville, *Democracy in America*, trans. Henry Reeve (London, 1838); Jakob Christoph Burckhardt, *The Civilization of the Renaissance in Italy*, trans. S. G. C. Middlemore (London, 1878); Johan Huizinga, *The Waning of the Middle Ages: A Study of the Forms of Life, Thought, and Art in France and the Netherlands in the Dawn of the Renaissance*, trans. F. Hopman (London, 1924); and Fernand Braudel, *The Mediterranean and the Mediterranean World in the Age of Philip II*, trans. Sian Reynolds (New York, 1972). See also my *Metahistory: The Historical Imagination in Nineteenth Century Europe* (Baltimore, 1973) and Hans Kellner, "Disorderly Conduct: Braudel's Mediterranean Satire," *History and Theory* 18, no. 2 (May 1979): 197–222.

4. Gerard Genette, "Boundaries of Narrative," *New Literary History* 8, no. 1 (Autumn 1976): 11. See also Jonathan Culler, *Structuralist Poetics: Structuralism, Linguistics, and the Study of Literature* (Ithaca, N.Y., 1975), chap. 9; Philip Pettit, *The Concept of Structuralism: A Critical Analysis* (Berkeley and Los Angeles, 1975); Tel Quel [Group], *Theorie d'ensemble* (Paris, 1968), esp. articles by Jean-Louis Baudry, Philippe Sollers, and Julia Kristeva; Robert Scholes, *Structuralism in Literature: An Introduction* (New Haven, Conn. and London, 1974), chaps. 4–5; Tzvetan Todorov, *Poétique de la prose* (Paris, 1971), chap. 9; and Paul Zumthor, *Langue, texte, énigme* (Paris, 1975), pt. 4.

5. Emile Benveniste as quoted by Genette, "Boundaries of Narrative," p. 9. Cf. Benveniste, *Problems in General Linguistics*, trans. Mary Elizabeth Meek (Coral Gables, Fla. 1971), p. 208.

6. See Louis O. Mink, "Narrative Form as a Cognitive Instrument," and Lionel Gossman, "History and Literature," in *The Writing of History: Literary Form and Historical Understanding*, ed. Robert H. Canary and Henry Kozicki (Madison, Wis., 1978), with complete bibliography on the problem of narrative form in historical writing.

7. For purposes of economy, I will use as representative of the conventional view of the history of historical writing Harry Elmer Barnes, *A History of Historical Writing* (New York, 1962), chap. 3, which deals with medieval historiography in the West. See also Scholes and Robert Kellogg, *The Nature of Narrative* (Oxford, 1976), pp. 64, 211.

8. I discuss Croce in *Metahistory*, pp. 381–85.

9. Peter Gay, *Style in History* (New York, 1974), p. 189.

10. *Annales Sangallenses Maiores, dicti Hepidanni*, ed. Idlefonsus ab Arx, in *Monumenta Germaniae Historica*, series *Scriptores*, ed. George Heinrich Pertz, 32 vols. (Hanover, 1826), I: 73–85; my translation.

11. This is Oswald Ducrot and Todorov's definition of what can count as narrative. See Ducrot and Todorov, eds., *Encyclopedic Dictionary of the Sciences of Language*, trans. Catherine Porter (Baltimore, 1979), pp. 297–99.

12. G. W. F. Hegel, *The Philosophy of History*, trans. J. Sibree (New York, 1956), pp. 60–61; all further references to Hegel's introduction will be cited parenthetically in the text.

13. Roman Jakobson and Morris Halle, *Fundamentals of Language* (The Hague, 1971), pp. 85–86.

14. See Barnes, *A History of Historical Writing*, pp. 65–68.

15. Richer, *Histoire de France, 888–995*, ed. and trans. Robert Latouche, 2 vols.

(Paris, 1930–37); all further references to this work will be cited parenthetically in the text; my translations.

16. *La cronica di Dino Compagni delle cose occorrenti ne'tempi suoi e La canzone morale Del Pregio dello stesso autore*, ed. Isidoro Del Lungo, 4th ed. rev. (Florence, 1902). Cf. Barnes, pp. 80–81.

17. Ibid., p. 5; my translations.

18. See Frank Kermode, *The Sense of an Ending: Studies in the Theory of Fiction* (Oxford, 1967), chap. 1.

19. Compagni, pp. 209–10.

3

THE COLLECTIVE STORY

Postmodernism and the Writing of Sociology

Laurel Richardson

At the 1987 American Sociological Association Meetings in Chicago, colleagues asked me the conventional convention question—our functional equivalent to "How are you?"—namely, "What are you working on?" Instead of responding ("Fine") by enumerating my projects in progress, I heard myself saying, "I don't know *what* I want to write about, *how* I want to write it, or *who* I want to write it for." The heresy just popped out. Nevertheless, my answer did not reflect only a temporary lapse of sensibility, a moment of unorthodoxy that would soon pass. Rather, these concerns with the writing of sociology are issues I have struggled with throughout my professional career. I embrace them now as priorities for myself and for the future of sociology: *What* do we write about? *How* do we write it? And for *whom* do we write?

My speech this afternoon will reflect my penchant for mingling the personal, the political, and the intellectual. I will first talk about "what to write about" and "how to write it" as postmodernist problems. I will defer the question of "for whom do we write" until the latter part of my speech, where I reflect upon my own writing decisions and processes.

Laurel Richardson, "The Collective Story: Postmodernism and the Writing of Sociology," *Sociological Focus*, Vol. 21, No. 3 (August 1988), pp. 199–208, reprinted by permission of the North Central Sociological Association, *www.ncsanet.org*.

Postmodernism and the Crisis of Representation

We ply our sociological craft within—not above—broader historical, social, and intellectual contexts. Today, the dominant intellectual context challenges all "grand theory" and all claims for a singular, correct style for organizing and presenting knowledge. Lacking a totalizing vision, the contemporary intellectual context lacks a name of its own. The period is defined not by what it is but by what it comes *after*. It is variously called *postparadigmatic*—postmodernism, post-Marxism, poststructuralism, postpositivism—some even say, post-feminism. Characteristic of this period is the loss of authority of "a general paradigmatic style of organizing research" (Marcus and Fisher, 1986:8). Ideas and methods are freely borrowed from one discipline to another, leading to a "blurring of genres" (Geertz, 1980). A totalizing vision is replaced by concerns with contextuality, exceptions, indeterminants, and the meanings to participants. Even the totalizing vision that feminism created is now being reassessed by feminists as we critique that vision as being, itself, contextually created, a product primarily of privileged women in a social movement which has glossed over meaningful differences in the experiences of differently situated women.

The loss of grand theory has affected all disciplines, although their responses have differed. In literary criticism, literature is aesthetically equivalenced. All texts can be "deconstructed" so that Dickens and Tolstoi, for example, are no better writers than their deconstructors. In law, The Critical Legal Studies movement abrogates the legal reasoning model (Livingston, 1982). In philosophy, the principles of uncertainty and contextuality undermine the possibility of universal systems of thought (Rorty, 1979). In physics and mathematics, the focus is on the inelegant, the disorderly, indeed even, "chaos" (Gleick, 1984). In sociology and the other social sciences, the critiques of grand theories have dislodged their hegemony; sociological production, like other human productions, is seen as socially produced (cf. Fiske and Shweder, 1986).

When there is no dominant paradigm, indeed, when the very grounds upon which paradigms can be considered valid are themselves subject to contextualization and indeterminacy, scholars face what Marcus and Fisher (1968:8) refer to as a "crisis in representation": uncertainty about what constitutes adequate depiction of social reality. When scholarly conventions are themselves contested, politics and poetics become inseparable and neither science nor art stands above the historical and linguistic processes (Clifford, 1986:2). As a result, the growing edges of the intellectual-sociological enterprise have shifted. Attention is focused on epistemology (cf. Cook and Fonow, 1986; Fonow and Cook, Forthcoming; Fiske and

Shweder, 1986), interpretive understanding (Diamond, Forthcoming; DiIorio, Forthcoming; Mishler, 1986), and the discursive forms of representation themselves (cf. Becker, 1986b; Long, 1987; Krieger, 1983; Stewart, Forthcoming; Clifford and Marcus, 1986; Strathem, 1987). Our commonsense understanding of method is extended to include epistemological assumptions, on the one hand, and the writing process on the other.

How in the midst of this ferment and uncertainty do we prevent a paralysis of intellect and the will to work? Why do any intellectual work at all? But, conversely, "why not?" We can be caught in the infinite regress of deconstructionism, where nothing is better than anything else, but we can also be drawn to infinite expansion. When there is a crisis of representation we are freed from the intellectual myopia of hyper-determined research projects and their formulaic write-ups, what Kuhn has termed "normal science." We can tum uncertainty to our advantage; we can be more sociologically imaginative in our thinking, apprehending, and writing of the social world. We can, as C. Wright Mills (1959:195) proposed, resist the "codification of procedures" stratagem for developing theory and methods and get on with the "exchange of information about . . . actual ways of working."

Science and Literature

At this historical point, I have chosen to think about my sociological work as telling what I term *the collective story.* A collective story tells the experience of a sociologically constructed category of people in the context of larger sociocultural and historical forces. The sociological protagonist is a collective. I think of similarly situated individuals who may or may not be aware of their life affinities as coparticipants in a collective story. My intent is to help construct a consciousness of kind in the minds of the protagonists, a concrete recognition of sociological bondedness with others, because such consciousness can break down isolation between people, empower them, and lead to collective action on their behalf.

People make sense of their lives, for the most part, in terms of specific events, such as the birth of a child, and sequences of events, such as the life-long impact of parenting a damaged child. Most people do not articulate how sociological categories such as race, gender, class, and ethnicity have shaped their lives or how the larger historical processes such as the Depression or the Women's Movement have affected them. Erik Erikson (1975) contends that only great people, people who see themselves as actors on the historical stage, tell their life stories in a larger social and historical context. Yet, as C. Wright Mills (1959:5) cogently argued, knowledge of the social context leads people to understand their own experiences and to "gauge . . . [their] own fates"; this is the promise of the "sociological imagination." What sociologists are capable of doing is to give voice to silenced people, to present them as historical actors by telling their collective story.

The notion of sociological writing as allegorical goes contrary to received wisdom about the separation of the literary from the scientific. From the 17th century onward, Western Science has rejected "rhetoric (in the name of 'plain' transparent signification), fiction (in the name of fact), and subjectivity (in the name of objectivity)" (Clifford, 1986:5). Rhetoric, fiction, and subjectivity were located in "literature," a new historical construction, aesthetically pleasing but scientifically ridiculed. Literature was denied truth value because it "invented" reality rather than observing it. Dependent on the evocative devices of metaphor and imagery, literature could be interpreted in different ways by different readers. Worse, "the narrating is always multi-vocal—it says one thing to illuminate something else" (De Certeau, 1983:128). Literature violates a major pretension of science: the single, unambiguous voice.

Science was to be written in "plain style," in words that did not, in John Locke's estimation, "move the Passions and thereby mislead the Judgment," unambiguous words unlike the "perfect cheats" of poetic utterances (quoted in Levine, 1985:3). The assault on poetic language intensified throughout the 18th Century. Locke urged parents to stifle any poetic tendencies in their children. Hume depicted poets as professional liars. Bentham proposed that the ideal language would be one where ideas were represented by symbols to eliminate the ambiguity of words. Samuel Johnson's dictionary sought to fix "univocal meanings in perpetuity, much like the univocal meanings of standard arithmetic terms" (Levine, 1985:4).

Such was the attitude toward language when the marquis de Condorcet introduced the term "social science" (Levine, 1985:4). De Condorcet contended that with precise language about moral and social issues "knowledge of the truth" would be "easy and error almost impossible" (quoted in Levine, 1985:6). Emile Durkheim affirmed the need for sociology to resolutely cleanse itself of everyday language. Even Max Weber urged the construction of ideal-types as a way to achieve univocity—the single voice of science.

By the 19th Century, intellectuals divided knowledge into two parts: literature and science. Literature was a bourgeois institution aligned with "art" and "culture." Given to literature were the "higher values" of taste, aesthetics, ethics, humanity, and morality as well as the privilege to be experimental, avante garde, multi-vocal, transgressing (Clifford, 1986:6).

Given to science was the *belief* that its words were objective, precise, unambiguous, non-contextual, non-metaphoric.

This historical separation between literature and science does not imply an immutable schism. Historical implies human construction. What humans construct, they can reconstruct. And, indeed a plethora of disciplines—communications, linguistics, English criticism, anthropology, folklore, women's studies, as well as the sociology of knowledge, science and culture—has been engaged in reconstructive analyses. Their analyses show that literary devices appear in all writing, including scientific writing. All works use such rhetorical devices as metaphor, image and narrative which affect how ideas are formed, how field notes are taken, how survey questions are phrased, how the work is written up, and how readers make sense of it. "Literary devices are inseparable from the telling of 'fact'" (Clifford, 1986:4).

Once we fully recognize this, it seems to me, we can lay claim to some of the "higher values" that were historically given to literature. We can lay claim to a *science* that is aesthetic, moral, ethical, moving, rich, and metaphorical as well as avante garde, transgressing, and multi-vocal. We can lay to rest our Faustian bargain, giving up our humanity for the illusion of objective knowledge.

Meta-Writing Issues: Metaphor and Narrative Voice

If we give up the ill-fitting conceit that our sociological concepts are precise, their referents clear, and our knowledge unambiguous, we are met with an interesting question: the *writing* of sociology. The final solution to the writing problem is not the extermination of jargon, redundancies, passive voice, circumlocution, and (alas) multisyllabic conceptualization referential indicators (for how to write see Becker, 1986a; Selvin and Wilson, 1984; Fox, 1985).

How we choose to write sociology raises two meta-writing issues: guiding metaphor and narrative voice. Our choices are simultaneously political, poetic, methodological, and theoretical.

Writing exists in the context of an implicit guiding metaphor that shapes the narrative. We have an implicit "story which we tell about the people we study," a story which is itself historically rooted (Bruner, 1986:2). Edward Bruner's analysis of the scientific discourse about Native Americans is highly instructive in this regard. In the 1930's and 1940's, the social scientific narrative of Native American social change viewed the present "as disorganization, the past as glorious, and the future as assimilation." Now, there is a new implicit narrative; "the present is viewed as a resistance movement, the past as exploitation, the future as ethnic resurgence" (Bruner, 1986:4). With great rapidity, the guiding concepts of assimilation and acculturation have been replaced with the concepts of exploitation, oppression, liberation, colonialism, and resistance.

The shift in story was more than a theoretical shift; it was a shift in syntax and politics. As science is the child of metaphor, metaphor is the child of politics. For the acculturation story, the writing problem was the description of past culture. Indian life had no future, and the present was interpreted in light of this futurelessness as pathology and disintegration. The political action consistent with this metaphor was to send Native American children to Anglo boarding schools, to create urban relocation projects, to undermine tribal tradition. For the contemporary resistance narrative, however, the writing problem concerns the future: the resistance of indigenous people to exploitation in their struggle to preserve ethnic identity. The writing describes the resistance in the present to preserve the past for the future. Political action consistent with this narrative is intervention to prevent cultural genocide.

Analogous implicit narrative shifts have occurred in the collective stories of other groups of people. Within American society, certain sociologists have positioned Blacks, women, gays and lesbians, the aging, and ethnics within a liberation narrative. And we have extended the liberation narrative to Third World countries, no longer conceptualizing them as "developing," a metaphor that implies their current inferiority but their eventual future as Western clonettes. Instead, the notion of ethnic nationalism is gaining ascendency. The implicit liberation narrative is consistent with liberation movements. Indeed, the outstanding success of feminist scholarship across disciplines arises from its explicit link to the feminist movement, a continuity of purpose between research and activism, namely, the empowerment of women.

The second meta-writing issue is the narrative voice. *Who* is telling the story? The researcher? The researched? Both? Postmodernist critique challenges the grounds for authority in the writings of positivists as well as phenomenologists, measurers as well as ethnographers because it rejects dichotomizing the "knower" and the "known." In scientific writing, authority has been accomplished through the "effacement of the speaking and experiencing" scientists (Pratt, 1986:32). Neither "I" nor "we" are used. With no apparent narrator, an illusion of objectivity is created. The implied narrator is godlike, an all-knowing voice from afar and above, stripped of all human subjectivity and fallibility. But, in fact, science does have a human narrator, the "camouflaged first person," hiding in the bramble of the passive voice. The scientist is not all-knowing. Omniscience is imaginary, possible only in fiction.

Ethnographies have depended upon two forms of authority: the personal experience of the ethnographer in the field and the presumed objective, factual report. Rather than fusing the two forms of knowledge into one, the ethnographer's first person account is separated from the objective account. Personal experiences, anxieties, and fears are marginalized, written about in introductions, appendices, memoirs, and "reflections" sections of qualitative journals.

Contemporary concern with the narrative voice problem has led some social scientists to what is termed "experimental writing," writing social science in non-traditional ways. Experimental writing includes the use of multiple voices, split pages with the storyteller's account filling one column and the analyst's another, and the writing of "true fiction" (cf. Stewart, Forthcoming; Marcus and Fisher, 1986; Clifford and Marcus, 1986; Krieger, 1983; Reinharz, 1979; Pfohl and Gordon, 1986). But the reasons for experimenting with literary style and genre are not simply to deal with the false dichotomization of subject and object; the writing experimentalists are raising political and ethical questions as well. Separating the researcher's story from the people's story implies that the researcher's voice is the authoritative one, a voice that stands *above* the text. But because people have differential access to the use of the authoritative voice—and for the most part the people we study have less access than we do—we may unwittingly colonize, overgeneralize or distort. Further, by objectifying ourselves out of existence, we void our own experiences. We separate our humanity from our work. We create the conditions of our own alienation.

Reflections

What I choose to write about, how I choose to write it, and for whom I write it say more about me than sociodemographics, personality inventories, or horoscopes. My sociological work has been the analysis of power inequalities; my activism, the challenge of those inequalities. To do my work, I have consciously chosen to use the liberation narrative. This narrative tells the collective story of the disempowered, not by judging, blaming or advising them, but by placing their lives within the context of larger social and historical forces, and by directing energy – changing those social structures which perpetuate injustice.

In my recent work (Richardson, 1985), I have told the collective story of a particular set of women, namely, single women involved in long term relationships with married men. Sociologically, their lives had been ignored, their experiences shrouded in secrecy and stigma, and their relationships told about and judged by others, not themselves. I wanted to give voice to this muted group of women: the second sex in a secondary world. I wanted to tell their collective story.

To do this, I first *listened* to the personal stories of single women involved with married men. I heard how single women got involved, fell in love, and ended their relationships with married men. Although the details of the single women's stories differed, the contours of their experiences were similar. My analytical task was to place their narratives in social and historical context, and to discern what in the contemporary world was disempowering them.

In a world where there were not enough eligible men, but where a woman's self esteem was still embedded in having the love of a man, and in a world where women were urged to achieve autonomy and career success, but where they were expected to put their lover's needs above their own, the tension between achieving both an independent identity and a satisfying intimate relationship was severe. One solution to an untenable situation was a relationship with a married man. Believing that these liaisons would be temporary, single women imagined they would achieve intimacy in them without sacrificing independence. However, because of the relationship's secrecy in conjunction with overarching gender inequalities, the woman ended up caring for her lover more than she had intended. The more she cared about him, the more dependent and less powerful she became, because she carried into the relationship the normative expectations for women in love—personal sacrifice.

I struggled with what to call these women. I finally chose the term, "The New Other Woman," or *collectively* "New Other Women." I consciously chose to claim the label, "*other woman*," but I capitalized it, wresting it from its stigmatized context. The capitalization continually reminds me and my readers that these women are not just "others" in the "some . . . others" grammatical construction: They are a distinct social category worthy of a collective story. The "New" in the name modifying "Other Woman" metaphorically suggests the women's simultaneous embrace of contradictions, modernity and traditionalism. Allegorically, we are reminded of the tensions between the old and the new within all modern societies and within our own psyches, as well. In some ways, we are all Other Women—striving to make a life in a contradictory world, torn between our needs for belonging and independence.

The narrative voice in which to tell their collective story troubled me. I was never able to resolve—nor have I yet—the mare's nest of authorial authority, the dichotomy between the observer and the observed. But if I did not "find" a voice, I feared I would descend into the Prince Hamlet Syndrome, frozen by indecision, and—Shakespeare please forgive me—eternally plagued with the question, "to write or not to write. . . ."

Remembering how C. Wright Mills (1959) grounded issues of "intellectual craftsmanship" in the work process rather than in the codification of procedures, I read sociology for style and voice. I rejected the sociological verite style, the publication of the interview transcript, because—to modernize Socratic wisdom—the unanalyzed transcript is not worth reading. I rejected the paraphrasing style because it lacked credibility and it's boring. I rejected the self-centered reflexive style, where the people studied are treated as garnishes and condiments, tasty only in relationship to the main course, the sociologist.

Struggling with finding my narrative voice, I first wrote a woman's story as a scene in which she and I were two "characters" engaged in dialogue. I used my mini-arsenal of literary devices. I set the scene and established the ambience. I showed the woman's feelings, rather than telling about them. I wrote in concrete detail. I quoted. I gave the women fictitious names that inscribed their "narrative essence." "Lisa Maxwell" used her liaison to get a new *lease* on life by changing careers, a change which was of *maximal value* to her. "Michelle Mitchell" was an avante garde architect, who used her liaison to explore and to eventually reject heterosexuality as a way of life. "Abby Goodman" was a psychologist who prided herself on her listening ability, her kindness, and her Jewish hospitality. She was duped by her lover. Each woman had her own story, her own chapter, her own analysis. I felt powerful. I felt like a "writer."

But this narrative voice did not work. The format implied that each story represented something *different* sociologically. Because each story was separately analyzed, I was in fact writing a collection of individual sociobiographies, rather than what I wanted to write, a *collective* story.

My final decision was to organize the research as a unified chronological narrative based on the women's narratives. I typified events and sequences of events, illustrating them through multiple voices and direct quotations. I was trying to simultaneously have the women speak of and for themselves, and for me to speak of and for "them, as a sociological analyst. I was constructing a collective story.

Deciding on my narrative voice was more than a literary and theoretical problem. It was a political issue: "Sociology for Whom?"—a question I have had since graduate school. At the defense of my dissertation on *Pure Mathematics*, a defense attended by a flock of university officials as part of a university wide evaluation of graduate programs, I was asked, "What do you plan to do now?" Being madly in love with sociology and desiring to communicate that passion to the world, I answered, probably with feeling, "I want to write for the public." A hush fell upon the examiners, and, like an errant child, I was excused from the room while they decided my fate. Despite my heretical answer, I passed. With great seriousness, my responsible, if embarrassed Ph.D. committee publicly advised me not to "waste my intelligence on people."

Over the years, I have wrestled with identifying the audience I want to write for, temporarily solving the problem, or perhaps absolving myself of my unwitting sins, by writing, alongside abstract articles on science, mathematics, and literature (cf. Richardson [Walum], 1965; Richardson [Walum], 1975), socially relevant sociology (cf. Richardson [Walum], 1970; Franklin and Richardson, 1972; Richardson [Walum], 1974; Kirshner and Richardson [Walum], 1978), and gender texts, accessible to students and their parents (cf. Richardson, 1977, 1981, 1988; Richardson and Taylor, 1983).

But the more my work on single women and married men progressed, the more I found myself saying, as I did in my dissertation defense, "Sociology is for the people." I decided to write words and sentences that could meet a different standard of science and truth: accessibility to lay audiences. Because I wanted the *sociological* analysis widely disseminated, I chose to write a trade book, working with a publishing house noted for its sociology list (Richardson, 1987).

But the writing story does not end here. Telling the collective story of these women has propelled me back into thinking and writing about very large and abstract sociological questions: questions about the sex and gender system and the social construction of intimacy (Richardson, 1988; Richardson, Forthcoming); about the complementariness of symbolic interactionism and feminist theory (Statham, Richardson, and Cook, 1988); about how gender interacts with other social characteristics, such as age, race, class, sexual orientation, marital status and ethnicity—how we are like each other, how we are different; and questions most of all about how to tell *well* the story of people. My image of sociological work now is an ever-widening spiral, where I write collective stories that are more and more accessible to more people, and then I write more and more sociologically abstract work directed to professionals, each kind of writing deepening the other.

When I was a preschooler, I would daily ponder the mystery of the Morton salt box, where a little dark-haired girl held a Morton salt box with a picture of a little girl holding a Morton salt box and so on and on and on. Was there ever an ending? As infinite regress riveted my attention in childhood, infinite expansion attracts me now. I welcome the writing of collective stories. I welcome metaphor, imagery, evocative prose. In them, I see the possibility of fulfilling sociology's promise—a sociology *of* and *for* the people.

References

Becker, Howard S. 1986a. *Writing for Social Scientists: How to Finish Your Thesis, Book, or Article*. Chicago: The University of Chicago Press.

———. 1986b. "Telling about Society." Pp.121–36 in *Doing Things Together*. Evanston: Northwestern University Press.

Bruner, Edward M. 1986. "Ethnography as Narrative." Pp. 137–55 in *The Anthropology of Experience*, edited by Victor Turner and Edward M. Bruner. Champagne-Urbana: The University of Illinois Press.

Clifford, James. 1986. "Introduction: Partial Truths." Pp. 1–26 in *Writing Culture: The Poetics and Politics of Ethnography*, edited by James Clifford and George E. Marcus. Berkeley, CA: University of California Press.

Clifford, James, and George E. Marcus. (eds.) 1986. *Writing Culture: The Poetics and Politics of Ethnography*. Berkeley, CA: University of California Press.

Cook, Judith A., and Mary Margaret Fonow. 1986. "Knowledge in Women's Interests: Issues in Epistemology and Methodology in Feminist Sociological Research." *Sociological Inquiry* 56:2–29.

De Certeau, Michel. 1983. "History: Ethics, Science and Fiction." Pp. 173–209 in *Social Science as Moral Inquiry*, edited by Norma Hahn, Robert Bellah, Paul Rabinow, and William Sullivan. New York: Columbia University Press.

De Man, Paul. 1979. *Allegories of Reading*. New Haven, CT: Yale University Press.

Diamond, Timothy. Forthcoming. *Making Gray Gold: The Everyday Production of Nursing Home Life*. Chicago: The University of Chicago Press.

DiIorio, Judi. Forthcoming. "Sex Glorious Sex." In *Feminist Frontiers: Rethinking Sex, Gender, and Society*, Second Revised Edition, edited by Laurel Richardson and Verta Taylor. New York: Random House.

Erikson, Erik H. 1975. "On the Nature of 'Psycho-Historical' Evidence." Pp. 113–68 in *Life Span Development and Behavior*. New York: Norton.

Fiske, Donald W., and Richard A. Shweder (eds.) 1986. *Metatheory in Social Science: Pluralisms and Subjectivities*. Chicago: University of Chicago Press.

Fonow, Mary Margaret, and Judith A. Cook (eds.) Forthcoming. *Feminist Methodology in the Social Sciences*. Bloomington, IN: University of Indiana Press.

Fox, Mary Frank (ed.). 1985. *Scholarly Writing and Publishing: Issues, Problems, and Solutions*. Boulder, CO: Westview Press.

Franklin, Clyde W., and Laurel Richardson. 1972. "Sex and Race: A Substructural Paradigm." *Phylon* 242:53.

Geertz, Clifford. 1980. "Blurred Genres." *American Scholar* 49:165–79.

Gleick, James. 1984. "Solving the Mathematical Riddle of Chaos." *The New York Times Magazine*, June 10th, pp. 30–32.

Kirschner, Betty Frankie, and Laurel Richardson [Walum]. 1978. "Dual Location Families: Married Singles." *Alternative Life Styles* 1:513–25.

Krieger, Susan. 1983. *The Mirror Dance: Identity in a Woman's Community*. Philadelphia: Temple University Press.

Levine, Donald N. 1985. *The Flight from Ambiguity: Essays in Social and Cultural Theory*. Chicago: University of Chicago Press.

Livingston, Debra. 1982. "'Round and 'Round the Bramble Bush: From Legal Realism to Critical Legal Scholarship." *Harvard Law Review* 95:1650–76.

Long, Judy. 1987. "Telling Women's Lives: The New Sociobiography." Presented at the American Sociological Association Meetings, Chicago, IL.

Marcus, George E., and Michael M. J. Fisher. 1986. *Anthropology as Cultural Critique: An Experimental Moment in the Human Sciences.* Chicago: University of Chicago Press.

Mills, C. Wright. 1959. *The Sociological Imagination.* New York: Oxford University Press.

Mishler, Elliot G. 1986. *Research Interviewing.* Cambridge, MA: Harvard University Press.

Pratt, Mary Louise. 1986. "Fieldwork in Common Places." Pp. 27–50 in *Writing Culture: The Poetics and Politics of Ethnography,* edited by James Clifford and George E. Marcus. Berkeley, CA: University of California Press.

Phohl, Stephen, and Avery Gordon. 1986. "Criminological Displacement: A Sociological Deconstruction." *Social Problems* 33:94–113.

Reinharz, Shulamit. 1979. *On Becoming a Social Scientist.* San Francisco: Jossey-Bass.

Richardson, Laurel. 1965. "Pure Mathematics Publications: 1939–1958." *American Mathematics Monthly* 73:192–95.

———. 1968. "Group Perception of Threat of Non-Members." *Sociometry* 3:278–84.

———. 1970. "Sociologists as Signers: Some Characteristics of Protestors of Vietnam War Policy." *American Sociologist* 5:161–65.

———. 1974. "The Changing Door Ceremony: Some Notes on the Operation of Sex-Roles in Everyday Life." *Urban Life and Culture* 2:506–15.

———. 1975. "The Art of Domination: An Analysis of Power in Paradise Lost." *Social Forces* 53:573–80.

———. 1985. *The New Other Woman: Contemporary Single Women in Affairs with Married Men.* New York: The Free Press.

———. 1987. "Disseminating Research to Popular Audiences: The Book Tour." *Qualitative Sociology* 10:164–76.

———. 1988. *The Dynamics of Sex and Gender: A Sociological Perspective.* Third Revised Edition. New York: Harper and Row.

———. 1988. "Secrecy and Status: The Social Construction of Forbidden Relationships." *American Sociological Review* 53:209–19.

———. Forthcoming. "Sexual Freedom and Sexual Constraint: The Paradox of Single Woman and Married Man Liaisons." *Gender & Society.*

Richardson, Laurel, and Verta Taylor. 1983. *Feminist Frontiers: Rethinking Sex, Gender, and Society.* New York: Random House.

Rorty, Richard. 1979. *Philosophy and the Mirror of Nature.* Princeton: Princeton University Press.

Selvin, Hanan C., and Everett K. Wilson. 1984. "On Sharpening Sociologists' Prose." *The Sociological Quarterly* 25:205–22.

Stewart, John. Forthcoming. *Drinkers, Drummers, & Decent Folk: Ethnographic Narratives of Village Trinidad.* New York: SUNY.

Statham, Anne, Laurel Richardson, and Judith A. Cook. 1988. *Any Questions: Gender and University Teaching.* Unpublished Manuscript: Department of Sociology. Ohio State University.

Strathern, Marilyn. 1987. "Out of Context: The Persuasive Fictions of Anthropology." *Current Anthropology* 28:251–70.

4

THE USE OF PERSONAL NARRATIVES IN SOCIAL SCIENCE AND HISTORY

Mary Jo Maynes, Jennifer L. Pierce, and Barbara Laslett

Introduction

The relationship between the individual and the social has been a problem of perennial concern to social scientists and humanists alike. In the second half of the twentieth century, theorists from various disciplines and often competing tendencies—ranging from structuralist sociologists to feminist theorists, and from the "new social historians" to their Foucauldian critics—converged around theories that undermined classical understandings of the individual as a purposive social actor. The critiques went to the core of much modern Western social, political, and historical analysis; more deeply, they raised new questions about selfhood as it is understood, articulated, and practiced by individuals.[1]

Beginning around the same time, ironically, there has been an outpouring of scholarly work based on personal narrative evidence—that is on retrospective first-person accounts of individual lives. The impulses behind the increased interest in individuals' personal narratives are multiple, as we discuss more fully below. One primary motivation is the desire to examine varieties of individual selfhood and agency "from below" and in practice, as constructed in people's articulated self-understandings.

More specifically, analyses of personal narratives have served to introduce marginalized voices (e.g., those of women or globally subaltern people) and they also have provided counternarratives that dispute misleading generalizations or refute universal claims. For some researchers, the goal of personal narrative analysis has simply been to work from an empirical base that is more inclusive. However, the grounding for many studies based on personal narratives is in critical traditions (such as Marxism, feminism, subaltern theory, or queer theory) that question the epistemological foundations of positivist social science, recognize the historical and social specificity of all viewpoints and subjectivities, and emphasize the perspectivity intrinsic to knowledge production.

Telling Stories enters into these discussions through a cross-disciplinary examination of analyses of personal narratives. We have been able to write this book at this juncture precisely because of the continuing groundswell of new and creative approaches to personal narrative analysis across disciplines. *Telling Stories* argues that analyses of personal narratives, beyond the contributions they make to specific areas of empirical research, can also serve to reorient theories about the relationship between the individual and the social by calling attention to the social and cultural dynamics through which individuals construct themselves as social actors. In so doing, they have the potential constructively to intervene in the theoretical impasse resulting from the collision between skepticism of hegemonic individualism, on the one hand, and the persistent, even increasingly urgent interest in understanding selfhood and human agency, on the other.

Personal narrative analysis, we argue, demonstrates that human agency and individual social action is best understood in connection with the construction of selfhood in and through historically specific social relationships and institutions. Second, these analyses emphasize the narrative dimensions of selfhood; that is, well-crafted personal narrative analyses not only reveal the dynamics of agency in practice but also can document its construction through culturally embedded narrative forms that, over an individual's life, impose their own logics and thus also shape both life stories and lives. Finally, *Telling Stories* calls attention to the subjective and intersubjective character of the analysis of personal narratives. In contrast with many other approaches to social-scientific and historical analysis, many of the insights that personal narrative analyses provide flow from tapping into subjective takes on the world (those of narrators, analysts, and readers). Moreover, the attempt to generate intersubjective understandings—between narrator and analyst and between analyst and audience—are a distinctive feature of this approach and of the knowledge it produces.

The connections among individual agency, historically and socially embedded processes of self-construction, and the culturally specific narrative forms in which individuals construct their life stories and subjectivities are interwoven throughout *Telling Stories*. These connections drive its arguments about theorizing the relationship between the individual and the social and also its arguments about methodologies for effective personal narrative analysis.

Personal Narratives: Connecting the Individual and the Social

For scholars who analyze personal narratives, it is important to recognize that stories that people tell about their lives are never simply individual, but are told in historically specific times and settings and draw on the rules and models in circulation that govern how story elements link together in narrative logics. *Telling Stories* thus necessarily draws on wide ranging understandings of and approaches to life stories and their analysis—historical, social-scientific, and literary. What people do and their understandings of why they do what they do are typically at the center of their stories about their lives. Empirically, they provide access to individuals' claims about how their motivations, emotions, imaginations—in other words, about the subjective dimensions of social action—have been shaped by cumulative life experience. Although life stories vary greatly in the detail they include, partly because of the variance in individual lives and personalities and partly because differing norms of storytelling shape life story plots, we argue that it is inappropriate to regard life stories primarily as idiosyncratic. Individual life stories are very much embedded in social relationships and structures and they are expressed in culturally specific forms; read carefully, they provide unique insights into the connections between individual life trajectories and collective forces and institutions beyond the individual. They thus offer a methodologically privileged location from which to comprehend human agency.

Personal narrative sources, moreover, are infused with notions of temporal causality that link an individual life with stories about the collective destiny. In analyses of life histories, two salient temporalities continually interact. Historical time contextualizes a life course, even while the narrator's moment in the life course affects how he or she experiences, remembers, and interprets historical events. Both temporalities, then, inform life histories: any methodologically sound employment of such stories for the purposes of social-scientific analysis needs to keep both temporalities in mind. In other words, when events happen within the individual life course and when they happen with reference to historical temporalities are, we suggest, analytical keys to understanding people's lives and the stories they tell about them.

Finally, personal narrative analysis pushes the investigator to move beyond the distinction between what sociologists call the macro and micro levels of analysis (or, put differently, between the social and the individual realms of experience) and instead to focus on the connections linking them. Once the individual life is explored in its subjective detail and temporal depth, the line between individual and social tends to dissolve. We are not arguing, of course, that the strong sense of self as distinct from a collectivity that marks personal narrative claims about agency, especially in Western cultures, is merely delusional. On the contrary, the problem of this relationship is precisely the focus of our book; it is our contention that personal narrative analysis that keeps an eye open toward the interconnectedness of the individual and the social provides a basis for a new understanding, even recovery of, the individual as a focus of social-scientific and historical inquiry.

Personal Narratives as Documents of Social Action and Self-Construction

Telling Stories emphasizes the *storied* quality of personal narratives, which rely simultaneously on literary and historical logics. Stories that people tell about their lives deploy individual "plots" in a way that resembles the construction of literary narratives; they also embed their subjects in larger narrative frames with historical plots and temporalities. *Telling Stories* thus draws on a wide range of approaches to narrative-historical, social-scientific, and literary. These stories, we argue, are individual creations but are never simply individual creations; they are told in historically specific times and places and draw on the rules and models and other narratives in circulation that govern how story elements link together in a temporal logic.[2]

Narrative analysis is not as common or well established across the social sciences as other forms of analysis, but scholars from a variety of disciplines now increasingly employ it in their research and also have generated an ongoing discussion of relevant epistemological and methodological issues.[3] The aims and techniques of narrative analysis are diverse. Our focus in *Telling Stories* is quite specific and differs in aim and focus from much of the narrative analysis now common in fields such as medical and legal sociology, social psychology, and social work. Our interest centers on a specific subset of narrative analyses; namely, on research employing the analysis of personal narratives. A *personal narrative* (we also sometimes use the more common term *life story*) in our usage is a retrospective first-person account of the evolution of an individual life over time and in social context. Specifically, we are primarily interested in social-scientific and historical analyses based on such forms of personal narrative as oral histories, autobiographies, in-depth interviews, diaries, journals, and letters.

Personal narratives according to our definition contrast in key ways with other types of narratives often used in social-scientific research such as narratives of illness that focus on one specific dimension of experience, or conversational transcripts that capture a self-presentation in a particular setting and moment in time. There are points where the issues we discuss here have a lot in common with narrative analysis in this broader sense. Temporality, for example, is an important dimension of most types of narrative analysis. However, it plays a different role in different types of narrative analysis. Close attention to sequencing or pauses in people's accounts may be a crucial aspect of temporality in conversational analysis or in the analysis of a narrative of illness, for example, whereas in personal narrative analysis of the sort that we discuss in *Telling Stories*, the temporality of the life course and its intersection with historical temporality are of the essence. And just to be clear, while narrative researchers employ the term "personal narratives" to describe a wide range of sources, we are defining the term more specifically and narrowly in this book. We focus on analyses of particular types of personal narratives as we pursue our general arguments about the relationship between the individual and the social. Despite this focus, we are concerned with many of the same theoretical and methodological questions that all narrative researchers confront.[4]

Subjectivity and Social Science: The Epistemology of Personal Narrative Analysis

Scholars in the social sciences have often regarded life histories with unease and suspicion. Many sociologists and political scientists dismiss analyses that focus on individual actions as guilty of the logical errors of methodological individualism or volunteerism. Within positivist strains of social science, life stories are reduced to the status of the anecdotal, adding color or personal interest but unreliable as a basis for generalization. In the 1960s and 1970s, social historians also contributed to this skepticism by criticizing the "great man" approach to history and emphasizing instead the relatively unforgiving structures and mentalities that change only slowly and constrain individual choices.

Life histories, and the individual subjectivities they presume, have also been subject to challenges from scholars operating within post-positivist epistemological frameworks and theoretical traditions. Poststructuralists, particularly those influenced by the work of Michel Foucault, regard individuals and the stories they tell about their experiences as primarily constituted through discourse. Similarly, in the 1980s, the narrative turn in anthropology undermined the transparency of the life history and ethnographic descriptions that had been a mainstay of the anthropological method by attending to the generic forms, rhetorical conventions, and authorial and institutional power relations that produce them. Importantly, feminist theorists in many disciplines have deconstructed the quintessential Western concept of the autonomous individual, a conception of the self that often masks the dependencies and inequalities on which its "autonomy"—and the basis it postulates for individual agency—rests.

Despite these forms of skepticism we argue that *it is precisely their subjective character* that has made personal narratives increasingly interesting to social scientists and historians aiming to open up space for new understandings of the relationship between the individual and the social. Within this broad theoretical and empirical agenda, personal narrative analyses address a range of specific aims. Some explore in depth a particular social, categorical, or positional location and thus address critical dimensions of social action that are otherwise opaque. Often the very titles or subtitles of personal narrative analyses of social-structural categories reveal such aims; for example, *Academics from the Working Class*, *The Polish Peasant in Europe and America*, "Life Stories in the Bakers' Trade," *Life Course in French and German Workers' Autobiographies in the Era of Industrialization*, *Auf dem Weg ins Burgerleben* (on the path to a bourgeois life), *Stories of a Lesbian Generation*, *An Intimate History of American Girls*, or *Family Firms in Italy*.[5] In these analyses, individual stories are treated as interesting in and of themselves, but their analytic value rests on their ability to reveal something new about a social position defined by and of interest to the analyst but more legible through an insider's view. Thus, for example, sociologists Daniel Bertaux and Isabelle Bertaux-Wiame started with the puzzle of how to account for the survival of artisanal baking in Paris. Their answers came from the life histories of male bakers, and their wives, that when analyzed together revealed the gender and generational dynamics of bakery succession.[6] Particular characteristics of personal narrative evidence—for example, its documentation of the lifelong consequences of transformative experiences, or the operation of temporal logics that data from one point in time cannot capture, or its revelation of details of everyday life that prove only in retrospect to have been salient—make it especially useful for capturing certain types of social-structural dynamics.

A large number of personal narrative analyses have been designed pointedly *to introduce marginalized voices into the record.* Feminist uses of personal narrative analysis provide a good illustration. While some feminist research has sought mainly to bring women's voices and perspectives to light, others focus on the analysis of gender as an organizing principle of social life. Personal narrative analyses have played a major role in both types of feminist projects; conversely, many scholars who use personal narrative analysis make claims based on feminist epistemological grounds. Initially echoing the political techniques of consciousness raising that emerged in second-wave feminist groups and organizations in the United States in the late 1960s, at the core of feminist epistemology is the claim that new insights about gender relations and power emerge from women telling stories about themselves and their lives and that the process of telling reveals past oppressions that had been suppressed or unrecognized. As the editors of *Interpreting Women's Lives: Feminist Theory and Personal Narratives* wrote in 1989, "For a woman, claiming the truth of her life despite awareness of other versions of reality that contest this truth often produces both a heightened criticism of officially condoned untruths and a heightened sense of injustice."[7] This insight was extended to the more general claim that just as social relations are embedded in a nexus of hierarchical gender relations, so too is knowledge production itself.[8]

In a similar vein, explorations of alternative sexualities have relied heavily on personal narrative analysis. Like consciousness raising, "coming-out stories" were a mainstay of gay and lesbian personal politics in the era of emergence of gay rights movements. Telling counternarratives moved readily from emancipatory politics to gay-lesbian-bisexual-transgender (GLBT) scholarship, often designed to reveal the damage inflicted by blatant homophobia suffered by homosexuals, or the more veiled dynamics of heteronormativity. Since the introduction of queer theory and feminist critiques of essentialism, personal narrative analysis more frequently has been used to document the construction and reconstruction of sexual identities understood to be unstable, rooted in particular practices, and mutable.[9] Personal narrative analysis can capture this dynamic construction process, even as the stories themselves document historic shifts and variations in the experience of particular sexual identities.

Beyond the women's and GLBT movements, an outpouring of oral histories from the late 1960s onward also drew political insights from the U.S. Civil Rights movement, peace movements, trade union movements, antipoverty movements, and Third World liberation struggles and applied them to critical scholarship in history and the social sciences. Not surprisingly, then, many of the best examples of personal narrative analysis have emerged in the areas of African American studies and ethnic studies more generally, labor and working-class history, Latin American studies, and African studies. Like feminist claims, the power of the analyses results from bringing new voices and previously untold stories into conversations on topics about which these voices provide invaluable witness, critique, and alternative narratives. In the arena of African American studies, the long tradition of testimony going back to slave narratives has offered a distinctive basis for knowledge about black history and culture.[10] Among historians, probably no field has been more creative in its use of personal narratives than African history. Prior to the 1960s, much African history was written from the perspective of colonial or former colonial powers and was based on their archival records. In the anticolonial movements and in postcolonial Africa, many historians of Africa (among them Africans, Europeans, and North Americans) sought out African perspectives, African voices, and African narrative traditions for their studies of the past and their revisions of history. Not surprisingly, oral histories and life stories featured prominently.[11]

Class analysis has also relied on personal narrative research. Labor and working-class history have almost always been written from a subaltern location within the discipline of history. Marxist epistemologies have at times explicitly informed these histories, especially when they emerged from socialist intellectual milieus; in some settings, such as the German Socialist Party of the late nineteenth and early twentieth centuries, workers were encouraged to tell their stories for the edification of fellow workers and for the betterment of social research. Their personal narratives were meant as substantiations of the class coming to consciousness. The energy with which labor history was infused beginning in the 1960s as a result of the developments of new social history and "history from below" led to a renewed interest in the stories of workers and labor organizers.[12] Within this enormous body of literature that rests on critical epistemologies and centers on marginalized voices, some studies deliberately use personal narratives as *sources of counternarratives to undermine misleading generalizations, correct commonly misused analytic categories, or refute historical claims based on other types of evidence or other modes of inquiry.* For example, historian Wally Seccombe turned to letters from working-class wives in early twentieth-century England to cast doubt on demographic generalizations about fertility control based on the common presumption among demographers that choices about fertility were made by married couples.[13] Seccombe's interpretation of the letters revealed how the category of "couple" disguised how men's and women's stakes in fertility decisions could differ and hid the power dynamics that affected whose desires prevailed in the outcome. He pointed to the significance of factors that cannot be captured by usual statistical correlations focused on family size, occupation, income, and education. Instead Seccombe argues that in accounting for European fertility decline, relationships between husbands and wives, and historical factors such as medical arguments in favor of contraception that could be used with authority by wives and then enforced through moral suasion, play a role even before male cooperation could be counted on as a "rational" response to changing economic conditions. The logic of his argument, then, is to point to truths found in personal narratives that lie beyond the reach of more commonly used techniques.

Closely related are personal narrative analyses that *reveal "hidden histories" or revisionist understandings* of a phenomenon or event because they bring to light not merely new or untapped perspectives but also suppressed or deliberately hidden histories. These kinds of analyses, whether based on life stories gathered by the researcher or on extant sources such as memoirs or letters, open possibilities for revealing "private" or "privileged" information that is relevant to our understanding of a historical or social phenomenon, but is normally beyond the reach of all except insiders. The claim here, then, is that personal narrative sources can reveal a social or historical dynamic that has been deliberately silenced or distorted by interested parties. For example, Mary Jo Maynes's analysis of the autobiographies published in the context of the German socialist movement emphasizes that movement's determination to present workers as competent historical subjects, and to counter the dominant culture's attempts to pathologize the working-class family. Still, as Maynes suggests and as some subaltern and feminist theorists have argued, there is never an "authentic" identity transparently revealed in personal narratives or any other sources.[14] The circulation and preservation of politicized identities are always matters of contest; personal narratives can be valuable documents of such contestation.

Some personal narrative analyses provide entrees into the black box of subjectivity by exploring its psychological as well as its social dimensions. Their knowledge claims rest on insights about deep motivations, irrationalities as well as rationalities, and their connections to actions— connections that are not transparent but emerge only when the narrator's psychological history is revealed. Relatively few in number since this sort of analysis is beyond the reach of most personal narrative evidence, these studies can nonetheless succeed as rich social-scientific accounts under the right circumstances. Historians and sociologists have ventured onto this terrain with personal narrative analyses that, while rooted in social relations nevertheless see the psychological and the social as intertwined. Letters, diaries, and other personal writings become keys to making sense of, not just an individual's motivations, but more generally the psychological construction of social action and the social construction of the psyche in a particular context. To offer one example, Barbara Laslett uses the personal writings and public papers of the prominent early twentieth-century American sociologist William Fielding Ogburn to suggest the interconnections between private aspects of his life story and the development of his ideas about how scientific sociology should be defined and practiced.[15]

Finally, some analyses of personal narratives result in forms of knowledge that are *accessible only through intersubjective or dialogic processes.* Sometimes this knowledge emerges only because of the emotional responses triggered by the interview situation itself. Obviously, these sorts of encounters become ethically difficult when narrators tell analysts something that might strike them as morally objectionable or personally offensive, One striking example is Helena Pohlandt-McCormick's reaction to a life history narrator who told her of having been involved in a killing during the Soweto uprising.[16] Paying close attention to such moments can be fruitful, for it is precisely the emotional intensity of the interview encounter that signals that revelations of an uncommon sort are occurring. Perceived silences can also be an indicator of boundary crossing, marking the distinction between publicly acceptable forms of discourse and private thoughts and feelings. Though analysts may not be able to get beyond a narrator's silence, discomfort, or reluctance, they can nevertheless read them productively for insights into norms about taboo topics, emotions, or opinions within different narratives and in different contexts.

Because personal narrative analysis is based on distinct epistemological and methodological presumptions, it produces a different type of knowledge than do many other types of social-scientific and historical analysis. It contrasts with much of the research in the social sciences—especially common in the disciplines of sociology, political science, and economics—that focuses on the statistical analysis of aggregate data about entire populations or large samples. In these types of analysis, the overarching purpose is to establish correlations between variables or to predict general patterns and trends.[17] Personal narrative analysis, by contrast, builds from the individual and the personal. It gleans insight not only from subjective perceptions about social phenomena and events as revealed through participants' stories, but more particularly through narrative forms of experiencing, recalling, and making sense of social action. Subjectivity and narrativity are at the core of the alternative epistemological presumptions associated with personal narrative analysis.

Personal narratives can offer interpretations about many aspects of social life, but given their epistemological and methodological assumptions, historical and social-scientific analysis of them can support corresponding types of knowledge claims. In contrast to demographic studies and survey research, which often reduce individuals to a cluster of variables such as race, ethnicity, gender, or political affiliation, effective personal narrative analysis provides evidence about individuals as whole persons. By offering insights from the point of view of narrators who see themselves as persons in context, and whose stories reflect their lived experiences over time and in particular social and historical settings, personal narrative analyses proceed from a logic that is quite different from other types of social-scientific analysis. The interest in *whole persons* is key to the distinctiveness of personal narrative approaches when compared with the types of social-scientific epistemology and practice that came to prevail in the United States in the course of the twentieth century. To consider whole persons involves understanding multiple aspects of an individual's life and experiences over the life course and in historical time. Studying whole persons involves an epistemological strategy that sees individuals *both* as unique *and* as connected to social and cultural worlds and relationships that affect their life choices and life stories. Learning about and interpreting these relationships, we are arguing, entails soliciting stories that individuals tell about their lives and in their own terms, rather than simply categorizing them in analytic terms that research questions impose on them. Personal narrative analyses are certainly appropriately informed by theories and conceptualizations derived from the analyst's interests and categories. But the analytic categories must also be responsive to the terms in which narrators make sense of their world.

It is worth elaborating this epistemological point here through reference to the evolution of American sociology and its presumptions. Within sociology, change in the organization and nature of empirical research after World War II made it more difficult to study "whole persons" because the criteria for drawing professionally acceptable "scientific" conclusions from empirical research were changing. In his study of the five top-ranked U.S. sociology departments (Columbia University, the University of Chicago, the University of Michigan, the University of Wisconsin, and Harvard University), George Steinmetz argues that a tolerance for methodological and epistemological diversity that characterized these departments before World War II began to erode shortly after it. By 1950, the earlier "balanced or splintered epistemic condition had disappeared. . . . Methodological positivism was becoming orthodox or even *doxic*, that is, its practices and proclamations were increasingly recognized even by its opponents as a form of scientific capital, however much they disliked it."[18] This did not mean, of course, that other methodologies ceased to exist. What it did mean is that the accumulation of rewards—professional status, respect, and recognition—supported methodological positivism and the accompanying use of quantitative methodologies. It therefore became less common to do the sort of in-depth research required for understanding the beliefs and actions of "whole persons"; favored methods tended to reduce and simplify the analytic categories that sociologists (and other social sciences) used; along with this limitation there evolved an overly simplified understanding of individuals and of human agency.

Writing up analyses based on personal narrative evidence also presents particular methodological and rhetorical challenges to social scientists and historians. The forms of evidence are distinctive, and logics of persuasion rest on epistemological grounds that are at odds with the assumptions embedded in much mainstream social science. What makes a personal analysis persuasive as argument? What kinds of truth claims can be made on the basis of individual life stories? What forms of generalization are appropriate in personal narrative analysis? Transparency and clarity about the processes that shape the production and analysis of the personal narratives, we argue, goes a long way toward making arguments persuasive. Furthermore, such transparency also serves to educate audiences who are perhaps more accustomed to other types of analysis about how to read and evaluate knowledge claims based on personal narrative evidence. In the end, we argue, the way of knowing that is characteristic of personal narrative analysis is necessarily distinctive from the knowledge claims of positivist social science.

Notes

1. Bridging this dualism has long been an important theoretical project among social theorists. See Anthony Giddens, *Central Problems in Social Theory* (Berkeley and Los Angeles: University of California Press, 1979); Philip Abrams, *Historical Sociology* (Ithaca, NY: Cornell University Press, 1982); Pierre Bourdieu, *Outline of a Theory of Practice* (Cambridge: Cambridge University Press, 1977) and *The Logic of Practice* (Stanford: Stanford University Press, 1980), both translated by Richard Nice; Pierre Bourdieu and Loic Wacquant, *An Invitation to Reflexive Sociology* (Chicago: University of Chicago Press, 1992); George Steinmetz, "Bourdieu's Disavowal of Lacan: Psychoanalytic Theory and the Concepts of 'Habitus' and 'Symbolic Capital'" *Constellations* 13, no. 4 (2006): 44 64; James Coleman, "Social Theory, Social Research and a Theory of Action" *American Journal of Sociology* 91, no. 6 (1986): 1309–1335 and *Foundations of Social Theory* (Cambridge, MA: Harvard University Press, 1990); Jurgen Habermas, *The Theory of Communicative Action*, vol. 2, *Lifeworld and System: A Critique of Functionalist Reason* (Boston: Beacon Press, 1985).
2. There is a considerable literature on the underpinnings of narrative and narrativity as well as empirical studies that adopt a narrative approach to social-scientific analysis. Works that are particularly helpful in terms of the approach we develop here include: Paul Ricoeur, *Time and Narrative*, 2 vols., translated

by Kathleen McLaughlin and David Pellauer (Chicago: University of Chicago Press, 1984—86); Charles Taylor, *Sources of the Self* (Cambridge, MA: Harvard University Press, 1989); Personal Narratives Group, *Interpreting Women's Lives: Feminist Theory and Personal Narratives* (Bloomington: University of Indiana Press, 1989); Margaret Somers, "Narrativity, Narrative Identity, and Social Action: Rethinking English Working-Class Formation," *Social Science History* 16, no. 4 (1992): 591–630; Patrick Ewick and Susan S. Silbey, "Subversive Stories and Hegemonic Tales: Toward a Sociology of Narrative," *Law and Society Review* 29 (1995): 197–226; Francesca Polletta, "Contending Stories: Narrative in Social Movements," *Qualitative Sociology* 21, no. 2 (1998): 419–446; Jaber F. Gubrium and James A. Holstein, "At the Border of Narrative and Ethnography," *Journal of Contemporary Ethnography* 28 (1999): 561–573; Richard Price, *The Political Use of Racial Narratives: School Desegregation in Mobile, Alabama, 1954–97* (Urbana: University of Illinois Press, 2002); Joseph Davis, ed., *Stories of Change: Narrative and Social Movements* (Albany: State University of New York Press, 2002); Ronald J. Berger and Richard Quinney, eds., *Storytelling Sociology: Narrative as Social Inquiry* (Boulder, CO: Lynne Riemer, 2005).

3. For examples of works demonstrating a wide range of approaches to narrative analysis in the social sciences beyond the subset we call analyses of personal narratives, see Jerome Bruner, *Actual Minds, Possible Worlds* (Cambridge, MA: Harvard University Press, 1986); Kenneth J. Gergen and Mary M. Gergen, "Narratives of the Self," in *Studies in Social Identity*, ed. Theodore R. Sarbin and Karle E. Scheibe, 254–273 (New York: Praeger, 1983); Susan Chase, *Ambiguous Empowerment: Work Narratives of School Superintendents* (Amherst: University of Massachusetts Press, 1995); Elliot Mishler, *Research Interviewing: Context and Narrative* (Cambridge, MA: Harvard University Press, 1986); Richard Delgado, "Legal Storytelling for Oppositionists and Others: A Plea for Narrative," *Michigan Law Review* 87 (1989): 2411–2441; Cheryl Mattingly, *Healing Dramas and Clinical Plots: The Narrative Structure of Experience* (Cambridge: Cambridge University Press, 1998); Francesca Polletta, *It Was Like a Fever: Storytelling in Protest and Politics* (Chicago: University of Chicago Press, 2006). English-language journals that have explored narrative analysis in the social sciences and history include, for example, *Narrative Inquiry, Qualitative Sociology, Journal of Narrative and Life History, History Workshop Journal, Oral History Review*, and *Auto/biography*.

4. For a useful discussion, see E. G. Mishler, *Storylines: Craftartists' Narratives of Identity* (Cambridge, MA: Harvard University Press, 1999), which includes a helpful account of the methods used in his research and its grounding in sociolinguistic research traditions. Susan E. Bell, "Intensive Performances of Mothers: A Sociological Perspective," *Qualitative Research* 4 (2004): 45–75, provides an interesting discussion of the author's use of artwork to trace a narrative of the meanings of intensive motherhood over the first year of an infant's life. See also Paul Atkinson and Sara Delamont, "Rescuing Narrative from Qualitative Research," *Narrative Inquiry* 16 (2006): 164–172; Mike Bury, "Illness Narratives: Fact or Fiction," *Sociology of Health & Illness*, 23 (2001): 263–285; Cheryl Mattingly, "Pocahontas Goes to the Clinic: Popular Culture as Lingua Franca in a Cultural Borderland," *American Anthropologist* 108 (2006): 494–501; E. G. Mishler, *Research Interviewing: Context and Narrative* (Cambridge, MA: Harvard University Press, 1986); Lee Quinney, "Narrative

in Social Work," *Qualitative Social Work* 4 (2005): 391–412; Catherine Kohler Reissman, "Beyond Reductionism: Narrative Genre in Divorce Accounts," *Journal of Narrative and Life History* 1(1991): 41–68 and *Narrative Methods for the Human Sciences* (Thousand Oaks, CA: Sage, 2007).

5. Jake Ryan and Charles Sackrey, *Strangers in Paradise: Academics from the Working Class* (New York: South End Press, 1984); William I. Thomas and Florian Znaniecki, *The Polish Peasant in Europe and America: A Classic Work in Immigration History* (Urbana: University of Illinois Press, 1996), ed. Eli Zaretsky (first published in five volumes in 1918–1920); Daniel Bertaux and Isabelle Bertaux-Wiame, "Life Stories in the Bakers' Trade," in *Biography and Society*, ed. Daniel Bertaux (London: Sage Publications, 1981), pp. 169–190; Mary Jo Maynes, *Taking the Hard Road: Life Course in French and German Workers' Autobiographies in the Era of Industrialization* (Chapel Hill: University of North Carolina Press, 1995); Gunilla-Friederike Budde, *Auf dem Weg ins Burgerleben: Kindheit und Erziehung in deutschen und englischen Burgerfamilien 1840–1914* (On the path to bourgeois life: childhood and education in German and English bourgeois families, 1840–1914) (Gottingen: Vandenhoeck & Ruprecht, 1994); Arlene Stein, *Sex and Sensibility: Stories of a Lesbian Generation* (Berkeley: University of California Press, 1997); Joan Brumberg, *The Body Project: An Intimate History of American Girls* (New York: Random House, 1997); Sylvia Yanagisako, *Producing Culture and Capital: Family Firms in Italy* (Princeton, NJ: Princeton University Press, 2002).

6. Bertaux and Bertaux-Wiame, "Life Stories."

7. Personal Narratives Group, *Interpreting Women's Lives*, pp. 7–8.

8. See, e.g., Dorothy Smith, *The Everyday World as Problematic: A Feminist Sociology* (Boston: Northeastern University Press, 1987); Joan Scott, "Gender: A Useful Category of Historical Analysis," in *Gender and the Politics of History* (New York: Columbia University Press, 1988); Donna Haraway, "Situated Knowledges: The Science Question in Feminism as a Site of Discourse on the Privilege of Partial Perspective," *Feminist Studies* 14, no. 3 (1988): 575–599; Gayatri Spivak, "Can the Subaltern Speak?" in *Marxism and the Interpretation of Culture*, ed. Cary Nelson and Lawrence Grossberg (Urbana: University of Illinois Press, 1988); Patricia Hill Collins, *Black Feminist Thought* (New York: Allen and Unwin, 1990); Sandra Harding, *Whose Science? Whose Knowledge? Thinking from Women's Lives* (Ithaca, NY: Cornell University Press, 1991).

9. We discuss examples in chapters 2 and 5. These include R. W. Connell, *Masculinities* (Berkeley and Los Angeles: University of California Press, 1995); Kath Weston, *Render Me, Gender Me: Lesbians Talk Sex, Class, Color, Nation, Studmuffins* (New York: Columbia University Press, 1996); Arlene Stein, *Sex and Sensibility*; Ken Plummer, *Telling Sexual Stories: Power, Change, and Social Worlds* (London: Routledge, 1995).

10. We discuss many examples of work in this vein in subsequent chapters. These include, for example, Sara Lawrence-Lightfoot, *I've Known Rivers: Lives of Loss and Liberation* (New York, Penguin Books, 1994) and *Respect: An Exploration* (Cambridge, MA: Perseus Books, 2000); Mamie Garvin Fields with Karen Fields, *Lemon Swamp and Other Places: A Carolina Memoir* (New York: The Free Press, 1983).

11. See, e.g., Marjorie Shostak, *Nisa: The Life and Words of a !Kung Woman* (Cambridge, MA: Harvard University Press, 2000); Jan Vansina, *Oral Tradition*

as History (Madison: University of Wisconsin Press, 1985); Allen Isaacman, *Cotton Is the Mother of Poverty: Peasants, Work, and Rural Struggle in Colonial Mozambique, 1938–1961* (London: Heinemann, 1995); Marcia Wright, *Strategies of Slaves and Women: Life-Stories from East/Central Africa* (London: Currey, 1993); Shula Marks, *Not Either an Experimental Doll: The Separate Worlds of Three South African Women* (Bloomington: Indiana University Press, 1988); Heidi Gengenbach, *Naming the Past in a "Scattered" Land: Memory and the Powers of Women's Naming Practices in Southern Mozambique* (Boston: African Studies Center, 2000).

12. Again, there are many examples, and we discuss a number of them in greater detail in subsequent chapters. See, e.g., Norbert Ortmayr, *Knechte: Autobiographische Dokumente und sozialhistorische Skizzen* (Vienna: Bohlau Verlag, 1992); James Amelang, *The Flight of Icarus: Artisan Autobiographies in Early Modern Europe* (Stanford: Stanford University Press, 1998); Elizabeth Faue, *Writing the Wrongs: Eva Valesh and the Rise of Labor Journalism* (Ithaca: Cornell University Press, 2005); Frederick Cooper, *Struggle for the City: Migrant Labor, Capital, and the State in Urban Africa* (Beverly Hills: Sage, 1983); Michael Keith Honey, *Black Workers Remember: An Oral History of Segregation, Unionism, and the Freedom Struggle* (Berkeley: University of California Press, 1999).

13. Wally Seccombe, "Starting to Stop: Working-class Fertility Decline in Britain," *Past and Present* 126 (1990): 153–178.

14. Maynes, *Taking the Hard Road*, esp. pp. 83–84. For the larger epistemological critique, see Spivak, "Subaltern"; and Joan Scott, "The Evidence of Experience," *Critical Inquiry* 17 (1991): 773–797.

15. Barbara Laslett, "Unfeeling Knowledge: Emotion and Objectivity in the History of Sociology," *Sociological Forum* 5 (1990): 413–433 and "Biography as Historical Sociology: The Case of William Fielding Ogburn," *Theory and Society* 20 (1991): 511–538.

16. Michelle Mouton and Helena Pohlandt-McCormick, "Boundary Crossings: Oral History of Nazi Germany and Apartheid South Africa—A Comparative Perspective," *History Workshop Journal* 48 (1999): 41–63.

17. See Harding, *Whose Science? Whose Knowledge?*; George Steinmetz, ed., *The Politics of Method in the Human Sciences: Positivism and Its Epistemological Others* (Durham, NC: Duke University Press, 2005).

18. George Steinmetz, "American Sociology before and after World War II: The (Temporary) Settling of a Disciplinary Field," in *Sociology in America: A History*, ed. Craig Calhoun (Chicago: University of Chicago Press, 2007), p. 339.

19. As discussed in the preface, our selection of personal narrative analyses also reflects our areas of interests and expertise in history and sociology.

Part IB

Does Narrative Explain?

Sociological analyses routinely *describe* social processes. Sociology's aspirations, however, rest on its ability to *explain* those processes. Sociological analyses, at their best, explain not just *what* occurred and *how*, but also *why* it occurred. Even the simplest of narratives does more than simply recount events. As we have suggested, narratives connect events in ways that convey understanding and create particular meanings. Because narratives answer the questions of why and how, we might then wonder whether the understanding produced by narrative constitutes a form of explanation.

The question of whether narrative explains contains three related questions. First, if "does narrative explain" means "can explanations take narrative form," then the answer is clearly yes. In everyday life, we routinely use—and often accept—narrative as explanation. Consider, for example, the response to the question, "Why were you late?" The question itself does not invite explanation in the sense of invoking universal laws that subsume a five- or ten-minute delay. Only the most intolerable pedant, sociologists included, would respond to a question about lateness with a detailed explication of how traffic increases with proximity to quitting hours or of how congestion of all sorts varies with the rhythms of daily human activity.

Although "Why were you late?" does not necessarily invite explanation in the sense of general laws, it does invite a narrative. "Why were you late?" "I was about to leave the office, but I got an important call. I was on the phone for nearly an hour. By the time I got on the road, I was in the thick of rush hour traffic." This explains an event by telling a story about it. The response includes the standard story elements. It has a protagonist who tells the story. It has a beginning and a setting; we do not need to go back any further than the phone call at the office. It has a middle, in which the teller is delayed first by the phone call and then by traffic. And it has an ending, although an implicit one, assuming the teller has reached home. And it has an explanatory point of view: "It wasn't my fault."

As an explanation, most people would consider the account of the phone call and rush hour traffic perfectly adequate and would not delve deeper. But does what counts for explanation in everyday life meet the (presumably) more rigorous standards of an academic discipline? One way of answering is by reformulating the question. Thus, the question becomes not whether narrative explains but under what conditions it explains. One answer would be when temporality is involved. Social life unfolds over time. As Richardson writes, "Everywhere people experience and interpret their lives in relationship to *time*. Time is the quintessential basis for and constraint upon the human experience" (1990: 124; emphasis original). The philosopher Paul Ricoeur claims it is no accident that human beings capture lived experience through narrative (1984–86). Questions like "why were you late," as well as "what did you do today" and "how was your weekend" are really questions about experience over time. Narrative's sequence depicts this unfolding, making it "interpretable in human terms" (Richardson 1990: 124). Narrative also works particularly well as an explanation, as in the example of lateness, where agency matters, where we assume there is some matter of choice or that actions are motivated. Narrative also works particularly well when we are interested in a specific question—why were *you* late *tonight*, rather than the general question of what causes lateness.

The second question leads to a third. If "does narrative explain" means "does narrative imply causality," then our answer is "sometimes."[1] The temporal aspects of narrative can make it seem as though the links between events are causal, but this is not necessarily the case. The linkage in "this happened *and* that happened" differs from the linkage in "this happened *because* that happened." The latter depicts an explicit *causal* link between events.

The excerpt by Donald Polkinghorne grapples with this difference. Polkinghorne points out that the concept of "cause" often carries with it the formal or technical-meaning baggage from science, where cause refers to a deductive-nomological model. Explanations by narrative are usually explanations of human action. They can explain why someone did something, but they do not develop laws that then hold whenever the same action occurs again. In a narrative explanation, most people would find references to laws irrelevant and unsatisfying.

Polkinghorne was well aware that his position did not represent anything approaching a consensus in the social sciences. In "From Causes to Events," Andrew Abbott challenges, in particular, the agentic aspects of narrative explanation. Abbott's approach to narrative differs significantly from the (mostly) hermeneutic approach taken in this volume. Abbott does not use narrative in the sense of personal narratives, life stories, or subjective accounts of experience. Instead, he takes a more formal approach, focusing on sequences of events in time, in the context of case studies. He frames narrative as a way to address the neglect of time and order by the dominant sociological methods. In particular, multivariate methods emphasize configurations of static variables in the search for causality. This produces a view Abbott (1988) has called "general linear reality," which has influenced sociology's image of how the social world works. Abbott retains an interest in causality, but emphasizes the temporal ordering of events. He proposes techniques to generate sociological explanations that are situated in time and space. For Abbott, "narrative" means "narrative positivism," which first uncovers "regularities" and "typical sequences" in social processes and then engages in "causal analysis of a more typical sort" (Abbott 2001: 182).

In "The Trouble with Stories," Charles Tilly discusses his trouble with the way stories explain. In our view, Tilly seems sometimes to confuse his problem with certain types of stories and certain contexts of storytelling with stories in general. The stories that trouble Tilly are "standard stories," or those that involve the "recounting of self-propelled people and events." Standard stories "pop up everywhere," Tilly writes. People tell them about the events of everyday social life. Students in sociology classes tell them about inequality and other social processes. Though vivid and often compelling, the trouble with standard stories is that they treat individuals as independent, conscious, and self-motivated. They attribute all the significant action to the dispositions and impulses of individual actors. In so doing, standard stories oversimplify cause-effect relationships. They create the idea that the actions of individuals or groups of individuals lead directly to historical outcomes. As Tilly wrote elsewhere, stories are troubling because they "minimize or ignore the intricate webs of cause and effect that actually produce human social life" (2008: 21; see also Eden 2008). Sociology's best insights about social processes, Tilly argues, often contradict the logic and causality of standard stories.

Note

1. The question of causality applies to explanations of other sorts, too, and not just those in narrative form. The analysis of explanations has long been a concern of philosophers of science, especially in the debate about the scientific study of human and social phenomena. For a full discussion, see Polkinghorne 1983.

References

Abbott, Andrew. 1988. "Transcending General Linear Reality." *Sociological Theory* 6(2): 169–86.

Abbott, Andrew. 2001. *Time Matters: On Theory and Method*. Chicago: University of Chicago Press.

Eden, Lynn. 2008. "Tilly's Trouble with Stories: The Narrator and the Case of the Missing Disposition." Presented at "Contention, Change, and Explanation: A Conference in Honor of Charles Tilly." New York: Social Science Research Council. Retrieved April 27, 2018 (*www.ssrc.org/hirschman/content/2008/texts/Eden .pdf*).

Martin, Douglas. 2008. "Charles Tilly, 78, Writer and a Social Scientist, Is Dead." *New York Times*, May 28. Retrieved April 27, 2018 (*www.nytimes.com/2008/05/02/ nyregion/02tilly.html*).

Polkinghorne, Donald. 1983. *Methodology for the Human Sciences: Systems of Inquiry*. Albany NY: The State University of New York Press.

Ricoeur, Paul. 1984–86. *Time and Narrative*, 2 vols. Translated by K. MacLaughlan and D. Pellauer. Chicago: University of Chicago Press.

Tilly, Charles. 2008. *Credit and Blame*. Princeton NJ: Princeton University Press.

Further Reading

Abbott, Andrew. 1997. "Of Time and Space: The Contemporary Relevance of the Chicago School." *Social Forces* 75(4): 1149–82.

Abell, Peter. 1987. *The Syntax of Social Life: The Theory and Method of Comparative Narratives*. Oxford: Clarendon.

Elliott, Jane. 2005. *Using Narrative in Social Research: Qualitative and Quantitative Approaches*. Thousand Oaks CA: SAGE.

Franzosi, Roberto. 2004. *From Words to Numbers: Narrative, Data, and Social Science*. Cambridge UK: Cambridge University Press.

Gotham, Kevin Fox, and William G. Staples. 1996. "Narrative Analysis and the New Historical Sociology." *The Sociological Quarterly* 37(3): 481–501.

Griffin, Larry J. 1993. "Narrative, Event-Structure Analysis, and Causal Interpretation in Historical Sociology." *American Journal of Sociology* 98(5): 1094–133.

Roth, Paul A. "How Narratives Explain." *Social Research* 56(2): 449–78.

Somers, Margaret R., and Gloria D. Gibson. 1994. "Reclaiming the Epistemological 'Other': Narrative and the Social Constitution of Identity." In *Social Theory and the Politics of Identity*. Edited by C. Calhoun. Cambridge, MA: Blackwell.

5

EXPLANATORY NARRATIVE RESEARCH

Donald E. Polkinghorne

The result of a research program aiming to give a narrative explanation is the same as one of the answers to the question of why something that has involved human actions happened. The research can address such questions as, "Why did a person crash his/her auto into a sign post?", "Why did the student become a merit scholar?", "Why did the company go bankrupt?", "Why did the Challenger space shuttle explode?", or "Why did the United States go to war in Vietnam?" Seeking to give a narrative account of why something has happened is not a new form of inquiry; it is already used in many studies undertaken to explain why a project has succeeded or failed. Investigative reports often take the form of narrative accounts that link together the events and actions that have led up to the outcome under investigation. In ordinary conversation we often provide explanations of our own or others' behavior by telling narratives. In answer to such a question as, "Why are you interested in classical literature?", we are apt to tell a story that provides a sequence of critical events accounting for the interest. In research of this type, the researcher is charged to provide an explanation for why an outcome has occurred.

It is the narrative explanation, as opposed to an explanation by law or correlation, that makes narrative research different from the research ordinarily undertaken in the human sciences. For example, the explanations of why the Challenger exploded can be given in terms of the physical properties of the o-rings that malfunctioned during the launch, in terms of the probabilities that a launch will fail, or in terms of the probabilities that equipment will malfunction. Although the knowledge of the laws that relate temperature and plasticity are important to include in a narrative explanation, they do not in themselves satisfy the need to know why, in this particular instance and in this context, the space shuttle exploded. A satisfactory answer to this question requires a narrative explanation. Narrative explanations are retrospective. They sort out the multitude of events and decisions that are connected to the launch, and they select those which are significant in light of the fatal conclusion. They draw together the various episodes and actions into a story that leads through a sequence of events to an ending. The story highlights the significance of particular decisions and events and their roles in the final outcome. The researcher's final report reads more like a historical account of why a country has lost a war or why an election has come out in a particular way than like a research report giving the correlations between scores on measuring instruments.

The results draw on all the evidence that is relevant to the outcome, including individuals' interpretations of information, the personal and social forces operating in the context, the individual stories of ambition and pressure, the lack of procedures to insure that appropriate and timely information has reached decision makers, and so on. The narrative research report recreates the history or narrative that has led to the story's end, and draws from it the significant factors that have "caused" the final event. The report does not develop generalizable laws that are supposed to hold whenever the initial conditions are repeated; it does locate the decision points at which a different action could have produced a different ending. The report is retrodictive rather than predictive, that is, it is a retrospective gathering of events into an account that makes the ending reasonable and believable. It is more than a mere chronicling or listing of the events along a time line: it configures the events in such a way that their parts in the whole story become clear.

We use the skill of constructing narrative explanations in our own lives to understand why we and others act in a particular way. The skill is part of our competence to understand the meaning of sentences or the facial expressions of others. The narrative research report differs from this everyday use of narrative explanation in its reflectiveness and consciousness: it seeks out information and calls on the investigator's enlarged experience of prototypical narrative explanations, which may make sense of the complex of events that contribute to explaining the ending.

Historians often use this type of research to give accounts of why small- or large-scale events have occurred, organizing natural occurrences and human actions into a linked and unified story. This is also the type of explanation therapists give in response to such questions as, "Why is the client afraid of taking a new job?" Their answers often take the form of case histories that describe the context in which past events have significantly affected the patients to bring about their present fearful condition.

Historians and therapists use narratives to explain states or events by recounting significant and critical past episodes. Yet the approach has not been generally adopted by the other human disciplines as an acceptable alternate model for research.[1]

Explanation. This study holds that narrative explanations are genuinely explanatory, for they can answer the question of why something has happened. As described in the chapter on history, this position has been challenged on the grounds that because narrative explanation does not derive from universal laws, it cannot provide a basis for prediction. Nevertheless, narratives can be explanatory, if they meet several conditions. Atkinson has addressed these conditions and concluded:

> The question is, then, what conditions have to be satisfied before "mere" narrative (writing about the past) can be counted explanatory. There would, I believe, be common consent that the truth of the individual assertions made is not enough, and that reporting events in chronological order is neither necessary nor sufficient. These are negative points. Positively what is required is some species of coherence—comprehensiveness with unity, nothing relevant omitted, everything irrelevant excluded—a coherence which carries with it intelligibility and explanatory power.[2]

Atkinson gives three characteristics of the kind of coherence required of a narrative account in order for it to be explanatory: it should be intelligible in human terms, it should have an appropriately unified subject matter, and it should be causally related.[3] Narrative explanation is also question-relative, that is, narratives are explanatory when they provide meaningful and complete answers to questions which are worth asking.

Explanation by narrative has the structure, "one because of the other." It includes rational explanation, in which the reasons a person gives for doing something-that is, his or her intentions-are acknowledged as the impetus for the performance. This type of explanation derives from the competence people possess for recognizing that an event is a human action and not a simple physical occurrence; that is, it recognizes that people can make something happen by intervening in the course of natural events, by setting a sequence of events in motion. It also involves the notion of teleological inference, in which something is done in order to accomplish a preconceived end: "Why did he enroll in a French class?" "He wanted to learn to speak French." But perhaps he wanted to learn to speak French specifically in order to be offered a new position in his company that required knowledge of French. Ricoeur calls explanations using teleological inference "intentional understanding," and practical inference (a knowledge of the practical consequences of intended actions) "singular causal imputation."[4]

Max Weber has described the logic of singular causal imputation in his work, "Critical Studies in the Logic of the Cultural Sciences."[5] This kind of logic consists essentially of a "what if" procedure: constructing by imagination a different course of events, weighing the probable consequences of the imagined course of events, and then comparing these consequences with the real course of events. As Weber puts it: "In order to penetrate the real causal interrelationships, *we construct unreal ones.*" (Emphasis in original)[6] For example, the researcher imagines that a participant in a narrative did not decide to write a particular letter, and then asks if this changed event would have produced a different outcome. If yes, then the actual event probably has a causal significance in relation to the actual outcome; if no, then it does not. The kind of events that can be submitted to the test for causal implication can be natural and chance events as well as human actions: for example, "What if the other driver had not lost control of the car at that specific moment?", or "What if it had not rained on that day?"

The test for causal significance suggested by Weber actually involves the testing of different plot schemes tried on the actual events. The procedure is a reportable thought experiment, and the reasons for accepting or rejecting particular events as causally significant can be defended through argument. The logical structure of the thought experiment is based on the notion that "things would have been different" if this particular event or combination of events had been different. In order to carry out the thought experiment, the researcher uses knowledge based on rules that describe how humans are prone to react under given situations. The consequences of the imagined, changed past are developed through the application of these rules to the imagined situation. These rules usually are not at the level of formal scientific physical laws; rather they cover knowledge of dispositions to act in certain ways. Ricoeur understands that this use of the rules of behavioral responses in the imaginative reconstruction of a changed past is "sufficient to show . . . how laws can be used in history, even though they are not established by history."[7]

In explanatory narrative research, the point is to provide a narrative account that supplies the events necessary or causal for the outcome under investigation to have occurred. The term "cause" is another of those concepts that has acquired a technical meaning through formal science, now being limited to the effects of general laws on particular events; for example, gravity "causes" the rock to fall. Cause is defined as the "constant antecedent." In general usage, however, "cause" means whatever produces an effect, result, or consequence, and it can include events, people's actions, or other conditions. Because narrative cause can relate to the antecedents of a peculiar sequence that may never be repeated, its meaning is different from that meaning of cause in formal science.[8] Gareth Williams, to avoid the confusion brought about by these two meanings, has suggested that narrative cause be designated by the word "genesis." Williams writes:

> Given the teleological form of narrative reconstruction, I employ the concept of "genesis" not for stylistic or rhetorical purposes, but in order to liberate myself from the semantic straitjacket imposed by the term "cause" as it has been generally understood since Hume, and so as to establish a connexion with the Greek tradition of reflection on origins of things which attained its apogee in Aristotle's doctrine of the four causes. . . . It [cause] is an analytic construct through which the respondent can be seen to situate a variety of causal connexions as reference points within a narrative reconstruction of the changing relationships between the self and the world.[9]

In spite of Williams's use of the term "genesis," I believe that the term "cause" should be maintained in explanatory narrative research, with cause by law acknowledged as only one of the broader range of types of causes—laws, rules, events, and actions. By recounting the connections between events and actions that have led to a particular occurrence, the researcher arrives at an appropriate statement of the reasons for the event.

Data collection. A narrative researcher's data—interviews, documents, and other sources—are the traces of past events; they help uncover the events leading up to the phenomenon under investigation. Of course, the kind of data collected depends on the kind of ending to be explained. An analysis of why negotiations over nuclear arms have broken down requires data from a great many sources covering a long historical period compared to data for an explanation of why a child has stayed home from school.

Narrative explanations are based on past facts. These are then organized into a unified story in which the links between the events are developed, and the significance provided. Because past "facts" are not open to direct, present observation, they must be established on the basis of traces, for instance, documents, memos, and personal memory. Events retained in memory as aspects of a narrative account are often reshaped by later happenings and by the plot line. The reconstruction of past facts thus frequently resembles detective work, with several personal accounts together with partial written records needed to infer what actually has happened.[10] For example, to establish whether or not a person received certain information before deciding to launch the Challenger, several types of evidence may be required. In some instances, the researcher may have cause to suspect that a person's story is false and cannot be relied on for establishing the event. Noting from the daily log that the message was received in the office at a certain time, that the person was in the office at the time the message arrived, and that the person has a habit of reading messages at the time they arrive, the researcher can deduce (but not with certainty) that the person probably read the message.

Courts of law have established procedures for arriving at an authentic story. The prosecutor and defendant bring conflicting stories before the bar; various witnesses are called to give evidence in support of one or the other stories. Rules of evidence and standards of argument have been designed to assist in deciding which of the stories is an accurate statement; for example, evidence based on hearsay or personal conclusions are not acceptable.[11] Thomas Seebohm has explored the relation between jurisprudence and hermeneutics.[12] Seebohm understands that jurists and historians use similar methods to determine the "facts" of what happened, including the intentions of the actors. The courts, however, have means for determining what "really happened" that are sometimes not available to human science researchers. They have direct communication with witnesses, testimonies of present persons, and often extensive circumstantial evidence and pleas. The court investigates present or almost present episodes. In Seebohm's view the interpretive problem is not determining "beyond reasonable doubt" the facts of the case (what I call narrative first-order referents). It is, rather, determining the plot or kind of story (second-order referents) that connects the facts and how the "original intention of the lawgiver" applies to a particular narrative.

Collecting past "facts" and placing them in correct chronological order, although necessary for a narrative explanation, is not sufficient. The researcher has to select from the multitude of past facts related to an incident, and the selection is made on the basis of the narrative that is under construction. The narrative may show gaps in the information base and may lead the researcher to search for the missing information. A narrative explanation draws the gathered past facts together into a whole account in which the significance of the facts in relation to the outcome to be explained is made clear. For example, that someone received a memo before making a decision may be a simple fact, but it is not an explanatory fact. In the narrative account, however, the meaning of the fact is described in relation to the sequence of events, and the fact becomes significant in light of the subsequent events. It becomes clear in the narrative account that the cause of the failure was the person's refusal to believe or act on the information, not that the information was not received.

Validity, significance, and reliability. As has happened with the concept of "cause" the general concept of "validity" has been redefined by formal science. It has become confused by the narrowing of the concept to refer to tests or measuring instruments. In narrative research, "valid" retains its ordinary meaning of well-grounded and supportable.[13] This ordinary meaning is distinguished from two more limited meanings. The first comes from the context of formal logic, where "valid" describes a conclusion that follows the rules of logic and is correctly drawn from the premises. The second is used in measurement theory, where "validity" refers to the relationship between the measuring instrument and the concept it is attempting to measure. A valid finding in narrative research, however, although it might include conclusions based on formal logic and measurement data, is based on the more general understanding of validity as a well-grounded conclusion.

Conclusions of narrative research are most often defended by the use of "informal" reasoning.[14] The researcher presents evidence to support the conclusions and shows why alternative conclusions are not as likely, presenting the reasoning by means of which the results have been derived. The argument does not produce certainty; it produces likelihood. In this context, an argument is valid when it is strong and has the capacity to resist challenge or attack. Narrative research does not produce conclusions of certainty, the ideal of formal science with its closed systems of mathematics and formal logic.[15] Narrative research, by retaining an emphasis on the linguistic reality of human existence, operates in an area that is not limited by formal systems and their particular type of rigor.

The results of narrative research cannot claim to correspond exactly with what has actually occurred-that is, they are not "true," if "truth" is taken to mean exact correspondence or conformity to actuality. Research

investigating the realm of meaning aims rather for verisimilitude, or results that have the appearance of truth or reality. Karl Popper has proposed that verisimilitude is the limit on all knowledge and that, at best,
we can demonstrate only the falsity of statements, not their truth.[16] The
conclusions of narrative research remain open-ended. New information
or argument may convince scholars that the conclusion is in error or that
another conclusion is more likely. Narrative research, then, uses the ideal
of a scholarly consensus as the test of verisimilitude rather than the test of
logical or mathematical validity.[17]

The concept of "significance" has also been redefined by formal science to designate a technical, statistical definition of the extent to which
a correlation found among variables is probably due to the chance of
random sampling. In general usage, the term "significance" points to the
notion of meaningfulness or importance. But because the same word is
used to designate both the broad and the limited concept, the more limited technical meaning has gathered to it the values of the general usage.
Thus, people often interpret statistical significance to mean that the finding is important, without considering the limited idea that the finding
probably resulted from the chance drawing of sample elements from the
population. In narrative research "significance" retains its more general
meaning. A finding is significant if it is important. Finding out that the
Challenger accident was caused by a faulty decision-making strategy
would be significant.

The ordinary meaning of "reliable" refers to the quality of dependability. To rely on someone is to have complete confidence and trust that
she or he will do what is asked or that what he or she says can be trusted.
Used in the context of quantitative research, "reliability" refers to the
consistency and stability of measuring instruments. Reliable instruments
continually yield the same score when the variable itself remains stable. If
in taking a second measurement the score differs, one can trust that the
difference is because of an actual change in the variable, not simply an
artifact of a "loose" instrument.

Reliability in narrative study usually refers to the dependability of the
data,[18] and validity to the strength of the analysis of the data. Attention
has been directed to the trustworthiness of field notes and transcriptions
of interviews. Mishler has reviewed the problems that arise in going from
tape recordings to written texts.[19] He recommends researchers keep returning to the original recordings and devise explicit transcription rules
and a well-specified notation system, including codes for pauses, talk-
over, and voice tone. Mishler notes that present interview theory is based
on a stimulus-response model. The interviewer's questions are treated as a
standard research stimulus and are expected to remain a constant so that

any variance in the response can be attributed to factors in the interview population. Mishler argues that interviewing needs to be understood as a discourse, not a constant stimulus provoking a measurable response.[20] Data generation in narrative studies is affected by the context and sequence in which interviews are given. Researchers undergo changes as they gather data, and the people interviewed affect those doing the interviewing. Yet interviewers do generate stories and gather information. It is the responsibility of researchers to establish a free flow of information from participants in their studies and to describe fully how it was accomplished. Narrative studies do not have formal proofs of reliability, relying instead on the details of their procedures to evoke an acceptance of the trustworthiness of the data.

Data analysis. Data collection results in a collection of stories. The goal of analysis is to uncover the common themes or plots in the data. Analysis is carried out using hermeneutic techniques for noting underlying patterns across examples of stories. A simple example of the use of these techniques can illustrate the process. Comparing two reports, "I approached the phone to call her for a date, but my stomach became so tense I couldn't pick up the phone, so I ended up not making the call and went back and watched TV for the evening," and "I saw this job advertised that really looked exciting, I was going to apply but I thought they would probably get a lot of better applications and it wouldn't be worth the effort," yields a number of possible themes. For example, both include initial attraction to a goal, followed by a retreat from pursuing the goal. Perhaps they experienced the debilitating thought that they might be rejected if they exposed themselves by asking for what they wanted. One reported physical symptoms as part of his fear. These notions would have to be held as possible descriptions until further information was given.

A test of the results of this type of linguistic analysis is asking if the identified general pattern would produce the specific stories given in the original data. Furthermore, adequate analysis does not produce idiosyncratic results; other researchers, given the data from which the results were drawn, can agree that the results follow.[21] The analysis of narrative data does not follow an algorithmic outline, but moves between the original data and the emerging description of the pattern (the hermeneutic circle). Amedeo Giorgi has developed a more formal, six-stage process for the analysis of linguistic data.[22] Two recent exemplar studies by Robert Bellah and associates and by Erik and Joan Erikson and Helen Kivnick demonstrate the responsible manner in which linguistic analysis can be carried out systematically and rigorously.[23] Linguistic analysis has a rich tradition as a research approach in literary criticism, providing the behavioral and social sciences a reservoir of principles and guidelines for use in narrative analysis.[24]

Notes

1. An exception in sociology is Robert N. Bellah, Richard Madison, William M. Sullivan, Ann Swidler, and Steven M. Tipton, *Habits of the Heart: Individualism and Commitment in American Life* (Berkeley and Los Angeles: University of California Press, 1985), and in anthropology the collection of articles in Victor W. Turner and Edward M. Bruner, eds., *The Anthropology of Experience* (Urbana: University of Illinois Press, 1986).
2. R. F. Atkinson, *Knowledge and Explanation* in *History: An Introduction to the Philosophy of History* (Ithaca, N.Y.: Cornell University Press, 1978), 131.
3. Ibid. 133–135.
4. Paul Ricoeur, *Time and Narrative*, trans. Kathleen McLaughlin and David Pellauer (Chicago: University of Chicago Press, 1984), 1:138.
5. Max Weber, "Critical Studies in the Logic of the Cultural Sciences." In Max Weber, *The Methodology of the Social Sciences*, trans. Edward Shils and Henry A. Finch (Glencoe, Ill.: The Free Press, 1949), 113–188.
6. Weber, 185–186.
7. Ricoeur, *Time and Narrative*, 1:185.
8. See Rom Harré and E. H. Madden, *Causal Powers: A Theory of Natural Necessity* (Totowa, NJ.: Rowman and Littlefield, 1975), for a discussion of the move from a classical Humean notion of cause applicable to the assumed closed systems of experimentation to the self-generation found in open systems. Their view of causal explanation does not contradict the notion of free will or self-determined human actions.
9. Gareth Williams, "The Genesis of Chronic Illness: Narrative Reconstruction," *Sociology of Health and Illness* 6 (1984): 179–180.
10. See William B. Sanders, "The Methods and Evidence of Detectives and Sociologists," in *The Sociologist as Detective: An Introduction to Research Methods*, ed. William B. Sanders (New York: Praeger, 1974), 1–17.
11. See H. L. A. Hart and A. M. Honoré, *Causation in the Law* (Oxford: Oxford University Press, 1959).
12. Thomas M. Seebohm, "Facts, Words, and What Jurisprudence Can Teach Hermeneutics." *Research in Phenomenology* 16 (1986): 25–40.
13. "Valid" is an adjective usually attached to a statement, argument, or reasoning. Its synonyms in ordinary usage are "sound," "convincing," "telling," and "conclusive." The synonyms designate the differences in the power of an argument to convince the hearer. "Valid" and "sound" both refer to the notion that the argument is able to resist attack. A "convincing" argument is slightly stronger than a "valid" one: it not only can withstand attack, it can silence the opposition. A "conclusive" argument is still stronger; it puts an end to doubt or debate.
14. John Eric Nolt, *Informal Logic: Possible Worlds and Imagination* (New York: McGraw-Hill, 1984).
15. See Murray Levine, "Scientific Method and the Adversary Model: Some Preliminary Thoughts," *American Psychologist* 29 (1974): 661–677, for comments

on the requirement that the relevance of statistical measures is dependent on the proposition that the mathematical model underlying them is a reasonable approximation of the nature of the effect being studied. It is the position of this study that the appropriate model for the realm of meaning is linguistic and not mathematical.

16. Karl Popper, *The Logic of Scientific Discovery* (London: Hutchinson, 1959), 53.

17. I agree with the criticism leveled at Habermas that he has made a "category mistake" by identifying consensus derived from argument as "truth." A statement is not "true" because after submission to public debate a general consensus in support of the statement is reached. Instead, the statement agreed to is to be understood as the best understanding we can reach at this time—"the best" meaning that which is judged most accurate given the present evidence and the rational considerations of free participants in a discussion. See Thomas A. McCarthy, "A Theory of Communicative Competence," in *Critical Sociology*, ed. Paul Connerton (Middlesex, England: Penguin Books, 1976), 478–496.

18. Jerome Kirk and Marc L. Miller, *Reliability and Validity in Qualitative Research* (Beverly Hills, Cal.: Sage, 1986), 51.

19. Elliot G. Mishler, *Research Interviewing: Context and Narrative* (Cambridge, Mass.: Harvard University Press, 1986), 47–50.

20. Ibid. 35–51.

21. Donald E. Polkinghorne, "Phenomenological Research Methods," in *Existential-Phenomenological Perspectives* in *Psychology*, eds. R. S. Valle and S. Halling (New York: Plenum, in press).

22. Amedeo Giorgi, "An Application of Phenomenological Psychology," in *Duquesne Studies in Phenomenological Psychology*, eds. Amedeo Giorgi, Constance T. Fischer, and Edward L. Murray (Pittsburgh: Duquesne University Press, 1975), 2:82–103. Giorgi's process was developed for the analysis of phenomenological descriptions; however, its principles of linguistic analysis are also applicable to narrative data.

23. Bellah et al; Erik H. Erikson, Joan M. Erikson, and Helen G. Kivnick, *Vital Involvement in Old Age: The Experience of Old Age in Our Time* (New York: WW Norton, 1986).

24. See P. D. Juhl, *Interpretation: An Essay in the Philosophy of Literary Criticism* (Princeton, N.J.: Princeton University Press, 1980) for a systematic review of the positions on linguistic analysis by literary critics.

6

FROM CAUSES TO EVENTS

Notes on Narrative Positivism

Andrew Abbott

In the last decade, a number of writers have proposed narrative as the foundation for sociological methodology. By this they do not mean narrative in terms of words as opposed to numbers and complexity as opposed to formalization. Rather, they mean narrative in the more generic sense of process, or story. They want to make processes the fundamental building blocks of sociological analyses. For them, social reality happens in sequences of actions located within constraining or enabling structures. It is a matter of particular social actors, in particular social places, at particular social times.

In the context of contemporary empirical practice, such a conception is revolutionary. Our normal methods parse social reality into fixed entities with variable qualities. They attribute causality to the variables—hypostatized social characteristics—rather than to agents; variables do things, not social actors. Stories disappear. The only narratives present in such methods are just-so stories justifying this or that relation between the variables. Contingent narrative is impossible.

There are, of course, empirical literatures within which process remains important. The various microsociologies—symbolic interactionism, interaction process analysis, ethnomethodology, conversational analysis—all focus on social processes, and particularly on the branchings and turnings of interaction. Historical sociology, especially in the study

Andrew Abbot, *Sociological Methods & Research* (20, no. 4: 428–455), copyright © 1992 by SAGE Publications, Inc. Reprinted by Permission of SAGE Publications, Inc.

of collective behaviors such as revolutions and strikes, likewise studies the unfolding of processes, although here the search is more for characteristic processes than for rules of interaction. (There are also literatures where process is of obvious conceptual importance, but where empirically no one has moved beyond the recipes of regression, the life-course literature being the best example.)

But the main empirical traditions of sociology ignore process altogether, and, as I have argued elsewhere (Abbott 1988a), this ignorance has gradually spread into much of our theory. Narrative methodology is a response to this twofold ignorance. In reviewing it here, therefore, I wish to propose an agenda of central questions in the conceptualization of process and to review the attempts, preliminary but exciting, to develop formal methodologies founded on such process conceptions. To that end, I shall first mention the status of process in classical sociological theories. I shall then discuss how process analysis gradually disappeared from empirical methods. This leads into a discussion of the major theoretical questions raised when process is reintegrated with empirical practice. This discussion is followed by a review of the new methodological approaches proposed to accomplish this reintegration.

Theory and Process

Although action and process have largely disappeared from empirical sociology, they are by contrast central to much of sociological theory, both classic and recent. Weber (1947) made action central in his theoretical writings. He wrote numerous contingent narratives in the areas of comparative religion and economics and put the search for ideal-typical narratives at the heart of his methodological writings. Marx, too, conceived of the world processually, although his processes of interest were the grand tides of Hegelian history. But like Weber, Marx wrote explanatory narratives with both facility and felicity (e.g., Marx 1963).

In the American tradition, it was above all the Chicago School that focused on process. Park and Burgess's (1921) textbook was organized around process headings. Their students gave "natural histories" of social processes, describing typical patterns observed in the development of gangs (Thrasher 1927), occupational careers (Cressy 1932), even revolutions (Edwards 1927). The central Chicago concept of "interaction" embodied an obsession with process, an obsession bequeathed to descendants such as Erving Goffman and the labeling theorists. But Chicago was not the only theoretical tradition interested in process. Even Parsons, particularly in his early work, made action, if not process, central to sociology (Parsons 1937). Today there is a recurrence of this long-standing sociological concern with action in yet another guise; rational choice theories focus directly on actors and decisions. Although many decry rational choice as "unsociological" in its resolute methodological individualism, the theory at least concentrates on agents and activity.

One might wish to summarize this common theoretical attention to process and action by saying that much of theory takes a "narrative approach" to social reality. But the word "narrative," unless it is seriously qualified, here obscures more than it reveals. One often assumes that narrative necessarily involves complexity of meaning and that it is inherently unformalizable. Nonetheless, in approaching social reality through process, one need not make either of these assumptions, however desirable they might be for other reasons. There is nothing about thinking processually that requires interpretive attention to complexity of meaning; certainly there is nothing about thinking processually that forbids representing social reality in a formal manner. If narrative is understood here in the broad sense of processual, action-based approaches to social reality, approaches that are based on stories, these conflations can be avoided, and the great theoretical traditions of sociology may be seen to have indeed taken a narrative approach to social reality.

The Disappearance of Process in Empirical Sociology

But the dominant empirical traditions have not taken this approach. The concept that has replaced process and narrative in empirical sociology is, of course, causality. Yet causality has a curious history in sociology. Although it is now central to empirical sociology's self-image, early sociological positivism avoided the concept (see Bernert 1983).

The contemporary concept of causality derives from logical positivism. Although Hume had held that causality was nothing more or less than correlation, early 20th-century natural science nonetheless used the cause concept with distinctly pre-Humean overtones of determination and forcing. Quantum mechanics challenged this concept by asserting the essentially indeterminate nature of reality and by claiming "probable determination" (determination of probability distributions by probability distributions) as the best approximation to "real" causality. In response to this development, the logical positivists recast the causality concept as a predicate of statements rather than of reality (see e.g., Reichenbach 1962, chap. 10).

This recast concept of causality is the one taught in the best sociological methods courses today. To say "x causes y" is to say something about the equations relating x and y and about the implicit theoretical framework in which they are embedded (the temporal priority of x and so on).

A good sociological methodologist (e.g., Lieberson 1985) will thus argue that the statement "education causes occupational achievement" is essentially a shorthand for the union of three statements: (a) education generally precedes occupational achievement in the life course, (b) the two are highly correlated across individuals, and (c) it is plausible (cause one can tell a little "plausibility story" that "gives a potential mechanism") to see the latter as flowing directly from the former. In this idealized view, "education causes occupational achievement" is not a statement about some causal force—education—that determines in some transcendent fashion an equally abstract thing called "occupational achievement." Rather, it is a quick way of summarizing many narratives in which education accounts for occupational achievement.

In practice, of course, such care is uncharacteristic. Many or most sociologists interpret statements such as "education causes occupational achievement" in precisely the realist fashion, seeing in the social world causal forces that push on other forces in a terrain removed from human activity. One has only to read the journals to find such a rhetoric of determinate "causal forces," even though any serious methodologist falls back, upon challenge, to the idealized "summary of narratives" view. (See Abbott forthcoming for such a detailed reading.)

The takeover of sociology by this reworked theory of causality began with the statistical revolution of Ogburn, Stouffer, Duncan, and Lazarsfeld. The first moves of this statistical revolution, in the 1920s, had been conducted in the name of association, rather than causation (Bernert 1983). In true Humean fashion, this first version refused altogether to talk about "causes." But as sociology gradually adopted the new statistics during and after the war, the logical positivist notion of causality as merely a predicate of statements justified a renewed use of causal language. Because talking about causality was merely talking about equations, it was philosophically proper to do so, Hume notwithstanding. This interpretation gave rise to the "causal language as shorthand" view that I have just outlined as the widely taught philosophical foundation of standard methodology.

But in practice, sociologists never took the separation of statement and reality all that seriously. By the time of Blalock's *Causal Inference in Non-Experimental Research* (1964), the language of determining causal forces, acting in the real world yet without real reference to specific individual actions, had become standard in the field. This metamorphosis was helped by the translation of Emile Durkheim's *Suicide* in 1951, with its seductive blend of resolute social emergentism and quantitative empiricism. Durkheim's almost medieval social realism seemed to justify ignoring agency and story altogether.

By this point, the methods themselves had begun to constrain theoretical thinking with a set of implicit assumptions. The methods have gradually become second nature to sociologists, so that these implicit assumptions have begun to dictate how sociologists imagine the social world to be constructed. I have analyzed these assumptions in detail elsewhere (Abbott 1988a), but it is useful to recall them here.

1. The social world is made up of fixed entities with varying attributes (demographic assumption)
    1a. Some attributes determine (cause) others
2. What happens to one case doesn't constrain what happens to others, temporally or spatially (casewise independence assumption)
3. Attributes have one and only one causal meaning within a given study (univocal meaning assumption)
4. Attributes determine each other principally as independent scales rather than as constellations of attributes; main effects are more important than interactions (main effects assumption).

Some of these assumptions have been attacked by various literatures. Thus, for example, the demographic assumption has been attacked by some studies of merger and division. But the general drift in demography has been away from the study of flows of entities (formal demography) toward the fixed entities/varying attributes approach (social demography). Although the organizational ecologists have addressed the question of merger and division, they treat the processes merely as the continuation of one group coupled with the death or birth of another, thus avoiding the central questions posed about the continuity between entity and attribute. Existence in such an argument becomes an attribute that it is somehow possible for an entity to lose, thus producing the philosophical monstrosity of an entity that can be defined as an entity but that doesn't exist.

The casewise independence assumption has also been attacked, in this case by the network literature. This substantial literature focuses on types of interrelations and conceives of the social world in spatial terms. It leans toward scaling, clustering, and similarly descriptive approaches to social structure, but remains within formalistic approaches. By contrast, the univocal meaning assumption has been attacked chiefly by the various interpretive literatures and thus has not been the focus of a formalizing or methodological literature, although one could imagine formal work on attributes with multiple causal relations to each other. In general, it is this third assumption that has provoked the major "soft" sociology critique of "hard" sociological empiricism.

The main effects assumption has not been directly challenged by a major literature. To be sure, the network literature implicitly argues that social relations come in constellations rather than simple links. But it has been left to applied social scientists—predominantly market researchers—to argue that complexes matter more than do main effects and to follow the methodological implications of this argument to the point of making classification and description of reality more central than the causal analysis of it. (But see Abbott 1990b on this issue.)

More important for my argument than these four assumptions, however, are the assumptions implicit in standard methodology that involve time and temporality. It is against these assumptions that the new "narrative positivism" has arisen.

5. Things happen in discrete bits of uniform length and are not aggregated into overlapping "events" of varying length (continuity or uniform time-horizon assumption)

5a. In cases where one must consider differential duration of attributes, determination flows from long duration attributes to shorter duration ones, from context to individual (monotonic causal flow assumption)

6. The order in which attributes change does not influence what changes occur; all cases follow the same "causal narrative" or model (non-narrative assumption).

Reflection will persuade the thoughtful reader that these are indeed the temporal assumptions basic to what I have elsewhere called "general linear reality." (I shall not elaborate them here; for detailed expositions, see Abbott 1988a, 1990b). A useful discussion of them, possibly the best in standard methodological sources, is found scattered through the pages of Blau and Duncan's *American Occupational Structure* (1967). Applying regression methods for the first time to a massive data set, Blau and Duncan discussed these matters at length. (Particularly interesting discussions are found on pp. 82–97, 121–28, 163–71, and 177–88.)

In summary, the methods adopted by sociology since World War II not only embodied a concept of causality as forcing: Along with that concept, they brought a set of implicit assumptions that were gradually imposed on sociological theorizing. It is these hidden assumptions, and particularly those concerning time and temporality, that are the concern of the people I am here calling narrative positivists.

Theoretical Questions about Narrative

The history of standard methods in sociology thus reminds us of a simple but important truth. Any methodological strategy (what we might call a Methodology with a capital "M") brings with it general constraints that are, properly speaking, theoretical. Because any social methodology must parse the social world in particular ways, it must contain elements of an implicit social theory. As one can see from the list of assumptions above, these elements comprise an ontology (Assumption 1), theories of structure (Assumption 2) and causality (Assumptions 3, 4, and 5a), and a concept of time (Assumptions 5 and 6).

Thus the first move in creating an alternative Methodology founded on narrative is to discover the theoretical strategy appropriate to such a methodology and to outline some central questions it poses for conceptual reflection. A narrative Methodology will, of course, itself make assumptions about social reality. The new narrativists claim no exemption from that necessity. Rather, they wish to pose new questions based on new assumptions. That would give us two strings to our bow instead of only one, as we have at present.

At present, the theoretical literature in this area is sparse. Although one can draw many theoretical insights from the scattered empirical literatures mentioned at the outset, none of these literatures is strongly interested in the creation of positive methods founded on narrative. The only self-conscious expositions are the various writings of Abbott (1983, 1984, 1988a, 1990b) and Abell (1984, 1985, 1987). Both follow much the same logic in their attack on what Abell called "the variable-centered model," but from there they have gone different ways.

Abbott's original argument drew as much on literatures in structural literary theory and the philosophy of history as on sociology. He has focused on the issue of the coherence and followability of social stories, the issue of whether it really makes sense to think that "social reality happens in stories." Originally, Abbott (1983) proposed three major story properties. The first was enchainment, defined as the nature of the narrative link from one step to the next; this was the narrative analogue of causality. The second was order, the degree to which a social story presupposed a particular, exact order of events. The third was convergence, the degree to which a social sequence approached a steady state, for which nonnarrative methods would then be appropriate. In later theoretical writing, as in methodological work, Abbott has generally focused on the order property, and in particular on the typical sequence problem—finding, a typical or characteristic order of events (Abbott 1990a contains a succinct exposition). In contrast to Abell, Abbott's theoretical stance seems rather indeterminate; he leaves room for varieties of enchainment and has spent little time focusing that concept. This follows from Abbott's major empirical concerns as a historical sociologist of institutions. Enchainment is theorized in diverse ways in institutional analysis (in professionalization, for example, see Abbott 1988b, chap. 1).

Writing from a more formal background, Abell has grounded his approach to narrative much more explicitly on a theoretical model of action, a focused concept of enchainment. Although, like Abbott, Abell claimed a unity and coherence to stories, he founded these chiefly on the philosophical literature concerning action. Abell defined enchainment explicitly in terms of individual action, which he categorized in terms of intention, positive activity, forbearance, and similar concepts. On this basis he has built a formidable algebraic approach to Abbott's typical sequence problem. For Abell, the central theoretical issues of narrative analysis lie in categorizing the types and modalities of action. Recently, Abell (1989, 1991) has become more explicitly wedded to the rational action paradigm, which he espouses as a "least worst alternative." Although this commitment makes Abell's theoretical grasp more focused and thus perhaps less catholic than Abbott's, his exposition of the narrative problem in *The Syntax of Social Life* (1987) remains the best extended treatment of it in sociology.

Although Abbott and Abell have begun to develop an agenda of theoretical questions and issues for a methodology of narrativism, they have both turned to more explicitly methodological concerns in order to persuade empirical sociologists of their theoretical insights. (I review these methodologies below.) Thus most of the theoretical agenda remains open for investigation. I shall discuss here some of the major problems (see also Abbott forthcoming). It is vitally important to note that these kinds of issues—issues of what might be called the "philosophy of method"—should not discourage one from seeing the social world in narrative terms. The same kinds of issues exist for standard methods but are largely ignored because of the paradigmatic quality of those methods. It is the novelty of the narrative approach that makes one conscious of these questions.

The first general category of theoretical problems concerns the handling of demographic questions within the narrative framework. Abbott (forthcoming) calls this the issue of "entity processes." These processes involve the transformation or fundamental change of the case itself. The most familiar (and best studied) are birth and death. But Abbott has also pointed to the importance of the merger and division of cases, problems that disappear in Abell's rather strong methodological individualism but that are conspicuously important at the institutional level that has been Abbott's chief concern (e.g., the discussions of merger and division in

Abbott 1988b). As I noted earlier, merger and division have been treated as death (of one case by merging out of existence) and birth (of one case by splitting off from another) in the event history literature, but this approach simply finesses an important theoretical problem.

Abbott has also argued that the micro/macro problem is inherently temporal (Abbott forthcoming) and hence that there are a variety of entity processes relating change and nonchange at micro and emergent levels. Again, this problem arises out of the theoretical concerns of institutionalism. Professions can continue in a constant position in a division of labor while their personnel turns over totally, or, conversely, a constant personnel can experience, as a collectivity, a complete shift of collective identity through changes in the general professional division of labor. These kinds of problems raise issues of micro- and macro-transformation that are important subjects for theoretical analysis. One must discover reasonable rules governing the conception of cases and of their integration into macro entities. All these are problems of theorizing "entity processes."

After these demographic concerns, a second general class of theoretical issues concerns events. Because he draws on a relatively formalistic model of narrative and on rational choice with its methodological individualism, Abell tends to see events as simple, unproblematic exchanges and responses. Abbott, by contrast, regards conceptualizing events as a central theoretical problem (see Abbott 1984). For the literature in philosophy of history, events are particularly problematic because a given set of "happenings" (Abbott has usually called them "occurrences") can be plotted in many different ways. (The analogous problem in standard methods is that a given empirical statistic can be used as an indicator of many different concepts.) Moreover, for the historian, events have duration and hence may overlap. This in turn raises havoc with the concept of order, which is central to that of narrative. Abbott's various writings have circled around these issues, but it remains a central question in applications (e.g., Abbott 1991b).

Moreover, once events become large, conceptual things indicated by "happenings" or "occurrences," there are then a whole variety of issues relating the two levels. To a large extent, these can be seen as measurement issues. Which are the crucial happenings that tell us that event x has taken place? Which new medical school finally persuades the public that the medical profession is becoming committed to education? These issues fold back into the problem of defining and theorizing events in the first place. Once one moves beyond the simple world of action/response sequences to a world where events have duration and overlap and are known largely by the happenings that indicate them, an enormously complex problem is confronted in deciding how the parts of stories go together. As Abbott has noted, there is a long and distinguished literature on this topic in the philosophy of history. It is nonetheless inconclusive for being long and distinguished.

A related set of theoretical issues concerns the multiple plot structures of the social world. If the social world is conceptualized in terms of stories, one immediately faces the problem that every event lies in many narratives at once. Every event has multiple narrative antecedents as well as multiple narrative consequences. (The same, of course, is true in standard methods with the word "causal" substituted for "narrative"; cf. Marini and Singer 1988.) That is, the full social process, when viewed in narrative terms, makes up a network of stories flowing into the present and future. Narratives vary in the tightness of this network. Certain narratives develop relatively independent of the others around them; these we call stage processes. Others are more contingent on environing narratives—for example, organizational careers in the majority of cases. Finally, others take place in systematic structures that constrain their unfolding in radical ways. The latter are "interaction systems" of mutually constraining narratives. Abbott's (1988b) analysis of the evolution of professions takes this position, as does Wallerstein's (1974) analysis of the world system. This problem of the mutual contingency of narratives clearly requires extensive theoretical study before one can think about methodologies to address it.

This issue can be generalized by considering the theoretical problem of how the narrative (or causal) meaning of an event varies with the ensemble of environing contemporary events and with the past events leading to the present. A fundamental argument of narrative methodology is that narrative meaning (the "causal force" of enchainments) is a function of present and past context. Synchronically, this is the argument that "reality doesn't happen in main effects but in interactions" (see Abbott 1988a, 1990b). Temporally, it is the argument that narrative force is inevitably sequential, that order makes a difference. These problems, too, are topics for important theoretical reflection.

Finally, perhaps the most important theoretical problem of all is that of formally representing processes that involve multiple contingent sequences of events that are "moving at different speeds," what I have elsewhere called the time-horizon problem (Abbott 1988a, 1990b). This, too, is a theoretical problem raised chiefly by the literature in historical sociology. I once set out to explain why there are no psychiatrists in American mental hospitals. The exodus, which dates from 1900–1930, reflects not only rational individual mobility decisions that are specifiable annually, but also outpatient community developments that are specifiable only every decade, and changes in knowledge and social control taking place over even longer periods. How is one to embrace all four processes?

There are a number of quick fixes to this problem; none is satisfactory. One is the traditional notion that historical study defines periods or intervals within which sociology studies causes in a basically synchronic manner. There is long-run change, within which one can specify short-run "causality." This argument (which dominates the historical sociology literature at present; see Abbott 1991a) unfortunately provides no way of accounting either for long-run (between period) changes or for the effects of long-run changes on short-run processes. Another answer is the more subtle "Markovian" answer that there is, in fact, no depth to historical causality, that all the effects of the deep past are expressed through an immediate past that shapes the present. Characteristic of both many philosophies (e.g., Whitehead) and of certain methods (e.g., event history analysis), this view makes problematic continuity assumptions about history (see Abbott 1990b). If events with duration really exist, which no sensible analyst would deny, the Markovian view has major problems. But beyond these two stopgaps, there is no easy answer to this issue of multiple sequences of differing speeds. Braudel's famous division of history into structure, conjuncture, and event is one way to start, but even there, the narrative linkages between the three levels are not theorized. The multiple time-horizon problem remains the central theoretical barrier to moving formalized narrative beyond the simple-minded analysis of stage processes and rational action sequences. Serious institutional analysis cannot be conducted without addressing it.

Author's note

This article is dedicated to the memory of Bruce Mayhew, who wrote two interesting papers on sequences (Mayhew, Gray, and Mayhew 1971; Mayhew and Levinger 1976) and who wrote me a wonderfully encouraging letter when I was trying to get some unorthodox work published early in my career. (As the reader can see, I am still trying.) I would also like to thank Harrison White for the original invitation to write this summary piece for the "Interfaces Conference" at Enfield, New Hampshire, 16 August 1991, and I would like to thank the participants at that conference, whose hostile comments have forced important clarifications. Finally, I would like to thank John Padgett for his advice on game theory and Peter Abell for many forms of collegiality.

References

Abbott, A. 1983. "Sequences of Social Events." *Historical Methods* 16(4):129.
———. 1984. "Event Sequence and Event Duration." *Historical Methods* 17(4):192.
———. 1988a. "Transcending General Linear Reality." *Sociological Theory* 6:169–86.

————. 1988b. *The System of Professions*. Chicago: University of Chicago Press.

————. 1990a. "A Primer on Sequence Methods." *Organization Science* 1:373–92

————. 1990b. "Conceptions of Time and Events in Social Science Methods." *Historical Methods* 23:140–50.

————. 1991a. "History and Sociology." *Social Science History* 15:201–38.

————. 1991b. "The Order of Professionalization." *Work and Occupations* 18:355–84.

————. Forthcoming. "What Do Cases Do?" In *What Is a Case?* edited by Charles Ragin and Howard Becker. Cambridge: Cambridge University Press.

Abell, P. 1984. "Comparative Narratives." *Journal for the Theory of Social Behavior* 14:309–31.

————. 1985. "Analyzing Qualitative Sequences." Pp. 99–115 in *Sequence Analysis*, edited by P. Abell and M. Proctor. Brookfield, VT: Gower.

————. 1987. *The Syntax of Social Life*. Oxford: Oxford University Press.

————. 1989. "Games in Networks." *Rationality and Society* 1:259–82.

————. 1991. *Narrative Analysis*. Paper for the Interfaces Conference, Enfield, New Hampshire, 17 August.

Bernert, C. 1983. "The Career of Causal Analysis in American Sociology." *British Journal of Sociology* 34:230–54.

Blalock, H. 1964. *Causal Inference in Non-Experimental Research*. Chapel Hill: University of North Carolina Press.

Blau, P. B., and O. D. Duncan. 1967. *The American Occupational Structure*. New York: Free Press.

Cressey, P. G. 1932. *The Taxi-Dance Hall*. Chicago: University of Chicago Press.

Edwards, L. P. 1927. *The Natural History of Revolution*. Chicago: University of Chicago Press.

Lieberson, S. 1985. *Making It Count*. Berkeley: University of California Press.

Marini, M. M., and B. L. Singer. 1988. "Causality in the Social Sciences." Pp. 347–409 in *Sociological Methodology 1988*, edited by Clifford Clogg. Washington, DC: American Sociological Association.

Marx, K. 1963. *The Eighteenth Brumaire of Louis Bonaparte*. New York: International Publishers.

Mayhew, B. H., L. N. Gray, and M. L Mayhew. 1971. "Behavior of Interaction Systems." *General Systems* 16:13–29.

Mayhew, B. H., and R. L. Levinger. 1976. "On the Frequency of Oligarchy in Human Interaction." *American Journal of Sociology* 81 :1017–49.

Park, R. E., and E.W. Burgess. 1921. *An Introduction to the Science of Sociology*. Chicago: University of Chicago Press.

Parsons, T. 1937. *The Structure of Social Action*. New York: McGraw-Hill.

Reichenbach, H. 1962. *The Rise of Scientific Philosophy*. Berkeley: University of California Press.

Thrasher, F. M. 1927. *The Gang*. Chicago: University of Chicago Press.

Wallerstein, I. 1974. *The Modern World System*. New York: Academic Press.

Weber, M. 1947. *The Theory of Social and Economic Organization*. Translated by A. M. Henderson and T. Parsons, edited by T. Parsons. New York: Free Press.

7

THE TROUBLE WITH STORIES

Charles Tilly

Born in England but soon transplanted to Ontario, Stephen Leacock left Canada to do a Ph.D. with Thorstein Veblen at the University of Chicago. After four years, Leacock returned definitively to Canada, but this time to Montreal; he eventually chaired McGill University's Department of Economics and Political Science. In that vein, his *Elements of Political Science* (Leacock 1921) merited translation into 17 languages. As Leacock grew older and wiser, however, he turned increasingly from economics and political science to humor such as his droll classic *Literary Lapses*. He titled that book's final story "A, B, and C. The Human Element in Mathematics." It concerns stories. Leacock ([1910] 1957) wrote,

> The student of arithmetic who has mastered the first four rules of his art, and successfully striven with money sums and fractions, finds himself confronted by an unbroken expanse of questions known as problems. These are short stories of adventure and industry with the end omitted, and though betraying a strong family resemblance, are not without a certain element of romance.
>
> The characters in the plot of a problem are three people called A, B, and C. The form of the question is generally of this sort:
>
> "A, B, and C do a certain piece of work. A can do as much work in one hour as B in two or C in four. Find how long they work at it." (p. 141)

Tilly, Charles. 1999. "The Trouble with Stories." In *The Social Worlds of Higher Education: Handbook for Teaching in a New Century*, edited by B. Pescosolido and R. Aminzade, 256–70 (Thousand Oaks CA: Pine Forge Press). Reprinted by permission of SAGE Publications, Inc.

A, B, and C rowed on rivers, pumped water from cisterns, dug ditches, and otherwise competed strenuously, always to the disadvantage of C. Leacock ([1910] 1957) reveals what he learned from survivor D: C died of exhaustion after yet another grueling contest with A and B. A then lost interest in competition as B languished in his grief until he "abjured mathematics and devoted himself to writing the history of the Swiss Family Robinson in words of one syllable" (p. 146).

Under Leacock's pen, the abstract relations of algebra give way to human interest stories. His readers can chuckle because they instantly recognize the conceit. Alas, the same does not hold for sociology's readers. The trouble with reading, writing, and learning sociology is straightforward but formidable; people ordinarily cast their accounts of social life as stories—stories, as we shall see, with distinctive causal structures. Such stories do crucial work in patching social life together. But sociology's strongest insights do not take the form of stories and often undermine the stories people tell.

By *stories*, I do not mean rhetoric, the artful use of language to convince readers that the writer tells the truth. Nor do I mean the straightforward chronologies of events that appear in sources such as personnel records, marriage registers, and machine inspection logs. Although reading notes, court proceedings, political tracts, and advertisements sometimes incorporate stories in the narrow sense I am pursuing here, I am not including all of them under the heading "stories." I mean the sequential, explanatory recounting of connected, self-propelled people and events that we sometimes call tales, fables, or narratives. Let us call these sequential, explanatory accounts of self-motivated human action *standard stories*.

Standard Stories

To construct a standard story, start with a limited number of interacting characters, individual or collective. Your characters may be persons, but they also may be organizations such as churches and states or even abstract categories such as social classes and regions. Treat your characters as independent, conscious, and self-motivated. Make all their significant actions occur as consequences of their own deliberations or impulses. Limit the time and space within which your characters interact. With the possible exception of externally generated accidents—you can call them "chance" or "acts of God"—make sure that everything that happens results directly from your characters' actions.

Now, supply your characters with specific motives, capacities, and resources. Furnish the time and place within which they are interacting with objects that you and they can construe as barriers, openings, threats, opportunities, and tools—as facilities and constraints bearing on their actions. Set your characters in motion. From their starting point, make sure that all their actions follow your rules of plausibility and produce effects on others that likewise follow your rules of plausibility. Trace the accumulated effects of their actions to some interesting outcome. Better yet, work your way backward from some interesting outcome, following all the same rules. Congratulations, you have just constructed a standard story.

In writing your standard story, you have crafted a text that resembles a play, a television sitcom episode, a fable, a news item, or a novel. But you also have produced something like the following:

- The account that a jury constructs from the testimony and evidence laid out during a trial
- A biography or an autobiography of a single character
- Explanations that people piece together at the scene of a grisly accident
- Histories that nationalists recount as they say why they have prior rights to a given territory
- Speeches of social movement leaders who are linking today's actions or demands to the movement's past
- The selective (and perhaps fanciful) account of his past with which a taxi driver regales his or her captive passengers during a long ride to the airport
- How people apologize for, or justify, their violations of other people's expectations: "I'm sorry, but . . ."
- What victims of a crime or a disaster demand when authorities say they do not know how or why it happened
- Conversations people carry on as they judge other people's sins, good deeds, successes, and failures
- How bosses and workers reply to the question "Why don't you folks ever hire any X's?"

Standard stories, in short, pop up everywhere. They lend themselves to vivid, compelling accounts of what has happened, what will happen, or what should happen. They do essential work in social life, cementing people's commitments to common projects, helping people make sense of what is going on, channeling collective decisions and judgments, spurring people to action they would otherwise be reluctant to pursue. Telling stories even helps people to recognize difficulties in their own perceptions, explanations, or actions, as when I tell a friend about a recent adventure only to remark—or to have my friend point out—a previously unnoticed contradiction among the supposed facts I have laid out.

Stories in Action

The sociological technique of interviewing (especially in the forms we call life histories or oral histories) benefits from the readiness of humans to package memory in standard stories. Although all of us have recollections we would prefer not to share with interviewers, in my own interviewing I have generally found people delighted to talk about past experiences and adept at placing those experiences in coherent sequences. Indeed, humans are so good at making sense of social processes after the fact by means of standard stories that skilled interviewers must spend much of their energy probing, checking, looking for discrepancies, and then reconstructing the accounts their respondents offer them.

In teaching sociology to North American and European students, I have been impressed by the ingenuity and persistence with which they pack explanations into standard stories. Whatever else we have learned about inequality, for example, sociologists have made clear that a great deal of social inequality results from indirect, unintended, collective, and environmentally mediated effects that fit very badly into standard stories. Yet, students discussing inequality tend to offer two competing variants on the same standard story: (1) that individuals or categories of individuals who differ significantly in ability and motivation arrive at various tests, judged by others, on which they perform with differential success, whereupon those others reward them unequally, *or* (2) that powerful gatekeepers follow their own preferences in sorting individuals or whole categories of individuals who arrive at certain choice points, thereby allocating them differential rewards.

Both variants respect the rules of standard stories—self-motivated actors in delimited time and space and conscious actions that cause most or all of the significant effects. Such a standard story shapes likely disagreements—over which variant is more accurate, over whether and why categories of people do differ significantly in ability and motivation, over whether existing performance tests measure capacities properly, over whether gatekeepers operate out of prejudice, and so on. Although many people in and out of sociology explain inequality in these ways, either variant of the story omits or contradicts major inequality-generating causal sequences well established by sociological research. Such a story conflicts, for example, with explanations in which inequality at work forms as a byproduct of hiring through existing, socially homogeneous personal networks of people already on the job, which happens to be the most common form of job recruitment through most of the contemporary capitalist world. That sort of confrontation between preferred standard stories and well-documented causal processes presents teachers and students of sociology with serious difficulties but also with great opportunities to rethink conventional explanations of social life. Later sections of this chapter examine the difficulties and opportunities in detail.

By no means does trouble with stories occur in pedagogy alone. It bedevils sociological analysis wherever that analysis takes place—in field observation, in historical reconstruction, in polling, on the editorial page, in everyday conversation, or in classrooms. Even veteran analysts of incremental, interactive, indirect, unintended, collective, and environmentally mediated causal processes in social life—I include myself—easily slip into interpreting new social situations as if standard stories adequately represented their causal structures. Although when discussing what we can do about weaknesses of stories I describe one sort of teaching that concentrates on the construction of more adequate stories, I see no yawning gulf between teaching and research; sophistication and effectiveness in one promotes sophistication and effectiveness in the other. At a minimum, teachers and researchers must learn the pitfalls of assuming that standard stories adequately represent causes and effects as they unfold in social processes.

For specialized purposes, of course, people often offer other sorts of accounts than the ones I have called standard stories. Novelists and poets occasionally write descriptions of humans who engage in inexplicable actions, respond to hidden forces, or experience all life as chaos. Patients reporting their medical histories commonly depart from standard stories to enumerate successions of mishaps. Religious and political doctrines often include great historical arcs that fulfill some powerful plan or immanent principle—progress, decline, destiny, or just retribution. A book titled *The Story of the Atom* may well include standard stories about Albert Einstein and Niels Bohr, but much of its account is likely to center on explications of physical principles. Standard stories stand out among all of the accounts we sometimes call stories by their combination of unified time and place, limited sets of self-motivated actors, and cause-and-effect relations centered on those actors' deliberated actions. Such stories predominate in everyday descriptions, explanations, and evaluations of human social behavior.

Why do standard stories occupy such central places in social life? I see two main possibilities that are not mutually exclusive. First, standard story structures might correspond closely to the ways in which human brains store, retrieve, and manipulate information about social processes. Brains seem to array objects, including social objects, in virtual spatial and temporal relations to each other; to assign objects attributes that are available as explanations of their behavior; and to assemble complex situations as interactions of self-motivated objects within delimited spaces and times. If so, then preference for standard story accounts and availability of storytelling as a wide-ranging social tool could spring from deep currents in the human organism.

Perhaps, however, brains and nervous systems do no more than accommodate storytelling as one of many possible ways of organizing social accounts. Perhaps people learn the structure of stories just as they learn maps of cities and melodies of favorite songs. In that case, we might reasonably expect different populations to vary in their emphases on storytelling and may well discover that Westerners acquired a preference for standard story packaging of social life through a long, distinctive history. Through that long history, we might find, people extended storytelling from an initial narrow invention to a wide range of applications.

Here, as always, the exact interplay between nature and nurture, between wired-in capacity and cultural immersion, and between genetic determination and historical transformation presents a great challenge to our long-term understanding and explanation of social life. But in the short run, we need only this conclusion: for whatever reasons, today's Westerners (and maybe all peoples) have a strong tendency to organize conversations about social processes in standard story form.

Disciplinary Stories

Each of the academic disciplines that concentrates on the explanation of some aspect of human behavior has made its own adjustment to the dominance of standard stories. Linguists, geographers, psychologists, historians, paleontologists, economists, anthropologists, political scientists, and sociologists all have characteristic ways of dealing with—or keeping their distance from—standard stories. Many historians, for example, insist that such stories accurately represent the causal structure of social life. They write their histories as tales of conscious, self-motivated actors. When they get to the large scales of wars, great transformations, and civilizations, however, historians split between those who refer to collective actors (e.g., classes, nations) in standard story form and those who resort to abstract causal forces such as mentalities, cultures, technologies, and forms of power.

Psychologists take other approaches to stories. They divide among a dwindling number of storytelling analysts who continue to treat whole individuals as conscious acting entities and a variety of reductionists who trace observable human behavior to the operation of genes, neurons, hormones, and/or subconscious mental processes. Economists divide differently; many analysts of individual economic behavior adopt a highly stylized version of the standard story that centers on deliberate decision making within well-defined constraints, whereas analysts of macroeconomic processes introduce non-story-mediating mechanisms—impersonal markets, technologies, resource endowments, and flows of information, capital, goods, or labor. For all their differences in other regards, political scientists, anthropologists, and sociologists maintain similar relations to standard stories. Within each of the three disciplines, some specialists conduct almost all of their analyses in standard story form, whereas others reject stories in favor of explanations based on non-story structures and processes such as markets, networks, self-sustaining cultures, physical environments, and evolutionary selection.

What place should stories occupy in sociology? In ordinary circumstances, well-told standard stories convey what is going on far more forcefully than do the mathematical equations, lists of concepts, statistical tables, or schematic diagrams sociologists commonly chalk up on their blackboards. Why, then, should sociologists not turn to fiction and biography as models for their own efforts? After all, nonsociologists often reserve their highest praise for sociological work that "reads like a novel." Would a course in story writing not, therefore, provide the best introduction to sociological analysis?

No, it would not, at least not if the point of sociology is to describe and explain social processes. The difficulty lies in the logical structure of storytelling. Remember its elements: (1) limited number of interacting characters; (2) limited time and space; (3) independent, conscious, self-motivated actions; and (4) with the exception of externally generated accidents, all actions resulting from previous actions by the characters. Standard stories work that way, but on the whole social processes do not.

Consider some examples:

- Within a high-fertility population, as improved nutrition or prevention of children's diseases reduces infant mortality, the population grows more rapidly and experiences a rise in life expectancy.
- Job seekers who get their information about employment opportunities from other people who are already close to them do less well in the job market, on average, than do job seekers who get their information from more distant acquaintances.
- Despite the sometimes sensational salaries of athletes, entertainers, and chief executive officers, the higher we go up the ladder of annual income in America, the larger looms inherited wealth and the smaller the share that wages of any type constitute current revenues.

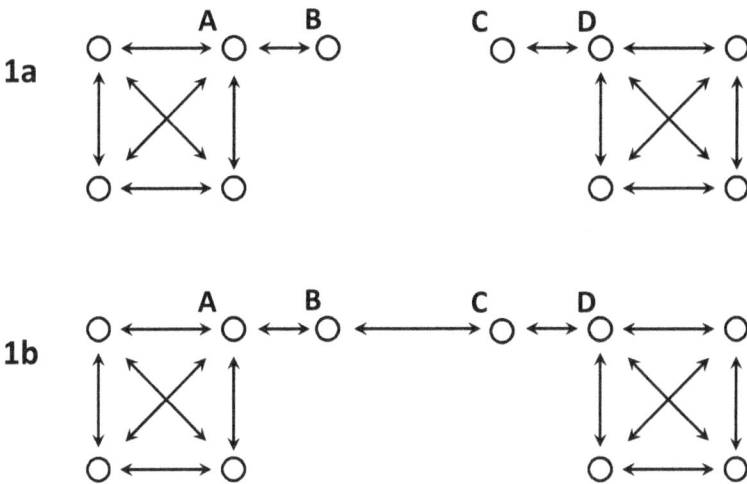

FIGURE 7.1

- In Figure 7.1, 1a, B and C obviously occupy peripheral locations, whereas A and D hardly differ from their neighbors in centrality. In Figure 7.1, 1b, however, the addition of connection between B and C has made them much more central than any of their predecessors, whereas A and D also have gained in their access to others.
- In American cities, children from low-income households often live in rundown, crowded housing where dust mites and cockroaches proliferate. Those pests trigger asthma attacks, which keep poorer children out of school or hamper their performance in school.

Each of these cases calls for qualifications and explanations. The rise in life expectancy as a consequence of declining infant mortality registers the passage of larger surviving cohorts into higher age groups and soon reaches a limit unless death rates start declining for those higher age groups as well. More distant acquaintances provide relatively effective news about available jobs not because individually they have better information but because collectively they connect job seekers with a wider range of opportunities than do close friends and kin. Inherited wealth actually places the bulk of rich Americans in their high positions and means that much of their income arrives as returns from capital rather than as salaries. Connecting apparently peripheral locations that possess complementary resources describes the work of effective entrepreneurs, brokers, and matchmakers; it frequently changes whole organizational configurations rapidly. Missing school and being sick in school not only reduce children's exposure to education but also promote children's confusion, inattention, and discouragement, which further damages learning.

The point of these obvious examples is twofold. In each case, strong, recurrent causal mechanisms are operating, but in none of them do the crucial causal mechanisms correspond to the structure of standard storytelling. Of course, we can tell standard stories about some aspects in each of these situations—how microbe hunters track down baby-killing diseases, how individual job seekers actually find employment, why parents bequeath wealth to their children, under what circumstances entrepreneurs notice good fits between unconnected locations, or how poor children experience schools. But these cases differ from the conventional matter of storytelling because central cause-and-effect relations are indirect, incremental, interactive, unintended, collective, or mediated by the nonhuman environment rather than being direct, willed consequences of individual actions. The standard stories we construct for such processes miss their central causal connections. Most significant social processes fall into a nonstory mode. Most of them do so because at least some crucial causes within them are indirect, incremental, interactive, unintended, collective, and/or mediated by the nonhuman environment.

Personally, I have nothing against standard stories. I read them eagerly, make arguments with them, remember things by telling myself stories, and gladly overhear stories people tell each other on the subway. I began this chapter with a standard story about Leacock. As a student of social processes, I have spent much of my career locating, transcribing, cataloging, analyzing, retelling, and pondering other people's standard stories. The pages of my books on popular contention overflow with stories in which ordinary people make collective claims. That massive effort to extract evidence concerning social processes from stories has brought me to appreciate the centrality of storytelling in human life, but it also has taught me the incompatibility in causal structure between most standard stories and social processes.

The Search for Causes

Refusal to recognize the limits of standard storytelling creates major problems for social analysts. In one light, the problems stem from distortion produced by forcing social processes into stories about self-motivated actors. In the opposite light, they consist of failures to specify causal mechanisms that actually drive social processes. To clarify what is at issue in the confrontation between standard storytelling and the social science explanation, we can use a rough distinction among the four dominant ontologies and explanatory strategies adopted by analysts of social life: methodological individualism, phenomenological individualism, systems realism, and relational realism. Let us review them and their connections with storytelling in turn.

Methodological individualism treats independent choice-making persons as the fundamental units and starting points of sociological analysis. Its explanations pivot on mental events—choices or decisions. People make choices that forward their interests, preferences, or utilities within constraints set by personal resources and environmental settings. What causes those choices? Other mental events in the form of calculations concerning the likely outcomes of different actions.

Methodological individualism has the great advantages of simplicity and generality—if and when it works. For the moment, it faces three large difficulties, two of them upstream and one of them downstream. Upstream (i.e., before the point of decision that constitutes its central object of explanation), (1) few actual human behaviors seem to fit its requirement of optimizing choices among well-defined alternatives and (2) supposedly fixed elements such as preferences and computations of outcomes actually wobble and interact in the course of social action. Downstream (i.e., once a decision supposedly is made), we confront difficulty in that (3) methodological individualism so far lacks a plausible account of the causal chains by which decisions produce their effects on individual action, social interaction, and complex social processes.

Methodological individualists, however, can take standard storytelling in their stride. They already are talking about self-motivated actors—the fewer, the better—within delimited times and places whose deliberated decisions produce all the effects worth mentioning. Their problem results not from intrinsic incompatibil*ity* of their causal accounts with storytelling but rather from the implausibility of the standard stories their causal accounts entail.

Phenomenological individualists, likewise, move easily on standard story terrain. They center descriptions and explanations of social processes on human consciousness. At the extreme of solipsism, indeed, the social world dissolves into individual consciousness, and systematic explanation of social processes faces an insuperable barrier—the impossibility of any observer's entering into his or her neighbor's awareness, much less explaining it. In less extreme forms, however, phenomenological individualists pursue a familiar variety of explanation. Through empathy, deduction, criticism, or some other means, they reconstruct the meanings, feelings, ideologies, and theories that presumably motivate social action. They can deal more easily than methodological individualists with collective actors such as churches, states, classes, or regions, to which they impute varieties

and degrees of shared consciousness. At that point, nevertheless, phenomenological individualists confront the same explanatory obstacles as
do methodological individualists—upstream, accounting for change and
interaction of the conscious states that presumably produce social action;
downstream, showing how those conscious states create their effects.

System realists have commonly prided themselves on escaping precisely
those obstacles by recognizing the interdependence of individual actions,
their constraint by previously existing social structure, and their coales-
cence into self-regulating systems. Structures sketched by system realists
range in scale from friendships to civilizations, in content from fluid communications to evolutionary universals, and in structure from gossamer
webs to iron cages. What unifies system approaches is their imputation
of self-generating properties to social aggregates and their explanation of
particular social events by connections to the larger social systems within
which they occur. The great failures of systems theories lie in two main
areas: (1) the absence of sturdy, well documented causal mechanisms that
actually are observable in operation and (2) the prevalence of poorly ex-
plicated functional explanations in which events, relations, institutions,
or social processes exist because they serve some requirement of the system as a whole. Although they certainly describe their major actors—social systems—as self-propelling and sometimes describe social systems as
having characteristic life histories, system realists usually avoid standard
storytelling.

Relational analysis focuses on the transaction, interaction, information
flow, exchange, mutual influence, or social tie as its elementary unit. For
relational realists, individuals, groups, and social systems are contingent,
changing social products of interaction. Relational realists vary greatly in
the prominence they ascribe to culture—to shared understandings and
their representations. At one extreme, hard-nosed network theorists treat
the geometry of connections as having a logic that operates quite independently of the network's symbolic content. At the other extreme,
conversational analysts treat the back-and-forth of social speech as ines-
capably drenched with meaning. In between, students of organizational
processes who reject the idea that organizations are self-maintaining systems often trace webs of culturally conditioned interdependency among
persons and positions within the organization.

At both extremes and in between, relational analysis maintains a curious
connection with storytelling. It simultaneously denies the self-propulsion
of a story's characters and affirms the centrality of mutual influences among
characters that give standard storytelling its continuity. Relational analyses enjoy the advantages of providing excellent descriptive templates for
social processes and of identifying robust regularities in social interaction.

At least in principle, they offer the promise of treating standard stories not as descriptions or explanations of social processes but as changing, contingent *products* of social interaction. In fact, they could account for the production and use of nonstandard stories as well.

To be sure, in real life and in sociology, most attempts at explanation of social processes involve syntheses, amalgams, and compromises among some or all of our four basic approaches: methodological individualism, phenomenological individualism, system realism, and relational analysis. It is not hard, for example, to conceive of individuals as making rational choices within strict limits set by encompassing and self-regulating social systems, as in the model of a buyer or seller who enters a competitive market. Similarly, relational analysts often go on to argue that the structures created by interaction—hierarchies, paired categories, industries, and so on—have emergent properties, operate according to powerful laws, and shape social relations among their participants; to that extent, relational realists edge toward systems theories. Still, each of the four explanatory traditions generates some relatively pure and exclusive accounts of social life, each (even in compromised form) presents characteristically different difficulties, and at the limit all four cannot be valid. Furthermore, none of the four offers an explanatory structure that fits comfortably with the standard stories in which people ordinarily cast their social accounts.

In most circumstances, standard storytelling provides an execrable guide to social explanation. Its directly connected and self-motivated actors, deliberated actions, circumscribed fields of action, and limited inventory of causes badly represent the ontology and causal structure of most social processes. There are exceptions; some games, some battles, some markets, and some decision making within formal organizations approximate the ontology and causal structure of standard stories. But these are extreme cases, notable especially for the hidden institutional supports that make them possible. Most social processes involve cause-and-effect relations that are indirect, incremental, interactive, unintended, collective, and/or mediated by the nonhuman environment.

How to Confront Storytelling

Hence, a three-faced problem: how to cut through the limits set by prevalent stories on the explanation of social processes, how to convey valid explanations of social processes when audiences customarily wrap their own explanations in storytelling, and how to describe and explain the creation, transformation, and effects of existing standard stories.

The first is, surprisingly, the easiest. All well-versed practitioners of methodological individualism, phenomenological individualism, system realism, and relational analysis have at times learned to resist standard story interpretations of their subject matter and to adopt formalisms that assist them in imposing an alternative frame—mathematical models, diagrams, simulations, conceptual schemes, measurement devices, and more. It might be painful, and some skilled practitioners abandon their training, but such learned self-discipline comes with apprenticeship to the trade.

Communication with nonspecialists who customarily cast their social accounts in standard stories sets a greater challenge. Teachers of mathematics' or chemistry's emphatically nonstory structures to novices have several advantages over sociologists; almost no one thinks mathematics or chemistry should or does follow the rules of storytelling, students have no previous training in mathematics or chemistry as a series of stories to shed before they can learn more adequate models, and students grudgingly or eagerly accept that learning the formal structure of mathematics or chemistry will give them future benefits. None of these, regrettably, applies to sociology.

On the contrary. Most people, including some teachers of sociology, think that social life actually does conform to the requirements of storytelling—self-motivated actors, deliberated actions, and the lot. In addition, people (or at least Western people) ordinarily carry on their moral reasoning in a standard story mode. They judge actual or possible actions by their conscious motives and their immediately foreseeable effects; this fact lies behind the frequent complaint that sociological explanations deny the responsibility, autonomy, and/or moral worth of individuals. In addition, people ordinarily join (1) moral judgments, (2) conceptions of what is possible, (3) ideas of what is desirable within that realm of possibility, and (4) causal accounts of social life. A discussion of what people should do presumes that they can do it, and the justification for their doing so usually includes judgments about the likely consequences of their doing so. As a result, people do not readily accept analysts' attempts to pry elements of moral thinking part. (Perhaps for that very reason, young people who are beginning to question the moral systems within which they grew up develop greater receptivity to sociology than do their fellows.)

That is not all. Before they encounter sociology as a discipline, students and nonspecialist readers have had years of practice in constructing social explanations by means of storytelling; they do not cast off that practice easily. Finally, the benefits of doing so are much harder to discern than in the case of mathematics or chemistry; indeed, what most students and some professionals hope to find in sociology is the ability to construct more persuasive standard stories. Sociologists do not easily cut through the veil of resistance.

What can sociologists do about it? Here are some of the possibilities:

- Study the social processes that condition how and why similar stories strike one audience as quite authentic and strike another as utterly phony

- Teach competing ways of representing particular social processes, not only as storytelling and as alternative social scientific models but also as metaphor, machine, and political rhetoric; compare premises, procedures, and results of these competing representations, showing what is distinctive and valuable about the social scientific ones

- Dramatize the existence of social processes, configurations, or outcomes for which available standard stories offer implausible explanations, demonstrably false explanations, contradictory explanations, or no explanations at all and for which coherent sociological explanations exist

- More precisely and aggressively, create and use simulations of social processes (whether simple games or complex symbolic representations) that challenge available standard stories, embody sociologically plausible causes and effects, produce empirically verifiable outcomes, and allow participants to investigate the consequences of altering inputs or causal structures

- Trace standard story shadows of nonstory processes, as by following a series of interdependent life histories, each itself in coherent standard story form, before examining the intersection and variation of those lives; how, for example, do variable relations to the same school system, firm, or labor market create contrasting trajectories and solidarities?

- Go even farther in the same direction and subvert storytelling; embed nonstory explanations in ostensibly storytelling form, for example, by recounting the same social process—a military battle, flow of information through a hospital, or racial integration of a school system—from multiple perspectives, one standard story per participant, until the problem shifts to accounting for differences and connections among the experiences of participants

- Observe how the relationship and conversation between interviewer and respondent shape the responses that survey analysts later interpret as evidence of respondents' individual traits, preferences, intentions, and/or propensities

- Simulate and investigate what happens when participants in standard stories become aware of and respond deliberately to cause-and-effect relations that are indirect, incremental, interactive, unintended, collective, and/or mediated by the nonhuman environment, thus approximating what many theorists have advocated as "reflexive" sociology

- Tunnel under standard stories themselves by creating compelling explanations for both (1) the stories that participants in social processes tell about what is happening to them or others and (2) the stories that analysts, critics, observers, and even other sociologists tell about particular social processes, situations, and outcomes; using systematic knowledge of the social processes involved, for example, explain how and why police, criminals, judges, prosecutors, priests, social workers, and criminologists come to tell different stories about crime

From the last alternative unfolds a huge, promising program of sociological work. Analysts of social construction have generally contented themselves with demonstrating that entities that earlier interpreters have taken to be irreducibly real—identities, nations, states, genders, and more—consist of or depend on elaborate, contingent, but compelling cultural webs. They have not offered verifiable descriptions or explanations of the processes by which the relevant social construction takes place. They have taken social construction to be a blank wall, an opaque screen, or an impenetrable thicket, impossible to tunnel under. Because standard stories constitute one of the major zones of social construction, however, any systematic account of the processes by which people generate, transform, respond to, and deploy standard stories will serve as a model for tunneling under constructionist analyses in general, taking them seriously but identifying the social constructions involved as objects of explanation.

Here is a challenge to social science worthy of a lifetime's effort. To explain how, why, and with what effects people fashion standard stories will require a commodious, sophisticated theory. It will entail mapping the various contents, forms, and contexts of stories; tracing how they change; pinpointing the social work people do with them; and saying how some of them become fixed in laws, national traditions, or religious rituals, others form and flow like jazz, and still others circulate as jokes, insults, potted biographies, excuses, moral pronouncements, and ad hoc explanations. Surely, hermeneutic and text-analytic methods will not suffice; attention will shift to the social processes that precipitate standard stories. We should enjoy the irony that a major obstacle to social explanation should become the object of social explanation.

We have some models for that sort of analysis. In the study of language, of art forms, of well-articulated ideologies, of contentious repertoires, of kinship systems, and of other phenomena where change in shared understandings clearly occurs and significantly affects participants' interactions, sociologists and other social scientists already have accumulated experience in tunneling under social construction. Not that they have reached high consensus or manufactured models that will easily export to the explanation of standard stories or other equally complex phenomena. However we evaluate the models currently available in these fields, their existence establishes the possibility in principle of taking the prevalence, variety, and power of standard stories as an explanatory challenge.

An even greater challenge lies farther along the same road. Sociologists eventually must reconcile three apparently contradictory features of social life:

- The recurrence of a limited set of causal mechanisms in a wide variety of situations
- The incessant improvisation that occurs in social interaction
- The great weight of particular histories, congealed as particular cultural configurations, on social interaction.

Each is so compelling that it has acquired its own advocates—advocates of general covering laws for human behavior, advocates of social life as nothing but piecemeal improvisation, and advocates of deep historical and cultural determinism cum particularism. In fact, all three operate and interact. The three features combine in producing path-dependent social processes that never quite repeat themselves, ceaseless flux in relations among participants, and strong but partial causal analogies from one iteration of a social process to the next.

We see the trio in the field of inequality, where similar processes of exploitation, resistance, and control recur in disparate circumstances, yet actual participants in any one of those circumstances negotiate, innovate, cheat, resist, and adapt without cessation, and all this improvisation occurs within strong limits, particular to the time and place, set by accumulated culture, so much so that within the same setting inequalities by gender, race, and citizenship operate as if they belonged to distinct idioms within a common language. We see the trio again in contentious politics, where an analyst of mobilization notices similar causal connections in a vast array of situations, where on the ground improvisation is not only prevalent but also essential, and where the forms of interaction themselves occur within or at the perimeters of previously established forms.

Although the production of standard stories surely conforms to causal principles and permits variation in storytelling style, storytelling lodges especially in the third category, in the social arrangements by which the accumulated collective past weighs on the present and the future. Social interaction generates stories that justify and facilitate further social interaction, but it does so within limits set by the stories people already share as a consequence of previous interactions. It would be a triumph of social analysis to tell the true story of how storytelling arises and how it affects our conduct of social life.

Enlightenment and Explanation

The prevalence of standard stories poses two significant problems for teachers and students of sociology. First, both teachers and students make choices, implicit and explicit, between conceiving of sociology as enlightenment or science, but for most people the paths to enlightenment pass through standard stories, substituting one standard story for another rather than complementing standard stories by means of science. Second, the actual causal structure of social processes, the indispensable core of any sociological explanation, usually contradicts the logical and causal structure of standard stories. As a consequence, teachers of sociology choose, however unconsciously, how to connect their presentation of the subject with standard stories.

Figure 7.2 schematizes the choice. At one extreme, teachers can emphasize sociology as enlightenment by formulating and telling superior stories. In what way superior? From a sociological viewpoint, superior stories have these qualities:

- They include all the major actors (including collective and non-human actors) that a valid causal account of the events in question would identify and relate.
- Within the social interactions they describe, they accurately represent cause-and-effect relations among actions of participants in the story, even if they neglect indirect, incremental, and other effects that are not visible in the participants' interactions.
- They provide effective means of connecting the story with times, places, actors, and actions outside its purview.
- They offer means of relating causes explicitly invoked by the story with other causes that are indirect, incremental, interactive, unintended, collective, and/or mediated by the nonhuman environment.

FIGURE 7.2

Superior stories, that is, do not identify all the relevant cause-and-effect relations, but they remain consistent with fuller, more adequate causal accounts.

In the case of social movements, for example, an *inferior* but commonly credited story says that people who have failed in fair, normal competition vent their frustration in collective complaints, to which right-thinking people respond by pointing to established channels for the expression of political preferences. The story is inferior because solid evidence concerning social movement recruitment and participation regularly contradicts its empirical implications and because the causal connections it alleges—notably the chain from failure, to frustration, to collective action—do not hold up to close observation.

A *superior*, sociologically validated story says that people join social movements as a consequence of their relations with other people who have already experienced injustice or otherwise become aware of fellow humans' experience with injustice. Neither story adequately represents the significance of network connections in recruitment to social movements, but within the social interactions it does represent, the second story comes much closer to social processes actually governing social movement activism. Thus, the superior story makes a contribution to the teaching of sociology as enlightenment.

At the other extreme, nonstory processes, we can decide to teach, learn, and use sociology as a deliberate integration of social interaction into causal chains, significant parts of which are indirect, incremental, interactive, unintended, collective, and/or mediated by the nonhuman environment. Thus, we can construct, verify, and communicate models of social movements in which intentions, awareness, and deliberated action take place in tight interdependence with social processes that are not immediately visible to social movement participants. This sort of teaching, learning, and using is essential to the discovery of new explanations and the full criticism of prevalent stories and, hence, is crucial to the education of professional sociologists. It is essential because cause-and-effect relations within social processes do not, in fact, conform to standard stories.

In between the two extremes, we also can choose to pursue sociology as an effort to contextualize existing stories or to generate them. *Contextualizing* stories involves identifying the social situations in which certain types of stories arise and tracing the consequences of adopting those stories rather than others that are, in principle, available. Thus, we might analyze the conditions under which a connected but previously unmobilized population forms a story about its distinctive national origins, makes claims for political recognition on the basis of that story, and then lives the consequences of having adopted that particular story rather than some other that may have been available.

The even more ambitious program of *generating* stories consists of analyzing the processes by which people actually create, adopt, negotiate, and alter the stories they employ in routine social life. Here, in principle, the analyst should be able to simulate and predict both form and content of stories as they enter the social interactions of juries, social movement activists, newscasters, coworkers, and people in general. Storytelling is such a fundamental, pervasive social process that it is hard to imagine effective generation of stories without deep understanding of nonstory processes. Thus, each rung in the ladder from explanation to enlightenment depends on those below it; construction of superior stories rests on some ability to contextualize them, contextualization requires some awareness of processes that generate stories, and the analysis of generation requires partial knowledge of the nonstory causal processes at work in social life.

To teach superior stories and the capacity to detect and criticize inferior stories, however, amply serves enlightenment. Sociology as enlightenment can profitably concentrate on critical examination and reconstruction of widely employed standard stories. Because most students of sociology go off into other walks of life, and because nearly all of them continue to conduct their lives by means of stories and responses to other people's stories, sociology as enlightenment should enrich and clarify social experience. An enlightenment-oriented sociological education can equip those nonspecialist citizens to identify, compare, classify, criticize, improve, or even deploy standard stories. On the presumption that knowing how powerful everyday processes actually work prepares the knowers for more effective encounters with social life, sociological teaching can serve well by concentrating on standard stories. If that sort of education then sensitizes nonspecialists to indirect, incremental, interactive, unintended, collective, and/or environmentally mediated causal links to the stories people tell, then so much the better.

Author's Note

Ronald Aminzade, Mustafa Emirbayer, Roberto Franzosi, Herbert Gans, Jan Hoem, John Krinsky, Charles Lemert, John Markoff, Ann Mische, Victor Nee, Bernice Pescosolido, Francesca Polletta, Marilynn Rosenthal, Harrison White, and Viviana Zelizer provided helpful comments on earlier drafts. I also have benefited from an electronic discussion of these issues initiated by Polletta and then joined energetically by Jeff Broadbent, Marco Giugni, Jack Goldstone, Jeff Goodwin, Michael Hanagan, Roger Karapin, Howard Lune, and Heather Williams. It is only fair to record that (1) Mische, Polletta, and some of the electronic debaters vigorously dispute my claims that what I call *standard stories* are relatively invariant in structure and dominant in everyday social analyses and that (2) I have done no formal collection and analysis of stories to back up my arguments. I base my assertions about the form and prevalence of standard stories not only on everyday observation, some experience in life history interviewing, and long exposure to written accounts (fictional and otherwise) of social life but also on impressions gained from cataloging and coding perhaps 150,000 reports concerning different types of popular contention that my collaborators and I have abstracted from periodicals, administrative correspondence, chronicles, and related sources. Fortunately, the dispute is open to empirical adjudication; it should encourage readers to bring their own observations and evidence to bear on the actual structure of everyday storytelling. However such an empirical inquiry comes out, its results will clarify the origins, structures, and effects of social stories and thereby help specify effective ways in which to teach, learn, investigate, and explain social processes.

References

Leacock, Stephen B. [1910] 1957. *Literary Lapses*. Toronto: McClelland and Stewart.
———. 1921. *Elements of Political Science*. Boston: Houghton Mifflin.

Part 1C
The Work Narratives Do

Sociologists are interested in narratives not only for their explanatory value, but also for the work they perform for listeners and other public audiences. At the most fundamental level, narratives make meaning, and, in doing so, they can animate our imagination, inspire action, and mobilize social movements. They can plot different possible futures in our own lives and those of others. They can also operate to repair disrupted relationships, reproduce normative behavior, justify the status quo, and extend domination without resort to force. Moreover, they do all this for (and to) both individuals and collectivities. The readings we have selected for this section illustrate, but do not exhaust, the possible work that narratives can do.

Though the term *narrative* was not widely used by sociologists until the 1980s, it has a number of intellectual predecessors, which, though not identical to narratives, contain some resonant features. This body of work calls attention to the role of spoken language in framing actions as culturally appropriate and socially acceptable. The earliest comes from C. Wright Mills's well-known 1940 article, "Situated Actions and Vocabularies of Motives." Mills challenges psychological theories of motive as internal to the individual, arguing instead that motives are constructed through social interaction. More specifically, motives or explanations of behavior arise when someone questions our actions. In response to queries, we give reasons to justify our behavior; acceptable reasons are understood as "motives." Further, Mills understood explanations of our behavior as constrained by institutional contexts because "institutionally, different situations have different *vocabularies of motive* appropriate to their behavior." (1940: 906, his emphasis). For example, a working-class, white, male teenager who steals a car may provide different reasons for his behavior to his friends, to his family, or to a judge in court. Motives then serve a social function: insofar as they help to make sense of "questioned conduct," they facilitate social interaction by satisfying the questioner about the appropriateness of that conduct.

Vocabularies of motive, however, are not narratives. A teenager's reason for stealing a car, for example, might hint at the plot of a narrative or be suggestive of a longer story (the chronology of events), but it does not constitute all the elements of a narrative as we, following Hayden White (1980), have defined it. Further, Mills's sociological conception of motive does not encompass internal feelings or self-understanding that a personal narrative might explore. Still, Mills's piece is the precursor to a large literature on the elements of narrative. We include Mills's article in full here because it highlights what narrative sociologists take seriously: the significance of social interaction in creating meaningful talk. Although vocabularies of motive often fall short of full-blown narratives, they point to how narratives, too, may speak to particular audiences, lead to the forgiveness of some actions, or inspire others.

Following Mills, other sociologists, particularly those in the symbolic interactionist and dramaturgical traditions, have focused on the social construction of explanations that serve particular goals (Goffman 1971; Sykes and Matza 1957). For example, Marvin Scott and Stanford Lyman (1968) examine "accounts," socially approved explanations that operate to neutralize negative evaluations of an action or its consequences when either has been called into question. Accounts are further divided into two categories: justifications and excuses. In justifications, actors accept responsibility for their action, but deny the pejorative evaluations attributed to it. For example, the teenager referenced above may admit to stealing the car to his parents, but may claim that he didn't hurt anyone because the car wasn't damaged. By contrast, with excuses the actor acknowledges that the act was bad or wrong or inappropriate, but denies responsibility for it. The same teenager may admit that stealing a car was wrong to the judge, but may argue that "the drugs and alcohol made me do it."

Other research that presaged narrative sociology and explored the elements of narrative includes Erving Goffman's (1971) concept of "remedial work," which describes how actors engage in a form of "damage control" through the interactive processes of apologizing and requesting. For Randall Stokes and John Hewitt (1976), strategies such as vocabularies of motive, accounts, and the like constitute a more general form of talk they term "aligning actions" (Hewitt and Stokes 1975; Stokes and Hewitt 1976). Stated simply, the concept refers to various attempts by a social actor to bring her behavior into alignment with the values of the dominant culture.

At the level of groups, organizations, and nations, sociologists have studied narratives under the rubric of "collective memory" (Schwartz 2000; Olick 2011; Linde 2009). These narratives include stories told, retold, and passed on from one generation of a family to another, the organizational myths of heroic founders, the rituals of religion, and, perhaps most importantly, the pageants and monuments that tell the story of a nation. Collective memory is typically more complex than individual accounts. These memories have multiple authors who might contend over how to tell a story. They are often written, as in the Passover *Haggadah* that tells the story of the Jewish exodus from Egypt, or the passages of the New Testament that tell the story of the resurrection of Jesus Christ, or even as high school textbooks, which purport to tell the history of a nation. Sometimes these stories are embodied in monuments or celebrated in films. These stories—told *by* collectivities *about* collectivities—often contribute to the bonds of the group, to the sense of family, to pride in a business, to a religious commitment, or to patriotism. They may also exclude and divide, marking the inclusion of some people and the exclusion of others. They may be used to mobilize against inequalities of all sorts, but they may also be used to suppress dissent.

What sociological terms like vocabularies of motive, accounts, aligning actions, and even collective memory conceptualize is the kind of talk that social actors construct when they are called upon to respond to a challenge, real or imagined. They may not be full narratives or even partial narratives, but they are all examples of sociological understanding of talk constructed through social interaction. What they do not explore is how these forms of talk contribute to self-understanding or the ways social actors make sense of their experiences and social world.

It is largely through scholarship on the stories people tell about their individual lives that the study of narrative entered sociology. As we pointed out in Part 1A, the narrative turn and scholarship on narrative came from fields and disciplines outside of sociology, such as literary theory, linguistics, psychology, and anthropology (Bruner 1987; Clifford and Marcus 1986; Gergen and Gergen1983; Labov 1972). One of the most influential essays in this work is psychologist Jerome Bruner's essay, "Life as Narrative." For Bruner, life and narrative exist in a reciprocal relationship. Narrative draws upon life for inspiration to create an imagined world; life draws upon narrative for resources to imagine our identity, and to interpret others, social situations, and the "real" world. As Bruner writes, "ways of telling and ways of conceptualizing that go with them have become so habitual that they become recipes for structuring experience itself, laying down routes into memory not only for guiding the life narrative up to the present but directing it into the future" (1987: 31).

Bruner's essay has had an enormous impact in many fields. We have included it in this section because it underscores how narrative, or "recipes for structuring experience," becomes the means through which social actors fashion identities and make sense of their lives. Narrative operates to give form to *how we tell our life stories* (i.e., with a beginning, middle, and end) and works to make these stories morally meaningful (i.e., the plot). Further, how a story is told can provide insights into how individuals see themselves and understand their social positions. In telling a story about sexual abuse, for example, do women depict themselves as victims, do they understand themselves survivors, or is there a bit of both? Of course, this is not to say that our life stories are always the same. They may change in light of particular audiences and they may alter over the course of a life. Indeed, researchers have found that journals of teenage women are often "anxious" and "future" oriented, while autobiographies written at mid-life about female adolescence are "backward looking" and "self-justifying" (Maynes, Pierce, and Laslett 2008: 80). Thus, our narratives change, but the importance of narrative in structuring our life stories and identities does not.

Just as narratives can help us to define who we are, they can also help us to understand changes in our lives that shatter our daily routines and threaten our sense of self (Frank 1995; Riessman 1990). The excerpt from Arthur Frank's 1994 article, "Reclaiming an Orphan Genre," illustrates this well. Frank's body of work analyzes personal narratives of serious, often terminal, illness, particularly in written form (see also Frank 1991, 1995). He characterizes illness narrative as an "orphan genre," lacking legitimacy as medical data and holding no promise as literature. Nevertheless, illness narratives accomplish other work, which Frank describes as "reclaiming." The illness narrative "reclaims the author's right to tell what is her own experience, it reclaims a voice over and against the medical voice, and it reclaims a life beyond illness, even if illness is the occasion of writing." As Frank has argued elsewhere, narratives "have the capacity to deal with human troubles, but also to make TROUBLE" (2010: 28; his emphasis).

Frank's three "voices of illness" presented here do different work. In the first example, what he calls "the restitution story," the narrative focuses on the process of becoming ill, finding treatment and getting better, and ultimately returning to one's previous social role(s). It operates not only to make sense of the experience as something temporary that can be fixed, but its conclusion (getting well) restores social order (restitution). In the second example, "the chaotic story," illness becomes so disorienting and overwhelming that the individual cannot construct a coherent narrative around it. This story points to the limits of narrative in making sense of experience. In the third and final type of narrative, "the quest story," illness is recognized as part of a psychological journey in one's life. The central theme is not restitution, but working out the changes that illness will bring. Pain and suffering are understood as teaching important lessons that give new meaning and insights to life. Frank captures how these types of illness narratives express a changing self as tellers mix the voices throughout their experience of suffering.

In "Narrative Freedom," Robert Zussman stresses the institutional sources of narratives—in effect, the limits of freedom. Introducing a framework we deploy in Part III, Zussman distinguishes narratives generated "from below" and those generated "from above" (see also Davis 2005). In the first case, tellers may be influenced by the groups to which they belong or the conventions of storytelling, but they at least appear to determine for themselves what they say, without control from above. In the second case, institutionally empowered authorities (doctors, lawyers, priests, social workers) determine the form and content of the narratives they hear. Zussman combines the dimensions of "from above" and "from below" with the narrative's intention and consequences. Narratives can restore the teller to a previous state or transform his or her identity. Using examples of narratives from confession, therapy, reunion, and autobiography, Zussman analyzes the social conditions that generate elements of freedom, both the freedom to tell stories as one likes and the freedom to keep silent.

References

Davis, Joseph E. 2005. *Accounts of Innocence: Sexual Abuse, Trauma, and the Self.* Chicago: University of Chicago Press.

Frank, Arthur W. 1991. *At the Will of the Body: Reflections on Illness.* Boston: Houghton Mifflin.

Frank, Arthur W. 1995. *The Wounded Storyteller: Body, Illness, and Ethics.* Chicago: The University of Chicago Press.

Clifford, James, and George Marcus, eds. 1986. *Writing Culture: The Poetics and Politics of Ethnography.* Berkeley: University of California Press.

Gergen, Kenneth J., and Mary M. Gergen. 1983. "Narratives of the Self." In *Studies in Social Identity.* Edited by T. Sarbin and K. Schelbe, 245–73. New York: Praeger.

Goffman, Erving. 1971. *Relations in Public: Microstudies of the Public Order.* New York: Basic Books.

Hall, Peter M., and John P. Hewitt. 1970. "The Quasi-Theory of Communication and the Management of Dissent." *Social Problems* 18(1): 17–27.

Hewitt, John P., and Randall Stokes. 1975. "Disclaimers." *American Sociological Review* 40:1–11.

Labov, William. 1972. *Language in the Inner City: Studies in Black English Vernacular.* Philadelphia: University of Pennsylvania Press.

Linde, Charlotte. 2008. *Working the Past: Narrative and Institutional Memory.* New York: Oxford University Press.

Maynes, M. J., Jennifer L. Pierce, and Barbara Laslett. 2008. *Telling Stories: The Use of*

Personal Narratives in the Social Sciences and History. Ithaca, NY: Cornell University Press.

Olick, Jeffrey, Vered Vinitzky-Seroussi, and Daniel Levy. 2011. *The Collective Memory Reader*. New York: Oxford University Press.

Riessman, Catherine Kohler. 1990. *Divorce Talk: Women and Men Make Sense of Personal Relationships*. New Brunswick, NJ: Rutgers University Press.

Schwartz, Barry. 2000. *Abraham Lincoln and the Forge of National Identity*. Chicago: University of Chicago Press.

Scott, Marvin B., and Stanford M. Lyman. 1968. "Accounts." *American Sociological Review* 33(1): 46–62.

Stokes, Randall, and John P. Hewitt. 1976. "Aligning Actions." *American Sociological Review* 41: 838–49.

Sykes, Gresham M., and David Matza. 1957. "Techniques of Neutralization: A Theory of Delinquency." *American Sociological Review* 22(6): 664–70.

Further Reading

Chase, Susan. 1995. *Ambiguous Empowerment: The Work Narratives of Women School Superintendents*. Amherst MA: University of Massachusetts Press.

DeGloma, Thomas. 2014. *Seeing the Light: The Social Logic of Personal Discovery*. Chicago: University of Chicago Press.

Ezzy, Douglas. 2001. *Narrating Unemployment*. New York: Ashgate.

Orbuch, Terri L. 1997. "People's Accounts Count: The Sociology of Accounts." *Annual Review of Sociology* 23: 455–78.

Williams, Gareth. 1984. "The Genesis of Chronic Illness: Narrative Re–Construction." *Sociology of Health & Illness* 6(2): 175–200.

8

LIFE AS NARRATIVE

Jerome Bruner

I would like to try out an idea that may not be quite ready, indeed may not be quite possible. But I have no doubt it is worth a try. It has to do with the nature of thought and with one of its uses. It has been traditional to treat thought, so to speak, as an instrument of reason. Good thought is right reason, and its efficacy is measured against the laws of logic or induction. Indeed, in its most recent computational form, it is a view of thought that has sped some of its enthusiasts to the belief that all thought is reducible to machine computability.

But logical thought is not the only or even the most ubiquitous mode of thought. For the last several years, I have been looking at another kind of thought,[1] one that is quite different in form from reasoning: the form of thought that goes into the constructing not of logical or inductive arguments but of stories or narratives. What I want to do now is to extend these ideas about narrative to the analysis of the stories we tell about our lives: our "autobiographies."

Philosophically speaking, the approach I shall take to narrative is a constructivist one—a view that takes as its central premise that "world making" is the principal function of mind, whether in the sciences or in the arts. But the moment one applies a constructivist view of narrative to the self-narrative, to the autobiography, one is faced with dilemmas. Take, for example, the constructivist view that "stories" do not "happen" in the real world but, rather, are constructed in people's heads. Or as Henry James once put it, stories happen to people who know how to tell them. Does that mean that our autobiographies are constructed, that

Jerome Bruner, "Life as Narrative," *Social Research* 7, no. 1 (1987): 11–32. Reprinted with permission of Johns Hopkins University Press via Copyright Clearance Center.

they had better be viewed not as a record of what happened (which is in any case a nonexistent record) but rather as a continuing interpretation and reinterpretation of our experience? Just as the philosopher Nelson Goodman argues that physics or painting or history are "ways of world making,"[2] so autobiography (formal or informal) should be viewed as a set of procedures for "life making." And just as it is worthwhile examining in minute detail how physics or history go about their world making, might we not be well advised to explore in equal detail what we do when we construct ourselves autobiographically? Even if the exercise should produce some obdurate dilemmas, it might nonetheless cast some light on what we might mean by such expressions as "a life."

Culture and Autobiography

Let me begin by sketching out the general shape of the argument that I wish to explore. The first thesis is this: We seem to have no other way of describing "lived time" save in the form of a narrative. Which is not to say that there are not other temporal forms that can be imposed on the experience of time, but none of them succeeds in capturing the sense of *lived* time: not clock or calendrical time forms, not serial or cyclical orders, not any of these. It is a thesis that will be familiar to many of you, for it has been most recently and powerfully argued by Paul Ricoeur.[3] Even if we set down *annales* in the bare form of events,[4] they will be seen to be events chosen with a view to their place in an implicit narrative.

My second thesis is that the mimesis between life so-called and narrative is a two-way affair: that is to say, just as art imitates life in Aristotle's sense, so, in Oscar Wilde's, life imitates art. Narrative imitates life, life imitates narrative. "Life" in this sense is the same kind of construction of the human imagination as "a narrative" is. It is constructed by human beings through active ratiocination, by the same kind of ratiocination through which we construct narratives. When somebody tells you his life—and that is principally what we shall be talking about-it is always a cognitive achievement rather than a through-the-clear-crystal recital of something univocally given. In the end, it is a narrative achievement. There is no such thing psychologically as "life itself." At very least, it is a selective achievement of memory recall; beyond that, recounting one's life is an interpretive feat. Philosophically speaking, it is hard to imagine being a naive realist about "life itself."

The story of one's own life is, of course, a privileged but troubled narrative in the sense that it is reflexive: the narrator and the central figure in the narrative are the same. This reflexivity creates dilemmas. The critic Paul de Man speaks of the "defacement" imposed by turning around on oneself to create, as he puts it, "a monument."[5] Another critic comments on the autobiographical narrator's irresistible error in accounting for his acts in terms of intentions when, in fact, they might have been quite otherwise determined. In any case, the reflexivity of self-narrative poses problems of a deep and serious order—problems beyond those of verification, beyond the issue of indeterminacy (that the very telling of the self-story distorts what we have in mind to tell), beyond "rationalization." The whole enterprise seems a most shaky one, and some critics, like Louis Renza, even think it is impossible, "an endless prelude."[6]

Yet for all the shakiness of the form, it is perfectly plain that not just any autobiography will do—either for its teller or for his listener, for that matter. One imposes criteria of rightness on the self-report of a life just as one imposes them on the account of a football game or the report of an event in nature. And they are by no means all external criteria as to whether, for example, one did or did not visit Santander in 1956. Besides, it may have been Salamanca in 1953 and by certain criteria of narrative or of psychological adequacy even be "right" if untrue. There are also internal criteria relating to how one felt or what one intended, and these are just as demanding, even if they are not subject to verification. Otherwise, we would not be able to say that certain self-narratives are "shallow" and others "deep." One criterion, of course, is whether a life story "covers" the events of a life. But what is coverage? Are not omissions also important? And we have all read or heard painfully detailed autobiographies of which it can be said that the whole is drastically less than the sum of the parts. They lack interpretation or "meaning," we say. As Peter Winch reminded us a long time ago, it is not so evident in the human sciences or human affairs how to specify criteria by which to judge the rightness of any theory or model, especially a folk theory like an account of "my life."[7] All verificationist criteria turn slippery, and we surely cannot judge rightness by narrative adequacy alone. A rousing tale of a life is not necessarily a "right" account.

All of which creates special problems, as we shall see, and makes autobiographical accounts (even the ones we tell ourselves) notably unstable. On the other hand, this very instability makes life stories highly susceptible to cultural, interpersonal, and linguistic influences. This susceptibility to influence may, in fact, be the reason why "talking cures," religious instruction, and other interventions in a life may often have such profound effects in changing a person's life narrative.

Given their constructed nature and their dependence upon the cultural conventions and language usage, life narratives obviously reflect the prevailing theories about "possible lives" that are part of one's culture. Indeed, one important way of characterizing a culture is by the narrative models it makes available for describing the course of a life. And the tool kit of any culture is replete not only with a stock of canonical life narratives (heroes, Marthas, tricksters, etc.), but with combinable formal constituents from which its members can construct their own life narratives: canonical stances and circumstances, as it were.

But the issue I wish to address is not just about the "telling" of life narratives. The heart of my argument is this: eventually the culturally shaped cognitive and linguistic processes that guide the self-telling of life narratives achieve the power to structure perceptual experience, to organize memory, to segment and purpose-build the very "events" of a life. In the end, we *become* the autobiographical narratives by which we "tell about" our lives. And given the cultural shaping to which I referred, we also become variants of the culture's canonical forms. I cannot imagine a more important psychological research project than one that addresses itself to the "development of autobiography"—how our way of telling about ourselves changes, and how these accounts come to take control of our ways of life. Yet I know of not a single comprehensive study on this subject.

How a culture transmits itself in this way is an anthropological topic and need not concern us directly. Yet a general remark is in order. I want to address the question of how self-narratives as a *literary* form, as autobiography, might have developed. For the issue may throw some light on how more modest, less formulated modes of self-telling have emerged as well. Autobiography, we are told, is a recent and a not very widely distributed literary genre. As the French historian Georges Gusdorf remarks, it is

> limited in time and space; it has not always existed nor does it exist everywhere. . . . [Its] conscious awareness of the singularity of each individual life is the late product of a specific civilization. . . . Autobiography becomes possible only under certain metaphysical preconditions. . . . The man who takes the trouble to tell of himself knows that the present differs from the past and that it will not be repeated in the future.[8]

Gusdorf sees the birth of literary autobiography as issuing from the mixed and unstable marriage between Christian and classical thought in the Middle Ages, further inflamed by the doubts kindled in the Copernican revolution. Doubtless the Reformation also added fuel to the passion for written self-revelation.

While the act of *writing* autobiography is new under the sun—like writing itself—the self-told life narrative is, by all accounts, ancient and universal. People anywhere can tell you some intelligible account of their lives. What varies is the cultural and linguistic perspective or narrative *form* in which it is formulated and expressed. And that too will be found to spring from historical circumstances as these have been incorporated in the culture and language of a people. I suspect that it will be as important to study *historical* developments in forms of self-telling as it is to study their ontogenesis. I have used the expression "forms of self-telling," for I believe it is form rather than content that matters. We must be clear, then, about what we mean by narrative form. Vladimir Propp's classic analysis of folktales reveals, for example, that the *form* of a folktale may remain unchanged even though its content changes.[9] So too self-told life narratives may reveal a common formal structure across a wide variety of content. So let us get to the heart of the matter: to the forms of self-narrative or, indeed, of narrative generally, of which self-narrative is a special case.

Forms of Self-Narrative

Let me start my account with the Russian formalists, who distinguished three aspects of story: *fabula, sjuzet,* and *forma*—roughly theme, discourse, and genre. The first two (*fabula* and *sjuzet*) have been described by modern literary theorists as, respectively, the *timeless* and the *sequenced* aspects of story. The timeless *fabula* is the mythic, the transcendent plight that a story is about: human jealousy, authority and obedience, thwarted ambition, and those other plights that lay claim to human universality. The *sjuzet* then incorporates or realizes the timeless *fabula* not only in the form of a plot but also in an unwinding net of language. Frank Kermode says that the joining of *fabula* and *sjuzet* in story is like the blending of timeless mystery and current scandal.[10] The ancient dilemmas of envy, loyalty, jealousy are woven into the acts of Iago, Othello, Desdemona, and Everyman with a fierce particularity and localness that, in Joyce's words, yield an "epiphany of the ordinary." This particularity of time, place, person, and event is also reflected in the mode of the telling, in the discourse properties of the *sjuzet*.

To achieve such epiphanous and unique ordinariness, we are required, as Roman Jakobson used to tell his Russian poets, to "make the ordinary strange."[11] And that must depend not upon plot alone but upon language. For language constructs what it narrates, not only semantically but also pragmatically and stylistically.

One word about the third aspect of narrative—*forma* or genre, an ancient subject dating from Aristotle's Poetics. How shall we understand it? Romance, farce, tragedy, *Bildungsroman*, black comedy, adventure story, fairy tale, wonder tale, etc. That might do. A genre is plainly a type (in the linguist's sense) of which there are near endless tokens, and in that sense it may be viewed as a set of grammars for generating different kinds of story plots. But it cannot be that alone. For genre also commits one to use language in a certain way: lyric, say, is conventionally written in the first person/present tense, epic is third person/past tense, etc. One question we shall simply pass over for the moment: Are genres mere literary conventions, or (like Jung's alleged archetypes) are they built into the human genome, or are they an invariant set of plights in the human condition to which we all react in some necessary way? For our present purposes, it does not matter.

We may ask then of any self-told life what is its *fabula* (or gist, or moral, or leitmotiv); how is it converted into an extended tale and through what uses of language; and into what genre is it fitted. That is a start, but it does not get us very far.

There is widespread agreement that stories are about the vicissitudes of human intention and that, to paraphrase Kenneth Burke's classic, *The Grammar of Motives*, story structure is composed minimally of the pentad of an Agent, an Action, a Goal, a Setting, an Instrument—and Trouble.[12] Trouble is what drives the drama, and it is generated by a mismatch between two or more of the five constituents of Burke's pentad: for example, Nora's Goals do not match either the Setting in which she lives nor the Instruments available to her in Ibsen's *A Doll's House*. The late Victor Turner, a gifted anthropologist who studied Western theater as carefully as he studied the Ndembu in West Africa, locates this "trouble" in the breaching of cultural legitimacy: an initial canonical state is breached, redress is attempted which, if it fails, leads to crisis; crisis, if unresolved, leads eventually to a new legitimate order.[13] The crisis, the role of agents in redress, the making of the new legitimacy—these are the cultural constituents of which the variety of drama is constructed in life as in literature. That is to say, Burke's dramatistic troubles are, for Turner, individual embodiments of deeper cultural crises.

We had better get on to a closer characterization of Agents in stories, since our interest is in self-told life narratives. Narrative studies began with the analysis of myth and folktale. And it is indeed the case that, in these genres, the plot even more than motive drives the Agent. You will find little about the doubts, desires, or other intentional states of either Beowulf or Grendel, nor do you get a clear sense from recorded myth about how Perseus decided to get involved with the Gorgon. Even Oedipus is not so much driven by motives as by plight. As Vladimir Propp put it, the *dramatis personae* of the classical folktale fulfill a function in the plot but do not drive it. But that is only one version of character: Agent as carrier of destiny, whether divine or secular.

As literary forms have developed, they have moved steadily toward an empowerment and subjective enrichment of the Agent protagonist.

The most revealing single analysis of this transformation is, I think, to be found in an essay by Amelie Rorty, in which she traces the shape of agency in narrative from the folktale *figure* "who is neither formed by nor owns experience," to *persons* defined by roles and responsibilities in a society for which they get rights in return (as, say, in Jane Austen's novels), to *selves* who must compete for their roles in order to earn their rights (as in Trollope), and finally to *individuals* who transcend and resist society and must create or "rip off" their rights (as, say, in Beckett).[14] These, you will see, are characterizations of the forms of relationship between an intention-driven actor and the settings in which he must act to achieve his goals.

Another word, then, about Agents. Narrative, even at its most primitive, is played out on a dual landscape, to use Greimas's celebrated expression.[15] There is a landscape of *action* on which events unfold. Grendel wreaks destruction on the drinking hall and upon its celebrating warriors in *Beowulf*. But there is a second landscape, a landscape of consciousness, the inner worlds of the protagonists involved in the action. It is the difference between Oedipus taking Jocasta to wife before and after he learns from the messenger that she is his mother. This duality of landscape, Greimas tells us, is an essential ingredient of narrative and accounts in some measure for the ubiquitousness of deceit in tales throughout history. In the modern novel—in contrast to the classic myth or the folktale—there is a more explicit treatment of the landscape of consciousness itself. Agents do not merely deceive; they hope, are doubting and confused, wonder about appearance and reality. Modern literature (perhaps like modern science) becomes more epistemological, less ontological. The omniscient narrator (like the prerelativity "observer") disappears, and with him so does hard-core reality.

As narrative has become "modernized," so too has its language changed. Since, say, Conrad, Proust, Hardy, and Henry James, the language of the novel has accommodated to the perspectivalism and subjectivism that replaced the omniscient narrator. In another place, I have used the term "subjunctivizing" to characterize this shift from expository to perspectival narrative language, a shift from emphasis on actuality to the evocation of possibility marked by the greater use of unpackable presuppositions, of subjunctive discourse, of Gricean conversational implicatures and the like. In the end, the reality of the omniscient narrator disappears into the subjective worlds of the story's protagonists.[16] Linguistically and in spirit as well, the modern novel may be as profound (and perhaps out of the same cradle) as the invention of modern physics.

One last point, for I have lingered too long introducing my subject. Jean-Paul Sartre remarks in his autobiography, "a man is always a teller of stories, he lives surrounded by his own stories and those of other people, he sees everything that happens to him *in terms of* these stories and he tries to live his life as if he were recounting it."[17] His point is a telling one: life stories must mesh, so to speak, within a community of life stories; tellers and listeners must share some "deep structure" about the nature of a "life," for if the rules of life-telling are altogether arbitrary, tellers and listeners will surely be alienated by a failure to grasp what the other is saying or what he thinks the other is hearing. Indeed, such alienation does happen cross-generationally, often with baleful effects. Later, we shall return to the issue of "life-story meshing" in a more concrete way.

Four Self-Narratives

Let me turn now to the business of how a psychologist goes about studying issues of the kind that we have been discussing. Along with my colleagues Susan Weisser and Carol Staszewski, I have been engaged in a curious study. While it is far from done (whatever that may mean), I would like to tell you enough about it to make what I have been saying a little more concrete.

We were interested in how people tell the stories of their lives and, perhaps simplemindedly, we asked them to do so—telling them to keep it to about half an hour, even if it were an impossible task. We told them that we were not interested in judging them or curing them but that we were very interested in how people saw their lives. After they were done—and most had little trouble in sticking to the time limits or, for that matter, in filling up the time—we asked questions for another half hour or so, questions designed to get a better picture of how their stories had been put together. Had we followed a different procedure, we doubtless would have obtained different accounts. Indeed, had we asked them to tell us their lives in two minutes, perhaps we would have obtained something more like a *fabula* than a *sjuzet*. But such variations will get their innings later. Many people have now sat for their portraits, ranging in age from ten to seventy, and their stories yield rich texts. But I want to talk of only four of them now: a family—a father, a mother, and their grown son and grown daughter, each of their accounts collected independently. There are two more grown children in the family, a son and daughter, both of whom have also told their stories, but four are enough to handle as a start.

We have chosen a family as our target because it constitutes a miniature culture, and provides an opportunity to explore how life stories are made to mesh with each other in Sartre's sense. Beyond that, of course, the individual autobiographies provide us the opportunity to explore the issues of form and structure to which I have already alluded.

If you should now ask how we propose to test whether these four lives "imitated" the narratives each person told, your question would be proper enough, though a bit impatient. The position I have avowed, indeed, leaves entirely moot what could be meant by "lives" altogether, beyond what is contained in the narrative. We shall not even be able to check, as Professor Neisser was able to do in his studies of autobiographical memory,[18] whether particular memories were veridical or distorted in some characteristic way. But our aim is different. We are asking, rather, whether there is in each account a set of selective narrative rules that lead the narrator to structure experience in a particular way, structure it in a manner that gives form to the content and the continuity of the life. And we are interested, as well, in how the family itself formulates certain common rules for doing these things. I hope this will be less abstract as we proceed.

Our family is headed by George Goodhertz, a hard-working heating contractor in his early sixties, a self-made man of moral principles, converted to Catholicism in childhood and mindful of his obligations, though not devout. Though plainly intelligent and well informed, he never finished high school: "had to go to work." His father was, by Mr. Goodhertz's sparse characterization, "a drinker" and a poor provider. Mr. Goodhertz is neither. Mrs. Goodhertz, Rose, is a housewife of immediate Italian descent: family oriented, imbedded in the urban neighborhood where she has lived for nearly thirty years, connected with old friends who still live nearby. Her father was, in her words, "of the old school"—arrogant, a drinker, a poor provider, and unfaithful to her mother. In the opening paragraph of her autobiography she says, "I would have preferred a better childhood, a happier one, but with God's influence, I prayed hard enough for a good husband, and she [sic] answered me."

Daughter Debby, in her mid-twenties, is (in her own words) "still unmarried." She graduated a few years ago from a local college that she never liked much and now studies acting. Outgoing, she enjoys friends, old and new, but is determined not to get "stuck" in the old neighborhood with the old friends of her past and their old attitudes. Yet she is not ambitious, but caught, rather, between ideals of local kindliness and of broader adventure, the latter more in the existential form of a desire for experience than by any wish to achieve. She lives at home—in Brooklyn with her parents in the old neighborhood. Her thirty-year-old brother, Carl, who is about to finish his doctorate in neurophysiology at one of the solid, if not distinguished Boston-area universities, is aware of how far beyond family expectations his studies have taken him, but is neither deferential nor aggressive about his leap in status. Like his sister Debby, he remains attached to and in easy contact with his parents though he lives on his own even when he is in New York working at a local university laboratory. At school Carl always felt "special" and different—both in the Catholic high school and then in the Catholic college he attended. The graduate school he chose is secular, and a complete break with his past. He is ambitious to get ahead, but he is not one to take the conventional "up" stairway. Both in his own eyes and, indeed, by conventional standards, he is a bit eccentric and a risk taker. Where his sister Debby (and his mother) welcomes intimacy and closeness, Carl (like his father) keeps people more at arm's length. Experience for its own sake is not his thing. He is as concerned as his sister about not being "tied down."

And that, I now want to assure you, is the end of the omniscient authorial voice. For our task now is to sample the texts, the narratives of these four lives—father's, mother's, son's, and daughter's—to see not what they are *about* but how the narrators *construct* themselves. Their texts are all we have—though we may seem to have, so to speak, the hermeneutical advantage of four narratives that spring from a common landscape. But as you will see, the advantage that it yields is in narrative power and possibility, not in the ontology of verification. For one view of the world cannot confirm another, though, in Clifford Geertz's evocative phrase, it can "thicken" it.

Let me begin the analysis with Kenneth Burke's pentad, his skeleton of dramatism, and particularly with the setting or Scene of these life stories. Most psychological theories of personality, alas, have no place for place. They would' not do well with Stephen Daedalus in Joyce's *Portrait of the Artist as a Young Man*, for he is inexplicable without the Dublin that he carries in his head. In these four life narratives too, place is crucial and it shapes and constrains the stories that are told or, indeed, that could be told. Place is not simply a piece of geography, an established Italian neighborhood in Brooklyn, though it helps to know its "culture" too. It is an intricate construct, whose language dominates the thought of our four narrators. For each, its central axis is "home," which is placed in sharp contrast to what they all refer to as "the real world." They were, by all their own accounts, a "close" family, and their language seals that closeness.

Consider the psychic geography. For each of our narrators, "home" is a place that is inside, private, forgiving, intimate, predictably safe. "The real world" is outside, demanding, anonymous, open, unpredictable, and consequently dangerous. But home and real world are also contrastive in another way, explicitly for the two children, implicitly and covertly for the parents: home is to be "cooped up," restricted by duties and bored; real world is excitement and opportunity. Early on, the mother says of the children, "We spoiled them for the real world," and the father speaks of "getting them ready for the real world." The son speaks of its hypocrisies that need to be confronted and overcome to achieve one's goals. It is a worthwhile but treacherous battlefield. The daughter idealizes it for the new experience to be harvested there. Each, in their way, creates a different ontological landscape out of "the real world" to give it an appropriate force as the Scene in the narratives they are constructing.

One thing that is striking about all four narratives is the extent to which the spatial distinction home—real world concentrates all four of them on spatial and locative terms in their autobiographical accounts. Take Carl. His account is laden with spatial metaphors: *in/out, here/there, coming from/going to, place/special place.* The movement forward in his story is not so much temporal as spatial: a sequential outward movement from home to neighborhood to Catholic school to the library alone to college to the Catholic peace movement to graduate school and then triumphantly back to New York. In his *Bildungsroman* of a life story, the challenge is to find a place, the right place, and then a special place in each of these concentric outgoings. For Carl, you get involved *in* things, or you feel "*out* of place." You "go to" Boston or to a course or a lab, and fellow students "come from" prestigious schools. Or "I started gaining a fairly special place in the Department," and later "I ended up getting a fairly privileged place in the Department." The "special places" *allow, permit, make possible.* "After about six months I really started settling in and enjoying the program and enjoying the opportunities it gave me." And later, about the students who get a special place, "The faculty are committed to shielding their graduate students from negative repercussions of failure."

Two things are both surprising and revealing about Carl's language. One is the extent to which his sentences take self as object, and the other is the high frequency of the passive voice. With respect to the latter, some 11 percent of his sentences are in the passive voice, which is surprisingly high for such an action-oriented text. But they both are of a piece and tell something interesting about his world making. Recall the importance for Carl of "place" and particularly of the "special place." Whenever he recounts something connected with these places, the places "happen" and then he acts accordingly. His sentences then begin with either a passive or with self-as-object, and then move to the active voice. At a particular colloquium where he knew his stuff, "It allowed me to deal with the faculty on an equal footing." Or of his debating team experience, "It taught me how to handle myself." Occasions in these "special places" are seen as if they had homelike privileges: allowing and permitting and teaching. It is as if Carl manages the "real world" by colonizing it with "special places" that provide some of the privileges of home.

With Debby, thirty-seven of the first hundred sentences in her life narrative contain spatial metaphors or locatives. The principal clusters are about her place in the family (the *gap* or *span* in ages); the life layout ("the house I was brought home to is the house I live in now"; or "I traveled, my relatives are all over the country"; or "I've been coming to the city by myself ever since I was fourteen"); the coming-back theme ("everybody except me has gone out and come back at one time or another").

So much for Scene, at least for the moment. Come now to the agentive, to Burke's Actor. Rorty's typology turns out to be enormously useful, for in all four self-portraits the tale moves from Actor as figure, figure becoming a person, person becoming a self, self becoming an individual. Well into her fifties, even Mrs. Goodhertz has finally taken a job for pay, albeit working as secretary for her husband's heating-contracting business, motivated by the desire for some independence and the wish not to get "stuck" raising her eldest daughter's child. She remarks that it is "her" job and that she now "works." The transformation of her language as she runs through the chronology of her life is striking. When speaking of her childhood, self is often an object in such sentences as: "everything was thrown at us." But finally, by the time she takes her first job as a young woman, "I decided to take things in my own hands." Throughout her account, she "owns her own experience," to use Rorty's phrase. More than eight in ten of her sentences contain a stative verb, a verb dealing with thinking, feeling, intending, believing, praying. (This contrasts with five in ten for her more action-oriented husband.) One is easily deceived, reading Mrs. Goodhertz's self-portrait, into thinking that she is accepting of fate, perhaps passive. Instead, she believes in fate, but she also believes that fate can be nudged by her own efforts. And we rather suspect that the style is cultivated. For a closer analysis of her language reveals a very high "subjectivity level" as carried in those stative verbs.

We must return again to Scene, or perhaps to what might better be called mise-en-scène. Both the elder Goodhertzes—unlike their children—construct their lives as if they constituted two sides of a deep divide. That divide is marked by an escape from childhood, an old life, indeed, an old *secret* life of suffering and shame as figures in unbearably capricious family settings. Personhood is on the other side of the divide. Mrs. Goodhertz gets to the other side, to personhood, by "praying for the right husband" and getting him, of which more in a moment. Mr. Goodhertz crosses the divide by work, hard work, and by the grace of "the owner [who] took me under his wing." To him, achieving mastery of your work and, as we shall see, helping others help themselves are the two dominant ideals. For her, it is somewhat more complex. The linguistic vehicle is the "*but* . . ." construction. She uses it repeatedly, and in several telltale ways, the most crucial being to distinguish what *is* from what *might have been*, as in talking about teenage drug taking, ". . . but I am blessed *my* kids didn't start in on it," or "I would have been stricter, but they turned out with less problems than others." The construction is her reminder of what *might* have been and, at the same time, a string on her finger to remind her that she is the agent who produces the better event on the other side of the . . . *but*. . . . Her courtship and marriage are a case in point. Yes, she was waiting for God to bring the right man, *but* in fact she decided the moment her eyes fell on Mr. Goodhertz that *he* was the man and knew not an instant's remorse in throwing over her then fiancé.

Their secret childhoods provide a unique source of consciousness for the elder Goodhertzes. It is a concealed secret that they share and that provides the contrast to what they have established as the organizing concept of "home." Mrs. Goodhertz's knowledge of her macho father as a bad provider, a drinker, and a philanderer is secret knowledge, quickly and hintingly told in her narrative in a way that brooked no probing. It was there only to let us know why she prayed for a good husband and a better life for her children. Mr. Goodhertz goes into even less detail. But note the two following quotations, both about hopes for the children, each said independently of the other. Mr. Goodhertz: "I wanted to give them all the things I didn't get as a kid." And Mrs. Goodhertz: "To a point, I think, we try not to make our children have too much of what we had."

So Debby and Carl start on the other side of the divide. Each of them tells a tale that is animated by a contrast between a kindly but inert, entrenched, or "given" world and a "new" one that is their own. Carl is a young Werther. His tale begins with the episode when, as an aspiring young football player, he and his teammates are told by the coach to knock out the opposing team's star quarterback. He keeps his own counsel, quits football, and starts on his own road. For Debby the tale is more like the young Stephen Hero in the discarded early version of *Portrait*. She exposes herself to experience as it may come, "trying" in the sense of "trying on" rather than of striving. Her involvement in acting is in the spirit of trying on new roles. Of life she says, "I don't like doing one thing, . . . the same thing all my life, . . . shoved into a house and cooped up with four kids all day." If Carl's autobiography is a *Bildungsroman*, Debby's is an existential novel. His account is linear, from start to end, but it is replete with what literary linguists call *prolepsis*. That is to say, it is full of those odd flash-forwards that implicate the present for the future, like "if I had known then what I know now" and "learning to debate would stand me in good stead later." His narrative is progressive and sequential: the story tracks "real time." It "accounts" for things, and things are mentioned because *they* account for things.

Privileged opportunities "happen to" him, as we have seen, and he turns them into ventures.

The exception to this pattern is the dilemma of moral issues—as with the coach's murderous instructions or his becoming a conscientious objector in the Vietnam war, inspired by the Berrigans. Then his language (and his thought) becomes subjunctive rather than instrumental, playing on possibilities and inwardness. In this respect, he is his father's son, for Mr. Goodhertz too is principally oriented to action (recall that half his sentences contain nonstative verbs) save when he encounters issues he defines as matters of morality. Don't condemn, he would say, "you never know the whole story." And in the same spirit, Mr. Goodhertz's self-portrait is laced with literally dozens of instances of the intransitive verb *to seem*, as if he were forever mindful of a feather edge separating appearance from reality. When Carl decided he would become a conscientious objector against the Vietnam draft, his father stood by him on grounds that Carl's convictions, honestly arrived at, were worthy of respect even though he did not agree with them. Carl unwittingly even describes his intellectual quest in the same instrumental terms that his father uses in describing his ducting work. Both emphasize skills and "know-how," both reject received ways of doing things. Theirs is "instrumental" language and thought, as well suited to talking about heat ducting as to Carl's strikingly procedural approach to visual physiology. The father confesses to having missed intimacy in his life. So, probably, will Carl one day. Their instrumental language leaves little room for it in their discourse.

Debby's highly stative language is specialized for the reception of experience and for exploring the affect that it creates. It is richly adjectival, and the adjectives cluster around inner states. Her own acts are almost elided from her account. The past exists in its own right rather than as a guide to the present or future. In recounting the present there are vivid analeptic flashbacks—as in an unbid memory of an injured chicken on the Long Island Expressway, the traffic too thick for rescue. Like so many of her images, this one was dense with plight and affect. It evoked her tenderness for helpless animals, she told us, then veering off to that topic. And so her order of telling is dominated not by real time sequences but by a going back and forth between what happens and what she feels and believes, and what she felt and believed. In this, and in her heavy use of stative verbs, she is her mother's daughter—and, I suspect, both are locked in the same gender language. Finally, in Debby's self-story "themes and variations" are as recursive as her brother's is progressive, and hers is as lacking in efforts to give causes as his are replete with causative expressions.

Recipes for Structuring Experience

You will ask whether the narrative forms and the language that goes with them in our four subjects are not simply expressions of their inner states, ways of talk that are required by the nature of those internal states. Perhaps so. But I have been proposing a more radical hypothesis than that. I believe that the ways of telling and the ways of conceptualizing that go with them become so habitual that they finally become recipes for structuring experience itself, for laying down routes into memory, for not only guiding the life narrative up to the present but directing it into the future. I have argued that a life as led is inseparable from a life as told—or more bluntly, a life is not "how it was" but how it is interpreted and reinterpreted, told and retold: Freud's *psychic reality*. Certain basic formal properties of the life narrative do not change easily. Our excursion into experimental autobiography suggests that these formal structures may get laid down early in the discourse of family life and persist stubbornly in spite of changed conditions. Just as Georges Gusdorf argued that a special, historically conditioned, metaphysical condition was needed to bring autobiography into existence as a literary form, so perhaps a metaphysical change is required to alter the narratives that we have settled upon as "being" our lives. The fish will, indeed, be the last to discover water—unless he gets a metaphysical assist.

My life as a student of mind has taught me one incontrovertible lesson. Mind is never free of precommitment. There is no innocent eye, nor is there one that penetrates aboriginal reality. There are instead hypotheses, versions, expected scenarios. Our precommitment about the nature of a life is that it is a story, some narrative however incoherently put together. Perhaps we can say one other thing: any story one may tell about anything is better understood by considering other possible ways in which it can be told. That must surely be as true of the life stories we tell as of any others. In that case, we have come full round to the ancient homily that the only life worth living is the well-examined one. But it puts a different meaning on the homily. If we can learn how people put their narratives together when they tell stories from life, considering as well how they *might* have proceeded, we might then have contributed something new to that great ideal. Even if, with respect to life and narrative, we discover, as in Yeats's line, that we cannot tell the dancer from the dance, that may be good enough.

Notes

1. For example, J. S. Bruner, *Actual Minds, Possible Worlds* (Cambridge: Harvard University Press, 1986).
2. Nelson Goodman, *Ways of Worldmaking* (Indianapolis: Hackett, 1978).
3. Paul Ricoeur, *Time and Narrative* (Chicago: University of Chicago Press, 1984).
4. See Hayden White, "The Value of Narrativity in the Representation of Reality," in W. J. T. Mitchell, ed., *On Narrative* (Chicago: University of Chicago Press, 1984).
5. Paul de Man, *The Rhetoric of Romanticism* (New York: Columbia University Press, 1984), p. 84.
6. Louis Renza, "The Veto of the Imagination: A Theory of Autobiography," in James Olney, ed., *Autobiography: Essays Theoretical and Critical* (Princeton: Princeton University Press, 1980).
7. Peter Winch, *The Idea of a Social Science* (London: Routledge & Kegan Paul, 1958).
8. Georges Gusdorf, "Conditions and Limits of Autobiography," in Olney, *Autobiography.*
9. Vladimir Propp, *The Morphology of the Folktale* (Austin: University of Texas Press, 1968).
10. Frank Kermode, "Secrets and Narrative Sequence," in Mitchell, *On Narrative.*
11. See J. S. Bruner, in *A Tribute to Roman Jakobson* (Berlin: Walter de Gruyter, 1983).
12. Kenneth Burke, *The Grammar of Motives* (New York: Prentice-Hall, 1945).
13. Victor Turner, *From Ritual to Theater* (New York: Performing Arts Journal Publications, 1982).
14. Amelie Rorty, "A Literary Postscript: Characters, Persons, Selves, Individuals," in A. O. Rorty, ed., *The Identity of Persons* (Berkeley: University of California Press, 1976).
15. A. Greimas and J. Courtes, "The Cognitive Dimension of Narrative Discourse," *New Literary History* 7 (Spring 1976).
16. For those of you interested in this type of linguistic analysis, I refer you to Tzvetan Todorov's *The Poetics of Prose* (Ithaca: Cornell University Press, 1977) and to my own recent volume, *Actual Minds, Possible Worlds.*
17. Jean-Paul Sartre, *The Words* (New York: Braziller, 1964).
18. Ulric Neisser, "Autobiographical Memory," unpublished manuscript, Emory University, 1987.

9

RECLAIMING AN ORPHAN GENRE

The First-Person Narrative
of Illness

Arthur Frank

Three Voices of Illness

Illness narratives can also be described by the different narrative voices that tell them. As contemporary North American illness experience is constructed, I can identify three culturally available narrative voices for telling stories of illness. I call these narratives the restitution story, the chaotic story, and the quest story. The uniqueness of the contemporary illness narrative also reflects the structure of differences among these three voices.

The voice of *restitution* speaks a desire to have health restored. The surface plot of most illness narratives concerns the search for a proper diagnosis, optimal treatment, and cure. This search can involve a therapeutic alliance with physicians, the need to avoid and even outwit certain physicians, and complementing medical care with alternative medical treatments. But the restitution voice is only one in a narrative mix. Along with this concern with cure, the writer of an illness narrative, as a writer, usually wants more than just health restored; that "more" is essential to the fascination of the text. However important the restitution voice is in the surface plot, this voice has limited narrative possibilities. To understand this limit, it is necessary to look outside the published illness narrative at more banal narratives of illness.

Frank, Arthur W. "Reclaiming an Orphan Genre: The First-Person Narrative of Illness." *Literature and Medicine* 13:1 (1994), 5–8. © 1994 The Johns Hopkins University Press. Reprinted with permission of Johns Hopkins University Press.

The paradigm restitution story is told in over-the-counter drug commercials on television. The opening shots depict suffering: a haggard face after a sleepless night or important engagements about to be missed because of illness. The second sequence of shots shows the remedy-product, often provided by a wife or mother who is also the household's primary consumer. In longer versions of this story there may be a subplot involving a crisis of whether the sufferer believes in the remedy and will take it. The final sequence shows the face restored to health, activities being resumed, and thanks offered to the remedy. The consumer-loved one who provided the remedy-product stands proudly in the background. The household order has been restored. The ill person did nothing but engage in a secondary act of consumption.

The academic version of this same narrative is Talcott Parsons's sociological conception of the *sick role*. As Parsons tells it, illness results from some conflict, tension, or overburden. Being sick is a legitimate form of withdrawal from a situation that cannot be sustained, and it forestalls complete breakdown. The ill person is absolved from normal work and familial responsibilities, with the proviso that he seek medical advice. The physician sanctions a time and space for withdrawal, but not so much time or such a comfortable space as to generate "secondary gain" from being sick. The role of the physician is to avoid either making moral judgments on the withdrawal or colluding in the "deviance" of illness. The cycle ends with the person restored to his working role in the social order. Being sick, then, is legitimate deviance. Sickness is functional for society because it acts as a safety valve, allowing temporary withdrawals to correct situations that could lead *to* more permanent deviation.

Parsons's sick-role narrative culminates in the person's restitution to his former role, and the restitution of the social order to its former functioning. The physician has general responsibility for this process, monitoring the progress toward restitution. The ill person's responsibility for getting well consists almost exclusively in following "doctor's orders." I underscore that Parsons situates the sick-role model in his more general discussion of social control, and thereby shows great (albeit uncritical) insight into how society understands the "problem" of illness.

Neither the commercial-remedy narrative nor the sick-role narrative makes very good storytelling from the ill person's perspective, because in these restitution narratives the ill person is only a mute object, not the protagonist. The active role is taken by a third party, the physician or his surrogate, the drug. So it is hardly surprising that the voice of restitution is not dominant in most illness narratives. The restitution voice can dominate in the narrative variant when the odds of health being restored are especially long and against these odds the author "makes it." Then there is a story. Otherwise, what is there to tell when illness is conceived within this narrative form? The narrative subject of the restitution narrative is not the ill person but the physician.

All those television commercials do influence cultural images of illness, and sociologists have good reason for still taking Parsons seriously forty years later. Most people seem to experience their illnesses within a general narrative of restitution. Writers of illness narratives are no less human in their desire for cure, and so restitution is always one voice in their narratives. But restitution is only one voice in illness narratives, and the plurality of voices is part of what sets writers apart in their experiences of illness.

The paradox of the *chaotic* voice is that it would seem to be incapable of storytelling. Here the losses, the pain, the incoherence of suffering become so overpowering that language cannot resocialize what has happened. In this heart of darkness, "the horror" cannot be told; any telling can only point toward what happened in the vaguest terms. When chaotic stories are told, they are told on the verge of their own irrelevance.

Finding examples of telling what cannot be told is difficult. Gilda Radner's autobiography of cancer, *It's Always Something*, tells of her wanting to videotape what happens during one of her chemotherapy treatments. She spends these treatments in a drug-induced haze and hates the sense of time "lost." Videotaping is intended as a partial recovery of an experience that is otherwise chaotic in the most literal sense of being out of time, place, and meaning. Through the tape she hopes to reconstruct a narrative: people come, do things, leave, return. Chaos becomes ordered as she witnesses their caring for her, but chaos is never entirely ordered. What is produced is a countertext that can never fill in what is lost.

As this example illustrates, the "pure" chaotic voice is a hole in the narrative: what is tellable *about* chaos is no longer the chaos itself. But the chaotic voice is hardly less important for being untellable, particularly in the move from written narrative to bedside narrative. The silence that marks many illnesses can be heard as speaking in this voice. Attention to chaos narratives teaches readers to hear, in what is not said, what cannot be said.

The dominant voice in most illness narratives speaks what I call the *quest* narrative. These narratives recall the journey of the mythological hero, described as stages by Joseph Campbell. The three basic stages are the call, the road of trials, and the return. The call in illness narratives consists of recognizing a symptom not just as the sign of a disease but as the beginning of a journey. Accepting the call means accepting the illness as affecting one's life. The issue is not restitution but working out the changes illness brings. These changes occur in the course of trials, including the sufferings of surgery and stigma. The trials are not minimized, but they are progressively understood as teaching something and thus they gain meaning.

The mythological hero is granted a boon on her return: how to plant corn, for example. As civilization progresses the boon becomes less material and more metaphysical: insight, gnosis, and enlightenment are the heroic boons in societies more certain of their material survival. The boon granted at the end of the trials of illness is generally an enhanced subjectivity, extending toward others specifically and toward life generally. Most illness narratives culminate in some expression of how the self has been changed by the experience of suffering.

For illness narratives to become self-conscious storytelling, the quest voice usually dominates. Other voices mix in the narrative, but the quest voice alone is capable of sustained storytelling. When the voice of restitution is not mixed with some element of quest, then whatever happens along the way takes place only to be subsumed in the restoration at the end, whether this restoration is completed or anticipated. And illness in restitution terms never is the ill person's own story anyway: the active subject is the medical agent who effects the cure. The chaotic voice is equally incapable of speaking in its pure form. This voice needs to express wounds that have taken the wounded one outside the social boundaries of speech, and so its stories can only tell what cannot be spoken directly.

Ill people tell primarily quest stories, with voices of restitution and chaos entering the narrative mix, confounding it, forcing the voice of the quest to find itself again. In this confounding and refinding of voice, the primary question of the illness narrative emerges: *Who* tells these stories? Who is the subject telling the illness narrative?

10

NARRATIVE FREEDOM

Robert Zussman

This article is based on the presidential address delivered by Robert Zussman at the 2012 annual meetings of the Eastern Sociological Society.

Introduction

In early October 1990, 10 days before his death from cancer, Anatole Broyard, the former book review critic of the *New York Times*, gave his wife permission to tell their two children a secret of sorts, a secret he had long kept from them. Broyard, his Swedish-born wife explained, was African American. At first glance, the revelation seems simply the last gasp of racial passing, a curious and atavistic incident in the peculiar U.S. history of race. I want to propose that, although it may be that, it was also something much more.

In the first instance, Broyard's revelation to his children was not exactly a secret. Not only Broyard's wife knew about his background. Broyard's sister, married to the former U.S. ambassador to Ghana, also knew, of course, that Broyard's parents were African Americans, New Orleans creoles who had moved in the 1930s to Brooklyn. Moreover, many of Broyard's friends and acquaintances from his youth in Greenwich Village also seemed to know his "secret" as, for that matter, did at least a few of his friends and acquaintances from later in his life. Many more, too polite to ask and alert to the odd etiquettes of race that relegate it to silence, apparently suspected (Broyard, 2008; Gates, 1996).

Robert Zussman, *Sociological Forum* (Vol. 27, No. 4, December 2012), pp. 807–24, copyright © 2012 by Eastern Sociological Society. Reprinted by Permission of John Wiley and Sons, Inc.

Neither does Broyard himself seem to have made extensive efforts to hide his origins. The notes on the author in an article Broyard published in a 1950 *Commentary* entitled, "A Portrait of the Inauthentic Negro," referred to Broyard, a little cryptically, as "someone intimately acquainted with the subject matter" (Broyard, 1950:66). Later, in *When Kafka Was the Rage*, a memoir of his youth in the Village, Broyard (1993) acknowledged that he had been born in New Orleans and that he had grown up in Bedford-Stuyvesant. Broyard, it seems to me, was not trying to hide his race so much as he was trying simply to ignore it. Even Henry Louis Gates, although generally critical of Broyard for his own inauthenticity, was prepared, in an article published in the *New Yorker* a half-dozen years after Broyard's death, to grant that Broyard was engaging in an act of self-invention. Broyard, as Gates (1996) argues, wanted to be known "as a writer rather than a Black writer, as an intellectual rather than as a Black intellectual." Broyard himself, in his posthumously published *When Kafka Was the Rage*, put it differently: "Nobody in the village had a family. We were all sprung from our own brows, spontaneously generated the way flies were once thought to have originated" (Broyard, 1993:29).

Broyard did not, of course, actually spring from his own brow. Sociologists know better than that (or at least we think we do). But what is at stake in my brief account of this episode is whether one can tell a story as if we were sprung from our own brows. Race may be a particularly inescapable aspect of identity in the contemporary United States, but other aspects of personal histories and identities, individual and collective, are also difficult to escape. Yet, self-invention is also possible, in small ways and large, in formal autobiographies and in everyday accounts, and, not least, in the ways we lead our lives. What I would like to propose, then, is that what was at stake in Broyard's secret and its revelation, in his selective silences and his equally selective writing, are the possibilities and limits of something I would like to call narrative freedom.

What Is Narrative Freedom?

By narrative freedom I mean simply the ability to tell stories about ourselves in the ways we want, not simply to muster particular facts and events but to draw meanings and morals about our own lives. In evoking narrative freedom I do not mean to include the ability to tell (or get away with) explicit and self-conscious lies: although lying certainly happens and raises interesting issues of its own, I have in mind here more the processes of selection and connection, the acts of imaginative construction that are basic to narrative. This selectivity is what makes narrative meaningful, what makes it something more than a mere list of events, what gives narrative an inherently moral quality that is independent and apart from any concerns about objectivity (Polkinghorne, 1988; White, 1981). Narrative freedom involves selecting among the categories and actions we identify with but also selecting and transforming the meanings we ascribe to those identities and actions. This is, I think, precisely the process of self-invention that Gates identified in Broyard's life and writing.

The effort at self-invention is perhaps nowhere more evident than in the long tradition of African-American autobiographical writing. In sharp contrast to Broyard, this is a literature that most often both claims blackness and attempts to transform its meaning. This effort is present in Frederick Douglass's (1999) *Narrative of the Life of Frederick Douglass* and Harriet Jacobs's (1973) *Incidents in the Life of a Slave Girl*, in James Baldwin's (1955) *Notes of a Native Son*, in the *Autobiography of Malcolm X* (1964), in Maya Angelou's (1970) *I Know Why the Caged Bird Sings*, and, more recently, in Barack Obama's (1995) *Dreams from My Father*. In each of these autobiographies, the narrative is an *expression* of self-invention, a matter of the author putting in words the process of his or her own self-discoveries. However, each is also itself an *act* of self-invention. The writing does not simply reflect a self but creates one, does not simply report an identity but claims one, does not simply claim an identity but transforms that identity.

Self-invention may be particularly notable in the African-American autobiographical tradition, but it is by no means limited to it. Fitzgerald's (1925) *Gatsby* was engaged in self-invention as was Melville's (2008) *Confidence Man*, to take just two prominent literary examples. There is, of course, also a strong feminist tradition of autobiographical self-invention as there is, as well, in virtually every identity movement anyone of us could imagine. Alongside the accounts reported in Elaine Showalter's (2001) aptly named *Inventing Herself* is the long stream of autobiographical writing organized, variously, around troubled childhoods, sexual identities, battles with illness, lives with disabilities, and much more, all of which are also part of this tradition.

I have begun by evoking literary examples, two novels and a smattering of published autobiographies, but the analysis I have in mind is not literary. I am not interested here in the internal structure of autobiographies, let alone novels, or in the use of metaphor or other literary devices. Neither am I interested here even in certain versions of cultural analysis: I am not, for example, going to address broad cultural developments out of which patterns of self-invention emerge. Neither will I address how the cultural codes of self-invention are organized.

Rather, I have in mind a set of more distinctively sociological questions. Written autobiographies (Bjorklund, 1998) are only a small part of a much more common set of practices I have elsewhere called auto-biographical occasions (Zussman, 1996, 2000, 2006). Autobiographical occasions include all those socially structured situations where we, formally and informally, orally and in writing, individually and collectively, tell our life stories in the course of confessions, reunions, and therapeutic accounts, as well as in efforts to transform ourselves. Taken together, autobiographical occasions are those events through which, at least discursively, we create our selves. My question, not just about literary autobiography but about autographical occasions more generally, is how much, under what conditions, and with what limits these occasions allow us to narrate our lives as we would like. To ask about the possibilities and limits of narrative freedom is also to ask about the possibilities and limits of self-invention. What I mean to focus on are the social conditions under which narrative freedom is possible.

Foucault and Goffman

In taking up this question, I rely heavily on two guides who might seem, at first, to be leading in different directions. My two guides are Michel Foucault and Erving Goffman. Foucault and Goffman, separated by an ocean but almost exact contemporaries, shared a joint intellectual project, to understand how people are made up.[1] Both denied that there is any essential self. However, they did so in different ways.

For Foucault, the self was created from the top down, as part of a process of pervasive social control. "One confesses," Foucault (1990:59) wrote, "or is forced to confess. When it is not spontaneous or dictated by some internal imperative, the confession is wrung from the person by violence or threat; it is driven from its hiding place in the soul, or extracted from the body." For Foucault (1990:60), autobiographical occasions cannot and should not be confused with narrative freedom. "[O]ne has to have an inverted image of power," he continued, "in order to believe that all the voices that have spoken so long in our civilization—repeating the formidable injunction to tell us what one is and what one does, what one is thinking and what one thinks he is not thinking are speaking to us of freedom."

If, for Foucault, the self is imposed on the speaker and as part of a process of control, for Goffman the self is more often created from the bottom up, as an act of self-aggrandizement, and as part of a process of self-transformation. To be sure, we can find in Goffman frequent examples of the power of institutions—most famously in his (1962) analysis of total institutions—but the power of these boarding schools, military installations, and even mental hospitals is always fleeting and always leave massive room for strategic maneuver. Goffman explicitly denies the significance of the self as an essence, but constantly (if only implicitly) celebrates the presence of an actor, in both the dramaturgical sense and in the sense of agency as that term is used in sociology.[2] This actor may work with collaborators and may face impediments, but is also fundamentally free.

In evoking Foucault and Goffman as my guides, I do not imagine that I am doing justice to either. Rather, I mean to use them for my own purposes, in particular to draw a contrast between narratives, particularly narratives of the self, that are driven from the top down and narratives that are driven from the bottom up. Neither do I mean to adjudicate between these two approaches to narrative. Rather, I mean, in a spirit that probably would have discomfitted both my guides, to treat the difference between them as an empirical question, to ask where and when narratives, particularly narratives of the self, are created from the top down and where and when they are created from the bottom up. I do not want to assume that narrative freedom is always limited or always possible. Rather, I want to ask what the social situations are that produce both freedom and its limits.

Autobiographical Occasions

Some autobiographical narratives are generated from above, insisted on by an authority that can not only demand that a story be told but that it be told in a particular form and with particular content. This is certainly the case for confessions, whether criminal or religious. It is also the case in many forms of therapy, whether in the form of a conventional medical history or the more elaborate form of a psychoanalytic case. In contrast, other autobiographical narratives are more or less voluntary. They are, to be sure, told to an audience but an audience that lacks the authority to insist either that the story be told or that it be told in a particular way. If anything, the issue here, at least from the point of view of the storyteller, is more likely to be capturing an audience's attention than evading that audience's authority. This would at least seem to be the case for many acts of self-invention, including not just the written autobiographies produced as part of identity movements, but also their less elaborate relatives found in the everyday talk of identity claims, as well as in the kind of talk that goes on within courting couples anxious to establish a connection by sharing a history or between old friends catching up with each other after a long separation.

One dimension, then, in distinguishing narratives is the authority of the audience for that narrative. In some cases, the audience (a police officer, a priest, a physician) is able to direct the narrative. These are narratives generated from the top down. In other cases, there may be an audience, actual or imagined, but one without authority over form or content. These are narratives generated from the bottom up.

But there is also a second dimension to narratives. Narratives, particularly narratives of the self, may be distinguished by intention and consequence. Some narratives are meant to be restorative and integrative: They are meant to restore society as it has been or, at least, as some group believes it should have been, by integrating or reintegrating a transgressor or stray. This is very much the case for confessions, again both criminal and religious, generated from above, but it is also the case at reunions, generated from below. By contrast, other narratives are meant not to restore but to transform the individuals who tell them and often, by implication, society as well. This is again the case among the kind of autobiographies created within identity movements, generated from below, typically meant self-consciously to transform the meaning or evaluation of an identity: the feminist consciousness-raising groups of the early 1970s are a particularly clear example. But something similar is also the case in many therapeutic moments, generated by an authority, but with the intention not of restoring the storyteller to some previous state so much as transforming him or her into something or someone new. A second dimension of narratives, then, is whether they are restorative or transformative.[3]

Taken together, these two dimensions generate four types of narrative, as shown in Table 1, each accompanied by an illustrative example. I do not mean to reify these types as they are, like most such types, far less distinct than a neatly drawn table makes them seem, but they do provide a way to think.

The top right-hand corner of Table 1, confession, comes closest to what Foucault had in mind. It represents the strictest limits of narrative freedom. The bottom left-hand corner comes closest to what Goffman had in mind: it represents the possibilities of narrative freedom. The top-left corner and the bottom-right corner are mixed cases.

TABLE 1. THE VARIETIES OF NARRATIVE

	Transformative	**Restorative**
Top Down	Therapy	Confession
	Psychoanalysis	Sacrament of penance
Bottom Up	Self-invention	Reunion
	Slave narrative	Collective memory

I should also note that I have talked, so far, about narrative forms without much attention to whether the tellers themselves are primarily individuals or collectivities. Narratives can, of course, be both. Confession may be the provenance of a lone penitent in a confessional speaking only to a priest pledged to respect confidentiality, but it may also be a form imposed on a large class of persons as, for example, in the truth and reconciliation commissions found in South Africa, Cambodia, Colombia, Chile, and a dozen other countries (Hayner, 2000; Nagy, 2002). Self-invention may be the provenance of a lone figure attempting to impress a date or a prospective employer, but it may also represent the collective effort of a minority group determined to challenge a stigmatized status. I do not mean to propose that the process of narration is the same for individuals and collectivities. I do, however, mean to propose that they involve similar issues.

Confession

Confession, as Foucault (1990) tells us, is pervasive in modern societies. It is widespread in criminal control but also found in education, workplaces, Maoist self-criticism, television talk shows, and anywhere else men and women are called on not just to reflect on their lives but to do so in a spirit of repentance (Bibas and Bierschbach, 2004; Moorti, 1998; Tavuchis, 1991). At a collective level, confession is the mode with which South Africa is attempting to deal with the cultural legacy of apartheid, by which Chile is dealing with the legacy of Pinochet, and Cambodia, least successfully, with the legacy of Pol Pot and the Khmer Rouge, all in the spirit of restorative justice. Yet, however pervasive it may be in other areas, the template for confession remains the sacrament of penance as it is practiced in the Catholic Church.[4]

That the sacrament of penance is about social control may seem obvious: it involves not simply the Church's establishment of standards of behavior but a requirement that the penitent himself or herself accepts those standards. Moreover, the sacrament is administered by an authority, the priest, who is himself an emissary of the broader authority of the Church. The widespread publication beginning in the Middle Ages of manuals of confession—and, in the last decade of a $1.99 IPhone app—meant to instruct penitent and priest alike of the proper forms and content of confession simply adds to the limits on narrative freedom. What is perhaps less obvious is that penance involves not just control but also reintegration into the Church (Donoghue and Shapiro, 1984; Turner and Hepworth, 1982).

Penance proceeds in four stages. The first is contrition, "a sorrow of soul and a hatred of sin," according to the sixteenth-century Council of Trent, accompanied by "the resolution not to sin again" (Herbermann et al., 1913:337). Contrition, in the Catholic tradition, must be sincere. It is followed by and, in the Catholic imagination, is the motivation for, confession proper, the explicit acknowledgment of sin to a priest. The third stage is absolution in which the priest, speaking in God's place, forgives the penitent his or her sins: "may God give you pardon and peace, and I absolve you from your sins in the name of the Father, and of the Son, and of the Holy Spirit" (U.S. Conference of Catholic Bishops, 2006:1449). The final stage is reconciliation of the penitent with the Church from which his or her sin had separated him or her. It is in this final stage that, from the point of view of both the Church and, often, the penitent, is the primary purpose of the sacrament, that confession is most clearly both integrative and restorative.

It is the possibility of reconciliation that gives confession its power to control. This power is not simply discursive. Rather, the priest's control of reintegration into the Church is a powerful resource, more so of course at those moments when membership in the Church was critical to membership in a society more generally. The same process is evident in the ability of a parole board to reduce a prison sentence, of a high school principal to suspend or reinstate a difficult student, of a parent to punish or forgive a misbehaving child, or a truth and reconciliation commission to pardon a political enemy. Moreover, it is precisely the social and material significance of the resources at stake in reconciliation that creates a constant temptation for the penitent merely to feign contrition and the constant preoccupation of all those who receive confessions to distinguish merely feigned contrition from sincere contrition.

Under these conditions, the "truth" that accompanies reconciliation is a truth thoroughly imbued with power. Confession, as Foucault has told us, provokes narrative but it does not provide the conditions for narrative freedom.

Mixed Cases: Therapy and Reunions

Therapy and reunions are both generic types of narratives. Both are mixed cases, sharing some of the aspects of confession and some aspects of self-invention.

Therapy is the work of the various helping professions—social workers, physicians, guidance counselors, and, in their secular roles, ministers and priests. But, just as the sacrament of penance is the clearest expression of confession, Freudian psychoanalysis is perhaps the clearest example, for my purposes here, of therapy (Illouz, 2008; Rieff, 1966). Psychoanalysis operates from the top down, driven by a psychoanalyst who purports to understand his or her narrating patient better than does the patient himself or herself. However, unlike confession, which is oriented to restoring the penitent to the church, psychoanalysis, like the work of the helping professions more generally, often purports to transform those whose narratives it shapes. As a result, the issue of sincerity takes a very different form in therapy than in confession. The success of the narrative of therapy depends, at least in the therapist's conception, precisely on the willingness and ability of the patient to give an account that is not only sincere but authentic.[5] In confession, the penitent's interest in instrumental benefits tempts insincerity and lies. In contrast, in therapy, at least in the therapist's conception, the patient hurts only himself or herself with efforts to deceive. Certainly, many of those who practice therapy in its various forms would claim that they deploy it in the interests of freedom, not, to be sure, from the therapist but from the dead weight of a dysfunctional past, but this claim is very much contested, not just by academic critics of therapy, but also in practice by patients themselves.

Indeed, struggles over the form and content of narrative accounts pervade therapy. Freud's most famous case, his analysis of "Dora," a young woman beset by various hysterical symptoms, begins with Dora's father asking Freud to bring his daughter "to reason" (Freud, 1963:42). But, as the case unfolds, it becomes clear that what it means to bring Dora "to reason" has different meanings (see, e.g., Decker, 1992; Marcus, 1984). For Dora's father, it seemed to mean simply to eliminate the most blatant symptoms of her illness and to make her behave more conventionally. For Freud, in contrast, it meant encouraging Dora to come to terms with her own sexuality, directed, in Freud's understanding, at her father, a neighbor and a friend of her father who had made advances to her, and even her own latent homosexual impulses. In Freud's account, one of the striking characteristics of neurosis entails the patient's inability to give a coherent account of his or her own illness. This "inability to give an ordered history of their life in so far as it coincides with the history of their illness is not merely characteristic of the neurosis," Freud wrote (1963:30). "It also possesses great theoretical significance." Indeed, for Freud, the task of psychoanalysis was precisely to provide the patient with an ability to narrate her own story: "Whereas the practical aim of the treatment," Freud wrote (1963:31), "is to remove all possible symptoms and to replace them by conscious thoughts, we may regard it as a second and theoretical aim to repair all the damages to the patient's memory."

In this sense, for Freud—and, we might imagine, for the host of well-meaning social workers, psychologists, guidance counselors, and ministers who have followed, however distally, in Freud's tradition—

therapy does seem to contribute to narrative freedom. Indeed it might. But we should also express skepticism. Dora herself did not accept Freud's analysis, instead breaking off her treatment. Freud himself believed this was simply "denial," an unwillingness on Dora's part to acknowledge the painful truths Freud believed he was revealing. But, while we do not know what Dora herself believed beyond her reluctance to continue therapy, we do know that generations of feminist critics of Freud have suggested a powerful counternarrative: that Freud's easy assumption of Dora's sexual attraction to her father's friend was implausible, a story Freud imposed on Dora. In the feminist reading, Dora was engaged in a struggle, personal and discursive, with an oppressive paternalism that treated her as a sexual object and in which her father, her father's friend, and Freud himself were all implicated (Decker, 1992; Ramas, 1980). By this reading, therapy, far from a contributor to narrative freedom, is a powerful system of social control. Not only was Dora's father, in his call to bring his daughter "to reason," engaged in an effort at reintegrating Dora into her family but so, too, was Freud, even while rejecting the father's call, engaged in an effort to reintegrate Dora into a patriarchal sexual order.

In the other quarters of therapy, struggles for narrative control will be nowhere nearly as explicit as they are in Freud's account of Dora and Dora's response to Freud, but those struggles will be present, even in less explicit form, wherever therapy is practiced. Perhaps the single most consistent finding from a significant number of studies of self-help groups, modeled roughly on Alcoholics Anonymous, is how thoroughly the accounts participants give are scripted. These scripted statements—about alcoholism, drug use, codependency, recovered memories, or false memory syndrome—may well be useful to those who participate in group therapy, but they are hardly expressions of narrative freedom (Davis, 2005; Irvine, 1999). It makes less sense, I submit, to think of therapy as a source of narrative freedom than as a site of narrative struggle.

Therapy is pervasive in contemporary life. So are reunions. In invoking reunions as a generic form, I mean to include what is probably the form most celebrated in popular culture, the high school reunion, but also something broader. Colleges, military units, and, although probably less often, workplaces also celebrate reunions. Even more frequently do families have reunions, both in the form of holiday celebrations that bring together extended families a few times a year or in the much more casual reunions of partners after a day at work. At a more public level, holidays, memorials, and all the other phenomena conventionally grouped together as instances of collective memory have many of the same characteristics. In particular, reunions originate from the bottom up: although there may be a high school reunion organizing committee or more or less official committees to organize public holidays, these authorities rarely exercise significant control over what is said or how it is said. But this, as anyone who has attended a high school reunion knows, does not mean that there is narrative freedom (Vinitzky-Seroussi, 1998).

Rather, the constant tension at reunions is between the pull of the past and the pull of the present. At high school reunions, college reunions, military reunions, and workplace reunions, there is a constant temptation to embellish current successes. But this temptation, as Vinitzky-Seroussi has shown in the case of high school reunions, is balanced by the pull of a group invoking the values and solidarity of the group as it once was, by a group that reaches out to demand reintegration, not through the account of current triumphs (which would threaten that reintegration) but through the ritual recitation of events long past (Vinitzky-Seroussi, 1998). A similar tension exists in collective memory as it is worked through in holidays and memorials. Here, there are pervasive tensions not only between the demands of the past and those of the present, but also among a wide variety of interested parties, with potentially divisive issues suppressed in the interest of celebrating—and creating—a joint history around which a common culture can be built (Wagner-Pacifici and Schwartz, 1991; Schwartz, 2003; Vinitzky-Seroussi, 2002). These conditions dramatically limit the possibilities for narrative freedom.

Self-Invention

This brings me to the bottom left-hand cell of Table 1, where narratives are bottom up and transformative. This is the cell of self-invention, where we will find the autobiographical accounts of personal (and, often, by extension, of social) self-discovery, self-realization, self-fulfillment and triumph, organized variously, among different groups and at different times, around humble beginnings, sexuality, disability, illness, troubled childhoods, and troubled adulthoods. These are stories told in writing and orally, told one to one, in the extraordinary array of consciousness-raising and self-help groups found in every nook and corner of U.S. life, and in the mass media. If we are to find narrative freedom anywhere, it is here.

Although there are many other examples, the issues around narrative freedom in these acts of self-invention seem to me nowhere as clear elsewhere as in the slave narratives widely circulated in the years before the U.S. Civil War. These narratives, as has been widely noted, are stories about the struggle for freedom in a very literal sense. As Frederick Douglass wrote at a key turning point in his *Narrative of the Life of Frederick Douglass*, probably the greatest of the slave narratives: "You have seen

how a man was made a slave. You shall see how a slave was made a man"
(Douglass, 1973:63).

For the slave narratives, in particular, the very fact of writing involved
not only an act of self-invention but an act of liberation, what Gates
(1985:xxx) has called "the will to power as the will to write." Slave owners
often viewed efforts to learn to read, let alone write, as insurrectionary
and attempted to repress them. Douglass himself recounted his master's
efforts to prevent his wife from teaching him to read.

> Mr. Auld found out what was going on, and at once forbade Mrs.
> Auld to instruct me further, telling her that it was unlawful, as
> well as unsafe, to teach a slave to read. . . . If you teach that nigger
> (speaking of myself) how to read, there would be no keeping him. It
> would forever unfit him to be a slave. (Douglass, 1973:38–39)

In the course of writing, the ex-slave demonstrated not only a successful
triumph over bans on literacy, not only an ability to do something that
slave owners thought dangerous or impossible. In the very course of writing, the ex-slave also demonstrated—and established—a humanity that
slavery had denied.

It is little wonder that the actual authorship of slave narratives was
often contested by slavery's apologists: The mere fact of authorship—
the simple instance of the subaltern's ability to speak—was itself deeply
subversive. Slave narratives and their successors, both in the African-
American autobiographical tradition and in the traditions of writing by
other excluded and stigmatized groups, should rightly be celebrated as
instances of narrative freedom, driven by the narrators, arrayed against
institutions of oppression, insistent in their transformative possibilities.
But, even here, that celebration needs qualifications.

The first qualification requires noting that the slave narratives were,
with very few exceptions, highly conventional in form. The second qualification, which helps explain the first, is that the ability of ex-slaves to
publish slave narratives was highly dependent on sponsors who often
insisted on particular narrative elements. Slave narratives began almost
uniformly with an engraved portrait signed by the narrator, followed by
a title page making a claim to authorship ("As Written by Himself"),
and testimonials to the truthfulness of the narrative, usually provided
by a white abolitionist (Olney, 1985). The narrative itself begins, equally
predictably, with the formulaic, "I was born," a phrase that operates both
as an insistence on the reality of the experience narrated but also as a concession to the doubts about the narrative's truth. To say that the slave narratives were formulaic is not to deny their power, but it is to acknowledge

that the narrative freedom they represent is collective, a freedom won only by participation in a social movement, rather than individual. And it is to acknowledge, in the words of Robert Stepto, "the former slave's ultimate lack of control over his own narrative, occasioned primarily by the demands of audience and authentication" (Stepto, 1985:237).

The qualifications that apply to slave narratives apply, perhaps even more powerfully, to self-invention more generally. Unlike the slave narrative, other forms of self-invention are only occasionally self-exemplifying, in the sense that the simple fact of literacy demonstrates humanity in the slave narratives. But the formulaic character of the slave narratives is very much in evidence in the equally formulaic statements well documented as standard to consciousness-raising groups, born-again Christians, and the various literatures of self-invention. I do not mean to claim that self-invention is impossible. I do mean to claim that it is very difficult. If in looking at confessions we find processes of control even more pervasive than we might have first imagined, in looking at self-invention we find the elements of freedom less pervasive than we might have imagined. Foucault, to my regret, gets the better of Goffman.

The Social Structures of Narrative Freedom

At first glance, the social conditions under which narrative freedom can be achieved—or at least approximated—are generally the same as those that, in the conventional sociological meta-narrative of modernity, produced contemporary individualism. Where there are high levels of physical and social mobility, where networks are loose, and where lives are segmented between work and family, there individual men and women should have the greatest freedom to tell their stories as they like, free from the corrective gazes of those who have known them since birth and from fellow members of communities they have abandoned. These are, of course, the conditions that allowed Anatole Broyard to pass as white, the conditions that allowed Gatsby to invent his own myth, and the conditions through which countless social climbers cultivate modes of dress, styles of speech, and patterns of self-presentation that obscure otherwise humble origins. It is these conditions, particularly as they are manifest in urban settings, which provoke both Freud's preoccupation with telltale signs in dreams, jokes, and slips of the tongue that may give away otherwise invisible biographical facts, and Goffman's preoccupation with the strategic acts of men and women intent on keeping those facts discreet (Kasson, 1990). It is these conditions that would make Facebook and its equivalents the apogee of narrative freedom.

I do not think this account is wrong. I do, however, think it is limited in at least two ways. First, insofar as the conventional sociological account is concerned with explicit deception, it runs the risk of trivialization. No doubt a young man new to the city can present himself as coming from a more elevated background or a young woman as in possession of more (or less) dramatic romantic histories than either could in a setting where they would be observed more closely by those who knew them earlier. It is certainly possible for a Facebook page to list an imaginary status, accompanied by doctored or mislabeled pictures, not to mention an altogether invented history. But these are instances when all that is at stake is typically a mostly vague impression without significant consequence. The conventional account, then, leaves out the massive apparatus of surveillance—background checks, credit checks, letters of reference—that is deployed when jobs, loans, and admission to schools are at stake. It leaves out the counterclaims that typically greet efforts to draw broader conclusions from public acts of self-invention: not just the controversies around the authorship of slave narratives, but also, among many others, the controversies about the authenticity of Betty Friedan's experiences as they informed her *Feminist Mystique* (Horowitz, 2000) or of James Frey's as they informed his *A Million Little Pieces* (Kipnis, 2010) or even the place of Obama's birth. The conditions of modernity do create the conditions of narrative freedom, but it is a negative freedom, an absence of restraint. The conditions of modernity make it more possible to tell our stories as we like but may simultaneously make it more difficult to achieve a positive freedom, to ensure that those stories are heard. The conditions of modernity may create narrative freedom but much less successfully when interests are at stake.

Second, the conventional meta-narrative leaves out power and inequality. Yet it is precisely inequality of various sorts that is central to the limits of narrative freedom. To be sure, poverty and wealth are probably only unevenly associated with confession. However, power, organizational and political, is a more certain guide. Confession, most clearly, is enforced by power relations. The penitent confesses to the priest, who grants penance not in his own name but in that of God and through authority vested in the priest by the Church. Similarly, the criminal confesses to the police officer, the unruly student to the principal, the child to the parent, not the other way around. There was no truth and reconciliation commission under the apartheid regime in South Africa or in Chile under Pinochet. Both required regime changes.

Conversely, the possession of power by a potential penitent typically exempts him or her from the requirement to confess. At various points, the Catholic Church took great pains to ensure that members of superior estates did not confess downward to priests of lower ranks: kings and nobility could often choose their own confessors, in effect limiting the Church's control over their actions (Hepworth and Turner, 1982:56–57). In contemporary daily life, it is precisely the child's moving out of his or her parents' house that also often marks the end of the parents' ability to compel confession, just as graduation from school marks the end of the authority of the principal. The inability of the Cambodian government to begin truth and reconciliation commissions until three decades after the fall of the Khmer Rouge and the weakness of that commission's findings, even when seated, have been widely attributed to the persistent influence of former Khmer Rouge officials in the succeeding Cambodian governments (McDonald, 2012). And much as many may believe George Bush—and perhaps others—responsible for war crimes in Afghanistan and Iraq, the power of the United States patently protects him from any need to confess.

My mixed cases, therapy and reunions, are, as one would expect, fraught with ambiguities, precisely because the character of the narration is also ambiguous. Access to some types of therapy, most notably psychoanalysis, should clearly be treated as a privilege, available only to those with the means to pay for a remarkably expensive course of treatment. It is, however, also likely that those who have, in fact, been subject to long courses of psychotherapy are also those who, within a privileged class, like Dora, who have the least authority within their own families. And, as is well documented, in many cases, therapy, typically in its less expensive form as group therapy, is court ordered as an alternative to jail or other punishment.

Reunions are as ambiguous as therapy. On the one hand, reunions are generally voluntary on the part of the group. Certainly, there are many individuals, whether out of genuine affection for the reconstituting group or a desire to parade successes, who actively seek out reunions as an occasion to tell their tales. On the other hand, once constituted, reunions express the power of groups over individuals, compelling even those who do "choose" not to return to reflect on their absence.

In the case of self-invention, resources, more often financial than organizational, do not exempt the narrator from the need to tell but to empower him or her with the means to do so. What, Virginia Woolf (1929) asked famously, does a woman need to write and answered, even more famously, "500 pounds and a room of her own." The ability to self-invent, as Woolf's answer implies, is not distributed evenly. It does not require but is made much easier by literacy, much in dispute in the case of slave narratives. It does not require but is made much easier by the resources—a typewriter, a computer, a sponsor, an independent income—that allow a narrator to narrate. Even more, if self-invention is to be not only personally transformative but socially transformative, it needs the resources that enable it to reach an audience. It needs access to the means of a narration—to publishers, to the hosts of talk shows, to the Internet—all of which, although to varying degrees, are structured by class, race, gender and class-, race-, and gender-based networks.

In general, then, subordination—a lack of power and authority within formal organizations, families, communities, and the state—results in a compulsion to confess. But it is wealth and network resources that make it easier to approximate narrative freedom. The great leveler, in regard to both power and wealth, is, of course, social movements. Slave narratives and the abolitionist movement fed on each other, as do feminist autobiographies and the feminist movement, as do coming-out stories and the gay liberation movement. But social movements cut both ways. Social movements may, on the one hand, oppose the imposition of narration on the powerless. This is the case for various rights groups addressing the needs of prisoners, children, and those with various disabilities. Social movements may also provide the means of self-invention to individuals and groups who would otherwise lack those means, as was the case for slave narratives supported by the abolitionist movement. But social movements, as was the case for slave narratives, are almost certainly more effective at encouraging narrative freedom in a collective form than in an individual form. Social movements counter the inequalities of wealth and power, providing new narratives for whole categories of people. At the same time, however, they also impose narratives on those individuals who fall into the very categories social movements are helping to create (Benford, 2002; Polletta, 2002). Just as ex-slaves wrote highly conventionalized narratives to satisfy the expectations of a sympathetic audience, so, too, have feminist narratives, narratives of triumph over disability, and coming-out narratives all also taken on highly conventionalized forms of sorts required by their various audiences (Plummer, 1995; Stein, 1997, 2011).

Conclusion: The Power of Silence

I have been more insistent on the limits of narrative freedom than its possibilities. Narrative freedom may not be impossible, but it is difficult. Narrative freedom requires resources, possessed by few, such that a story may not simply be told but also heard. Narrative freedom is limited by authorities who require confession as a condition of access to the benefits of membership in groups of various sorts. It is limited by therapists who, with the best of intentions, insist on particular forms of speech. It is limited by friends, family, classmates, and colleagues who reach out from the past. Even where self-invention seems most promising, when it is at-tached to a social movement, when it is deployed in the interests of social transformation, the narrator often finds himself or herself a captive of the very audience that encouraged him or her in the first place.

Let me, however, at this late point in this article, introduce another pos-sibility—that narrative freedom consists not so much in the ability to tell one's story but in the ability to remain silent. Anatole Broyard was no hero. His effort to ignore his own blackness reads badly at a moment when si-lence about race has become a major form for the extensions of racial in-equality and when the narrative embrace of race has become a major means of its transformation. Broyard could not escape race because race in the United States is inescapable.[6] But Broyard's silence also suggests another route to narrative freedom, even if he was himself unable to achieve it.

If some resources provide an ability to speak, others provide an ex-emption from speaking. The parent calls the child to account more often than the child calls the parent to account. The priest, the police officer or the judge, the high school principal, the therapist call the penitent, the prisoner, the student, the patient to account—not the other way around. In confession, we are compelled to speak. But, so, too, are we compelled to speak at reunions and in therapy. We are, in contrast—and by defini-tion—rarely compelled to reinvent ourselves but, even when we do, we reinvent ourselves in terms of the very categories we are trying to escape. Even acts of self-invention cannot avoid categories. In claiming identities, we also reify those identities. In claiming a racial identity, we reify race. In claiming a sexual identity, we reify sexuality. In claiming a disability identity, we reify disability. Where identities, individual and collective, are oppressive, narrative freedom may provide some relief. But an even greater freedom would be found in an ability to ignore those identities altogether.

The closest approximation of narrative freedom may, then, reside not in any particular form of narrative but in the right not to narrate. This is not a privilege often extended to the subaltern. For the subaltern we are most often preoccupied with efforts to find a voice of his or her own. But these efforts to find a voice are themselves made necessary only by the insistent calls to account by superordinates. A thoroughgoing freedom, then, might involve not an ability to make up our stories as we choose but a choice to avoid making up stories altogether, not so much a choice of identities as a choice to avoid identities altogether. Foucault remarks somewhere that the point is not to liberate sexuality but to liberate our-selves from sexuality. In a similar spirit, I would like to suggest that true freedom may not involve liberating narrative, but to liberate ourselves from narrative.

Notes

Thanks to Naomi Gerstel, Vered Vinitzky-Seroussi, Mary Ann Clawson, and the members of the Narrative Reading Group and my course on Narrative Sociology for their comments on earlier drafts of this article.

1. Goffman lived from 1922 through 1982; Foucault from 1926 to 1984. For a provocative comparison of Foucault and Goffman, see Hacking 2004.
2. Goffman's denial of any essential self is most explicit in *Stigma* (1963:51–56). His emphasis on the actor oozes out of virtually every page of *Presentation of the Self* (1959) and *Strategic Interaction* (1969) as well as *Stigma*.
3. My distinction here parallels Scott and Lyman's (1968) distinction between excuses, which restore a moral order, and justifications, which threaten that order. But where Scott and Lyman emphasize the point of view of the account giver, I am emphasizing the point of view of the audience for the account.
4. Besides confession, this cell also includes applications of various sorts, most notably for jobs and admission to schools. Applications and confessions share various attributes. Both are driven from above. Both require a celebration of existing values, although slightly more explicitly in the case of confessions than of applications. Moreover, both confessions and applications pose similar problems for their audiences judging the honesty of the profession. They differ, however, in that confessions typically demand both contrition and, related to that contrition, a transformation of an inner state of a sort that is usually absent, or at least far weaker, in applications for jobs and schools. Because this inner state is particularly hard to observe, "effective" confession, at least from the point of view of those who hear that confession, is much harder to evaluate than an application. For a slightly different view of applications, see, for example, Lamont et al. (2000).
5. The distinction is Trilling's (1972). Sincerity refers to a profession of truth made without regard to external consequences. Authenticity refers to a profession of truth made on the basis of often difficult to attain self-understanding.
6. Broyard (1950:63) clearly had something like this in mind: "In fact, one can say that, in many cases, the inauthentic Negro almost entirely occupies himself with either affirming (ingratiation) or denying by his behavior what the anti-Negro says about him, until his personality is virtually usurped by a series of maneuvers none of which has any necessary relation to his true self. . . . Authenticity, as I take it, would mean stubborn adherence to one's essential self, in spite of the distorting pressures of one's situation. By the Negro's essential self, I mean his innate qualities and developed characteristics as an individual, as distinguished from his preponderantly defensive reactions as a member of an embattled minority." Broyard's article was a response to and an extension of Sartre's *Anti-Semite and Jew*, which had originally been published as a series of articles in *Commentary*. For those looking for intellectual continuities—and underlying orientations—compare Broyard's use of Sartre's notions of authenticity and inauthenticity with what Hacking (2004) sees as a similar spirit in Goffman and Foucault.

References

Angelou, Maya. 1970. *I Know Why the Caged Bird Sings*. New York: Random House.
Baldwin, James. 1955. *Notes of a Native Son*. Boston, MA: Beacon.

Benford, Robert D 2002. "Controlling Narratives and Narratives as Control within Social Movements," in Joseph E. Davis (ed.), *Stories of Change: Narrative and Social Movements*: pp. 54–75. Albany, NY: State University of New York Press.

Bibas, Stephanos, and Richard A. Bierschbach. 2004. "Integrating Remorse and Apology into Criminal Procedure," *Yale Law Journal* 114: 85–148.

Bjorklund, Diana. 1998. *Interpreting the Self: Two Hundred Years of American Autobiography*. Chicago, IL: University of Chicago Press.

Broyard, Anatole. 1950. "Portrait of the Inauthentic Negro: How Prejudice Distorts the Victim's Personality," *Commentary* 10: 56–64.

———. 1993. *When Kafka Was the Rage*. New York: Carol Southern Books.

Broyard, Bliss. 2008. *One Drop: My Father's Hidden Life—A Story of Race and Family Secrets*. New York: Little, Brown and Co.

Davis, Joseph E. 2005. *Accounts of Innocence: Sexual Abuse, Trauma, and the Self*. Chicago, IL: University of Chicago Press.

Decker, Hannah. 1992. *Freud, Dora and Vienna 1900*. New York: Free Press.

Donoghue, Quentin, and Linda Shapiro. 1984. *Bless Me Father, For I Have Sinned*. New York: Donald I. Fine.

Douglass, Frederick. 1973. *Narrative of the Life of Frederick Douglass*. New York: Oxford University Press (Orig. pub. 1845).

Fitzgerald, F. Scott. 1925. *The Great Gatsby*. New York: Scribner.

Foucault, Michel. 1990. *The History of Sexuality: An Introduction*, vol. I. New York: Vintage Books.

Freud, Sigmund. 1963. *Dora: An Analysis of a Case of Hysteria*. New York: Macmillan.

Gates, Henry Louis. 1985. "Introduction: The Language of Slavery," in Charles T. Davis and Henry Louis Gates (eds.), *The Slave's Narrative*: pp. xi–xxxiv. New York: Oxford University Press.

———. 1996. "White Like Me," *New Yorker*, June 17: 66–81.

Goffman, Erving. 1959. *Presentation of Self in Everyday Life*. Garden City, NY: Doubleday.

———. 1962. *Asylums: Essays on the Social Situation of Mental Patients and Other Inmates*. Chicago, IL: Aldine.

———. 1963. *Stigma: Notes on the Management of Spoiled Identity*. Englewood Cliffs, NJ: Prentice Hall.

———. 1969. *Strategic Interaction*. Philadelphia, PA: University of Pennsylvania Press.

Hacking, Ian. 2004. "Between Michel Foucault and Erving Goffman: Between Discourse in the Abstract and Face-to-Face Interaction," *Economy and Society* 33: 277–302.

Hayner, Priscilla B. 2000. *Unspeakable Truths: Confronting State Terror and Atrocities*. New York: Routledge.

Hepworth, Mike, and Bryan S. Turner. 1982. *Confession: Studies in Deviance and Religion*. London: Routledge & Kegan Paul.

Herbermann, Charles G., Edward A. Pace, Conde B. Pallen, Thomas J. Shahan, and John J. Wynne (eds.). 1913. *Catholic Encyclopedia*, vol. 4. New York: Encyclopedia Press.

Horowitz, Daniel. 2000. *Betty Friedan and the Making of "The Feminine Mystique": The American Left, the Cold War, and Modern Feminism*. Amherst, MA: University of Massachusetts Press.

Illouz, Eva. 2008. *Saving the Modern Soul: Therapy, Emotions, and the Culture of Self-Help*. Berkeley, CA: University of California Press.

Irvine, Leslie. 1999. *Codependent Forevermore: The Invention of Self in a Twelve Step Group*. Chicago, IL: University of Chicago Press.

Jacobs, Harriet. 1973. *Incidents in the Life of a Slave Girl*. New York: Harcourt Brace Jovanovich (Orig. pub. 1861).

Kasson, John F. 1990. *Rudeness & Civility: Manners in Nineteenth Century Urban America*. New York: Hill and Wang.

Kipnis, Laura. 2010. *How to Become a Scandal: Adventures in Bad Behavior*. New York: Metropolitan Books.

Lamont, Michele, Jason Kaufman, and Michael Moody. 2000. "The Best of the Brightest: Definitions of the Ideal Self among Prize-Winning Students," *Sociological Forum* 15: 187–224.

Malcolm X. 1964. *The Autobiography of Malcolm X*. New York: Ballantine Books.

Marcus, Steven. 1984. "Freud and Dora: Story, History, Case History," in Steven Marcus (ed.), *Freud and the Culture of Psychoanalysis*. New York: Norton.

McDonald, Mark. 2012. "The Tortuous Path to Justice in Cambodia," *International Herald Tribune*, March 27.

Melville, Herman. 2008. *The Confidence Man: His Masquerade*. New York: Oxford University Press (Orig. pub. 1857).

Moorti, Sujata. 1998. "Cathartic Confessions or Emancipatory Texts? Rape Narratives on the Oprah Winfrey Show," *Social Text* 57: 83–102.

Nagy, Rosemary. 2002. "Reconciliation in Post-Commission South Africa: Thick and Thin Accounts of Solidarity," *Canadian Journal of Political Science / Revue Canadienne de Science Politique* 35: 323–346.

Obama, Barack. 1995. *Dreams from My Father: A Story of Race and Inheritance*. New York: Times Books.

Olney, James. 1985. "'I Was Born': Slave Narratives, their Status as Autobiography and Literature," in Charles T. Davis and Henry Louis Gates (eds.), *The Slave's Narrative*: pp. 148–174. New York: Oxford University Press.

Plummer, Ken. 1995. *Telling Sexual Stories: Power, Change and Social Worlds*. London: Routledge.

Polkinghorne, Donald. 1988. *Narrative Knowing and the Human Sciences*. Albany, NY: State University of New York Press.

Polletta, Francesca. 2002. "Plotting Protest: Mobilizing Stories in the 1960s Student Sit-Ins," in Joseph E. Davis (ed.), *Stories of Change: Narrative and Social Movements*: pp. 31–52. Albany: State University of New York Press.

Ramas, Maria. 1980. "Freud's Dora, Dora's Hysteria," *Feminist Studies* 6: 472–510.

Rieff, Phillip. 1966. *The Triumph of the Therapeutic: The Uses of faith After Freud*. New York: Harper & Row.

Schwartz, Barry. 2003. *Abraham Lincoln and the Forge of National Memory*. Chicago, IL: University of Chicago Press, 2003.

Scott, Marvin B., and Stanford M. Lyman. 1968. "Accounts," *American Sociological Review* 33: 46–62.

Showalter, Elaine. 2001. *Inventing Herself: Claiming a Feminist Intellectual Heritage*. New York: Scribner.

Stein, Arlene. 1997. *Sex and Sensibility: Stories of a Lesbian Generation*. Berkeley, CA: University of California Press.

———. 2011. "The Forum: Therapeutic Politics—An Oxymoron?" *Sociological Forum* 26(1): 187–193.

Stepto, Robert Burns. 1985. "I Rose and Found My Voice: Narration, Authentication, and Authorial Control in Four Slave Narratives," in Charles T. Davis and Henry Louis Gates (eds.), *The Slave's Narrative*: pp. 225–241. New York: Oxford University Press.

Tavuchis, Nicholas. 1991. *Mea Culpa: A Sociology of Apology and Reconciliation.* Stanford, CA: Stanford University Press.

Trilling, Lionel. 1972. *Sincerity and Authenticity.* Cambridge, MA: Harvard University Press.

U.S. Conference of Catholic Bishops. 2006. *United States Catholic Catechism for Adults.* Washington, DC: USCC Publishing Services.

Vinitzky-Seroussi, Vered. 1998. *After Pomp and Circumstances: High School Reunions as an Autobiographical Occasion.* Chicago, IL: University of Chicago Press.

———. 2002. "Commemorating a Difficult Past: Yitzhak Rabin's Memorial," *American Sociological Review* 67: 30–52.

Wagner-Pacifici, Robin, and Barry Schwartz. 1991. "The Vietnam Veterans Memorial: Commemorating a Difficult Past," *American Journal of Sociology* 97: 376–420.

White, Hayden. 1981. "The Value of Narrativity in the Representation of Reality," in W. J. T. Mitchell (ed.), *On Narrative*: pp. 1–23. Chicago, IL: University of Chicago Press.

Woolf, Virginia. 1929. *A Room of One's Own.* New York: Harcourt, Brace and Co.

Zussman, Robert. 1996. "Autobiographical Occasions," *Contemporary Sociology* 25: 143–148.

———. 2000. "Autobiographical Occasions: Introduction to the Special Issue," *Qualitative Sociology* 23: 5–8.

———. 2006. "Picturing the Self: My Mother's Photograph Album," *CONTEXTS* 5: 28–34.

11

SITUATED ACTIONS AND VOCABULARIES OF MOTIVE

C. Wright Mills

The major reorientation of recent theory and observation in sociology of language emerged with the overthrow of the Wundtian notion that language has as its function the "expression" of prior elements within the individual. The postulate underlying modern study of language is the simple one that we must approach linguistic behavior, not by referring it to private states in individuals, but by observing its social function of coordinating diverse actions. Rather than expressing something which is prior and in the person, language is taken by other persons as an indicator of future actions.[1]

Within this perspective there are suggestions concerning problems of motivation. It is the purpose of this paper to outline an analytic model for the explanation of motives which is based on a sociological theory of language and a sociological psychology.[2]

As over against the inferential conception of motives as subjective "springs" of action, motives may be considered as typical vocabularies having ascertainable functions in delimited societal situations. Human actors do vocalize and impute motives to themselves and to others. To explain behavior by referring it to an inferred and abstract "motive" is one thing. To analyze the observable lingual mechanisms of motive imputation and avowal as they function in conduct is quite another. Rather than fixed elements "in" an individual, motives are the terms with which interpretation of conduct *by social actors* proceeds. This imputation and

C. Wright Mills, "Situated Actions and Vocabularies of Motive." *American Sociological Review* Vol. 5, No. 6 (Dec., 1940), pp. 904–13.

avowal of motives by actors are social phenomena to be explained. The differing reasons men give for their actions are not themselves without reasons.

First, we must demarcate the general conditions under which such motive imputation and avowal seem to occur.[3] Next, we must give a characterization of motive in denotable terms and an explanatory paradigm of why certain motives are verbalized rather than others. Then, we must indicate mechanisms of the linkage of vocabularies of motive to systems of action. What we want is an analysis of the integrating, controlling, and specifying function a certain type of speech fulfils in socially situated actions.

The generic situation in which imputation and avowal of motives arise, involves, first, the *social* conduct or the (stated) programs of languaged creatures, i.e., programs and actions oriented with reference to the actions and talk of others; second, the avowal and imputation of motives is concomitant with the speech form known as the "question." Situations back of questions typically involve *alternative* or *unexpected* programs or actions which phases analytically denote "crises."[4] The question is distinguished in that it usually elicits another *verbal* action, not a motor response. The question is an element in *conversation.* Conversation may be concerned with the factual features of a situation as they are seen or believed to be or it may seek to integrate and promote a set of diverse social actions with reference to the situation and its normative pattern of expectations. It is in this latter assent and dissent phase of conversation that persuasive and dissuasive speech and vocabulary arise. For men live in immediate acts of experience and their attentions are directed outside themselves until acts are in some way frustrated. It is then that awareness of self and of motive occur. The "question" is a lingual index of such conditions. The avowal and imputation of motives are features of such conversations as arise in "question" situations.

Motives are imputed or avowed as answers to questions interrupting acts or programs. Motives are words. Generically, to what do they refer? They do not denote any elements "in" individuals. They stand for anticipated situational consequences of questioned conduct. Intention or purpose (stated as a "program") *is* awareness of anticipated consequence; motives are names for consequential situations, and surrogates for actions leading to them. Behind questions are possible alternative actions with their terminal consequences. "Our introspective words for motives are rough, shorthand descriptions for certain typical patterns of discrepant and conflicting stimuli."[5]

The model of purposive conduct associated with Dewey's name may briefly be stated. Individuals confronted with "alternative acts" perform one or the other of them on the basis of the differential consequences which they anticipate. This nakedly utilitarian schema is inadequate because: (a) the "alternative acts" of *social* conduct "appear" most often in lingual form, as a question, stated by one's self or by another; (b) it is more adequate to say that individuals act in terms of anticipation of *named* consequences.

Among such names and in some technologically oriented lines of action there may appear such terms as "useful," "practical," "serviceable," etc., terms so "ultimate" to the pragmatists, and also to certain sectors of the American population in these delimited situations. However, there are other areas of population with different vocabularies of motives. The choice of lines of action is accompanied by representations, and selection among them, of their situational termini. Men discern situations with particular vocabularies, and it is in terms of some delimited vocabulary that they anticipate consequences of conduct.[6] Stable vocabularies of motives link anticipated consequences and specific actions. There is no need to invoke "psychological" terms like "desire" or "wish" as explanatory, since they themselves must be explained socially.[7] Anticipation is a subvocal or overt naming of terminal phases and/or social consequences of conduct. When an individual names consequences, he elicits the behaviors for which the name is a redintegrative cue. In a *societal* situation, implicit in the names for consequences is the social dimension of motives. Through such vocabularies, types of societal controls operate. Also, the terms in which the question is asked often will contain both alternatives: "Love or Duty?", "Business or Pleasure?" Institutionally different situations have different *vocabularies of motive* appropriate to their respective behaviors.

This sociological conception of motives as relatively stable lingual phases of delimited situations is quite consistent with Mead's program to approach conduct socially and from the outside. It keeps clearly in mind that "both motives and actions very often originate not from within but from the situation in which individuals find themselves. . . ."[8] It translates the question of "why"[9] into a "how" that is answerable in terms of a situation and its typal vocabulary of motives, i.e., those which conventionally accompany that type situation and function as cues and justifications for normative actions in it.

It has been indicated that the question is usually an index to the avowal and imputation of motives. Max Weber defines motive as a complex of meaning, which appears to the actor himself or to the observer to be an adequate ground for his conduct.[10] The aspect of motive which this conception grasps is its intrinsically social character. A satisfactory or adequate motive is one that satisfies the questioners of an act or program, whether it be the other's or the actor's. As a word, *a motive tends to be one which is to the actor and to the other members of a situation an unquestioned answer to questions concerning social and lingual conduct.* A stable motive is an ultimate in justificatory conversation. The words which in a type situation will fulfil this function are circumscribed by the vocabulary of motives acceptable for such situations. Motives are accepted justifications for present, future, or past programs or acts.

To term them justification is *not* to deny their efficacy. Often anticipations of acceptable justifications will control conduct. ("If I did this, what could I say? What would they say?") Decisions may be, wholly or in part, delimited by answers to such queries.

A man may begin an act for one motive. In the course of it, he may adopt an ancillary motive. This does not mean that the second apologetic motive is inefficacious. The vocalized expectation of an act, its "reason," is not only a mediating condition of the act but it is a proximate and controlling condition for which the term "cause" is not inappropriate. It may strengthen the act of the actor. It may win new allies for his act.

When they appeal to others involved in one's act, motives are strategies of action. In many social actions, others must agree, tacitly or explicitly. Thus, acts often will be abandoned if no reason can be found that others will accept. Diplomacy in choice of motive often controls the diplomat. Diplomatic choice of motive is part of the attempt to motivate acts for other members in a situation. Such pronounced motives undo snarls and integrate social actions. Such diplomacy does not necessarily imply intentional lies. It merely indicates that an appropriate vocabulary of motives will be utilized—that they are conditions for certain lines of conduct.[11]

When an agent vocalizes or imputes motives, he is not trying to *describe* his experienced social action. He is not merely stating "reasons." He is influencing others—and himself. Often he is finding new "reasons" which will mediate action. Thus, we need not treat an action as discrepant from "its" verbalization, for in many cases, the verbalization is a new act. In such cases, there is not a discrepancy between an act and "its" verbalization, but a difference between two disparate actions, motor-social and verbal.[12] This additional (or "*ex post facto*") lingualization may involve appeal to a vocabulary of motives associated with a norm with which both members of the situation are in agreement. As such, it is an integrative factor in *future* phases of the original social action or in other acts. By resolving conflicts, motives are efficacious. Often, if "reasons" were not given, an act would not occur, nor would diverse actions be integrated. Motives are common grounds for mediated behaviors.

Perry summarily states the Freudian view of motives "as the view that the real motives of conduct are those which we are ashamed to admit

either to ourselves or to others."[13] One can cover the facts by merely saying that scruples (i.e., *moral* vocabularies of motive) are often efficacious
and that men will alter and deter their acts in terms of such motives. One
of the components of a "generalized other," as a mechanism of societal
control, is vocabularies of acceptable motives. For example, a business
man joins the Rotary Club and proclaims its public-spirited vocabulary.[14]
If this man cannot act out business conduct without so doing, it follows
that this vocabulary of motives is an important factor in his behavior.[15]
The long acting out of a role, with its appropriate motives, will often induce a man to become what at first he merely sought to appear. Shifts in
the vocabularies of motive that are utilized later by an individual disclose
an important aspect of various integrations of his actions with concomi-
tantly various groups.

The motives actually used in justifying or criticizing an act definitely
link it to situations, integrate one man's action with another's, and line
up conduct with norms. The societally sustained motive-surrogates of
situations are both constraints and inducements. It is a hypothesis worthy and capable of test that typal vocabularies of motives for different
situations are significant determinants of conduct. As lingual segments of
social action, motives orient actions by enabling discrimination between
their objects. Adjectives such as "good," "pleasant," and "bad" promote
action or deter it. When they constitute components of a vocabulary of
motives, i.e., are typical and relatively unquestioned accompaniments of
typal situations, such words often function as directives and incentives
by virtue of their being the judgments of others as anticipated by the
actor. In this sense motives are "social instruments, i.e., data by modifying which the agent will be able to influence [himself or others]."[16] The
"control" of others is not usually direct but rather through manipulation
of a field of objects. We influence a man by naming his acts or imputing
motives to them—or to "him." The motives accompanying institutions
of war, e.g., are not "the causes" of war, but they do promote continued
integrated participation, and they vary from one war to the next. Working vocabularies of motive have careers that are woven through changing
institutional fabrics.

Genetically, motives are imputed by others before they are avowed by
self. The mother controls the child: "Do not do that, it is greedy." Not
only does the child learn what to do, what not to do, but he is given stan-
dardized motives which promote prescribed actions and dissuade those
proscribed. Along with rules and norms of action for various situations,
we learn vocabularies of motives appropriate to them. These are the motives we shall use, since they are a part of our language and components
of our behavior.

The quest for "real motives" supposititiously set over against "mere rationalization" is often informed by a metaphysical view that the "real" motives are in some way biological. Accompanying such quests for something more real and back of rationalization is the view held by many sociologists that language is an external manifestation or concomitant of something prior, more genuine, and "deep" in the individual. "Real attitudes" versus "mere verbalization" or "opinion" implies that at best we only infer from his language what "really" is the individual's attitude or motive.

Now what *could we possibly* so infer? Of precisely *what* is verbalization symptomatic? We cannot *infer* physiological processes from lingual phenomena. All we can infer and empirically check[17] is another verbalization of the agent's which we believe was orienting and controlling behavior at the time the act was performed. The only social items that can "lie deeper" are other lingual forms.[18] The "Real Attitude or Motive" is not something different in kind from the verbalization or the "opinion." They turn out to be only relatively and temporally different.

The phrase "unconscious motive" is also unfortunate. All it can mean is that a motive is not explicitly vocalized, but there is no need to infer unconscious motives from such situations and then posit them in individuals as elements. The phrase is informed by persistence of the unnecessary and unsubstantiated notion that "all action has a motive," and it is promoted by the observation of gaps in the relatively frequent verbalization in everyday situations. The facts to which this phrase is supposedly addressed are covered by the statements that men do not always explicitly articulate motives, and that *all* actions do not pivot around language. I have already indicated the conditions under which motives are typically avowed and imputed.

Within the perspective under consideration, the verbalized motive is not used as an index of something in the individual but *as a basis of inference for a typal vocabulary of motives of a situated action*. When we ask for the "real attitude" rather than the "opinion," for the "real motive" rather than the "rationalization," all we can meaningfully be asking for is the controlling speech form which was incipiently or overtly presented in the performed act or series of acts. There is no way to plumb behind verbalization into an individual and directly check our motive-mongering, but there is an empirical way in which we can guide and limit, in given historical situations, investigations of motives. That is by the construction of typal vocabularies of motives that are extant in types of situations and actions. Imputation of motives may be controlled by reference to the typical constellation of motives which are observed to be societally linked with classes of situated actions. Some of the "real" motives that have been imputed to actors were not even known to them. As I see it, motives are circumscribed by the vocabulary of the actor. The only source for a terminology of motives is the vocabularies of motives actually and usually verbalized by actors in specific situations.

Individualistic, sexual, hedonistic, and pecuniary vocabularies of motives are apparently now dominant in many sectors of twentieth-century urban America. Under such an ethos, verbalization of alternative conduct in these terms is least likely to be challenged among dominant groups. In this milieu, individuals are skeptical of Rockefeller's avowed religious motives for his business conduct because such motives are not *now* terms of the vocabulary conventionally and prominently accompanying situations of business enterprise. A medieval monk writes that he gave food to a poor but pretty woman because it was "for the glory of God and the eternal salvation of his soul." Why do we tend to question him and impute sexual motives? Because sex is an influential and widespread motive in our society and time. Religious vocabularies of explanation and of motives are now on the wane. In a society in which religious motives have been debunked on rather wide scale, certain thinkers are skeptical of those who ubiquitously proclaim them. Religious motives have lapsed from selected portions of modern populations and other motives have become "ultimate" and operative. But from the monasteries of medieval Europe we have no evidence that religious vocabularies were not operative in many situations.

A labor leader says he performs a certain act because he wants to get higher standards of living for the workers. A business man says that this is rationalization, or a lie; that it is really because he wants more money for himself from the workers. A radical says a college professor will not engage in radical movements because he is afraid for his job, and besides, is a "reactionary." The college professor says it is because he just likes to find out how things work. What is reason for one man is rationalization for another. The variable is the accepted vocabulary of motives, the ultimates of discourse, of each man's dominant group about whose opinion he cares. *Determination of such groups, their location and character, would enable delimitation and methodological control of assignment of motives for specific acts.*

Stress on this idea will lead us to investigations of the compartmentalization of operative motives in personalities according to situation and the general types and conditions of vocabularies of motives in various types of societies. The motivational structures of individuals and the patterns of their purposes are relative to societal frames. We might, e.g., study motives along stratified or occupational lines. Max Weber has observed:

> . . . that in a free society the motives which induce people to
> work vary with . . . different social classes. . . . There is normally
> a graduated scale of motives by which men from different social
> classes are driven to work. When a man changes ranks, he switches
> from one set of motives to another.[19]

The lingual ties which hold them together react on persons to constitute frameworks of disposition and motive. Recently, Talcott Parsons has indicated, by reference to differences in actions in the professions and in business, that one cannot leap from "economic analysis to ultimate motivations; the institutional patterns *always* constitute one crucial element of the problem."[20] It is my suggestion that we may analyze, index, and gauge this element by focusing upon those specific verbal appendages of variant institutionalized actions which have been referred to as vocabularies of motive.

In folk societies, the constellations of motives connected with various sectors of behavior would tend to be typically stable and remain associated only with their sector. In typically primary, sacred, and rural societies, the motives of persons would be regularly compartmentalized. Vocabularies of motives ordered to different situations stabilize and guide behavior and expectation of the reactions of others. In their appropriate situations, verbalized motives are not typically questioned.[21] In secondary, secular, and urban structures, varying and competing vocabularies of motives operate coterminously and the situations to which they are appropriate are not clearly demarcated. Motives once unquestioned for defined situations are now questioned. Various motives can release similar acts in a given situation. Hence, variously situated persons are confused and guess which motive "activated" the person. Such questioning has resulted intellectually in such movements as psychoanalysis with its dogma of rationalization and its systematic motive-mongering. Such intellectual phenomena are underlaid by split and conflicting sections of an individuated society which is characterized by the existence of competing vocabularies of motive. Intricate constellations of motives, for example, are components of business enterprise in America. Such patterns have encroached on the old style vocabulary of the virtuous relation of men and women: duty, love, kindness. Among certain classes, the romantic, virtuous, and pecuniary motives are confused. The asking of the question: "Marriage for love or money?" is significant, for the pecuniary is now a constant and almost ubiquitous motive, a common denominator of many others.[22]

Back of "mixed motives" and "motivational conflicts" are competing or discrepant situational patterns and their respective vocabularies of motive. With shifting and interstitial situations, each of several alternatives may belong to disparate systems of action which have differing vocabularies of motives appropriate to them. Such conflicts manifest vocabulary patterns that have overlapped in a marginal individual and are not easily compartmentalized in clear-cut situations.

Besides giving promise of explaining an area of lingual and societal fact, a further advantage of this view of motives is that with it we should be able to give sociological accounts of other theories (terminologies) of motivation. This is a task for sociology of knowledge. Here I can refer only to a few theories. I have already referred to the Freudian terminology of motives. It is apparent that these motives are those of an upper bourgeois patriarchal group with strong sexual and individualistic orientation. When introspecting on the couches of Freud, patients used the only vocabulary of motives they knew; Freud got his hunch and guided further talk. Mittenzwey has dealt with similar points at length.[23] Widely diffused in a postwar epoch, psychoanalysis was never popular in France where control of sexual behavior is not puritanical.[24] To converted individuals who have become accustomed to the psychoanalytic terminology of motives, all others seem self-deceptive.[25]

In like manner, to many believers in Marxism's terminology of power, struggle, and economic motives, all others, including Freud's, are due to hypocrisy or ignorance. An individual who has assimilated thoroughly only business congeries of motives will attempt to apply these motives to all situations, home and wife included. It should be noted that the business terminology of motives has its intellectual articulation, even as psychoanalysis and Marxism have.

It is significant that since the Socratic period many "theories of motivation" have been linked with ethical and religious terminologies. Motive is that in man which leads him to do good or evil. Under the aegis of religious institutions, men use vocabularies of moral motives: they call acts and programs "good" and "bad," and impute these qualities to the soul. Such lingual behavior is part of the process of social control. Institutional practices and their vocabularies of motive exercise control over delimited ranges of possible situations. One could make a typal catalog of religious motives from widely read religious texts, and test its explanatory power in various denominations and sects.[26]

In many situations of contemporary America, conduct is controlled and integrated by *hedonistic* language. For large population sectors in certain situations, pleasure and pain are now unquestioned motives. For given periods and societies, these situations should be empirically determined. Pleasure and pain should not be reified and imputed to human nature as underlying principles of all action. Note that hedonism as a psychological and an ethical doctrine gained impetus in the modern world at about the time when older moral-religious motives were being debunked and simply discarded by "middle class" thinkers. Back of the hedonistic terminology lay an emergent social pattern and a new vocabulary of motives. The shift of unchallenged motives which gripped the communities of Europe was climaxed when, in reconciliation, the older religious and the hedonistic terminologies were identified: the "good" is the "pleasant." The conditioning situation was similar in the Hellenistic world with the hedonism of the Cyrenaics and Epicureans.

What is needed is to take all these *terminologies* of motive and locate them as *vocabularies* of motive in historic epochs and specified situations. Motives are of no value apart from the delimited societal situations for which they are the appropriate vocabularies. They must be situated. At best, socially unlocated *terminologies* of motives represent unfinished attempts to block out social areas of motive imputation and avowal. Motives vary in content and character with historical epochs and societal structures.

Rather than interpreting actions and language as external manifestations of subjective and deeper lying elements in individuals, the research task is the locating of particular types of action within typal frames of normative actions and socially situated clusters of motive. There is no explanatory value in subsuming various vocabularies of motives under some terminology or list. Such procedure merely confuses the task of explaining specific cases. The languages of situations as given must be considered a valuable portion of the data to be interpreted and related to their conditions. To simplify these vocabularies of motive into a socially abstracted terminology is to destroy the legitimate use of motive in the explanation of social actions.

Notes

Revision of a paper read to The Society for Social Research, University of Chicago, August 16–17, 1940.

1. See C. Wright Mills, "Bibliographical Appendices," Section I, 4: "Sociology of Language" In *Contemporary Social Theory,* Ed. by Barnes, Becker & Becker, New York, 1940.

2. See G. H. Mead, "Social Psychology as Counterpart of Physiological Psychology," *Psychol. Bul.*, VI: 401–8, 1909; Karl Mannheim, *Man and Society in an Age of Reconstruction*, New York, 1940; L. V. Wiese-Howard Becker, *Systematic Sociology*, part I, New York, 1932; J. Dewey, "All psychology is either biological or social psychology," *Psychol. Rev.*, vol. 24: 276.

3. The importance of this initial task for research is clear. Most researches on the verbal level merely ask abstract questions of individuals, but if we can tentatively delimit the situations in which certain motives *may* be verbalized, we can use that delimitation in the construction of *situational* questions, and we shall be *testing* deductions from our theory.

4. On the "question" and "conversation," see G. A. DeLaguna, *Speech: Its Function and Development*, 37 (and index), New Haven, 1927. For motives in crises, see J. M. Williams, *The Foundations of Social Science*, 435 ff, New York, 1920.

5. K. Burke, *Permanence and Change*, 45, New York, 1936. I am indebted to this book for several leads which are systematized into the present statement.

6. See such experiments as C. N. Rexroad's "Verbalization in Multiple Choice Reactions," Psychol. Rev., Vol. 33: 458, 1926.

7. Cf. J. Dewey, "Theory of Valuation," *Int. Ency. of Unified Science*, New York, 1939.

8. K. Mannheim, *Man and Society*, 249, London, 1940.

9. Conventionally answerable by reference to "subjective factors" within individuals. R. M. MacIver, "The Modes of the Question Why," *J. of Soc. Phil.*, April 1940. Cf. also his "The Imputation of Motives," *Amer. J. Sociol.*, July 1940.

10. *Wirtschaft und Gesellschaft*, 5, Tubingen, 1922, "'Motiv' heisst ein Sinnzusammenhang, Welcher dem Handelnden selbst oder dem Beobachtenden als sinnhafter 'Grund' eines Verhaltens in dem Grade heissen, als die Beziehung seiner Bestandteile von uns nach den durchschnittlichen Denk- und Gefühlsgewohnheiten als typischer (wir pflegen in sagen: 'richtiger') Sinzusammenhang bejaht Wird."

11. Of course, since motives are communicated, they may be lies; but, this must be proved. Verbalizations are not lies merely because they are socially efficacious. I am here concerned more with the social function of pronounced motives, than with the sincerity of those pronouncing them.

12. See F. Znaniecki, *Social Actions*, 30, New York, 1936.

13. *General Theory of Value*, 292–293, New York, 1936.

14. *Ibid.*, 392.

15. The "profits motive" of classical economics may be treated as an ideal-typical vocabulary of motives for delimited economic situations and behaviors. For late phases of monopolistic and regulated capitalism, this type requires modification; the profit and commercial vocabularies have acquired other ingredients. See N. R. Danielian's *AT&T*, New York, 1940, for a suggestive account of the *noneconomic* behavior and motives of business bureaucrats.

16. *Social Actions*, 73.

17. Of course, we could infer or interpret constructs posited in the individual, but these are not easily checked and they are not explanatory.

18. Which is not to say that, physiologically, there may not be cramps in the stomach wall or adrenalin in the blood, etc., but the character of the "relation" of such items to social action is quite moot.

19. Paraphrased by K. Mannheim, *op. cit.*, 316–317.

20. "The Motivation of Economic Activities," 67, in C. W. M. Hart, *Essays in Sociology*, Toronto, 1940.

21. Among the ethnologists, Ruth Benedict has come up to the edge of a genuinely sociological view of motivation. Her view remains vague because she has not seen clearly the identity of differing "motivations" in differing cultures with the varied extant and approved vocabularies of motive. "The intelligent understanding of the relation of the individual to his society . . . involves always the understanding of the types of human motivations and capacities capitalized in his society . . ." "Configurations of Culture in North America," *Amer. Anthrop.*, 25, Jan.–Mar. 1932; see also: *Patterns of Culture*, 242–243, Boston, 1935. She turns this

observation into a quest for the unique "genius" of each culture and stops her research by words like "Apollonian." If she would attempt constructively to observe the vocabularies of motives which precipitate acts to perform, implement programs, and furnish approved motives for them in circumscribed situations, she would be better able to state precise problems and to answer them by further observation.

22. Also motives acceptably imputed and avowed for one system of action may be diffused into other domains and gradually come to be accepted by some as a comprehensive portrait of *the* motive of men. This happened in the case of the economic man and his motives.

23. Kuno Mittenzwey, "Zur Sociologie der psychoanalystischer Erkenntnis," in Max Scheler, ed. *Versuche zu einer Sociologie des Wissens*, 365–375, Munich, 1924.

24. This fact is interpreted by some as supporting Freudian theories. Nevertheless, it can be just as adequately grasped in the scheme here outlined.

25. See K. Burke's acute discussion of Freud, *op. cit.*, Part I.

26. Moral vocabularies deserve a special statement. Within the viewpoint herein outlined many snarls concerning "value-judgments," etc., can be cleared up.

Part II
Sociological Narrative Forms

This section differs from the other parts of this book in two ways. First, the readings included here do not address narratives as objects of analysis but are themselves narratives. They use stories, broadly understood, to make arguments, albeit arguments of very different sorts. Second, these narratives are the work of sociologists. Whereas in preceding sections the readings acknowledge that "narrative analysis crosses several borders" (Gubrium and Holstein 2009: vii), this particular section is not interdisciplinary. The use of narrative by novelists and historians should surprise no one. Its use by sociologists is more surprising. This section calls attention to how sociologists deploy narrative, both as a particular way of presenting sociological knowledge and as a way to structure text. Thus, the readings constitute what we call *sociological narrative forms*.

A dedicated section on sociological narrative forms implies that these forms are uncommon. Indeed, as a glance through *American Sociological Review*, *American Journal of Sociology*, and other top-ranked journals reveals, narrative forms appear infrequently. Their scarcity, at least in the major journals, suggests that narrative forms are less highly valued within the discipline compared to other forms of writing (Reed 1989; Richardson 1990). To some degree, this reflects the division of sociological labor into quantitative and qualitative research, with narrative forms more commonly used in the latter. The scarcity of narrative forms stems from sociology's longstanding effort to legitimize itself as a science. After all, science (purportedly) does not tell stories; it uses Bruner's (1986) paradigmatic mode of thinking, which draws conclusions and reports results.

Attempts to imitate science have led many sociologists to write lengthy and impenetrable treatises. The form of writing that results from this effort has long come under criticism. For example, in *The Sociological Imagination*, C. Wright Mills (1959) famously condensed two pages of writing by Talcott Parsons into one neat paragraph, without losing the point. By contrast, sociological narrative forms emphasize that "sociological work is communicative work" (Maines 1993: 32). Indeed, because the story is such a common form, it is more readily understood by many different kinds of audiences than a scientific report might be.

The attempt to imitate science also silences the voice of the author. The "facts" allegedly speak for themselves. As Kathy Charmaz and Richard Mitchell explain, "Scholarly writers have long been admonished to work silently on the sidelines, to keep their voices out of the reports they produce, to emulate Victorian children: be seen (in the credits) not heard (in the text)" (1996: 285). By contrast, feminist scholars have called for transparency about the role of sociologists in doing fieldwork and conducting interviews, asking that they write about the ways their positioning influences the people and communities they study. As Mary Jo Maynes, Jennifer L. Pierce, and Barbara Laslett argue, personal narrative analyses can be enriched when these kinds of relationships and their effects are openly discussed in the text, rather than ignored or suppressed (2008: 102).

The selections we have included here work in two main ways. Diane Vaughan and Jerome Karabel's excerpts are exemplars of what might be called organizational narratives. Although both speak to larger issues (the collective management of mistakes in Vaughan, the maintenance of inequality in Karabel) they do so by looking at particular cases. Both are epic books—the sociological equivalents of *War and Peace* or *Lord of the Rings*—where the accumulation of massive detail, a type of thick description organized around a sequence of events, is critical to understanding intentions (in Karabel's case) or a failure to act (Vaughan's case). Both books also aspire to explanation. Vaughn's account of the *Challenger* launch shows how each event follows a previous event, each decision follows a previous decision, in a series of complex contingencies resulting eventually (but not inevitably) in a tragic failure. In other cases, narrative serves as an organizing trope to stress the intentionality of social change. In a brief but critical excerpt from his history of ethnically exclusive admission policies at elite universities, Karabel shows how Harvard president A. Lawrence Lowell's altogether self-conscious effort to limit the number of Jewish students was the source of what we now think of as standard admission policies.

The selections from Teresa Gowan and Alice Goffman work differently. Both show people caught up in structures well beyond their control. But where Karabel and Vaughan attempt to explain particular events, Gowan and Goffman use stories to illustrate processes that drive men and women in situations familiar and unfamiliar. Here the argument proceeds by a kind of social logic rather than by sampling, saying, in effect, that anyone caught in the same structures would act the same way. Gowan and Goffman put self-conscious actors at the center of their analysis even more clearly than Karabel and Vaughan do. They do so not to stress their freedoms so much as to exemplify the limited choices available even to more or less rational actors. For instance, Gowan's excerpt from *Hobos, Hustlers, and Backsliders* shows how one man slid from marginal employment working and living in a single-room occupancy hotel to an even more marginal life in jail and in a shelter, making do on the little income he could generate searching for glass and plastic to recycle. The excerpt from the opening pages of Goffman's widely read *On the Run*, a study of how the fear of arrest shapes the lives of young Black men, shows how "Alex," on parole, refused to go to a hospital for fear of discovery, after *he* had been robbed and badly beaten.

Despite their absence from prominent journals, instances of both forms of narrative sociology abound, primarily in books, which provide the space for extended stories. Explanatory narratives, like those of Karabel and Vaughan, are particularly prominent in the study of social movements (McAdam 1988; Morris 1984; Ganz 2009; Hochschild 2016). Illustrative narratives, like those of Gowan and Goffman, are found even more widely, prominent in classic studies of group dynamics (Whyte 1943), deviance (Venkatesh 2008), family (Stacey 1998; Gamson 2015), and medicine.

References

Bruner, Jerome. 1986. *Actual Minds, Possible Worlds*. Cambridge MA: Harvard University Press.

Charmaz, Kathy, and Richard G. Mitchell. 1996. "The Myth of Silent Authorship: Self, Substance, and Style in Ethnographic Writing." *Symbolic Interaction* 19(4): 285–302.

Gamson, Joshua. 2015. *Modern Families: Stories of Extraordinary Journeys to Kinship*. New York: New York University Press.

Ganz, Marshall. 2009. *Why David Sometimes Wins: Leadership, Organization and Strategy in the California Farm Worker Movement*. New York: Oxford.

Gubrium, Jaber F., and James A. Holstein. 2009. *Analyzing Narrative Reality*. Thousand Oaks CA: SAGE Publications.

Hochschild, Arlie Russell. 2016. *Strangers in Their Own Land. Anger and Mourning on the American Right*. New York: The New Press.

McAdam, Doug. 1988. *Freedom Summer*. New York: Oxford University Press.

Mills, C. Wright. 1959. *The Sociological Imagination*. New York: Oxford University Press.

Morris, Aldon. 1984. *The Origin of the Civil Rights Movement: Black Communities Organizing for Change*. New York: Free Press.

Reed, John Shelton. 1989. "On Narrative and Sociology." *Social Forces* 68(1): 1–14.

Richardson, Laurel. 1990. "Narrative and Sociology." *Journal of Contemporary Ethnography* 19(1): 116–35.

Stacey, Judith. 1998. *Brave New Families: Stories of Domestic Upheaval in Late–Twentieth Century America*. Berkeley: University of California Press.

Venkatesh, Sudhir. 2008. *Gang Leader for a Day: A Rogue Sociologist Takes to the Streets*. New York: Penguin.

Whyte, William Foote. 1943. *Street Corner Society: The Social Structure of an Italian Slum*. Chicago: University of Chicago Press.

12

THE NORMALIZATION OF DEVIANCE, 1981–1984

Diane Vaughan

For NASA, 1981–84 was an extraordinary time. The developmental period of the Space Shuttle Program gave way to the operational phase, thus apparently moving the space agency closer to the goal of a "space bus" that would routinely carry people and equipment back and forth to a yet-to-materialize space station. In glaring contrast to this public image, the engineers and technicians conducting risk assessments prior to each launch grappled with an uncertain technology that continuously produced anomalies—evidence that the shuttle was developmental, not operational. In this chapter, we trace the production of culture by the work group into the operational phase of the Shuttle Program. We examine the major turning points in the history of decision making to show (1) how the work group continued to normalize technical deviation as flight data accumulated and (2) the contrast between posttragedy interpretations of these events and the meanings these events had for insiders at the time. By immersing ourselves in work group routines, we see the incrementalism behind this historic event. We witness the gradual accrual of information, action, and definitions that shaped the work group's cultural construction of risk. We are reminded of how repetition, seemingly small choices, and the banality of daily decisions in organizational life—indeed, in most social life—can camouflage from the participants a cumulative directionality that too often is discernible only in hindsight.[1]

Dianne Vaughan, *The Challenger Launch Decision: Risky Technology, Culture, and Deviance at NASA*. (Chicago: University of Chicago Press, 1997). Excerpt reprinted with permission of the University of Chicago Press.

During these years, the work group continued to learn about the dynamics of their unique joint design. They were surprised by new signals of potential danger: among them, the first occurrence of "impingement erosion" on STS-2 and the first evidence of "blow-by" on STS 41-D. These incidents did not alter the work group's cultural construction of risk, however. To the contrary, their definition of the situation received repeated affirmation, becoming institutionalized in response to new signals of potential danger, the five-step decision-malting sequence was repeated. The work group calculated and tested to find the limits and capabilities of joint performance. Each time, evidence initially interpreted as a deviation from expected performance was reinterpreted as within the bounds of acceptable risk. By the end of 1984, the work group had, in a problem-driven, incremental fashion, developed a three-factor technical rationale consisting of a "safety margin," the "experience base," and the "self-limiting" aspects of joint dynamics that convinced them that impingement erosion and blow-by were within the bounds of acceptable performance. And in FRRs, the work group's official definition of the situation was conveyed up the hierarchy, creating at NASA a uniform cultural construction of risk for the booster joints.

As ethnographic history, this chapter necessarily reveals aspects of NASA decision rules that work group members took into account as they assessed risk. In so doing, it revises conventional posttragedy interpretations of controversial NASA actions: among them, continuing to fly with the existing design after the first—and extensive—occurrence of erosion on STS-2; publicly declaring the Space Shuttle "operational," despite an SRB joint that was not performing as expected; waiving the newly imposed C 1 status of the joint just before the flight of STS-6; and failing to report information about SRB joint performance to upper-level NASA administrators during FRR_3. As we relocate these controversial actions in the stream of actions of which they were a part, we see the native view: the meaning they had for participants when they occurred. Again we find the effects of cultural understandings on choice at NASA: actions that analysis defined as deviant after the disaster were acceptable and nondeviant within the NASA culture.

Erosion

The second developmental flight, STS-2, flew in November 1981. Thiokol always sent a team of four or five engineers and a photographer to Kennedy Space Center to inspect the boosters when they were returned from the sea. When Thiokol engineers disassembled the booster segments, they found the first in-flight O-ring anomaly. Thiokol's Jack Buchanan, permanently assigned to Kennedy Space Center as manager of Thiokol operations, was one of the first to see the damage: "At first we didn't know what we were looking at, so we got it to the lab. They were very surprised at what we had found."[2] Hot motor gases had eroded 0.053— of the primary O-ring in the right SRB's aft field joint.[3] Although erosion was a known phenomenon in the aerospace industry, neither Marshall nor Thiokol expected it because Titan tests showed none. Also, in Thiokol's static firings of four developmental motors and three qualifying motors and in the flight experience of STS-1, the rings had not eroded.

Thiokol engineers began reviewing the evidence. They discovered that "blowholes" in the zinc chromate putty that lined the space between the booster segments had caused the erosion. This putty, which after the disaster appeared to some to be a Band-Aid, on-the-cheap correction (e.g., when I talked about my research in progress to colleagues, invariably someone would comment derisively, "You mean they tried to patch it with putty?"), had two functions: (1) to protect the O-rings from direct exposure to the hot motor gases coming from the propellant at the center of the booster and (2) to act like a piston at ignition to compress the air in the joint and thus seal the primary O-ring.[4] Unknown to the engineers, however, tiny bubbles had formed in the putty when the booster segments were stacked. These bubbles left weak spots. At ignition, the hot propellant gases moved through these weak spots, -blowing holes in the putty and eating away, or "impinging" on, portions of the O-ring. Since erosion occurred on only one of the 16 O-rings on the two boosters, the cause appeared to be a deficiency in the putty in only that location. As Marshall S&E engineer Ben Powers explained, "the putty was creating a localized high temperature jet which was drilling a hole right into the O-ring."[5]

Once they had established cause, the Acceptable Risk Process required the work group to determine the "relative probability of the hazardous condition occurring." Despite 0.053— erosion, they found that the SRB field joint primary O-ring had sealed the gap created at ignition between the tang and the clevis. They calculated the "safety margin"—the maximum impingement erosion that could occur under an in-flight WOW condition—finding it was 0.090—.[6] Then they performed tests to find conditions under which the primary would both seal and fail. Cutting pieces out of a primary O-ring to simulate an erosion depth of 0.095—, they found it would still seal the joint under pressure of 3,000 psi—three times the amount the rings would experience at the peak of ignition pressure during a launch. They concluded that the joint was an acceptable risk because the STS-2 primary erosion was 0.053— —well within these parameters. This safety margin was an important precedent for future risk assessment: a numerical boundary was established defining the parameters of normal and/or deviant joint performance. It was the first of three in-house standards that would, by the end of 1984, constitute the full technical rationale that would be used repeatedly in assessing the risk of O-ring erosion.

Thiokol's Jack Kapp described the definition of the situation at the time:

> We didn't like that erosion, but we still had a couple of mitigating circumstances. First of all, it occurred very early on in firing, within a couple hundred milliseconds, and if the primary O-ring was burnt right through that early in the ignition sequence the secondary should be in a good position to catch it. In addition to that, we came home and we took our little extrusion test rig and we sliced off some rather significant amounts of the O-ring up to about 90,000ths and reran some extrusion tests. We found out that even with major portions of the O-ring missing, once it gets up into that gap in a sealing position it is perfectly capable of sealing at high pressures—2–3,000 psi.
>
>   So that gives us another little comfort zone in that, from the standpoint of O-ring material removal, what we were seeing was fairly minor compared to what would be critical for the O-ring. There was no question in our minds, as a matter of fact, and I want to state it again, that even if the primary O-ring failed to seal initially we felt that there was a high probability under those circumstances that the secondary would pick it up.[7]

The Acceptable Risk Process also required that the work group "implement hazard reduction": a corrective action that would reduce risk. Because the problem was defined as a "putty problem, not a joint rotation problem, the working engineers immediately began running tests on the putty composition and its ability to insulate the joint.[8] They altered the putty composition and the putty "lay-up"—the way it was applied to the booster segments—in order to eliminate the bubbles that formed when the segments were stacked. Thiokol engineer Howard McIntosh, stated that at the time impingement erosion was viewed as a "solvable problem."[9] Engineering analysis and tests would continue; redesign was not considered. Neither Marshall nor Thiokol working engineers viewed erosion as a constraint to flight. It had not occurred on STS-1. This was the only occurrence; they thought they correctly understood it and had taken necessary actions to control it. The construction of risk affected the procedural response: correct and fly.

This erosion was the most extensive prior to the fatal *Challenger* flight, but it was not discussed in FRRs for the next launch, STS-3, nor was it reported in the Marshall Problem Assessment System (MPAS), a computer system for tracking serious problems. After the *Challenger* tragedy, this reporting failure was interpreted as the first of many attempts by Level Marshall managers to keep bad news about the joint from top NASA officials. Indeed, the STS-2 erosion was not discussed in FRR until erosion occurred again nearly three years later. However, it was working engineers, not managers, who were responsible for the failure to report. Their inaction might appropriately be attributed to what Arthur Stinchcombe labeled "the liability of newness."[10] Although Stinchcombe had in mind difficulties that beset new organizations, new programs in existing organizations also face obstacles. Thiokol engineer Roger Boisjoly explained that the emphasis on the first four flights was on "R&D."[11] Consequently, so many physical instruments were on each flight to measure performance and feed the data into the system that the workload between flights was unusually heavy during the developmental period. Boisjoly remarked, "It was a major task just to turn around that data and assimilate it into the system."[12] The heavy instrumentation revealed many anomalies. These were important data, for they provided the first opportunity to compare engineering design predictions and test results with performance.

When Thiokol engineers spotted the STS-2 erosion immediately upon postflight disassembly at Kennedy, much analysis and discussion occurred between engineers; tests began. However, after analysis and putty corrections the engineers considered it a resolved problem. Marshall's Leon Ray said that the erosion discovery "generated quite a bit of excitement at the time," but it was not reported because only the generic problems—the things that could happen on the next flight—were mentioned in FRR.[13] Overwhelmed by the need to process and report the masses of data each developmental flight was producing, the engineers did not write up the erosion discovery and analysis for their Level IV FRR presentation for STS-3, and so it was not carried up the hierarchy.[14] The belief in redundancy was fundamental to their decision not to report. Marshall's George Hardy, then SRB Project Manager, explained: "On STS-2, we had no secondary erosion. Therefore, the joint performed as it was supposed to. The system was working exactly the way it was supposed to. You don't build in redundancy and never expect to use the back-up. If you never use your back-up, you're wasting money."[15]

Hardy made additional comments that support a "liability of newness" explanation. Procedures were also in a developmental phase. Not only was the work group doing baseline learning about how the technology operated during flight, but they were also trying out the rules for FRR

presentations for the first time. What should and should not be reported
in Level IV FRR may not have been clear to all the working engineers.[16]
They did record the incident, however. Catching up on its paperwork
much later, Thiokol completed a postflight report on STS-2 that, unlike
an FRR analysis, includes a complete rundown on all flight data.[17]

Accepting erosion was a major turning point in the work group's normalization of technical deviation. The engineers expanded the boundaries of
acceptable risk from test results that deviated from predictions to include
deviation from the in-flight performance expectation. The five-step decision sequence shows the pattern characterizing their interpretive work,
indicating the work group's production of culture.

Signals of potential danger. Postflight analysis of the SRB joints showed
that the primary ring on the aft field joint of the right SRJ had 0.053— of
its surface eroded by hot motor gases. The appearance of erosion deviated
from design expectations, creating uncertainty about the future performance of the joints.

Official act acknowledging escalated risk. The work group initiated no administrative action mandating special treatment when erosion first was
discovered. They were concerned, but erosion was not as remarkable to
the work group at the time as it was to outsiders after the *Challenger*
disaster. Although erosion bad not been predicted by the SRB design, de-
viations from design expectations are common during the developmental
phase of an innovative technology. The context mattered. At Marshall,
erosion was one of many flight anomalies that occurred on STS-2 and
required risk assessment.

Review of the evidence. Marshall and Thiokol working engineers examined
the aft field joint, measuring erosion and trying to pinpoint the cause
of the problem. They identified it as an idiosyncratic incident: a localized deficiency in the putty allowed hot gases to impinge on the primary
O-ring. Following guidelines of the Acceptable Risk Process, they calculated a safety margin that quantified the amount of erosion that could
occur without interfering with the ability of the primary O-ring to seal
the joint. Their analysis affirmed their belief in redundancy. The safety
margin was a yardstick against which the STS-2 erosion was measured
and assessed. They altered the putty and its lay-up in order to increase
the margin of safety, concluding that the design was an acceptable risk.

Official act indicating the normalization of deviance: accepting risk. In FRR for STS-3, the working engineers' analysis, conclusions, and recommendation that the SRBs were an acceptable risk were presented and discussed. The SRBs were certified as flight-ready at each review level. As a result of the "liability of newness," erosion was one of many resolved anomalies not included in engineers' FRR presentations. Contrary to the outsider interpretation that this was intentional managerial concealment of a highly dangerous situation, the engineers' failure to report reflected the prosaic meaning the problem held for them after their risk analysis.

Shuttle launch. STS-3 was launched in March 1982. Since no erosion occurred, the postflight analysis convinced the work group that the alterations to the putty had done the trick. It confirmed the belief that the SRB joint was an acceptable risk. The postflight analysis also affirmed the procedural responses to the problem: correcting the joint rather than redesigning it and flying despite data that the joint deviated from expected performance.

Notes

1. For a parallel, see also Diane Vaughan, *Uncoupling: Turning Points in Intimate Relations* (New York: Oxford University Press, 1986).
2. Jack Buchanan, interview transcript, 25 March 1986, Morton Thiokol, Inc., files, National Archives, Washington, D.C., pp. 34–37.
3. Presidential Commission on the Space Shuttle Challenger Accident. *Report to the President by the Presidential Commission on the Space Shuttle Challenger Accident* (Washington, D.C.: Government Printing Office, 1986), 1:125.
4. U.S. Congress, House, Committee on Science and Technology, *Investigation of the Challenger Accident: Hearings* (Washington, D.C.: Government Printing Office, 1986), 1:762.
5. Ben Powers, interview transcript, 12 March 1986, Marshall Space Flight Center files, National Archives, Washington, D.C., p. 42.
6. Presidential Commission, *Report 1*: 133.
7. Jack R. Kapp, interview transcript, 2 April 1986, Morton Thiokol, Inc., files, National Archives, Washington, D.C., pp. 44–48
8. Arnold R. Thompson, interview transcript, 4 April 1986, Morton Thiokol, Inc., files, National Archives, Washington, D.C., p. 28.
9. Howard McIntosh, interview transcript, 2 April 1986, Morton Thiokol, Inc., files, National Archives, Washington, D.C., p. 77.
10. Arthur L. Stinchcombe, "Social Structure and Organizations," in *Handbook of Organizations*, ed. James G. March (Chicago: Rand McNally, 1965).
11. Roger M. Boisjoly, telephone interview by author, 18 March 1993.
12. Ibid.
13. W. Leon Ray, telephone interview by author, 27 January 1993.
14. Boisjoly, telephone interview, 18 March 1993.

15. George B. Hardy, telephone interview by author, 7 April 1993.
16. Ibid.
17. Morton Thiokol, Inc., "Post-Flight Evaluation of STS-2 SRM Components," Report TRW-13 286, January 1983, National Archives, Washington, D.C.

13

HARVARD

The Quota Controversy and the Quest for Restriction

Jerome Karabel

As the nation moved to limit the number of Jewish immigrants, the Big Three confronted their own "Jewish problem." Harvard, just minutes away from the nation's fourth-largest concentration of Jews and long considered more open and democratic than Yale and Princeton, was particularly vulnerable to a "Jewish invasion."[1] By 1918, when the Association of New England Deans first discussed this issue, Harvard's freshman class was 20 percent Jewish. This was by far the highest proportion in the Big Three: three times the percentage at Yale, six times that at Princeton.[2]

A vice president of the Immigration Restriction League, President A. Lawrence Lowell was no friend of the Jews. But even had he been free of anti-Semitic sentiments, he would have had reason to worry about the consequences for Harvard of its growing Jewish presence on campus. For at a certain point, the arrival of the Jews would mean the departure of the sons of the Protestant upper and upper-middle classes whom Harvard most wished to enroll. Far more than an expression of cultural prejudice, Harvard's preference for these young men—which it shared with all the other leading private colleges—was quite rational from an organizational perspective. After all, who but the sons of the Protestant elite would provide the "paying customers," the gentlemanly atmosphere, and the future leaders in business and government—not to mention generous donors—on which Harvard's claims to preeminence ultimately rested?

For anyone who doubted the existence of a "tipping point" of Jewish enrollment beyond which the WASP elite would abandon a college, Columbia served as a sobering example. Located at the epicenter of European immigration, Columbia could hardly ignore New York's vast Jewish population, which dwarfed that of any other American city. As early as 1908, the headmaster of Horace Mann, a leading private school in New York, reported to Columbia's president Nicolas Murray Butler that the prevailing view among parents with children in private school was that "the University undergraduate body contains a prepondering element of students who have had few social advantages and that as a consequence, there is little opportunity of making friendships of permanent value among them. As a result, most of the parents sent their children out of the city for college."[3] One year later, a visitor to Princeton reported sentiment among the students that the Jews had already ruined Columbia.[4] And by the 1910s a college song offered a revealing glimpse into students' perceptions of Columbia:

> Oh, Harvard's run by millionaires,
> And Yale is run by booze,
> Cornell is run by farmers' sons,
> Columbia's run by Jews.
> So give a cheer for Baxter Street,
> Another one for Pell,
> And when the little sheenies die,
> Their souls will go to hell.[5]

By 1914, the "Jewish problem" was so great at Columbia that its dean, Frederick Keppel, openly acknowledged the widespread perception that the large number of immigrants had made it "socially uninviting to students who come from homes of refinement." While publicly insisting that "Columbia is not 'overrun' with Jews any more than it is with Roman Catholics or Episcopalians," Keppel privately admitted that "boys whose families are in New York society" had a strong tendency to go out of town for college and that no conceivable plans that Columbia could devise would attract them.[6] In truth, New York's upper class had begun to abandon Columbia as early as the 1890s. But the arrival of large numbers of Jews in the years after 1910 seems to have decisively accelerated the process; still attracting 16 percent of the sons of New York's elite between 1900 and 1909, the proportion dropped precipitously the following decade to 6 percent.[7]

By the time Columbia finally moved vigorously to repel the "Jewish invasion," it was far too late. Though the proportion of Jews, which had reached perhaps 40 percent, was reduced to 22 percent by 1921, the sons of the Protestant elite had abandoned Morningside Heights, never to return.[8] In the 1920s, just 4 percent enrolled at Columbia; meanwhile, 84 percent matriculated at the Big Three.[9] A contemporary observer, writing under the veil of anonymity, captured what had happened to the Columbia campus:

> As one casually observes the men of the College, one is struck by the complete lack of undergraduate atmosphere about any group of them. Singularly absent is the grace, the swagger, the tall attractive sleekness which, if it does not always dominate the usual college group, at least always touches it importantly. These men, one senses at once, are not of the highest caste, nor have they among them an influential sprinkling of members of the highest caste for their models. . . . Seen quickly, there is even a certain grubbiness about them. One somehow expects them all to be Jews, for it is usually the Jewish members of such a group who lower the communal easy handsomeness.[10]

As the case of Columbia had demonstrated, the possibility of "WASP flight" was a clear and present danger for any institution with a substantial Jewish presence.[11]

The specter of Columbia was very much on the mind of President Lowell as he confronted Harvard's "Jewish problem." With Columbia and NYU taking active measures to limit Jewish enrollment, Lowell moved in February 1920 to inquire about the number of Jews at Harvard College.[12] Although the dean's office did not provide a precise estimate, Lowell had ample reason to worry; a study of higher education enrollment patterns in 1918–1919 among the leading private colleges revealed that only Columbia and the University of Pennsylvania—the very institutions that many members of the eastern upper class believed had already been "ruined" by the Jews—had a higher percentage of Jewish students than Harvard.[13]

Though the proportion of Jews in Harvard's freshman class had ranged from 13 to 20 percent between 1912 and 1919, Harvard retained its close connection to Boston's upper class throughout the 1910s. Indeed, the link between Harvard and Brahmin Boston was far tighter than the historical ties between the upper classes of New York and Philadelphia with Columbia and Penn, respectively.[14] By the 1910s, Harvard enrolled 85 percent of the sons of the Boston upper class, whereas just 52 and 6 percent of their counterparts in Philadelphia and New York matriculated at Penn and Columbia.[15] Harvard, moreover, enjoyed a close relationship with the upper class of New York City, which in recent decades had come to dwarf Boston in economic importance; in the 1910s, nearly a third of the sons of New York's elite enrolled at Harvard.[16] To Lowell, Harvard's rising Jewish enrollment posed a threat to these crucial relationships, making it imperative to bring the "Jewish invasion" under control.

In a letter to the Harvard philosophy professor William Earnest Hocking, who had proposed enlisting the Jewish alumni to assist in eliminating the "undesirable Jews" (as he claimed had already occurred at Williams),[17] Lowell explained that his main concern was that the sheer number of Jews would cause the flight of the Protestant elite and thereby "ruin the college":

> The summer hotel that is ruined by admitting Jews meets its fate,
> not because the Jews it admits are of bad character, but because
> they drive away the Gentiles, and then after the Gentiles have left,
> they leave also. This happened to a friend of mine with a school in
> New York, who thought, on principle, that he ought to admit Jews,
> but who discovered in a few years that he had no school at all.[18] A
> similar thing has happened in the case of Columbia College; and
> in all these cases it is not because Jews of bad character have come;
> but the result follows from the coming in large numbers of Jews
> of any kind, save those few who mingle readily with the rest of the
> undergraduate body. Therefore any tests of character in the ordinary
> sense of the word afford no remedy.[19]

Lowell's personal preference was "to state frankly that we thought we could do the most good by not admitting more than a certain proportion of men in a group that did not intermingle with the rest, and give our reasons for it to the public." But he also anticipated quite presciently that "the Faculty, and probably the Governing Boards, would prefer to make a rule whose motive was less obvious on its face, by giving to the Committee on Admission authority to refuse admittance to persons who possessed qualities described with more or less distinctness and believed to be characteristic of the Jews." For Lowell, however, it was crucial that "the Faculty should understand perfectly well what they are doing, and that any vote passed with the intent of limiting the number of Jews should not be supposed by anyone to be passed as a measurement of character really applicable to Jews and Gentiles alike."[20]

In frankly endorsing a double standard, Lowell was rejecting the argument that applying ostensibly neutral criteria such as "character" would be sufficient to reduce the number of Jews. On this issue, as on many others, Lowell was utterly forthright: his goal was restriction itself. In a letter to Julian Mack, a member of Harvard's Board of Overseers and a federal judge, Lowell made explicit some of the cultural assumptions behind his commitment to a Jewish quota: "It is the duty of Harvard to receive just as many boys who have come, or whose parents have come, to this country without our background as it can effectively educate: including in education the imparting, not only of book knowledge, but of the ideas and traditions of our people. Experience seems to place that proportion at about 15%."[21]

By the spring of 1922, when Lowell moved decisively, the proportion of Jews had already reached 21.5 percent. Unless immediate measures were taken, Lowell wrote in a letter on May 20, it would suffer the fate of Columbia. At Harvard, he warned, "the danger would seem to be imminent."[22]

Compared to rural and small-town institutions such as Dartmouth, Princeton, Williams, and Amherst—which had already taken measures to limit the size of the freshman class and overhaul their admissions policies—Harvard was particularly vulnerable.[23] An urban institution with a long tradition of openness to graduates of public as well as private secondary schools, Harvard was not insulated from the growing numbers of public school graduates who met its entrance requirements. Between 1900 and 1920, the number of male graduates from the nation's high schools had risen from 95,000 to 311,000—an increase of over 300 percent.[24] The democratization of the opportunity to graduate from high school was a mixed blessing for institutions such as Harvard. While their numbers meant a much larger pool of academically qualified students, it also meant a surge in the number of applicants who lacked the social graces of an earlier generation.[25] Many of these students were from urban areas, and a disproportionate number of them—especially in the college preparatory track—were the children of Russian and Polish Jews.[26]

Left to his own devices, the authoritarian Lowell would have been more than willing to impose his own solution to the "Jewish problem." Indeed, that is precisely what he tried to do when he asked the Committee on Admission to admit as transfers only those "Hebrews . . . possessed of extraordinary intellectual capacity together with character above criticism" and to impose a higher standard for admission to the freshman class on members of the "Hebrew race." This was a covert attempt to impose a quota, but it was rejected by Chairman Henry Pennypacker, a graduate of Harvard (1888) who had served as headmaster of Boston Latin School from 1910 to 1920. Though Lowell's subordinate, Pennypacker told him that the group's members "felt that the Committee should not practice discrimination without the knowledge and assent of the Faculty," of which it was "merely the administrative servant."[27] The stage was thus set for a conflict between the autocratic Lowell and a faculty that, while hardly free of anti-Semitism, was reluctant to publicly endorse a policy of discrimination.

By this time, the faculty was actively involved in the debate about the "Jewish problem" that Lowell had initiated. At a meeting on May 23, Lowell's brother-in-law and personal friend, James Hardy Ropes, the Hollis Professor of Divinity, introduced a three-part motion; its most controversial elements instructed the Committee on Admission "to take into account the proportionate size of racial and national groups in the membership of Harvard College" and declared that "it is not desirable that the number of students in any group which is not easily assimilated into the common life of the College should exceed fifteen percent of the whole college." These proposals, which clearly had Lowell's support, generated a complex and at times bewildering array of amendments and countermotions, some of them supporting the basic thrust of Ropes's proposals and others opposed. Though the motion proposing a 15 percent quota on "any group which is not easily assimilated" (an unsubtle euphemism for Jews) was not approved, the meeting was a partial triumph for Lowell, for a slightly revised version of the other controversial element was passed by a vote of 56–44. It called upon the Committee on Admission, "pending further action by this Faculty . . . to take into account the . . . proportionate size of racial and national groups in the membership of Harvard College."[28] This was a dramatic departure from Harvard's historic commitment to nondiscrimination and, for that very reason, was warmly welcomed by Lowell.

Yet even before the faculty meeting, opposition to Lowell's efforts to limit Jewish enrollment had been growing. In addition to Mack, who had exchanged a series of increasingly tense letters with Lowell, further opposition was expressed by Jerome D. Greene, who had served as secretary to President Eliot (1901–1905) and then secretary to the Corporation (1905–1911).[29] Reportedly Eliot's top choice as his successor, Greene left Harvard to become an important banker in New York two years after Lowell took office.[30] On the Board of Overseers, he was generally thought to represent the views of Eliot, who remained a towering figure at Harvard (and a troublesome presence for Lowell) even though he had retired thirteen years earlier and was nearing the age of ninety.

After conferring with several Harvard officials, including Director of Admission Pennypacker, Greene wrote to Lowell, expressing his view that the "Jewish problem" resided less in any deficiencies among Harvard's Jewish students than in the response of their non-Jewish classmates to their very presence on campus: "The real kernel of this problem seemed to consist not in any question of the relative delinquency of the class of students in question as to either scholarship or conduct, but in the actual disinclination, whether justified or not, on the part of non-Jewish students to be thrown in contact with so large a proportion of Jewish undergraduates." Yet even Greene did not propose maintaining Harvard's policy of admitting students almost exclusively on the basis of academic criteria. Instead, he suggested a faculty study whose objective would be to devise a new policy of admissions "whereby numbers would be kept down or reduced, and the student body limited to the most promising individuals without reference to any question of race or religion." While insisting that these criteria be applied equally to Jews and Gentiles, Greene assured him that the consequence of the new policy "would undoubtedly be to reduce materially the number of those Jews who are of objectionable personality and manners."[31]

That men of goodwill like Greene apparently believed that Jews were far more likely than non-Jews to possess disagreeable personal qualities suggests that even principled opponents of Lowell were not immune to the anti-Semitic sentiments taken for granted in their milieu. Indeed, even Eliot, the leading public critic of Lowell's policy and long a defender of Jews and immigrants, believed that Jews had many "undesirable qualities" rooted in the "century-long persecution to which they have been subjected in the European and Asiatic countries through which they have been scattered."[32] In a 1919 article sympathetic to Zionism that he published in *The Maccabean*, Eliot described many Jews as having "feebled, stunted, undeveloped bodies, and morbid nervous systems"—qualities that made "the Jewish element of the population . . . dreaded at all the large public and private hospitals and dispensaries because it provides so many neurasthenic patients, the treatment of whom is always prolonged and tedious and not infrequently unsuccessful." According to Eliot, Jews' susceptibility "to sudden attack from their Christian neighbors . . . had the inevitable depressing effect on the spirit of the people," rendering them "subservient rather than independent, submissive rather than resistant." Lacking "the good elements in the martial spirit," Jews met "the indignities and cruelties to which they were subjected not with indignant protest but with lamentations, both public and private." Excluded from many occupations, "Jews in all generations developed skill in buying at low prices and in selling at high and also skill in lending money at high rates to impecunious Christians"—qualities that led to their acquiring "among Christians a reputation for being grasping and sharp in their money transactions." "The present Christian generation of European and American origin," Eliot wrote, "dread the clannishness of the Hebrew people who live among them." And although Christians considered "the refined, educated, and public-spirited Jew . . . a thoroughly satisfactory friend and neighbor, the coarse, ignorant, ostentatious Jew is a peculiarly disagreeable product of free institutions, especially if he be newly rich."[33]

This was the classic litany of complaints against Jews, and such sentiments were likely commonplace among the Harvard faculty. Yet faced with the full implications of its actions at the May 23 meeting, the faculty drew back from its implicit endorsement of discrimination. By May 29, Lowell had received four separate petitions requesting that he call a special meeting to permit the faculty to reconsider the motions it had passed less than a week earlier. One petition, signed by 31 faculty members, described the "action of the Faculty relating to controlling the percentage of the Jews in Harvard College" as "a radical departure from the spirit and practice of the College" and declared "that racial considerations should not influence the Committee on Admission before a careful and deliberate study of the whole question of the Jews shall be made by the Faculty."[34] Faced with broad sentiment within the faculty that the actions taken on May 23 were too precipitous and required reconsideration, Lowell had little choice but to call a new meeting.

By now the eyes of the public were fixed on Harvard, and the meeting of the faculty convened on June 2 was a historic one. Early in the meeting, Professor of Biological Chemistry Lawrence Joseph Henderson, a close ally of Lowell's who held strong anti-Semitic views, introduced a motion: "That the Committee on Admission be instructed, pending the report of the special committee, to keep the proportion of Jews in Harvard College what it is at present."[35] This motion would in fact mean the imposition of a Jewish quota. The faculty voted down Henderson's motion, 64–41—a major setback for Lowell.[36] Yet the call to set a ceiling on Jewish enrollment was supported by some of Harvard's most eminent professors; among them were Albert Bushnell Hart (History), George Lyman Kittredge (English), Richard C. Cabot (Medicine and Social Ethics), and James Bryant Conant (Chemistry), the man who would succeed Lowell in 1933.[37]

Compounding Lowell's defeat was the faculty's decision to rescind by a vote of 69–25 the motions passed at the May 23 meeting.[38] But the faculty stopped short of rejecting Lowell's initiatives altogether, leaving in place the earlier decision to appoint a special committee "to consider principles and methods for more effectively sifting candidates for admission." A key concession, it implicitly recognized Lowell's major point: the "Jewish problem" facing Harvard was a genuine one. Never one to shrink from blunt public declarations, Lowell made it explicit in a statement that was incorporated into the minutes of the June 2 meeting: "The primary object in appointing a special Committee," he declared, "was to

consider the question of Jews." If any member of the faculty did not con-
cur, Lowell warned: "Let him speak now or forever after hold his peace."[39]

Utterly convinced of the rectitude of his position, Lowell was confident that he could persuade others that there was no alternative to a
quota. But in addition to the equivocal response of the faculty, there
was the overwhelmingly negative reaction of the press. Within days of
the announcement of Lowell's plan, the *Boston Telegram* ran an editorial:
"Down Hill from Harvard to Lowell." In New York, the *Times* responded
with an article, "Discrimination Against Jews Suspected in New Harvard
Policy on Admission."[40] And the *Nation*, despite its reference to "pushing
young men with a foreign accent, accustomed to overcome discrimination by self-assertion," came out unequivocally against Jewish quotas. "A
university which bars a persecution-scarred race," its editorial of June 14,
1922, declared, "cannot keep alive the traditions of intellectual integrity,
of *noblesse oblige*, and of essential democracy which have made our elder
universities play so great a role in American life—or it must open its doors
frankly and fairly to all who can meet its requirements of scholarship."[41]

Lowell's proposal also created a storm of political controversy. In addition to an attack from Boston's mayor James Michael Curley ("If the
Jew is barred today, the Italian will be tomorrow, then the Spaniard and
the Pole, and at some future date the Irish") and a formal resolution of
opposition from Samuel Gompers, president of the American Federation
of Labor, the proposal also generated a call for a legislative committee, to
be appointed by Governor Channing Harris Cox, to investigate whether
Harvard was acting in violation of a bill already on the books that mandated equality of opportunity.[42] But Lowell was undeterred.

Believing that the meeting of June 2 had been a success, Lowell wrote
to Professor Kittredge, offering his own assessment: "We . . . attained by
far the most important object, which was that of making substantially
every member of the Faculty understand that we had before us a problem, and that that problem was a Jew problem and not something else.
We had also brought the Faculty to the point of being ready to accept
a limitation of the number of Jews, for their own benefit as well as that
of the college, if the Committee should, on investigation, report that it
is necessary. I have no doubt that they will so report, because I think I
know the situation well enough to be persuaded that there is no other
solution."[43] However confident Lowell may have been about the faculty's
eventual decision, he was not about to delay all action until it had finished its deliberations. In January 1922, four months *before* the faculty
began its debate, Lowell instructed the dean's office to use the allocation
of scholarships to limit the number of Jews. In an internal memorandum,
the dean's office reported that "Mr. Lowell feels pretty strongly that of

the scholarships controlled by us the percentage allotted to Jews in their first year at Harvard should not exceed the percentage of Jews in the Freshman Class." In essence, Lowell had imposed a quota on the number of scholarships awarded to Jews regardless of academic performance and need. Though awards were still to be given "primarily on the basis of high scholarship," recipients henceforth were required to be "men of approved character and promise."[44]

At the same time, Harvard was also beginning to gather the information that would permit it to identify which applicants were Jewish. Starting in the fall of 1922, applicants were required to answer questions on "Race and Color," "Religious Preference," "Maiden Name of Mother," "Birthplace of Father," and "What change, if any, has been made since birth in your own name or that of your father? (Explain fully.)" Lest any Jews slip through this tightly woven net by failing to disclose their background (a pattern thought to be rather common, given their alleged lack of character), the high school principal or private school headmaster was asked to fill out a form that asked him to "indicate by a check [the applicant's] religious preference so far as known . . . Protestant . . . Roman Catholic . . . Hebrew . . . Unknown."[45]

While moving behind the scenes to stem the flow of Jewish students, Lowell was publicly taking great pains to constitute a visibly balanced Committee on Methods of Sifting Candidates for Admission. Realizing that this committee, which was entrusted with reviewing Harvard's admissions policies, needed to have Jews among its members if it was to have any public legitimacy, Lowell appointed three—Paul J. Sachs ('00, associate professor of Fine Arts), Harry G. Wolfson ('12, professor of Jewish Literature and Philosophy), and Milton J. Rosenau (Honorary '14, professor of Medicine)—to the thirteen-member body. Sachs and Wolfson had voted against Henderson's motion. But Lowell also appointed three men who had voted for the motion (Professor of Hygiene Roger I. Lee '02, Chairman of the Committee on Admission Henry Pennypacker '88, and Henderson himself) and a fourth (Dean Wallace B. Donham '98 of the business school) known to share his position.[46] Though the committee's members represented a wide range of views, Lowell believed that it would in the end give his proposed policy of restriction a much-needed seal of approval.

Lowell managed to resist strong pressure to place Felix Frankfurter on the committee. The most visible Jewish member of the faculty, the brilliant law professor was an obvious choice. Such, in any case, was the view of Julian Mack, the sole Jewish member of the Board of Overseers, who urged Lowell to appoint him. In making the case for Frankfurter, who had been his close friend for more than a decade, Mack wrote: "If a Jewish member of any of the Faculties is to be on, I think it would be the unanimous judgment of those interested that Frankfurter, by training and by personal experience, is the most fitted to study and deal with the problem. While a Viennese by birth and belonging to the German Jewish, not the East European Jewish, element, he understands the latter as he has grown up side by side with them."[47] But Lowell, who had tangled with Frankfurter on a number of matters and despised his generally liberal political views, was not moved. "All members of the Committee ought," Lowell wrote to Mack, "to be persons in whom all Harvard men feel confidence, and you know that there are many people—including many on the Governing Boards of the University—who have not that feeling towards Professor Frankfurter. Many people with a high opinion of Professor Frankfurter's ability do not trust the solidity of his judgment."[48]

In refusing to appoint Frankfurter, Lowell was doing his utmost to ensure a favorable report from the committee.[49] A formidable debater with a strong personality, Frankfurter might well sway others to his viewpoint, which was strongly against restriction. Equally worrisome, the irascible Frankfurter had a powerful streak of independence and might issue a stinging dissent even if a majority of the committee supported Lowell—a trait that later became visible on the Supreme Court where he wrote 291 dissents.[50] There were still three Jews on the committee. But none of them posed the threat that Frankfurter would have; Sachs was an upper-class German Jew "far removed from the element" that Lowell was targeting, Wolfson was a "scholar pure and simple," and Rosenau was scheduled to be abroad while the committee would do much of its work. From Lowell's perspective, it seemed designed to produce the desired outcome but with enough variety to ensure public legitimacy.[51]

The committee's internal organization gave Lowell little reason to worry. Divided into four subcommittees, the larger committee assigned all three Jewish members to the subcommittee that would meet and correspond with prominent Jews as well as Harvard's Jewish alumni. Jews were not represented on the three other subcommittees, two of which— the subcommittee assigned to see how other colleges were handling their "Jewish problem" (chaired by Henry Pennypacker) and the subcommittee assigned to gather statistics about Jewish students at Harvard—were far more important than the one on which the Jewish faculty served.[52] The fourth subcommittee was enjoined to sample undergraduate opinion, which Lowell believed was largely in favor of restriction.[53]

Of the four, the Subcommittee to Gather Statistics arguably held the greatest potential for long-term impact. In order to count the number of Jews, one had to develop techniques for identifying them—techniques that could later be used to identify Jewish applicants. The subcommittee went about its work with a chilling enthusiasm. It consulted "the original enrollment cards or entries in admissions books" (which included the student's name, place of birth, father's name and occupation, mother's maiden name, home address, and school or college last attended), "bondsmen's names," and "individual college records (as obtained from the Senior Album)." Armed with this information, the group proceeded to classify each Harvard student into one of four categories: "J1," "J2," "J3," and "Other." A "J1" was assigned "when the evidence pointed conclusively to the fact that the student was Jewish," a "J2" when a "preponderance of evidence" suggested the student was Jewish, and a "J3" where "the evidence suggested the possibility that the student might be Jewish." This classification system provided the framework—right down to the tripartite distribution among "J1s," "J2s," and "J3s"—that would be used three years later to limit Jewish enrollment.[54]

After seven months, the subcommittee received a 104-page report with the conspicuously dry title "Statistical Report of the Statisticians."[55] But its contents were anything but dry. A remarkable investigation into the lives of Harvard students between 1900 and 1922, it was designed to provide the statistical evidence that Lowell hoped would clinch his case. Yet the results of the study, which had been conducted with great care, offered ammunition to both sides in the increasingly heated debate.

For those worried that the number of Jews at Harvard was rising, the study offered ample confirmation of their fears. Just 7 percent of freshmen in 1900, Jews had increased steadily over the entire period, rising to 10 percent in 1909, 15 percent in 1915, and 21.5 percent in 1922.[56] But nothing in the study suggested that this growth posed an *academic* problem for Harvard; on the contrary, the Jewish students outperformed their Gentile classmates by a considerable margin. Massively underrepresented among students reported for unsatisfactory academic records (15 percent of Jews vs. 37 percent of non-Jews), they were heavily overrepresented among those who received degrees with distinction (28 vs. 15 percent).[57] Were Harvard committed to raising the academic level of its student body, the proportion of Jews, the evidence suggested, should be increased rather than decreased.

Yet Lowell, aware of these numbers and inclined to dismiss them as the product of the Jewish students' greater dependence on scholarships, had never rested his case for quotas on academic grounds. Convinced that deficiencies in the "character" and ethical standards of Jews resulted in more frequent "discipline for offenses of a moral nature," he planned to press this issue.[58] Even before the faculty had begun to discuss the issue of quotas, Lowell had launched his own investigation. Having received a preliminary report on the misdeeds of Harvard's Jewish and non-Jewish students, he wrote back to the dean's office: "You have basely gone back on me. Somebody told me that of the fourteen men discussed last year for cheating and lying about it, thirteen were Jews. Now you make out that there were twelve of them, of whom only five were Jews. Please produce at once six more!"[59] Around this time, Lowell also told a distinguished alumnus that 50 percent of the students found guilty of stealing books from the library were Jewish. But when asked how many students had been apprehended, Lowell told him, "Two."[60]

The statistical report offered more systematic data on the distribution of offenses of a moral nature. Here Lowell found some apparent support; for the period covered, 4.7 percent of Jews, but only 3.0 percent of non-Jews, were found to be "under discipline." Though less likely to have been found guilty of drunkenness (0.1 vs. 0.5 percent), Jewish students were more likely to have committed "offences invoking dishonesty" (3.7 vs. 2.0 percent). These findings may, of course, have reflected genuine group differences in the propensity to commit such offenses; on the other hand, they may also have reflected a discriminatory pattern of treatment by the university authorities—a possibility compatible with the barely mentioned finding that over 25 percent of Jewish students "under discipline" were expelled compared to only 11 percent of non-Jews.[61] Though the numbers were small, the statisticians did not hesitate to draw out their implications: "The [higher] proportion of Jews under discipline . . . adds much to the strength of any case that could be based on the records."[62] In its final report, the committee as a whole wrote of the Jewish Harvard student in its cover note to President Lowell: "In morals, he seems to be more prone to dishonesty and sexual offenses, but much less addicted to intemperance."[63]

The findings on patterns of student participation in extracurricular and social activities also seemingly lent some support to Lowell. It was his belief that Jewish students were less likely to "do something for Harvard" than their Gentile classmates, and the results of the study confirmed that they were in fact less involved in the nonacademic side of college life. In athletics, which occupied such a central place in campus culture during the 1920s, non-Jews were almost twice as likely to participate as Jews: 48 vs. 25 percent. The discrepancy was even more pronounced off the playing field; there the figure was 33 percent for non-Jews and 11 percent for Jews."[64] But the meaning of these figures was not self-evident. It was possible that the relative paucity of Jews in Harvard's extracurricular life reflected the lower participation rate of commuting students in general—a group among whom Jews were heavily overrepresented.[65] It was also possible that the Jewish students' low participation rate was in no small part a response to exclusion or hostility on the part of Gentile students.[66]

The committee's findings on social as opposed to extracurricular life in Cambridge offered ample confirmation of the hypothesis that anti-Semitism was a powerful force among the undergraduates. Segregation between Jewish and non-Jewish students was the rule rather than the exception; only 3.6 percent of Jews belonged to social clubs (other than the six Jewish fraternities), compared to 58.6 percent of non-Jewish students.[67] Particularly striking were the committee's findings on the final clubs; for the seven classes that entered Harvard between 1912 and 1918, not a single Jew was elected to any of the five most prestigious clubs: Porcellian, AD, Fly, Spee, and Delphic (Gas).[68] The total exclusion of Jews from the summit of Harvard's social system confirmed what many had long suspected: the sheer fact of being Jewish—regardless of background, education, and personal demeanor—remained a serious social handicap at Harvard.

Lowell hoped that findings like these would convince the "better class" of Jews, many of them of German background, that something needed to be done to stem the flow of "undesirable" Jews. This hope was not unrealistic; at Williams, well-established Jewish alumni had reportedly assisted the college in excluding their "less fit" brethren, and some years later their counterparts did the same at Dartmouth, expressing satisfaction that their alma mater was admitting only "the better type of Jews and not the Brooklyn and Flatbush crowd."[69] At Harvard, hostility on the part of upper-class Jews toward their working-class and immigrant ethnic brethren was hardly unknown. Jesse Isidor Straus, an eminent businessman with three generations of ties to Harvard, reported to Charles Eliot that the "catastrophe" (the bitter controversy over Lowell's proposed policy) had been caused by the increase in Jewish students commuting from East Boston. Though opposed to blanket quotas, he wondered whether "there might have been found some less obnoxious method of discriminating against *them*."[70]

If Lowell was hoping for a prominent Jew to come out in favor of his policy, few prospects seemed more promising than Walter Lippmann '10. Already a renowned writer, Lippmann was an upper-class German Jew who shared Lowell's visceral distaste for the immigrant Jews from Poland and Russia. About the Jewish masses, Lippmann had written: "I worry about upper Broadway on a Sunday afternoon where everything that is feverish and unventilated in the congestion of a city rises up as a warning that you cannot build up a decent civilization among people who, when they are at last, after centuries of denial, free to go to the land and cleanse their bodies, now huddle together in a steam-heated slum." Those Jews of modest origin who had been lucky enough to succeed fared even worse with Lippmann: "The rich and vulgar and pretentious Jews of our big

American cities are perhaps the greatest misfortune that has ever befallen the Jewish people. . . . They are the real fountain of anti-Semitism. When they rush about in super-automobiles, bejeweled and furred and painted and overbarbered . . . they stir up the latent hatred against crude wealth, and that hatred diffuses itself." Rejecting the cultural pluralism of fellow intellectuals such as Randolph Bourne and Horace Kallen, Lippmann believed that the only solution for Jews, who were more "conspicuous" than Gentiles, was total assimilation. In the words of his biographer Ronald Steel, "The good Jew should lie low, dress and behave unobtrusively and be as indistinguishable as possible from the crowd."[71]

Given these sentiments, it is not surprising that, when Harvard's "Jewish problem" erupted into public view, Lippmann's first inclination was to find a discreet way to reduce the number of Jews. Accepting Lowell's premise that it would be "bad for the immigrant Jews as well as for Harvard if there were too great a concentration," he went so far as to suggest that Massachusetts set up a state university led by Jews to "persuade Jewish boys to scatter." Later, in a draft of a letter to a member of the faculty's committee considering admission criteria, he wrote that "I am fully prepared to accept the judgment of the Harvard authorities that a concentration of Jews in excess of fifteen percent will produce a segregation of culture rather than a fusion." In the clash between the culture of Jews and that of Christians, he added, "My sympathies are with the non-Jew. His personal manners and physical habits are, I believe, distinctly superior to the prevailing manners and habits of the Jews."[72]

Yet, in the end, even Lippmann could not bring himself to endorse an outright quota. Contacted by both Judge Mack and Felix Frankfurter (who was very active behind the scenes), he arranged to meet with Laurence Henderson on October 25, 1922. While sharing his hostility to Polish and Russian Jews, Lippmann was appalled when Henderson—who professed to favor higher intellectual standards—proposed a loophole for students who could not pass the examination if they showed promise of being "business and social leaders." A higher required grade on the entrance examination, Lippmann said, "would be a form of selection wholly without offence to the Jewish people." Though sympathetic to the idea of recruiting students from a wider geographical area—a change that he realized might reduce the number of Jews from New York and Boston—he was opposed to any direct methods of restriction.[73]

By January 1923, as the committee was nearing the end of its deliberations, Lippmann turned militantly against Lowell's policy. In an editorial in the *New York World*, he wrote that at Harvard there had been "a change of soul at the top. . . . In the place of Eliot, who embodied the stern but liberal virtues of New England, there sits a man who has lost his grip on the great tradition which made Harvard one of the true spiritual centers of American life. Harvard, with the prejudices of a summer hotel; Harvard, with the standards of a country club, is not the Harvard of her greatest sons."[74] In articulating these sentiments, Lippmann was expressing the views of not only the Jewish alumni of Harvard but of Jews nationwide. In carrying out its work, the committee had interviewed eighty "representative Hebrews on the subject of our Jewish problem." Though of diverse views, "all, or virtually all, were of one accord in vehement opposition to any system based on racial proportion."[75]

Not convinced that Lowell's distinction between "desirable" and "undesirable" Jews would not in the end be used against *all* Jews, Julian Mack and Felix Frankfurter had been successful in convincing Jews on and outside the committee that the best response to Lowell's attempts to divide the Jewish community was one of principled solidarity. But their success in temporarily blocking Lowell's initiative would have not been possible without the active and vigorous support of many distinguished Protestant alumni of Harvard. Particularly crucial was the support of Eliot, then eighty-eight years old, and Greene, Eliot's disciple and an influential member of the Board of Overseers. Throughout the controversy, Eliot and Greene were in close contact, united by their conviction that Lowell had violated fundamental Harvard principles. Believing Lowell to be flawed and untrustworthy, Eliot worked assiduously to block his efforts to impose a quota.[76] Assisted by the tireless and combative Greene and working closely with Mack and Frankfurter, he was able to convince the Board of Overseers that supporting Lowell's proposal would constitute an abdication of Harvard's best traditions.[77]

Completed on April 7, 1923, the final report of the Committee on Methods of Sifting Candidates for Admission was a major setback for Lowell. In the letter accompanying the report, Chairman Charles H. Grandgent wrote that of 100 "Harvard graduates not of Hebrew stock" (many of them "persons of high distinction"), "nearly all protested with earnestness . . . against the principle of racial discrimination." "A few suggested restriction," Grandgent wrote, but "hardly one favored frank limitation." Discussion "in the public and academic press," he noted, was of "like tenor."[78]

A man of extraordinary hubris, Lowell had made a grave error in making public his plan to impose a Jewish quota. As his counterparts at Yale and Princeton grasped intuitively, the public declaration of an intent to discriminate violated core American principles and was likely to lead to a bitter public controversy. This is precisely what happened at Harvard, with Jewish and non-Jewish foes of restriction mobilizing both inside and outside Harvard. Yet Lowell was utterly forthright about his intentions, making it impossible for Harvard to take measures in full public view that more prudent administrators elsewhere were already carrying out behind closed doors. It was a mistake that Lowell would not repeat.

To Eliot's great satisfaction, the committee's members were unanimous in recommending that "no departure be made from . . . the policy of equal opportunity for all regardless of race and religion," adding, "Any action liable to interpretation as an acceptance of the principle of racial discrimination would to many seem like a dangerous surrender of traditional ideals." In the context of 1923, this was a double rebuke to Lowell, for it overturned his policy of excluding African Americans from the freshmen dormitories at the same time that it repudiated his proposed Jewish quota.[79] The committee further stated that "even so rational a method as a personal conference or an intelligence test, if now adopted here as a means of selection, would inevitably be regarded as a covert device to eliminate those deemed racially or socially undesirable and . . . could not fail to arouse damaging suspicion." Finally, in an effort to thwart any attempt by Lowell to circumvent its stand, the committee expressed its opposition to "an arbitrary limitation of the number of students to be admitted" and specified that "if the size of our Freshman class is to be reduced, the reduction can best be accomplished by raising the standard for admission."[80]

To be sure, the report did not give the Mack-Eliot coalition everything that it wanted; in particular, it opposed the committee's recommendation that Harvard admit students "whose scholastic rank places them in the highest seventh of the boys of their graduating class" and "who have satisfactorily completed an approved school course" at "schools which do not ordinarily prepare their pupils for college examinations."[81] Designed to facilitate the admission of "a new group of men from the West and South," the top one-seventh plan seemed to men like Eliot and Frankfurter a thinly disguised attempt to lower the Jewish proportion of the student body by bringing in boys some of them academically ill equipped for Harvard—from regions of the country where there were few Jews. Despite the opposition of a number of faculty members, however, the top seventh was formally approved at a special meeting of the faculty on April 24, 1923, by a vote of 73–20.[82]

Despite the faculty's approval of the top-seventh plan, Lowell realized that the report constituted a major defeat. While publicly professing support for the committee's work, Lowell wasted little time in working to undermine it. Barely two months later, he persuaded the Fellows of the Harvard Corporation to let him commission a faculty study to determine "whether it might be wise to limit the number of students admitted to the Freshman class to one thousand."[83] A ceiling on the size of the class, he realized, was the necessary precondition for addressing the "Jewish problem," for as long as Harvard had an absolute standard of admission, a discretionary selection policy using nonacademic as well as academic criteria would not be possible. Lowell's revival of the limitation idea—in direct contravention of the committee's guidelines—thus signaled the beginning of a new, more subtle campaign to restrict Jewish enrollment. It was precisely the kind of devious action that Rosenau had anticipated a few months earlier when he told Eliot that "Lowell and the Committee on Admission to Harvard College will exclude Jews all the same."[84]

Indeed, by the end of 1923, Lowell's Committee on the Limitation of Students issued a report recommending a limit of 1,000 on the size of the freshman class and introduced additional changes in the criteria for admission. Whereas selection decisions had been made almost solely on the basis of scholarship, the committee—which included Henry Pennypacker and James Bryant Conant—proposed using letters from teachers and personal interviews to shed light on the candidates' "aptitude and character."[85] It was a major victory for Lowell.

Recognizing the potential for discrimination in the new reliance on nonacademic criteria, Eliot and Mack launched a last-ditch effort to block the new policy before it was approved by the Board of Overseers. But despite letters from Eliot and Mack's decision to return from a trip to Florida for the express purpose of opposing the new policy, it passed easily at the board's meeting on February 25, 1924.[86] Though the Committee on the Sifting of Candidates for Admission had explicitly rejected the idea of "an arbitrary limitation of the number of the students to be admitted" and the use of "a personal conference" in making admissions decisions, the authors of the new policy insisted that "the proposals now made are not in conflict with any of the recommendations of that Committee."[87] The Board of Overseers stipulated that the limit "be reconsidered at the earliest possible time" and that the president of the board should appoint a Special Committee comprising members of the Corporation, the overseers, and the faculty to review and evaluate the policy of limitation.

While these stipulations suggested that the policy was a provisional one, this was not Lowell's interpretation. Seizing on the opening provided by the Overseers' action, he immediately wrote to Pennypacker that the admissions committee was now fully empowered to seek information on the "character" of candidates from "persons who know the applicants well" and that it was "under no obligation" to apply the top-seventh plan "to any school if it does not think it best to do so" and was "at liberty to withdraw the privilege from other schools."[88] Without saying so explicitly, Lowell was telling Pennypacker that he now had the authority to begin reducing the number of Jewish students as long as he did so discreetly.

In his continuing push for the restriction of Jews, Lowell was assisted by the growing momentum of the movement to further limit immigration. Since the passage of the Immigration Act of 1921, anti-Semitism, xenophobia, and racism were all on the rise. Propelled by the exponential growth of the Ku Klux Klan, whose membership peaked at over three million in 1924, and by the mass dissemination of anti-Semitic propaganda in Henry Ford's *Dearborn Independent*, hostility to Jews, blacks, and immigrants escalated from the already high levels of 1921.[89] The nativist wave, which had ebbed and flowed over the course of the nation's history, would reach its crest in 1924.

Adding fuel to the popular sentiment against immigrants were the writings of important Anglo-Saxon intellectuals, many of them alumni of Harvard, Yale, and Princeton. Joining Grant, Osborn, and Stoddard as scientific racism's most prominent proponents were the eugenicist Harry N. Laughlin and Princeton's professor Carl Brigham, himself a 1912 graduate of Princeton.[90] Laughlin claimed to have shown higher rates of genetically based "degeneracy" and "social inadequacy" among the newer immigrant groups, and he served as the "expert eugenics agent" for the House Committee on Immigration and Naturalization.[91] In 1923, Brigham published *A Study of American Intelligence*, a widely publicized work based on the testing of army recruits in World War I—the first mass testing of a population ever conducted. Using the categories of Nordic, Alpine, and Mediterranean developed by Madison Grant, Brigham offered seemingly scientific documentation for the intellectual superiority of Nordics. With considerable alarm, he reported that the average intelligence of Americans was declining—a product, he believed, of increasing immigration from southern and eastern Europe as well as miscegenation between white and black Americans. Contributing to this decline was the growing number of Jews, whom he classified as Alpines because they shared "the head form, stature, and color" of their Slavic neighbors. The results of his study, Brigham claimed, "disprove the popular belief that the Jew is highly intelligent," instead showing immigrant Jews to have I.Q.'s well below average. Unless the United States wished the average intelligence of its population to continue to decline, drastic action was needed. Such action, he wrote, would include not only a much more restrictive and selective immigration policy but also "the prevention of the continued propagation of defective strains in the present population."[92]

Also contributing to the nativist upsurge was the Yale alumnus Burton J. Hendrick (1895), whose widely read book, *The Jews in America*, was published in 1923. Though pleased to inform his readers that the Jew was not as serious an economic threat as many believed (a review of a list of rich New Yorkers revealed the good news that "the racial stocks which founded the United States one hundred and fifty years ago still control its wealth"), Hendrick believed that the Jew did pose a grave political threat. Declaring that "there is a great mass of radicalism among the Polish Jews"—a community that showed "enthusiasm for the doctrines of Karl Marx, in preference to the doctrines of Washington and Jefferson and Franklin and Lincoln and Roosevelt"—he maintained that they were "devoid of patriotism" and "unsympathetic with the thing known as Americanism." Jews, he argued, could best be judged by the newspapers they edited, published, and read—newspapers such as the *Forward* (circulation 160,000), which preached "political principles whose success means the destruction of the American system of government."[93]

Buoyed by the works of sympathetic intellectuals and scientists as well as popular support, the Immigration Restriction League was finally poised to realize its goal: the passage of legislation that would preserve America's predominantly Anglo-Saxon character. With the coalition supporting immigration restriction now ranging all the way from the crude racists of the Ku Klux Klan to the refined gentlemen of the Immigration Restriction League and with the nativist cause now invested with unprecedented intellectual and scientific respectability, the passage of new legislation was all but inevitable.[94] But the proposal favored by leading restrictionists in Congress—to reduce the number of immigrants from southern and eastern Europe by basing the annual quotas on the 1890 rather than 1920 census—seemed to many transparently discriminatory and hence faced strong political opposition. The solution was provided by John B. Trevor, the Harvard alumnus who had played a critical role in passing the Immigration Act of 1921. A truly fair immigration policy, he argued, should be based not on the number of foreign-born in the United States but on the national origins of the entire current population of the United States. By this standard, going back to the 1890 census was more than fair; it was actually generous, for it would allocate 15 percent of the slots for immigrants from the nations of southern and eastern Europe even though only about 12 percent of Americans traced their origins there. With this brilliant rhetorical sleight-of-hand assuaging the consciences of reluctant senators, the watershed Immigration Act of 1924 passed the Senate easily, with only six negative votes, and was signed into law by President Coolidge on May 26, 1924.[95] Reducing the number of immigrants from 350,000 to 150,000 per year while slashing the annual quota for southern and eastern Europeans to fewer than 20,000 (compared to its average annual prewar level of 738,000), the act constituted a historic triumph for the small band of patricians who, thirty years earlier, had formed the Immigration Restriction League.[96]

For Lowell, a former national vice president of the league, the passage of the immigration act was deeply gratifying. But as he surveyed the situation in Cambridge that year, he could not have been equally pleased with the progress of his campaign for restriction at Harvard. Despite his best efforts, Jewish enrollment continued to rise—a striking contrast to the situation at Yale and Princeton, which had moved quietly to limit the number of Jews. By 1924, their measures had succeeded in dramatically cutting Jewish enrollment—at Yale from 13.3 percent in 1923 to 10.0 percent, at Princeton from 3.6 percent to 2.0 percent.[97] Meanwhile, Harvard was nearly 25 percent Jewish and already having difficulty, Lowell believed, in getting applicants from western cities and the "great preparatory schools" because of its "reputation of having so many Jews."[98]

With an eye on his chief rivals, Lowell decided that he could no longer tolerate half-measures. The seriousness of the situation became fully apparent in the fall of 1925, when statistics from the dean's office reported that the proportion of Jewish freshmen had risen to 27.6 percent—not even counting the additional 3.6 percent in the "J3" category.[99] Ironically, it was the top-seventh plan—a measure intended to reduce the proportion of Jewish students that was in good part responsible. Of the 276 students admitted under this plan, 42 percent were Jews. Designed to bring Harvard "a new group of men from the West and the South," the plan was in fact admitting more Jews from the Middle Atlantic states and New England.[100]

As Lowell was contemplating the disturbing figures, he was also receiving letters from alumni expressing concern that Harvard was being overrun by Jews. Among these letters was one from W. F. Williams '01, of Greenwich, Connecticut. Williams, who had attended a recent Harvard-Yale game, was profoundly troubled by the change in Harvard's atmosphere since his undergraduate days. As an expression of the sentiments held by a segment of the alumni, his letter is worth quoting at length:

> Naturally, after twenty-five years, one expects to find many changes but to find that one's University had become so Hebrewized was a feaful [sic] shock. There were Jews to the right of me, Jews to the left of me, in fact they were so obviously everywhere that instead of leaving the Yard with pleasant memories of the past I left with a feeling of utter disgust of the present and grave doubts about the future of my Alma Mater. One thought that kept recurring in my mind was as to what the future of the University would be when the Jew graduates of the present and future would have a possible preponderating vote for the Overseers and the right to fill the "Seats of the Mighty" in University Hall. A pleasant prospect to consider!
>
> My recent re-introduction to my University was when I left the

street car at Beck Hall on my way to the Union to get my ticket for
the game. Being uncertain what entrance to use I stopped a boy,
evidently a student, to ask directions—he was a Jew. Rounding
the corner of the Union, being still in doubt where to go I made
enquiries from three other boys, also very evidentl [sic] students,—
two Jews and a Negro, fraternizing. I was ushered to my seat at
the game by a Jew and another of the same "breed" followed me
to my seat and required me to sign my ticket And not one of these
appeared to be of the same class as the few Jews that were in college
in my day but distinctly of the class usually denominated "Kikes."

Shades of my New England parents that Harvard University
should come to such a pass that its graduates not only feel doubts
about sending their sons to their University but that they are in
many, many cases actually sending them elsewhere—on account of
the Jews.

My business life has been spent in New York where one stumbles
over Jews at every step and I am not anxious for my boys to come in
contact with them until they absolutely have to. They are without
doubt the Damned of God and the skunks of the human race.
I grant you that there are many Jews like the Straus family who
cannot be even remotely criticized, but generally speaking they're a
menace to decent society and the American race. I cannot but feel
that your New England blood must run cold when you contemplate
their ever-increasing numbers at Harvard but what I cannot fathom
is why you and the other Overseers don't have the backbone to put
you [sic] foot down on this menace to the University . . .

The Jew is undoubtedly of high mental order, desires the best
education he can get CHEAPEST, and is more persistent than
other races in his endeavors to get what he wants. It is self evident,
therefore, that by raising the standard of marks he can't be eliminated
from Harvard, whereas by the same process of raising the standard
"White" boys ARE eliminated. And is this to go on? Why the
Psychology Test if not to bar those not wanted? Are the Overseers so
lacking in genius that they can't devise a way to bring Harvard back to
the position it always held as a "white man's" college?[101]

Lowell told Williams that he "had foreseen the peril of having too large
a number of an alien race and had tried to prevent it," but that "not one
of the alumni ventured to defend the policy publicly: He concluded
by indicating that he was "glad to see from your letter, as I have from
many other signs, that the alumni are beginning to appreciate that I

was not wholly wrong three years ago in trying to limit the proportion of Jews."[102]

Yet Lowell still faced serious obstacles. Apart from the continued opposition of the redoubtable Eliot, he still had to gain the approval of the Special Committee on the Limitation of the Size of the Freshman Class.[103] Chaired by Henry James (1899), the son of the great philosopher William James and later the author of a two-volume biography of Eliot that won the Pulitzer Prize, the committee had the power to frustrate Lowell's plans.[104] Sensing that James might not share his views, Lowell turned his considerable energies to the task of convincing him that there was no realistic alternative to restriction.

Receiving a first draft of the Special Committee's report, which conspicuously failed to offer any specific measures to limit Jewish enrollment, Lowell responded with a confidential letter in which he noted that "questions of race," though "delicate and disagreeable," are not solved by ignoring them, Declaring that "the presence of Jews in large numbers tends to drive Gentiles elsewhere," he reminded James that "a few years ago many of us thought the proportion of Jews in Harvard College was reaching a dangerous point." Then, Lowell said, the figure was 21.7 percent; now it was more than 27 percent. Moreover, "the measures adopted at the time of the previous inquiry" which included the limitation of the freshman class to 1,000, the creation of the top-seventh plan, and the use of letters and interviews to assess applicants—"have produced no effect."[105]

From Lowell's perspective, there was no alternative but to act immediately.

> To prevent a dangerous increase in the proportion of Jews, I know at present only one way which is at the same time straightforward and effective, and that is a selection by a personal estimate of character on the part of the Admission authorities, based upon the probable value to the candidate, to the college and to the community of his admission. Now a selection of this kind can be carried out only in case the numbers are limited. If there is no limit, it is impossible to reject a candidate who passes the admission examinations without proof of defective character, which practically cannot be obtained. The only way to make a selection is to limit the numbers, accepting those who appear to be the best.

The Overseers, Lowell told James, had only three choices: "They must either assume the responsibility for the increase in the percentage of Jews, or they must assume the responsibility of saying what should be done about it, or they must leave the administrative officers of the University free to deal with it." And should they choose the last option, which Lowell clearly favored, it would require "a limitation of numbers" that "must be continued as long as there is need for it."[106]

James's initial reaction was less than enthusiastic. "*Everything* in my education and bringing up," he wrote, "makes me shrink from a proposal to begin a racial discrimination at Harvard—there's no use my pretending this isn't the case." Yet he acknowledged that Lowell was "quite right in saying that a situation which contains serious and unfortunate elements ought to be faced again." He then assured Lowell that he would "endeavor to bring an open mind to its consideration and not to follow my predisposition blindly."[107]

Sensing James's irresoluteness, Lowell insisted that he was not proposing discrimination against the Jews but rather "discrimination among individuals in accordance with the probable value of a college education to themselves, to the University, and the community," carefully adding that "a very large proportion of the less desirable, upon this basis, are at the present time the Jews."[108] While hardly the kind of argument that would have persuaded Frankfurter or Mack, it apparently persuaded James. Declaring that he agreed in principle with Lowell's notion of "a sound and discerning 'discrimination' among individuals," he expressed confidence that "such a discrimination would inevitably eliminate most of the Jewish element which is making trouble." Then, revealing that he was himself not immune to the anti-Semitism common in his milieu, he added: "I don't think that all Jews are particularly intelligent by any means. What intelligence they have seems to ripen early. But apart from their precocity and a certain advantage it gives them in the way of a head start, I am not afraid of any competition." Nevertheless, James could not go along with those Overseers who advocated "a candid regulation excluding all but so many or such a proportion of 'Jews.'"[109] More subtle measures, he advised Lowell, would provide the best means of reducing the number of Jews at Harvard.

With James now on board and Judge Mack having completed his term as an Overseer, there was no one left to block Lowell's plans. When the Report of the Special Committee Appointed to Consider the Limitation of Numbers was approved by the Board of Overseers on January 11, 1926, Lowell had every reason to be pleased. In addition to endorsing a limit of 1,000 freshmen, it recommended that "the application of the rule concerning candidates from the first seventh of their school be discretionary with the Committee on Admission"—a provision that would make it possible to eliminate schools that sent too many Jews to Harvard. Equally important, the committee decisively rejected an admissions policy based on scholarship alone, stating that "it is neither feasible nor desirable to raise the standards of the College so high that none but brilliant scholars can enter" while stipulating that "the standards ought never to be too high for serious and ambitious students of average intelligence."[110]

When the faculty formally approved the report eight days later, Lowell was further elated, for they also approved measures making the admissions process even more subjective. In particular, the faculty called on Penny-packer to interview as many applicants as possible to gather additional information on "character and fitness and the promise of the greatest usefulness in the future as a result of a Harvard education." Henceforth, declared the faculty, a passport-sized photo would be "required as an essential part of the application for admissions."[111]

The actions of the faculty and the Committee on Limitation, Lowell realized, provided a tremendous opportunity to impose, at long last, the policy of restriction he had favored since 1922. But as he had learned from his bitter experience with the Committee on Methods Sifting Candidates for Admission, the wrong personnel could frustrate the best-laid plans. This time Lowell would ensure that the men on the Committee on Admission, which had final authority over applicants, shared his views. Toward this end, he appointed two new members, Kenneth B. Murdock and Robert DeCourcy Ward. The appointment of Ward was especially significant, for he had been one of the founders of the Immigration Restriction League and a critical congressional witness on behalf of the Immigration Act of 1924.[112] All in all, the Committee on Admission in 1925–1926 had seven members, four of whom had voted for Henderson's 1922 failed motion in favor of restriction and none of whom had voted against it.[113] And whereas the earlier committee on sifting candidates had three Jewish members, not a single Jew served on the Committee on Admission.

By the fall of 1926, a new admissions regime was in place. In a visit with Henry Pennypacker in late 1926, Dean Clarence W. Mendell of Yale learned that Harvard was "now going to limit the Freshman Class to 1,000. . . . After this year they are going to discontinue—for the East at least—the 'first seventh' arrangement which is bringing in as high as 40% Jews. They are also going to reduce their 25% Hebrew total to 15% or less by simply rejecting without detailed explanation. They are giving no details to any candidate any longer."[114]

Less than four months before Mendell's visit, Charles W. Eliot had died at the age of ninety-two. With Lowell no longer in his shadow, Harvard entered a new era.

Notes

1. In the U.S. Government 1926 Religious Census, the first ever conducted, Boston was reported as having 90,000 Jews, placing it fourth in the country.

First was New York with 1,765,000, second was Chicago (325,000), and third was Philadelphia (270,000). Bureau of the Census, *Religious Bodies: 1926*, vol. 1 (Washington D.C.: Government Printing Office, 1930), 360. The second and last Government Religious Census was conducted in 1936.

2. Marcia Graham Synnott, *The Half-Opened Door: Discrimination and Admissions at Harvard, Yale, and Princeton, 1900–1970* (Westport, Conn.: Greenwood Press, 1979), 96, 182; Daniel A. Oren, *Joining the Club: A History of Jews and Yale* (New Haven, Conn.: Yale U.P., 1985), 320.

3. Elsewhere in the report, Horace Mann's headmaster, Virgil Prettyman, wrote that "the conditions and environment in which youth is to pass into manhood, the associations and friendships which may be formed within the student body, are popularly esteemed not less important factors in the value of a college education than the academic training and knowledge that may be acquired. Every undesirable student admitted is not an advantage but a detriment to the University" (Wechsler, Qualified Student, 148). Prettyman's views expressed in lay terms an idea with striking affinities to the concept of "social capital" as articulated on a more theoretical level by Pierre Bourdieu. For a discussion of his concept of social capital, see Pierre Bourdieu and Loic Wacquant, *An Invitation to Reflexive Sociology* (Chicago: Univ. of Chicago Press, 1992), 119.

4. Edwin E. Slosson, "Princeton University," *Independent*, 4 March 1909, 476.

5. Quoted in Stephen Steinberg, *The Ethnic Myth: Race, Ethnicity, and Class in America* (Boston: Beacon Press, 1989), 233.

6. Frederick Paul Keppel, *Columbia* (New York: Oxford U.P., 1914), 179; Harold Wechsler, *The Qualified Student: A History of Selective College Admission in America* (New York: John Wiley, 1977), 153, 181.

7. While only 6 percent of the scions of New York City's upper class attended Columbia in the 1910s, 73 percent attended the Big Three: 32 percent at Harvard, 25 percent at Yale, and 16 percent at Princeton (Richard Farnum, "Patterns of Upper-Class Education in Four American Cities: 1875–1975," in *The High-Status Track: Studies of Elite Schools and Stratification*, ed. Paul William Kingston and Lionel S. Lewis [Albany: State Univ. of New York Press, 1990], 60).

8. The figures for 1919 and 1921 are from "May Jews Go to College?" *Nation*, 14 June 1922, 708, and are cited in Wechsler, *Qualified Student*, 163–64. Though Farnum has expressed skepticism about whether Jewish enrollment at Columbia ever reached 40 percent, Yale's director of admission reported in 1922, after conferring with the dean of Columbia, that the proportion of Jews had been "reduced from about forty percent to about twenty." See Marcia Graham Synnott, "A Social History of Admissions Policies at Harvard, Yale, and Princeton, 1900–1930" (Ph.D. diss., Univ. of Massachusetts, 1974), 18; Richard Farnum, "Prestige in the Ivy League: Meritocracy at Columbia, Harvard, and Penn, 1870–1940" (Ph.D. diss., Univ. of Pennsylvania, 1990), 125.

9. The University of Pennsylvania, located in another of the nation's great centers of Jewish population, showed a parallel but even more precipitous decline, dropping from 52 percent in the 1910s to 14 percent in the 1920s. Whereas in the 1910s only 19 percent of the sons of Philadelphia's upper class enrolled at a Big Three college, by the 1920s the proportion had risen to 55 percent. The shift was in good part a product of the abandonment of Penn for Princeton, with the proportion at Old Nassau rising from 11 percent in the 1910s to 40 percent in the 1920s (Farnum, "Patterns of Upper-Class Education," 62).

10. Torch, "The Spirit of Morningside," *Menorah Journal*, March 1930, 255.

11. In 1984, I defined "WASP flight" as "the proclivity of upper-class Protestants to abandon an institution (e.g., a college, club, neighborhood, or vacation resort) in the face of entry into it by members of a low-status ethnic group. Structurally, it is strikingly similar to 'white flight,'—a term that has been used to describe the tendency of whites to flee public schools facing large-scale integration. In the cases of both 'WASP flight' and 'white flight,' there is evidence that institutions may reach a 'tipping point' beyond which the further entry of members of the 'outgroup' (typically Jews in the first case and blacks in the second) will cause members of the dominant group to abandon them" (Jerome Karabel, "Status-Group Struggle, Organizational Interests, and the Limits of Institutional Autonomy: The Transformation of Harvard, Yale, and Princeton, 1918–1940," *Theory and Society* 13). I have drawn on this article at several points in this chapter.

12. Synnott, *Half-Opened Door*, 16–19, 59.

13. *American Jewish Year Book, 5681: September 13, 1920, to October 2, 1921*, vol. 22 (Philadelphia: Jewish Publication Society, 1920), 387–90.

14. On the unusually close historical link between Harvard and Boston's upper class, see Ronald Story, *The Forging of an Aristocracy: Harvard & the Boston Upper Class, 1800–1870* (Middletown, Conn.: Wesleyan U.P., 1980), and E. Digby Baltzell, *Puritan Boston and Quaker Philadelphia: The Protestant Ethic and the Spirit of Class Authority and Leadership* (New York: Free Press, 1979), 246–80.

15. As far back as the 1880s, just as mass immigration from eastern and southern Europe was becoming visible in the large cities of the Northeast, there was a powerful tendency among the upper classes of Boston, New York, and Philadelphia to send their children to boarding schools in rural and small-town settings (Steven Levine, "The Rise of American Boarding Schools and the Development of a National Upper Class," *Social Problems* 28, no. 1 [October 1980]; E. Digby Baltzell, *The Protestant Establishment: Aristocracy and Caste in America* [New York: Vintage, 1964]). But Boston's upper class remained faithful to Harvard, sending 78 percent of its sons there in the 1880s. The parallel figures for Philadelphia (Penn) and New York (Columbia) in the 1880s were 49 and 25 percent, respectively (Farnum, "Patterns of Upper-Class Education," 57, 60, 62).

16. Ibid., 60.

17. In his letter to Lowell, Hocking expressed particular concern about the increasing numbers of "rootless and religionless Jews" Hocking to Lowell, 18 May 1922, Harvard University Archives [hereafter HUA]).

18. The case of the New York City school referred to by Lowell—in which growing Jewish enrollment led to the flight of Christian students, reportedly then leading to the departure of many Jews—is described in detail in Henry A. Yeomans, *Abbot Lawrence Lowell, 1856–1943* (Cambridge, Mass.: Harvard U.P., 1948), 210–12.

19. Lowell to Hocking, 19 May 1922, HUA.

20. Ibid.

21. Lowell to Mack, 29 March 1922, HUA. Characteristically, the fact that Judge Mack was not only a Jew but was actively involved in Jewish affairs (ex-president of the American Jewish Congress, president of the Palestine Development Council) did not deter Lowell from writing him a letter that implied that Jews were less than fully American while explicitly proposing a quota. Nevertheless,

Lowell may have had a sense of common class membership with Mack, who belonged to seven different social clubs, including the Cosmos Club of Washington, D.C., the Harvard Club of Boston, and the City Club in his home city of Chicago (*Who's Who in America, 1926–1927*).

22. Lowell to Tucker, 20 May 1922, HUA.

23. The proportion of undergraduates at these institutions in 1918–1919 was 2.8 percent at Dartmouth, 2.6 percent at Princeton, 1.9 percent at Amherst, and 1.4 percent at Williams (*American Jewish Yearbook, 1918–1919*, 386–89).

24. Bureau of the Census, *Historical Statistics*, Part I, 379.

25. At Columbia, it was the failure of the high school "to eliminate students . . . considered socially unqualified" that led to the adoption of selective admissions and of measures specifically designed to reduce the number of Jews. A generation earlier, when only an elite few graduated from high school, Columbia had been happy to "relegate [this function] to the secondary school" (Wechsler, *Qualified Student*, 133).

26. George S. Counts, *The Selective Character of American Secondary Education* (Chicago: Univ. of Chicago Press, 1922), 112.

27. Synnott, *Half-Opened Door*, 61.

28. Synnott, "Social History," 321–24. I have drawn extensively in the following section on Synnott's richly detailed discussion on the deliberations of the Harvard faculty in the spring of 1922 on "the Jewish problem."

29. On the exchange of letters between Mack and Lowell, see letters from Lowell to Mack, 29 March 1922, 31 March 1922, 4 April 1922, 7 June 1922, HUA; letters from Mack to Lowell, 27 March 1922, 30 March 1922, 6 June 1922, 9 June 1922, 13 June 1922, HUA.

30. John Bethell, *Harvard Observed: An Illustrated History of the University in the Twentieth Century* (Cambridge, Mass.: Harvard U.P., 1998), 40. A prominent banker, Greene had strong ties to the centers of financial power in both New York and Boston, with links to both John D. Rockefeller and the firm of Lee Higginson & Co.

31. Synnott, "Social History," 310–11.

32. Charles Eliot, "Zionism," in *A Late Harvest* (1919; Boston: Atlantic Monthly Press, 1924), 253. While concurring with Lowell that Jews had many disagreeable attributes, Eliot differed fundamentally from him in seeing these "undesirable" traits as products of oppression. Unlike Lowell, who believed that many Jews, especially those from eastern Europe, were unassimilable, Eliot was convinced that in the freer atmosphere of the United States, they would shed the negative qualities rooted in their history and become fully American. In his many writings on Jews, Eliot also stressed their many positive contributions to Western history. For all these reasons, the Jewish community at Harvard and elsewhere considered him a loyal friend and frequently published his writings. For examples of Eliot's writings on Jews, see Charles Eliot, "The Potency of the Jewish Race," *Menorah Journal*, June 1915, 141–44; Charles Eliot, "Three Lines of Action for American Jews," *Menorah Journal*, February 1918, 1; and Charles Eliot, "The Jewish Contribution to Modern Social Ethics," *Menorah Journal*, June 1919, 149–51.

33. Eliot, "Zionism," 253–57. Four years earlier, Eliot had warned, "If the [Jewish] race is to meet successfully the test of liberty, it will get over its apparent tendency of the moment towards materialism and reliance on the power of money" ("Potency of the Jewish Race," 144).

34. Synnott, "Social History," 326–34.

35. In a 1922 conversation with Julian Mack and Paul Sachs, both Jewish, Henderson referred to "the very objectionable and morally inferior" behavior and manners of many students of "the new Russian or Polish Jewish element" (Synnott, *Half-Opened Door*, 89).

36. Synnott, "Social History," 334–35.

37. "Minutes of Special Meeting of the Faculty of Arts and Sciences," 2 June 1922, HUA.

38. Synnott, "Social History," 324–25.

39. Ibid., 335–36.

40. Ibid., 356; "Discrimination Against Jews Suspected in New Harvard Policy on Admission," *NYT*, 2 June 1922.

41. "Jews have retained an extraordinary respect for learning," wrote the *Nation*, despite "all their hunt for money" ("May Jews Go to College?").

42. Synnott, "Social History," 357–58; "Governor Orders an Inquiry at Harvard Under Law Calling for Equal Opportunity," *NYT*, 7 June 1922.

43. Lowell to Kittredge, 3 June 1922, HUA.

44. Synnott, *Half-Opened Door*, 59.

45. Ibid., 258. As Michel Foucault has demonstrated, the gathering of knowledge by bureaucratic organizations is never a neutral process but rather an exercise of power; in the case of Harvard's admissions practices, the generation of the knowledge of an applicant's religious background was a precondition for the exercise of the power to discriminate. By the fall of 1922, this power was in the hands of administrators committed to turning back "the Jewish invasion." Of Foucault's many writings on surveillance, knowledge, and power, see especially *Discipline and Punish: The Birth of the Prison* (New York: Vintage, 1979) and *Power/Knowledge: Selected Interviews & Other Writings 1972–1977* (New York: Pantheon Press, 1980). For a brilliant study that demonstrates how seemingly neutral forms of knowledge such as maps and censuses can be used as instruments of control, see James C. Scott, *Seeing Like a State: How Certain Schemes to Improve the Human Condition Have Failed* (New Haven, Conn.: Yale U.P., 1998).

46. Synnott, *Half-Opened Door*, 70.

47. Mack to Lowell, 6 June 1922, HUA. Born in Vienna in 1882, Frankfurter came to the United States in 1894. The son of a retail fur merchant, he lived on the Lower East Side, attended public schools, and graduated from City College in 1902. In 1903, he entered Harvard Law School, where he was first in his class and a member of the *Law Review*. In 1914, he was appointed professor of law at Harvard. During his quarter of a century at the Law School, no other Jew was appointed to the faculty. In 1939, Frankfurter left Harvard to join the Supreme Court, where he served until 1962. See Leonard Baker, *Brandeis and Frankfurter: A Dual Biography* (New York: Harper & Row, 1984), 41–44, 490; and Seymour Martin Lipset and David Riesman, *Education and Politics at Harvard* (New York: McGraw-Hill, 1975), 149; *WWA, 1926–1927*.

48. Lowell to Mack, 7 June 1922, HUA. In questioning Frankfurter's "judgment," Lowell was echoing a charge made six years earlier against Frankfurter's mentor, Louis Brandeis, the first Jew to serve on the Supreme Court. In a statement signed by William Howard Taft, Elihu Root, and five other past presidents of the American Bar Association, Brandeis was described "as not a fit person to be a

member of the Supreme Court of the United States" by reason of his "reputation, character, and professional career." Brahmin Boston (but not Charles W. Eliot) was overwhelmingly against Brandeis's appointment, and Lowell himself joined 54 other Bostonians in a petition opposing his selection (Baltzell, *Protestant Establishment*, 192–93).

49. Even after Lowell had informed Mack of his decision not to appoint Frankfurter, Mack continued to press the issue, warning Lowell that "to leave off the Committee the one Jew of the Faculties who is uniquely fitted for this work would carry an obvious danger" (Mack to Lowell, 13 June 1922, HUA).

50. As a member of the Supreme Court, Frankfurter also wrote 263 opinions and 171 concurrences (Baker, *Brandeis and Frankfurter*, 491).

51. If Lowell was hostile to Frankfurter, it is clear from their correspondence that the feeling was mutual. In a testy exchange of letters when the committee was being constituted, Frankfurter accused Lowell of claiming to welcome "a Jewish member who shares Judge Mack's views" while in fact preferring someone who "passively" entertained them rather than a member who had "the power to render them effective by one's training and experience" (Frankfurter himself). When he wrote of someone who "passively" held Judge Mack's views, Frankfurter seems to have meant Wolfson, whom he described as "a naive and bookish man, without talent or training which would enable him to share effectively the direction of such an inquiry" (Frankfurter to Lowell, 29 June 1922, Harvard University [hereafter HU]). See also Frankfurter to Lowell, 19 June 1922, 21 June 1922, HU, and Lowell to Frankfurter, 20 June 1922, 24 June 1922, HU. But Frankfurter may have underestimated the Lithuanian-born Wolfson, who had written to Lowell criticizing the possible use of interviews in admissions, saying that "outward appearance is a proper test for selecting book agents, bond salesmen, social secretaries and guests for a week-end party," but not "a proper test for the selection of future scholars, thinkers, scientists, and men of letters" (Synnott, *Half-Opened Door*, 67, 71, 87).

52. Ibid., 86.

53. For evidence that there was in fact considerable support among the students for Lowell's effort, see Harry Starr, "The Affair at Harvard," *Menorah Journal*, October 1922, 263–76, and Lipset and Riesman, *Education and Politics*, 148–49.

54. Hettinger Jr. and Edward Gay, "Statistical Report of Statisticians to the Subcommittee Appointed to Collect Statistics," 1922, HUA, 1–3; Synnott, *Half-Opened Door*, 107. See also the cover letter from A. J. Hettinger Jr. to Chester Greenough, chairman of the Subcommittee to Gather Statistics, 21 December 1922, HUA. On systems of classification and their relationship to systems of power, see David Karen, "Toward a Political-Organizational Model of Gatekeeping: The Case of Elite Colleges," *Sociology of Education* 63, October 1990; Pierre Bourdieu and Luc Boltanski, "Formal Qualifications and Occupational Hierarchies: The Relationship Between the Production System and the Reproduction System," in *Reorganizing Education*, vol. 1, ed. Edward Sage (Beverly Hills, Calif.: Sage, 1977); Luc Boltanski, "Taxonomies socials et luttes de classes: la mobilization de 'la classe moyenn' et l'invention des 'cadres,'" *Actes de la recherche en sciences socials*, September 1979; Michele Lamont and Virag Molnar, "The Study of Boundaries in the Social Sciences," *Annual Review of Sociology* 28, 2002; and Geoffrey Bowker and Susan Leigh Star, *Sorting Things Out: Classification and Its Consequences* (Cambridge, Mass.: MIT Press, 2000).

55. The report was compiled by two Harvard statisticians, Dr. A. J. Hettinger Jr. of the Graduate School of Business Administration and Edward R. Gay, a dean of Harvard College, who were not formal members of the subcommittee (Synnott, *Half-Opened Door*, 93).

56. These figures did not even include students classified as "J3s," estimated to make up about 2.5 percent of the student body between 1918 and 1923 (Hettinger and Gay, "Statistical Report," HUA, 3, 8).

57. Ibid., 28–29.

58. Lowell to Mack, 4 April 1922, HUA.

59. Synnott, *Half-Opened Door*, 60.

60. Lipset and Riesman, *Education and Politics*, 146.

61. Among students found guilty of "offenses involving dishonesty," 29 percent of the Jews were expelled or dismissed compared to 11 percent of non-Jews (Hettinger and Gay, "Statistical Report," HUA, 39, 44–45).

62. Hettinger to Greenough, 21 December 1922, HUA.

63. Synnott, *Half-Opened Door*, 85.

64. Totally absent from dramatics and barely represented on student papers and in class office (4 and 5 percent, respectively), Jews did, however, participate heavily in musical and debating activities (19 and 38 percent) (Hettinger and Gay, "Statistical Report," HUA, 48, 53, 57).

65. Between 1912 and 1921, the proportion of Jewish students at Harvard who were commuters exceeded 40 percent eight times, with the figure reaching a high of 49.5 percent in 1915 (the low was 29.1 percent in 1920). This was roughly double, and perhaps in some years triple, the proportion of non-Jewish commuters (ibid., 77–79).

66. Synnott makes a similar point, writing: "Although impossible to measure, Gentile social attitudes probably accounted for the limited participation in or exclusion of Jewish students from extracurricular activities" (*Half-Opened Door*, 101).

67. Nearly a quarter (23.8 percent) of Jewish students belonged to one of the six Jewish fraternities, bringing their total participation in social clubs to 27.4 percent (Hettinger and Gay, "Statistical Report," HUA, 61).

68. Only a handful of Jews managed to enter even the lower-ranking clubs, which included Owl, Delta Upsilon (DU), Phoenix, and Iroquois (numbers six, eight, nine, and ten, according to Boston Brahmin and Harvard alumnus Cleveland Amory) (ibid., 61–75; Amory, *The Proper Bostonians* (New York: Dutton, 1947), 300; Synnott, *Half-Opened Door*, 101.

69. Hocking to Lowell, 18 May 1922, HUA; David O. Levine, *The American College and the Culture of Aspiration 1915–1940* (Ithaca, N.Y.: Cornell U.P., 1986), 155.

70. Synnott, *Half-Opened Door*, 78.

71. Ronald Steel, *Walter Lippmann and the American Century* (New York: Vintage, 1981), 191–92.

72. Ibid., 194.

73. Synnott, *Half-Opened Door*, 89; Steel, *Walter Lippmann*, 194–95.

74. Steel, *Walter Lippmann*, 195.

75. Grandgent to Lowell, 7 April 1923, cover letter to the Report of the Committee on Methods of Sifting Candidates for Admission, HUA.

76. Eliot had written to Greene of Lowell's "defects of judgment and good feeling" and had described "four generations of Lowells" as "eager to win in any

controversy upon which they entered, credulous in regard to alleged facts which go their way and incredulous with regard to alleged facts which do not go their way." See Eliot to Greene, 7 June 1922, 25 January 1923, 17 February 1923, HUA; Greene to Eliot, 10 June 1922, 13 January 1923, 20 January 1923, 24 January 1923, 9 February 1923, HUA.

77. Synnott, *Half-Opened Door*, 88. Another prominent alumnus whose intervention influenced the committee's decision to oppose the Jewish quota was Learned Hand (B.A. 1893, LL.B. 1896). A widely respected federal judge who later became known as the "tenth justice" because of his profound influence on the Supreme Court, Hand wrote an eloquent and forceful letter to the committee on 14 November 1922. While acknowledging that Harvard's growing heterogeneity had created tensions, he believed that restricting Jewish enrollment was not an appropriate solution: "If the Jew does not mix well with the Christian, it is no answer to segregate him. Most of those qualities which the Christian dislikes in him are, I believe, the direct result of that very policy in the past. Both Christian and Jew are here; they must in some way learn to live on tolerable terms, and disabilities have never proved tolerable. . . . But the proposal is not segregation or exclusion but to limit the number of Jews. That, however, is if anything worse. Those who are in fact shut out are of course segregated; those who are left in are effectively marked as racially undesirable. Intercourse with them is with social inferiors; there can be no other conceivable explanation for the limitation." Hand also expressed his firm opposition to the use of nonacademic criteria such as "character," which were clearly designed to restrict Jewish enrollment by indirect means. Until someone should "devise an honest test for character," the only legitimate criterion for admission was scholarly excellence. "A college may gather together men of a common tradition," he concluded, "or it may put its faith in learning" (Irving Dilliard, ed., *The Spirit of Liberty: Papers and Addresses of Learned Hand* [New York: Knopf, 1960], 21). For more on Learned Hand, see the monumental biography by his former law clerk Gerald Gunther, *Learned Hand: The Man and the Judge* (Cambridge, Mass.: Harvard U.P., 1994).

78. Grandgent to Lowell, 7 April 1923, HUA.

79. On the controversy over the admission of blacks to the dormitories, see Nell Painter, "Jim Crow at Harvard: 1923," *New England Quarterly* 44, no. 4 (December 1971); Synnott, *Half-Opened Door*, 49–50, 81–84; and the eloquent letter to Lowell from Roscoe Conkling Bruce, an African American from the Class of 1902 who had graduated magna cum laude and Phi Beta Kappa (Bruce to Lowell, 4 January 1923, HUA).

80. "Report of the Committee Appointed 'To Consider and Report to the Governing Boards Principles and Methods for More Effective Sifting of Candidates for Admission to the University,'" 10 April 1923, HUA, 1–2.

81. Ibid., 3–6.

82. Synnott, "Social History," 432–34.

83. Ibid., 438.

84. Eliot to Greene, 13 January 1923, HUA.

85. "Report of the Committee on the Limitation of Students," 18 December 1923, HUA.

86. Synnott, "Social History," 441–46.

87. "Report of the Committee Appointed 'To Consider and Report to the Governing Boards,'" HUA, 2; "Report of the Committee on the Limitation of Students," 18 December 1923, HUA.

88. Lowell to Pennypacker, 24 March 1924, HUA.

89. Higham, *Strangers in the Land: Patterns of American Nativism, 1860–1925* (1955; New Brunswick, N.J.: Rutgers U.P., 1992), 282–85, 312–24; Neil Baldwin, *Henry Ford and the Jews: The Mass Production of Hate* (New York: Public Affairs, 2001).

90. For biographical profiles of Brigham, whose ancestors included William Brewster, the fourth signer of the Mayflower Compact, see Matthew T. Downey, *Carl Campbell Brigham: Scientist and Educator* (Princeton, N.J.: Educational Testing Services, 1961), and *American National Biography*.

91. Gary Gerstle, *American Crucible: Race and Nation in the Twentieth Century* (Princeton, N.J.: Princeton U.P., 2001), 105.

92. Carl C. Brigham, *A Study of American Intelligence* (Princeton, N.J.: Princeton U.P., 1923), 189–90, 207–10. Seven years later, Brigham explicitly repudiated the conclusions about racial differences that he had reached in his book, writing that "one of the worst of these comparative racial studies—the writer's own—was without foundation." See Carl C. Brigham, "Intelligence Tests of Immigrant Groups," *Psychological Review* 37, 1930. For a sharp critique of Brigham's earlier work on intelligence, see Stephen Jay Gould, *The Mismeasure of Man* (New York: Norton, 1981), 224–33.

93. Burton Hendrick, *The Jews in America* (Garden City, N.Y.: Doubleday, Page, 1923), 89, 134, 145, 168.

94. Among the most outspoken advocates of restrictive legislation was Henry Fairfield Osborn. Of the I.Q. tests that Brigham had used, Osborn wrote in 1923: "I believe those tests were worth what the war cost, even in human life, if they served to show clearly to our people the lack of intelligence in our country, and the degrees of intelligence in different races who are coming to us, in a way which no one can say is the result of prejudice. . . . We have learned once and for all that the Negro is not like us. So in regard to many races and subraces in Europe we learned that some which we had believed possessed of an order of intelligence perhaps superior to ours [read Jews] were far inferior" (Gould, *Mismeasure of Man*, 231).

95. Higham, *Strangers*, 319–24.

96. Gerstle, *American Crucible*, 109; Desmond King, *Making Americans: Immigration, Race, and the Origins of the Diverse Democracy* (Cambridge, Mass.: Harvard U.P., 2000), 191, 206.

97. Oren, *Joining the Club*, 320; Freshman Herald: Class of 1927, PU, 33; Freshman Herald: Class of 1928, PU, 31.

98. Lowell to Tucker, 20 May 1922, HUA.

99. Delmar Leighton to Lowell, memorandum, 9 November 1925, HUA.

100. In 1925, the top-seventh plan brought Harvard 91 Jews from New England and the Middle Atlantic states compared to a total of just 22 students (6 of them Jewish) from the western and South Central states combined ("Table II: Geographic Distribution of Schools from Which New Freshmen Were Admitted, Percentage of Jews in Each Group, and Award of Freshman Aid," 23 November 1925, HUA).

101. Williams (pseudonym) to Lowell, 17 December 1925, HUA. (To protect

the privacy of alumni who sent private letters to Big Three administrators, I have generally used pseudonyms.) In implying that Jews, especially those from eastern Europe, were not "white," Williams was expressing a viewpoint common in the 1920s. Among the many scholars who have analyzed the fluidity of the position of Jews within the systems of racial classification of the period, see especially Matthew Frye Jacobson, *Whiteness of a Different Color: European Immigrants and the Alchemy of Race* (Cambridge, Mass.: Harvard U.P., 1998); Karen Brodkin, *How Jews Became White Folks: And What That Says About Race in America* (New Brunswick, N.J.: Rutgers U.P., 1998); and Robert Singerman, "The Jew as Racial Alien: The Genetic Component of American Anti-Semitism," in *Anti-Semitism in American History*, ed. David Gerber (Urbana: University of Illinois Press, 1986). Among Jewish students themselves at the time was the category of the "white Jew"—those who accepted the dictates of the dominant student culture and "put themselves forward for judgment and acceptance by their Gentile peers" (Harold Wechsler, "The Rationale for Restriction: Ethnicity and College Admission in America, 1910–1980," *American Quarterly* 36, no. 5 [Winter 1984], 657–58). For a brief but fascinating discussion of the participation of a Jewish congressman in placing the Japanese in a stigmatized racial category totally ineligible to emigrate to the United States, see Gerstle, *American Crucible*, 118–22. According to Gerstle, Jewish complicity in the racial denigration of the Japanese helped consolidate their status as members of a single superior European race and their placement "on the right side of the racial divide."

102. Lowell to Williams, 18 December 1925, HUA. In another letter to an alumnus that same month, Lowell offered assurances that "the matter [of the Jews] is thoroughly understood by the authorities here," adding of his attempt at restriction in 1922, "My plan was crude, and its method was very probably unwise," Lowell to Cyrus Brewer, 11 December 1925, HUA.

103. As late as April 1925, Lowell was forced to reply to Eliot's request that he have the opportunity to meet with the Special Committee to present his views (Synnott, "Social History," 447).

104. James's biography of Eliot was published just five years after his service as chairman of the Special Committee on the Size of the Freshman Class. See Henry James, *Charles W. Eliot: President of Harvard University 1869–1909*, 2 vols. (Boston: Houghton Mifflin, 1930). For a brief profile of James, a prominent New York lawyer with close connections to the Rockefellers, see *WWA, 1944–1945*.

105. Lowell to James, 3 November 1925, HUA.

106. Ibid.

107. James to Lowell, 4 November 1925, HUA.

108. Lowell to James, 6 November 1925, HUA.

109. James to Lowell, 10 November 1925, HUA.

110. "Report of the Special Committee Appointed to Consider the Limitation of Numbers," 11 January 1926, HUA, 11–12.

111. Synnott, *Half-Opened Door*, 109–10.

112. After the passage of the Immigration Act of 1924, Ward wrote to President Coolidge to declare that "in signing the immigration bill you have approved one of the most important measures which has ever been put upon our statute books. You have done a very great service to the country. You have lived up

to the words of your Message of last December, that America must be kept American" (quoted in King, *Making Americans*, 191). So loyal was Ward to the Immigration Restriction League that in nineteen years he missed only a single meeting except when he was away from Boston (Higham, *Strangers*, 102). For a portrait of Ward, a leader of the Immigration Restriction League for thirty years and an enthusiastic proponent of eugenics, see Barbara M. Solomon, *Ancestors and Immigrants: A Changing New England Tradition* (New York: John Wiley, 1956), 99–102, 104–5, 147–51, 168–69.

113. The membership of the Committee on Admission is listed in the "Report of the Committee on Admission, 1925–1926," HU, 297. An examination of the vote at the faculty meeting of 2 June 1922, at which the Henderson motion was defeated with 64 "nays" and 41 "ayes," reveals that four of its members (Pennypacker, Ward, Abbott, and Birkhoff) voted for the measure and none opposed it. "Minutes of the Special Meeting of the Faculty of Arts and Sciences," 2 June 1922, HUA.

114. Clarence Mendell, "Harvard," 8 December 1926, Yale University Archives.

14

PROLOGUE

From On the Run: Fugitive Life in an American City

Alice Goffman

Mike, Chuck, and their friend Alex were shooting dice on the wall of the elementary school. It was approaching midnight and quite cool for mid-September in Philadelphia. Between throws, Chuck cupped his hands together and blew heat into his fingers.

Mike usually won when the guys played craps, and tonight he was rubbing their noses in it, shrugging into a little victory dance when he scooped the dollar bills off the ground. After a pair of nines, Alex started in on Mike.

"You a selfish, skinny motherfucker, man."

"Niggas is always gonna hate," Mike grinned.

"You think you better than everybody, man. You ain't shit!"

Chuck laughed softly at his two best friends. Then he yawned and told Alex to shut his fat ass up before the neighbors called the law. A short time later, Chuck called it a night. Mike announced he was going to get cheesesteaks with his winnings and asked if I wanted to come with.

"Can *I* get a cheesesteak?" Alex interjected.

"Man, take your fat ass in the house," Chuck laughed.

"Oh, so I'm walking?!"

Alice Goffman, *On the Run: Fugitive Life in an American City* (Chicago: University of Chicago Press, 2014). © 2014 by The University of Chicago Press. All rights reserved.

Mike and I were halfway to the store in his car when his cell phone started ringing. When he picked up I could hear screams on the other end. Mike shouted, "Where you at? Where you at?"

He screeched the old Lincoln around and headed back to 6th Street, pulling up in front of the corner store. There in the headlights we saw Alex, all 250 pounds of him, squatting by the curb, apparently looking for something. When he glanced up at us, blood streamed from his face, down his white T-shirt, and onto his pants and boots. Alex mumbled something I couldn't decipher, and then I realized he was looking for his teeth. I started searching on the ground with him.

"Alex," I said, "we have to take you to the hospital."

Alex shook his head and put up his hand, struggling to form words with his mangled lips. I kept pleading until finally Mike said, "He's not fucking going, so stop pushing."

At this point I remembered that Alex was still on parole. In fact, he was quite close to completing his two years of supervision. He feared that the cops who crowd the local emergency room and run through their database the names of Black young men walking in the door would arrest him on the spot, or at least issue him a violation for breaking the terms of his parole. If that happened, he'd be back in prison, his two years of compliance on the outside wiped away. A number of his friends had been taken into custody at the hospital when they sought care for serious injuries or attempted to attend the birth of their children.

Mike took off his shirt and gave it to Alex to soak up the blood from his face. Chuck had come back around by this point, and carefully helped him into the front seat of Mike's car. We drove to my apartment a few blocks away. We cleaned Alex up a bit, and then he began to explain what had happened. On his way home from the dice game, a man in a black hoodie stepped out from behind the corner store and walked him into the alley with a gun at his back. This man pistol-whipped him several times, took his money, and smashed his face into a concrete wall. Later, Alex found out that this man had mistaken him for his younger brother, who'd apparently robbed the man the week before.

Over the next three hours, Mike and Chuck made a series of futile calls to locate someone with basic medical knowledge. Mike's baby-mom, Marie, was in school to become a nurse's aide, but she hadn't been speaking to him lately—not since she'd caught him cheating and put a brick through his car window. Finally, at around six in the morning, Alex contacted his cousin, who came over with a plastic bag full of gauze and needles and iodine, and stitched up his chin and the skin around his eyebrow. His jaw was surely broken, she said, as well as his nose, but there was nothing she could do about it.

The next afternoon, Alex returned to the apartment he shared with his girlfriend and young son. Mike and I went to visit him that evening. I again pleaded with Alex to seek medical treatment, and he again refused.

> All the bullshit I done been through [to finish his parole sentence], it's like, I'm not just going to check into emergency and there come the cops asking me all types of questions and writing my information down, and before you know it I'm back in there [in prison]. Even if they not there for me, some of them probably going to recognize me, then they going to come over, run my shit [check for his name in the police database under open arrest warrants]. I ain't supposed to be up there [his parole terms forbade him to be near 6th Street, where he was injured]; I can't be out at no two o'clock [his curfew was 10:00 p.m.]. Plus, they might still got that little jawn [warrant] on me in Bucks County [for court fees he did not pay at the end of a trial two years earlier]. I don't want them running my name, and then I got to go to court or I get locked back up.

At this point his girlfriend emerged from the bedroom, ran her hands over her jeans, and said, "He needs to go to the hospital. Better he spends six months in jail than he can't talk or chew food. That's the rest of his life."

———————

Alex's attack occurred over ten years ago. He still finds it difficult to breathe through his nose and speaks with a muffled lisp. His eyes don't appear at quite the same level in his face. But he didn't go back to prison. Alex successfully completed his parole sentence, a feat of luck and determination that only one other guy in his group of friends ever achieved.

15

A LITTLE ROOM FOR MYSELF

Teresa Gowan

I got to know Declan early in my recycling career. I was sitting in a Chinatown alleyway with a meager load of bottles and cans, writing in my notebook, when Declan pushed his cart into the same alleyway. I saw a slight, balding man with a forward lean.

"Just coming through. I'll leave you the findings," he muttered to me, pushing on fast.

"That's OK, take what you can. I'm taking a break."

Declan nodded. "That's right. You can't be getting frantic about this job."

"Do you want to join me? I have a couple of cans of soda."

"Soda! That's a new one. All right, then," he said hesitantly, sitting down nearby.

After a couple of minutes he asked me what I was writing. "I'm doing a study of recycling," I answered.

"So you are doing this for fun?" he said in a neutral tone.

I remarked on his Irish accent and told him that for a while I had made a living playing Irish music in pubs and factory clubs. Declan seemed pleased by the connection and agreed that we should go recycling together on Friday morning, a couple of days later.

These kinds of rendezvous were often unsuccessful so I was pleased when Declan showed up outside Vesuvio's Friday morning. We worked well together. He was not really nimble enough to vault over into the big dumpsters, so I clambered in and threw bottles and cans out to him. After gathering a substantial load over a three-hour period, we pushed it across the South of Market neighborhood to the recycling company on Rhode Island. Though the cart was piled high and wide, we were able to move fast. Declan pulled strenuously from the front with a "rope" made from two pairs of jeans and I did my best to stabilize the cart from the back.

After the last breathless push up the slope between the freeway and Rhode Island we swung into the great dim expanse of the plant's weighing area. It reeked with stale beer, and more distant clanks and engine sounds from inside the processing zone mixed with the sharper crash of bottles thrown into sorting bins by several other homeless recyclers, already in the process of separating and weighing their loads. Declan seemed wary of contact, keeping his eyes down. I wasn't sure if this was just shyness or fear, but I acquiesced, and we started our sorting in silence and a few yards away from the others.

As we were collecting our sixteen dollars, Desmond and Bill swung their carts into the plant. Bill was a generous middle-aged white man who had befriended me during my first days of fieldwork, teaching me the basic tricks of the trade. African American Desmond, a former musician, was another man I trusted deeply. My feeling was that Declan was isolated and that it would be good for him to get to know these two. Declan stiffened but seemed to be reassured when Bill and I hugged each other vigorously. Though Declan's tentative, polite manner was unusual on the street, Desmond treated him kindly, explaining the intricacies of the rates for different kinds of plastic. "OK, yes, that's good to know," Declan muttered, looking rather dazed.

After getting our money we waited around for Bill and Desmond and shared a couple of cigarettes outside the plant. Bill continued Declan's recycling education, telling him his own tips for how to collect and sell wine bottles without raising the wrath of the weighers. (At that time wine bottles were not covered by the California Bottle Bill's redemption scheme.) Declan paid careful attention, but his look of underlying bewilderment persisted. He seemed to be still in the "shock stage," as some in the recycling scene called it, not quite able to understand or accept that he was really homeless.

Sitting in Washington Park after some more hours of work, Declan and I watched a couple of older Chinese ladies doing their evening tai chi exercises. I didn't want to push him yet on how he had become homeless, so I turned the conversation toward our migrations to America.

"So why did you come?" I asked him.

"It's hard to say now. I can't really remember what I was thinking. . . . I do remember buying the ticket because I was so pleased with myself that

I saved the money, because it was expensive. . . . I think really it was less about coming to America and more about leaving Ireland. America was just . . . this place where everyone was supposed to do so well. But I wasn't so sure that I would do well. I never seemed to be cut out for success, but you can't help hoping."

Declan smiled ruefully, avoiding eye contact.

"Why did you want to leave Ireland?"

"That was clear enough. Ireland is awful strong on the family, you know. The family and the religion. And I, well, I had no luck with the first and no taste for the second. Bunch of hypocrites, if you ask me."

Later I found out that Declan was the illegitimate child of an absent and unmentioned mother. As a baby he had been reluctantly taken in by an aunt and uncle in a provincial town. Uncle James and Aunt Kathleen were "lace-curtain Irish," respectable, inhibited folks who never acknowledged Declan as their nephew in front of strangers. If necessary they would tell some vague story about how he was an orphan from Aunt Kathleen's village on the coast. In the evening, Kathleen would serve him food after the other children, and when I got to know him, he was still bitter about the rarity of meat on his plate as a child.

Like many others circulating in and out of homelessness, Declan had grown from unwanted child to isolated adult. At sixteen he found work washing dishes in a hotel: "I was doing all right with my work; that wasn't so much the problem. But, of course, I wasn't making enough for to rent my own place yet. I was lodging with another family for a few shillings a week, but they were a damn miserable lot. The place was so damp; my bed was always soaking.

"So I went to my other uncle, my Uncle Patrick, in the hopes that maybe I could stay with them for while. I was willing to pay my way, of course. He took me down to the pub and was quite friendly, but he said his wife wouldn't want it. They were always ashamed of my existence, all of them. I was a stain on the family."

"Were you the only one?"

"I don't know. They would never speak of my mother, so I don't know what happened to her, but fasure it was no good."

Thirty-five years after immigrating to America, Declan still led a solitary, unloved existence. Although he could talk up a storm when the mood took him, most of the time he seemed deeply depressed, his shoulders bowed and his forehead permanently drawn into a large, central crease.

My impressions turned out to be accurate: Declan had been homeless for only a few weeks. For the previous eleven years, he had been living in a Chinatown SRO hotel, cleaning the hallways and bathrooms in exchange for rent. It was a tiny nest, but he had made it quite cozy, even growing flowers and tomatoes on the roof. In 1994 the hotel manager had decided that Declan needed to come up with some money to supplement his work-for-rent trade.

"I mean, it was outrageous. This fella was already working me thirty hours a week for rent alone, so I was having to work another janitor position for my other living expenses. . . . They put the rent up to $500 a month, and they were getting people in who had that kind of money."

"How much were you making?"

"Ooh, I was making $8.25 an hour at my outside job, but the hours were not regular enough for me. I couldn't get my rent in on time, and they threatened me with eviction . . . like I walked in off the street last week. I didn't want to stay anymore. After that, I was too angry. I could not look the fella in the eye anymore. I wanted to punch him."

"Did you?"

"No. I'm not a violent man."

Far from it. Declan said that he had not had a fight since he was a teenager, and it was easy to believe. If anything, he had not enough fight in him, but seemed browbeaten into passivity by his harsh childhood and a life of lonely, menial labor.

He had accepted the prospect of temporary homelessness, moving some of his possessions into a storage locker and buying a twenty-year-old Corolla for somewhere to sleep. Another man living in a van suggested to him that he start recycling, as the chaos of car living was making it hard for him to keep regular hours with the day labor agencies.

As long as he had his car, where he could sleep or relax with the racing news, Declan was willing to push around a shopping cart without the shame that plagued most of the homeless men. "See," he told me, "you can tell that I'm not really homeless like some of these fellas, because I just have the bottles and cans in my shopping cart. There's no clothes in there. I'm not carrying broken-down pieces of junk. And I keep myself clean. Altogether there's not much reason for anyone to think I was sleeping out on the street."

During this period, Declan was parking overnight in an old industrial section of eastern So-Ma, now pocked with the upscale condominiums classified misleadingly as live-work "lofts." He chose this neighborhood because at that time many of the buildings were still warehouses and there was little competition for parking spaces. He would eat his breakfast on a picnic table in the small park and brush his teeth at the drinking fountain. But even though parking places were still plentiful, new parking restrictions had followed on the heels of the upscale urban pioneers. Frequently posted signs now announced, "NO VEHICLE LIVING 10 PM-6 AM."

"I want to stay in the neighborhood because there's plenty of parking and it feels safe-like. You've got good streetlights, not too many bad characters around. But this law, it's a right pain in the ass. You have to somehow make it look like you're not in the car. Like it's not hard enough fitting your whole life into a little car, you have to even hide the evidence inside the damn car. It's easier if you have a van; you can cover up the windows. But with a car, you look suspicious if you do that. Tinted windows, that's what you need. But you don't see your Civics and Corollas with tinted windows."

Declan decided to get rid of his much-loved plants, which had been stashed along the rear window shelf. He also sold his collections of Father Brown detective novels and Dick Francis thrillers, making more room for basic necessities in the trunk. None of these concessions worked. After police officers woke him three nights in a row, demanding he move on, Declan moved south into Dogpatch, one of the last remaining corners moderately safe from either robbers or nighttime rousting by the police.

The neighborhood's odd mixture of families and loners, wage workers, recyclers, sidewalk peddlers, and thieves provided solitary Declan with a more lively social circle than he had known for years. His prejudice against other homeless people disappeared, and he started talking about some as "neighbors." He befriended one person in particular: a big, shy redhead called Mitch with a lumberjack look to him.

A couple of months later, the Corolla's clutch finally gave out completely, and he had to push it from one side of the road to the other to avoid parking tickets. Mitch came to the rescue, helping Declan acquire and install a replacement clutch, and in return Declan let him use the car to visit his terminally ill father in Antelope Valley. Declan went along, as he had nowhere else to stay.

I did not see Declan for some weeks after this trip. But one morning about eleven o'clock he called me in a state of panic.

"Look, I'm sorry, but I need your help. I'm having a terrible time with my car."

"What's the matter?"

"The bastards towed it this morning. I didn't know what time it was because my watch was stopped!"

Declan asked me if I could come down and help him deal with the towing company. I could not afford the $130 he needed to get the car out of the pound, but he thought it would help if I came down. "Dressed nicely like?" he hinted. He was desperate to get his things out of the car. "I can't see why they would mind, you know. They will still have the car and all." Declan's shallow breathing and sweaty fidgeting gave the lie to his optimistic words.

When we got to the towing company, Declan told them respectfully that he did not have enough money for the fine right now, but could he please get his things out of the car.

At first the person at the desk was merely officious in his refusals. I had been trying to reach someone at the Coalition on Homelessness to find out what rights Declan had in this situation. Unfortunately, there was no one around at that moment that knew. There wasn't much that we could do. I tried to appeal to the desk clerk's sympathy.

"It's like being evicted from your house and not being able to get any of your things out," I pleaded.

"That's not our problem," he snapped, hardened no doubt by years of dealing with enraged car owners. "I can't make exceptions to the rule!"

Declan asked to speak to a manager, and the clerk pointedly ignored him.

"If you can't handle the responsibility of a car, you shouldn't have one," he told us.

This poverty-as-irresponsibility stab worked wonders. Declan stormed out, his fists clenched. Outside on the street the cars roared by, forcing us to shout.

I could tell Declan had given up on me.

"It's all right, it's all right," he kept repeating. "I'll figure something out. You haven't the time for all this."

It was embarrassing to be so useless, but I had no more authority than Declan did. He wouldn't speak his fear, so I could not easily console him. I offered him a couch for the night. He looked doubtful, but said he would call later, and we parted quickly.

I was not surprised that Declan did not call me that night, but when I had not heard from him in a week I started to worry. I went over to Dogpatch and managed to find Mitch. He also had no information and was equally concerned. I went home and reluctantly picked up the phone to call the usual trinity: the jail, the hospital, and the morgue. Suicide was my biggest worry, but pushing morbid thoughts aside, I called the jail first. To my surprise I was told that he was indeed there. I could not find out the charge, but assumed it was minor, for Declan had never been in trouble with the law.

When I went down to see him, his face looked gray and creased under the fluorescent lights of the jail.

"What did you do, Declan?"

"I don't know what I was thinking. I was wandering round the place for a few hours and, you know, I could see my car. I didn't know what to do. So when it got to about three in the morning I tried to jump the fence and get my papers out of the car. I couldn't see anyone around."

"But you got caught?"

"Mmmm." Declan looked at the table. We sat in silence.

"Are you OK?"

"You can't relax. There's all this fighting and bully boy tactics like."

I gave Declan some money for cigarettes and phone calls. I was going away for a few weeks, and I was sure that within a week or two he would be out. I could not imagine that a first offender would be given any serious jail time for trying to get his car back. Many of the recyclers cycled regularly in and out of jail for minor offenses, rarely staying more than a few weeks.

What Declan had not told me was that he had got into a scuffle with the security guard who had caught him. He was charged and convicted of both attempted burglary and assault.

I was out of town when his case came up, but I gleaned that Declan's clean record may have stood for something, but his lack of employment and legitimate housing had sent another, more important message. The judge seemed convinced by the security guard's tale of being attacked by a fearsome, demented intruder, though Declan assured me that this was "damn lies." ("Crikey. You never heard such a tall story. And him a big strapping lad, twice my size.")

Declan's courtroom manner would not have helped. When dealing with authority he vacillated between self-deprecation and resentment. Like so many of the always poor, he could not display the righteous indignation of a man who believes he deserves better.

Declan did nine months in the county jail, coming out noticeably grayer and even more stooped, his manner more meek and distracted than ever. He stumbled hopelessly into the shelter system with nothing beyond the clothes on his back.

Mr. Haven, his case manager at MSC South, helped him get some clothes, but although Declan picked up occasional days of work at a day labor agency, it seemed impossible that he would ever get together enough money to move back inside. It was now impossible to find even the meanest studio for less than $800 a month and inconceivable that he could pay such sums without a regular job.

As a client with neither a fiery attitude nor a serious substance abuse problem, Declan had won the sympathy of Mr. Haven, who eventually helped him to find a semipermanent bed in a Marin County shelter in exchange for kitchen work. This was a passable compromise for a while, but the last time I spoke to him, Declan was chafing over the lack of privacy.

"I'm asking myself, is it possible I'll ever have my own room again?" he told me as we sat alone in the shelter's grim cafeteria. "I'm dreaming about it constantly, like. That's all I want, just a little room for myself, away from people coughing, people snoring, people fighting. I've never been much of a sociable fella, you know, and I find the noise, the chatter, the quarrelling, and complaining makes me want to shout out BE BLOODY QUIET! ... I'm not sure how long I can do this job without going loony!'

"What do you think you will do?" I asked.

"What can you do? Mr. Haven says if I was American he could maybe get me some help to go home. But even if they could send me to Ireland, I don't know where I would go."

Declan looked up at me, shaking his head, then turned away as tears came into his eyes. "I'm finished, if you ask me. I'm finished."

> Home is the place where, when you have to go there,
> They have to take you in.

Thus ruminates the sympathetic farmer's wife in Frost's poignant poem about the death of the old tramp Silas. There was no such place for Declan. He would have to make do with today's poorhouse.

PART III

Narrative and Institutional Contexts

Part IIIA
Narratives from Above

To paraphrase Marx, women and men tell stories, but they do not tell them under conditions of their own choosing. In previous sections, we have addressed what narrative is, how it does (or does not) explain, and the purposes it serves. In Part III, we address how—and under what conditions—narratives are produced. We have divided Part III into two sections. The first encompasses what we call narratives "from above." By this we mean narratives that are imposed on individuals and groups by culture, by institutions, and sometimes simply by powerful figures. The second section addresses what we call narratives "from below." By this, we mean narratives that women and men produce in resisting the authority of that culture, those institutions, and those powerful figures.

In making this distinction, we readily admit to drawing sharper lines than exist in the social world. In practice, any particular narrative typically comes both from above and below. Nobody is completely free to make up stories on her or his own. A narrator uses language and conventions of plot, matters of explanation and connection that are drawn broadly from a surrounding culture. Social settings prescribe, even if loosely, characteristic sequences for telling stories. These have been defined as "narrative structures" or "master frames" (Bridger and Maines 1998), or as a "narrative formula" (Irvine 1999). Very few narrators can escape the institutional contexts in which they tell stories: police, courts, schools, religions, workplaces, even family and friends, all have criteria and rules, sometimes explicit, sometimes not, about what constitute *acceptable* narratives.

Pressures "from above" shape but do not determine people's narratives. It is rare, at most, for cultures and institutions to impose narratives without resistance. Imagine, as an extreme instance, a bully standing over a victim, twisting the victim's arm, insisting on hearing what may be the most primitive of narratives: "Say uncle." Even here, the victim may resist, refusing to "say uncle" despite pain and humiliation, perhaps murmuring something very different under her breath or discounting the narrative because it was coerced. Even more does culture, as it limits our choices, provide bits and pieces of ideas from which we can construct narratives to suit our own purposes. In addition, institutions, even those with explicit rules about acceptable narratives, such as religions, schools, and courts, typically allow at least some wiggle room for women and men to invent their stories, if not entirely, at least in part. People can employ standard stories from one setting in another (Holstein and Gubrium 2000). Moreover, "particular settings are often governed by multiple, ambiguous, and/or conflicting storytelling norms" (Polletta 2012: 230). For example, in Irvine's study of a twelve-step group, participants use the same narrative formula to tell very different stories (1999: 50).

Although we characterize some narratives as coming "from above," people don't necessarily experience them as oppressive. Narratives from above circulate at the level of the taken-for-granted background of everyday life, as part of what "everybody knows." An observant Catholic, for example, might have no knowledge of the institutional history of confession (Bridger and Maines 1998; Hepworth and Turner 1982). For most, going to confession is just what good Catholics do.

The tensions between narratives from above and narratives from below, between narrative control and narrative freedom, often overwhelm the ability to narrate clearly. Nowhere, perhaps, is this more evident than in the various forms of therapy, and particularly psychotherapy (Rose 1998). As no less significant a figure than Sigmund Freud announced in his famous case study of Dora, "Fragment of an Analysis of a Case of Hysteria" (1905), a patient's problems, compounded by repression and denial, manifest in an inability to tell a coherent story of one's own life. The "theoretical" aim of therapy, Freud argues, is "to repair all the damages to the patient's memory." In short, the point of therapy is to restore the patient's ability to tell her own story, to achieve a form of narrative freedom. And yet, as Freud himself acknowledges—and several generations of feminist critics of Freud have insisted—Dora resisted Freud's narrative, breaking off analysis, and the case Freud characterized as "hysteria" is better understood as sexual abuse.

Therapy unambiguously organizes itself around narratives. However, does therapy constitute an effort to give the patient tools to construct her own narrative, as its defenders would insist, or does it (as its critics would insist) impose a narrative on the patient from above? No doubt, it involves both, with the balance depending on the particular characteristics of the patient, the therapist, and the therapy. We can find similar ambiguities in the narratives produced by national truth commissions (Andrews, this volume), in narratives of autism (Gray 2001), in twelve-step programs (Irvine 1999), and in many other realms.

Despite the ambiguities, we keep to our "from above/from below" distinction while understanding its limits. Tendentious as the distinction may be, we believe it marks a fundamental difference in the ways narratives are produced and in the kinds of tensions we see in response to those narratives.

In one of the most striking passages of perhaps his best known book, *The History of Sexuality*, which we include here, Michel Foucault declares that, "the confession [has become] one of the West's most highly valued techniques for producing truth. We have become a singularly confessing society" (1978: 59). Foucault traces the rise of confession to the codification of the sacrament of penance in the Catholic Church. However, whatever its origins, the confessional mode has spread everywhere. Foucault writes:

> It plays a part in justice, medicine, education, family relations and love relations, in the most ordinary affairs of everyday life, and in the most solemn rites; one confesses one's crimes, one's sins, one's thoughts and desires, one's illnesses and troubles; one goes about telling, with the greatest precision, whatever is most difficult to tell. One confesses in public and in private, to one's parents, to one's educators, to one's doctors, to those one loves. (1978: 59)

The confession, a distinctive form of narrative, produces what we take for truth. While Foucault is notoriously elusive about the sources of social power, there is no ambiguity but that confession is deeply implicated in power—the power of professions, of institutions and, not least, of discourse. "One confesses," Foucault continues, "or is forced to confess" (1978: 59).

The archetype of confession is, as Foucault suggests, Catholic confession. Catholic confession can be read as "functional" in the rough sense that it is of value to those who confess as well as those to whom one confesses. In this light, confession can be understood to contribute to the health (mental and spiritual) of the penitent, to provide a means of reintegrating the sinner into society, and, at the same time, to articulate the basic values of that society. Nonetheless, as Hepworth and Turner (1982) argue, Catholic confession is better understood as a form of social control, based on a "priestly monopoly" of the right to hear confession, which both expressed and consolidated the authority of the Church. The very act of confession, they argue, involves an inequality between penitent and priest, which itself mirrors broader social inequalities. Most importantly, they argue, Catholic confession has "worked to police the behavior of subordinate classes while legitimating actions and beliefs . . . within the ruling classes" (1982: 55–56).

Catholic confession may be the archetype but there are many other forms and variants. In criminal confessions, for example, the power imbalance between confessor and confessee, or interrogator and suspect, is particularly coercive (Leo 2008). Consider also the sexual confessions of indescribable variety once frequent on television's syndicated afternoon talk shows, where coercion is much less visible (Gamson 1998). In the taking of a medical history, where confession is driven by the doctor's agenda, the claim to need knowledge is presented as being in the patient's best interest. ("How many cigarettes a day to do you smoke?" "Have you had unprotected sex?") So, too, are there confessions in much less structured situations, in the routine events of everyday life where one confesses to one's teachers ("I'm sorry. I didn't study as hard as I could have"), to one's parents ("I'm sorry I'm late"), even to one's friends ("I'll try to do better next time").

Catholic confession also provides a guide to the features of confession. The sacrament of penance involves not simply confession proper, or the acknowledgment of one's sins, but also contrition, satisfaction, and absolution. Although the three editors disagree on this point, at least one would argue that, while an acknowledgment of sin—or at least of responsibility—appears in most narratives from above, the other elements of penance appear with varying frequency and importance. "Satisfaction" (in effect, repayment for one's sins) and "absolution" (forgiveness for one's sins) are fundamental accompaniments of criminal confessions (with both aspects neatly covered in the notion of "paying one's debt to society"). So, too, are they present in the multitudinous confessions of everyday life ("Okay, but get it in tomorrow," "You're grounded," and extended pleas for forgiveness). However, *contrition*, sincere sorrow for one's sins, is most important to how narratives from above operate as systems of social control.

For a narrative from above to operate effectively as a system of control, the narrator must sincerely believe the story she is required to tell and recognize the authority of those people or institutions requiring the story. This is both the strength and the weakness of confession. On the one hand, insofar as the penitent believes her own story and recognizes the authority of the confessor, narratives from above are remarkably efficient. If the Catholic penitent believes herself to be a sinner and the priest to be capable of absolution, the Church need not supervise its parishioners directly to ensure obedience to its rules. Similarly, if the slave believes—and internalizes—the slave owner's story about slavery, if the factory worker believes the factory owner's story about markets, if the student believes the teacher's story about what a student should do and be, if the patient believes the therapist's story about the sources of his illness and what she must do to get better, to that degree the slave owner and the factory owner and the teacher and the therapist have achieved a level of control all the more effective because the slave or factory worker or student or patient seems a willing participant in her own domination. At the same time, however, the slave owner's or factory owner's or teacher's or therapist's control of *material* resources (less odious work, better pay, better grades, or exemptions from responsibility) invites cynical narration: the telling of stories that the narrator does not believe with the aim of gaining immediate advantage, but with no guarantee of future behavior. This tension, between the internalization of beliefs and their cynical adoption, is the fundamental tension in both confession and narratives from above more generally.

Molly Andrews's article, "Grand National Narratives," a comparative analysis of truth and reconciliation commissions in South Africa and Germany, switches attention from individual narratives to collective narratives. Granted, all narratives from above are socially structured—and in that sense collective—but the stories told in confessionals and interrogation rooms, as well as in therapists' offices and elsewhere are, for the most part, stories told by individuals about themselves. In contrast, collective narratives are stories told by collectivities—including nations, businesses, ethnic groups, schools, and families—about themselves. Often studied under the general rubric of "collective memory," collective narratives appear in textbooks, museums, company histories, yearbooks, and the rituals surrounding both religious and secular holidays. If the fundamental tension in individual narratives driven from above is between sincerity and cynicism, collective narratives are marked by a parallel tension between stories that are meaningful to members of the collectivity and those that are empty or meaningless.

Andrews is alert to this tension in truth and reconciliation commissions, an increasingly common way in which many nations with troubled pasts have attempted to come to terms with those pasts. These commissions mimic aspects of individual penance, with "truth" standing for elements of both contrition and confession and "reconciliation" approximating satisfaction and absolution. Yet, as Andrews argues, the collective character of the truth and reconciliation commissions adds an additional dimension. The German commission, formed to come to terms with East Germany's disturbing dependence on secret police before unification, intended to establish "a shared history for all of the newly united Germany." But this story, imposed from above, came at the cost of "silencing . . . the stories of the majority of East Germans, for whom state socialism was not the focus of resistance but merely a fact of everyday life." Even in South Africa, where the truth and reconciliation commission, as part of an effort to achieve a kind of national catharsis after the fall of apartheid, used a "bottom-up" approach in collecting testimony from more than twenty thousand individuals, not all groups within South Africa accept the particular truth that commission arrived at. Truth commissions, like other forms of collective memory, are not simply "conduits for stories." They are, instead, shaped by competing groups, often with distinctive political agendas, and thus "wield an important influence on which stories are told and how they are to be interpreted."

References

Bridger, Jeffrey C., and David R. Maines. 1998. "Narrative Structures and the Catholic Church Closings in Detroit." *Qualitative Sociology* 21(3): 319–40.

Freud, Sigmund. 1905. "Fragment of an Analysis of a Case of Hysteria." *Standard Edition*, Vol. 2. London: Hogarth.

Gamson, Joshua. 1998. *Freaks Talk Back: Tabloid Talk Shows and Sexual Nonconformity*. Chicago: University of Chicago Press.

Gray, David E. 2001. "Accommodation, Resistance, and Transcendence: Three Narratives of Autism." *Social Science & Medicine* 53(9): 1247–57.

Hepworth, Mike, and Bryan S. Turner. 1982. *Confession: Studies in Deviance and Religion*. London: Routledge and Kegan Paul.

Holstein, James A., and Jaber F. Gubrium. 2000. *The Self We Live By: Narrative Identity in a Postmodern World*. New York: Oxford University Press.

Irvine, Leslie. 1999. *Codependent Forevermore: The Invention of Self in a Twelve Step Group*. Chicago: University of Chicago Press.

Leo, Richard A. 2008. *Police Interrogation and American Justice*. Cambridge MA: Harvard University Press.

Polletta, Francesca. 2012. "Analyzing Popular Beliefs about Storytelling." In *Varieties of Narrative Analysis*. Edited by J. Holstein and J. Gubrium, 229–50. Thousand Oaks CA: SAGE.

Rose, Nikolas. 1998. *Inventing Ourselves: Psychology, Power, and Personhood*. Cambridge UK: Cambridge University Press.

16

SCIENTIA SEXUALIS

Michel Foucault

I suppose that the first two points will be granted me; I imagine that people will accept my saying that, for two centuries now, the discourse on sex has been multiplied rather than rarefied; and that if it has carried with it taboos and prohibitions, it has also, in a more fundamental way, ensured the solidification and implantation of an entire sexual mosaic. Yet the impression remains that all this has by and large played only a defensive role. By speaking about it so much, by discovering it multiplied, partitioned off, and specified precisely where one had placed it, what one was seeking essentially was simply to conceal sex: a screen-discourse, a dispersion-avoidance. Until Freud at least, the discourse on sex—the discourse of scholars and theoreticians—never ceased to hide the thing it was speaking about. We could take all these things that were said, the painstaking precautions and detailed analyses, as so many procedures meant to evade the unbearable, too hazardous truth of sex. And the mere fact that one claimed to be speaking about it from the rarefied and neutral viewpoint of a science is in itself significant. This was in fact a science made up of evasions since, given its inability or refusal to speak of sex itself, it concerned itself primarily with aberrations, perversions, exceptional oddities, pathological abatements, and morbid aggravations. It was by the same token a science subordinated in the main to the imperatives of a morality whose divisions it reiterated under the guise of the medical norm. Claiming to speak the truth, it stirred up people's fears; to the least oscillations of sexuality, it ascribed an imaginary dynasty of evils destined to be passed on for generations; it declared the furtive customs of the timid, and the most solitary of petty manias, dangerous for the whole society; strange pleasures, it warned, would eventually result in nothing short of death: that of individuals, generations, the species itself.

It thus became associated with an insistent and indiscreet medical practice, glibly proclaiming its aversions, quick to run to the rescue of law and public opinion, more servile with respect to the powers of order than amenable to the requirements of truth. Involuntarily naïve in the best of cases, more often intentionally mendacious, in complicity with what it denounced, haughty and coquettish, it established an entire pornography of the morbid, which was characteristic of the *fin de siècle* society. In France, doctors like Garnier, Pouillet, and Ladoucette were its unglorified scribes and Rollinat its poet. But beyond these troubled pleasures, it assumed other powers; it set itself up as the supreme authority in matters of hygienic necessity, taking up the old fears of venereal affliction and combining them with the new themes of asepsis, and the great evolutionist myths with the recent institutions of public health; it claimed to ensure the physical vigor and the moral cleanliness of the social body; it promised to eliminate defective individuals, degenerate and bastardized populations. In the name of a biological and historical urgency, it justified the racisms of the state, which at the time were on the horizon. It grounded them in "truth."

When we compare these discourses on human sexuality with what was known at the time about the physiology of animal and plant reproduction, we are struck by the incongruity. Their feeble content from the standpoint of elementary rationality, not to mention scientificity, earns them a place apart in the history of knowledge. They form a strangely muddled zone. Throughout the nineteenth century, sex seems to have been incorporated into two very distinct orders of knowledge: a biology of reproduction, which developed continuously according to a general scientific normativity, and a medicine of sex conforming to quite different rules of formation. From one to the other, there was no real exchange, no reciprocal structuration; the role of the first with respect to the second was scarcely more than as a distant and quite fictitious guarantee: a blanket guarantee under cover of which moral obstacles, economic or political options, and traditional fears could be recast in a scientific-sounding vocabulary. It is as if a fundamental resistance blocked the development of a rationally formed discourse concerning human sex, its correlations, and its effects. A disparity of this sort would indicate that the aim of such a discourse was not to state the truth but to prevent its very emergence. Underlying the difference between the physiology of reproduction and the medical theories of sexuality, we would have to see something other and something more than an uneven scientific development or a disparity in the forms of rationality; the one would partake of that immense will to knowledge which has sustained the establishment of scientific discourse in the West, whereas the other would derive from a stubborn will to nonknowledge.

This much is undeniable: the learned discourse on sex that was pronounced in the nineteenth century was imbued with age-old delusions, but also with systematic blindnesses: a refusal to see and to understand; but further—and this is the crucial point—a refusal concerning the very thing that was brought to light and whose formulation was urgently solicited. For there can be no misunderstanding that is not based on a fundamental relation to truth. Evading this truth, barring access to it, masking it: these were so many local tactics which, as if by superimposition and through a last-minute detour, gave a paradoxical form to a fundamental petition to know. Choosing not to recognize was yet another vagary of the will to truth. Let Charcot's Salpêtrière serve as an example in this regard: it was an enormous apparatus for observation, with its examinations, interrogations, and experiments, but it was also a machinery for incitement, with its public presentations, its theater of ritual crises, carefully staged with the help of ether or amyl nitrate, its interplay of dialogues, palpations, laying on of hands, postures which the doctors elicited or obliterated with a gesture or a word, its hierarchy of personnel who kept watch, organized, provoked, monitored, and reported, and who accumulated an immense pyramid of observations and dossiers. It is in the context of this continuous incitement to discourse and to truth that the real mechanisms of misunderstanding (*méconnaissance*) operated: thus Charcot's gesture interrupting a public consultation where it began to be too manifestly a question of "that"; and the more frequent practice of deleting from the succession of dossiers what had been said and demonstrated by the patients regarding sex, but also what had been seen, provoked, solicited by the doctors themselves, things that were almost entirely omitted from the published observations.[1] The important thing, in this affair, is not that these men shut their eyes or stopped their ears, or that they were mistaken; it is rather that they constructed around and apropos of sex an immense apparatus for producing truth, even if this truth was to be masked at the last moment. The essential point is that sex was not only a matter of sensation and pleasure, of law and taboo, but also of truth and falsehood, that the truth of sex became something fundamental, useful, or dangerous, precious or formidable: in short, that sex was constituted as a problem of truth. What needs to be situated, therefore, is not the threshold of a new rationality whose discovery was marked by Freud—or someone else—but the progressive formation (and also the transformations) of that "interplay of truth and sex" which was bequeathed to us by the nineteenth century, and which we may have modified, but, lacking evidence to the contrary, have not rid ourselves of. Misunderstandings, avoidances, and evasions were only possible, and only had their effects, against the background of this strange endeavor: to tell the truth of sex. An endeavor that does not date from the nineteenth century, even if it was then that a nascent science lent it a singular form. It was the basis of all the aberrant, naïve and cunning discourses where knowledge of sex seems to have strayed for such a long time.

Historically, there have been two great procedures for producing the truth of sex.

On the one hand, the societies—and they are numerous: China, Japan, India, Rome, the Arabo-Moslem societies—which endowed themselves with an *ars erotica*. In the erotic art, truth is drawn from pleasure itself, understood as a practice and accumulated as experience; pleasure is not considered in relation to an absolute law of the permitted and the forbidden, nor by reference to a criterion of utility, but first and foremost in relation to itself; it is experienced as pleasure, evaluated in terms of its intensity, its specific quality, its duration, its reverberations in the body and the soul. Moreover, this knowledge must be deflected back into the sexual practice itself, in order to shape it as though from within and amplify its effects. In this way, there is formed a knowledge that must remain secret, not because of an element of infamy that might attach to its object, but because of the need to hold it in the greatest reserve, since, according to tradition, it would lose its effectiveness and its virtue by being divulged. Consequently, the relationship to the master who holds the secrets is of paramount importance; only he, working alone, can transmit this art in an esoteric manner and as the culmination of an initiation in which he guides the disciple's progress with unfailing skin and severity. The effects of this masterful art, which are considerably more generous than the spareness of its prescriptions would lead one to imagine, are said to transfigure the one fortunate enough to receive its privileges: an absolute mastery of the body, a singular bliss, obliviousness to time and limits, the elixir of life, the exile of death and its threats.

On the face of it at least, our civilization possesses no *ars erotica*. In return, it is undoubtedly the only civilization to practice a *scientia sexualis*; or rather, the only civilization to have developed over the centuries procedures for telling the truth of sex which are geared to a form of knowledge-power strictly opposed to the art of initiations and the masterful secret: I have in mind the confession.

Since the Middle Ages at least, Western societies have established the confession as one of the main rituals we rely on for the production of truth: the codification of the sacrament of penance by the Lateran Council in 1215, with the resulting development of confessional techniques, the declining importance of accusatory procedures in criminal justice, the abandonment of tests of guilt (sworn statements, duels, judgments of God) and the development of methods of interrogation and inquest, the increased participation of the royal administration in the prosecution of infractions, at the expense of proceedings leading to private settlements, the setting up of tribunals of Inquisition: all this helped to give the confession a central role in the order of civil and religious powers. The evolution of the word *avowal* and of the legal function it designated is itself emblematic of this development: from being a guarantee of the status, identity, and value granted to one person by another, it came to signify someone's acknowledgment of his own actions and thoughts. For a long time, the individual was vouched for by the reference of others and the demonstration of his ties to the commonweal (family, allegiance, protection); then he was authenticated by the discourse of truth he was able or obliged to pronounce concerning himself. The truthful confession as inscribed at the heart of the procedures of individualization by power.

In any case, next to the testing rituals, next to the testimony of witnesses, and the learned methods of observation and demonstration, the confession became one of the West's most highly valued techniques for producing truth. We have since become a singularly confessing society. The confession has spread its effects far and wide. It plays a part in justice, medicine, education, family relationships, and love relations, in the most ordinary affairs of everyday life, and in the most solemn rites; one confesses one's crimes, one's sins, one's thoughts and desires, one's illnesses and troubles; one goes about telling, with the greatest precision, whatever is most difficult to tell. One confesses in public and in private, to one's parents, one's educators, one's doctor, to those one loves; one admits to oneself, in pleasure and in pain, things it would be impossible to tell to anyone else, the things people write books about. One confesses—or is forced to confess. When it is not spontaneous or dictated by some internal imperative, the confession is wrung from a person by violence or threat; it is driven from its hiding place in the soul, or extracted from the body. Since the Middle Ages, torture has accompanied it like a shadow, and supported it when it could go no further: the dark twins.[2] The most defenseless tenderness and the bloodiest of powers have a similar need of confession. Western man has become a confessing animal.

Whence a metamorphosis in literature: we have passed from a plea-sure to be recounted and heard, centering on the heroic or marvelous narration of "trials" of bravery or sainthood, to a literature ordered ac-cording to the infinite task of extracting from the depths of oneself, in be-tween the words, a truth which the very form of the confession holds out like a shimmering mirage. Whence too this new way of philosophizing: seeking the fundamental relation to the true, not simply in oneself—in some forgotten knowledge, or in a certain primal trace—but in the self-examination that yields, through a multitude of fleeting impressions, the basic certainties of consciousness. The obligation to confess is now re-layed through so many different points, is so deeply ingrained in us, that we no longer perceive it as the effect of a power that constrains us; on the contrary, it seems to us that truth, lodged in our most secret nature, "de-mands" only to surface; that if it fails to do so, this is because a constraint holds it in place, the violence of a power weighs it down, and it can finally be articulated only at the price of a kind of liberation. Confession frees, but power reduces one to silence; truth does not belong to the order of power, but shares an original affinity with freedom: traditional themes in philosophy, which a "political history of truth" would have to overturn by showing that truth is not by nature free—nor error servile—but that its production is thoroughly imbued with relations of power. The confession is an example of this.

One has to be completely taken in by this internal ruse of confession in order to attribute a fundamental role to censorship, to taboos regard-ing speaking and thinking; one has to have an inverted image of power in order to believe that all these voices which have spoken so long in our civilization—repeating the formidable injunction to tell what one is and what one does, what one recollects and what one has forgotten, what one is thinking and what one thinks he is not thinking—are speaking to us of freedom. An immense labor to which the West has submitted generations in order to produce—while other forms of work ensured the accumulation of capital—men's subjection: their constitution as subjects in both senses of the word. Imagine how exorbitant must have seemed the order given to all Christians at the beginning of the thirteenth cen-tury to kneel at least once a year and confess to all their transgressions, without omitting a single one. And think of that obscure partisan, seven centuries later, who had come to rejoin the Serbian resistance deep in the mountains; his superiors asked him to write his life story; and when he brought them a few miserable pages, scribbled in the night, they did not look at them but only said to him, "Start over, and tell the truth." Should those much-discussed language taboos make us forget this millennial yoke of confession?

From the Christian penance to the present day, sex was a privileged theme of confession. A thing that was hidden, we are told. But what if, on the contrary, it was what, in a quite particular way, one confessed? Suppose the obligation to conceal it was but another aspect of the duty to admit to it (concealing it all the more and with greater care as the confession of it was more important, requiring a stricter ritual and promising more decisive effects)? What if sex in our society, on a scale of several centuries, was something that was placed within an unrelenting system of confession? The transformation of sex into discourse, which I spoke of earlier, the dissemination and reinforcement of heterogeneous sexualities, are perhaps two elements of the same deployment: they are linked together with the help of the central element of a confession that compels individuals to articulate their sexual peculiarity—no matter how extreme. In Greece, truth and sex were linked, in the form of pedagogy, by the transmission of a precious knowledge from one body to another; sex served as a medium for initiations into learning. For us, it is in the confession that truth and sex are joined, through the obligatory and exhaustive expression of an individual secret. But this time it is truth that serves as a medium for sex and its manifestations.

The confession is a ritual of discourse in which the speaking subject is also the subject of the statement; it is also a ritual that unfolds within a power relationship, for one does not confess without the presence (or virtual presence) of a partner who is not simply the interlocutor but the authority who requires the confession, prescribes and appreciates it, and intervenes in order to judge, punish, forgive, console, and reconcile; a ritual in which the truth is corroborated by the obstacles and resistances it has had to surmount in order to be formulated; and finally, a ritual in which the expression alone, independently of its external consequences, produces intrinsic modifications in the person who articulates it: it exonerates, redeems, and purifies him; it unburdens him of his wrongs, liberates him, and promises him salvation. For centuries, the truth of sex was, at least for the most part, caught up in this discursive form. Moreover, this form was not the same as that of education (sexual education confined itself to general principles and rules of prudence); nor was it that of initiation (which remained essentially a silent practice, which the act of sexual enlightenment or deflowering merely rendered laughable or violent). As we have seen, it is a form that is far removed from the one governing the "erotic art." By virtue of the power structure immanent in it, the confessional discourse cannot come from above, as in the *ars erotica*, through the sovereign will of a master, but rather from below, as an obligatory act of speech which, under some imperious compulsion, breaks the bonds of discretion or forgetfulness. What secrecy it presupposes is not owing to the high price of what it has to say and the small number of those who are worthy of its benefits, but to its obscure familiarity and its general baseness. Its veracity is not guaranteed by the lofty authority of the magistery, nor by the tradition it transmits, but by the bond, the basic intimacy in discourse, between the one who speaks and what he is speaking about. On the other hand, the agency of domination does not reside in the one who speaks (for it is he who is constrained), but in the one who listens and says nothing; not in the one who knows and answers, but in the one who questions and is not supposed to know. And this discourse of truth finally takes effect, not in the one who receives it, but in the one from whom it is wrested. With these confessed truths, we are a long way from the learned initiations into pleasure, with their technique and their mystery. On the other hand, we belong to a society which has ordered sex's difficult knowledge, not according to the transmission of secrets, but around the slow surfacing of confidential statements.

The confession was, and still remains, the general standard governing the production of the true discourse on sex. It has undergone a considerable transformation, however. For a long time, it remained firmly entrenched in the practice of penance. But with the rise of Protestantism, the Counter Reformation, eighteenth-century pedagogy, and nineteenth-century medicine, it gradually lost its ritualistic and exclusive localization; it spread; it has been employed in a whole series of relationships: children and parents, students and educators, patients and psychiatrists, delinquents and experts. The motivations and effects it is expected to produce have varied, as have the forms it has taken: interrogations, consultations, autobiographical narratives, letters; they have been recorded, transcribed, assembled into dossiers, published, and commented on. But more important, the confession lends itself, if not to other domains, at least to new ways of exploring the existing ones. It is no longer a question simply of saying what was done—the sexual act—and how it was done; but of reconstructing, in and around the act, the thoughts that recapitulated it, the obsessions that accompanied it, the images, desires, modulations, and quality of the pleasure that animated it. For the first time no doubt, a society has taken upon itself to solicit and hear the imparting of individual pleasures.

A dissemination, then, of procedures of confession, a multiple localization of their constraint, a widening of their domain: a great archive of the pleasures of sex was gradually constituted. For a long time this archive dematerialized as it was formed. It regularly disappeared without a trace (thus suiting the purposes of the Christian pastoral) until medicine, psychiatry, and pedagogy began to solidify it: Campe, Salzmann, and especially Kaan, Krafft-Ebing, Tardieu, Molle, and Havelock Ellis carefully assembled this whole pitiful, lyrical outpouring from the sexual mosaic. Western societies thus began to keep an indefinite record of these people's pleasures. They made up a herbal of them and established a system of classification. They described their everyday deficiencies as well as their oddities or exasperations. This was an important time. It is easy to make light of these nineteenth-century psychiatrists, who made a point of apologizing for the horrors they were about to let speak, evoking "immoral behavior" or "aberrations of the genetic senses," but I am more inclined to applaud their seriousness: they had a feeling for momentous events. It was a time when the most singular pleasures were called upon to pronounce a discourse of truth concerning themselves, a discourse which had to model itself after that which spoke, not of sin and salvation, but of bodies and life processes—the discourse of science. It was enough to make one's voice tremble, for an improbable thing was then taking shape: a confessional science, a science which relied on a many-sided extortion, and took for its object what was unmentionable but admitted to nonetheless. The scientific discourse was scandalized, or in any case repelled, when it had to take charge of this whole discourse from below. It was also faced with a theoretical and methodological paradox: the long discussions concerning the possibility of constituting a science of the subject, the validity of introspection, lived experience as evidence, or the presence of consciousness to itself were responses to this problem that is inherent in the functioning of truth in our society: can one articulate the production of truth according to the old juridico-religious model of confession, and the extortion of confidential evidence according to the rules of scientific discourse? Those who believe that sex was more rigorously elided in the nineteenth century than ever before, through a formidable mechanism of blockage and a deficiency of discourse, can say what they please. There was no deficiency, but rather an excess, a redoubling, too much rather than not enough discourse, in any case an interference between two modes of production of truth: procedures of confession, and scientific discursivity.

And instead of adding up the errors, naïvetés, and moralisms that plagued the nineteenth-century discourse of truth concerning sex, we would do better to locate the procedures by which that will to knowledge regarding sex, which characterizes the modern Occident, caused the rituals of confession to function within the norms of scientific regularity: how did this immense and traditional extortion of the sexual confession come to be constituted in scientific terms?

1. *Through a clinical codification of the inducement to speak.* Combining confession with examination, the personal history with the deployment of a set of decipherable signs and symptoms; the

interrogation, the exacting questionnaire, and hypnosis, with the recollection of memories and free association: all were ways of re-inscribing the procedure of confession in a field of scientifically acceptable observations.

2. *Through the postulate of a general and diffuse causality.* Having to tell everything, being able to pose questions about everything, found their justification in the principle that endowed sex with an inexhaustible and polymorphous causal power. The most discrete event in one's sexual behavior—whether an accident or a deviation, a deficit or an excess—was deemed capable of entailing the most varied consequences throughout one's existence; there was scarcely a malady or physical disturbance to which the nineteenth century did not impute at least some degree of sexual etiology. From the bad habits of children to the phthises of adults, the apoplexies of old people, nervous maladies, and the degenerations of the race, the medicine of that era wove an entire network of sexual causality to explain them. This may well appear fantastic to us, but the principle of sex as a "cause of any and everything" was the theoretical underside of a confession that had to be thorough, meticulous, and constant, and at the same time operate within a scientific type of practice. The limitless dangers that sex carried with it justified the exhaustive character of the inquisition to which it was subjected.

3. *Through the principle of a latency intrinsic to sexuality.* If it was necessary to extract the truth of sex through the technique of confession, this was not simply because it was difficult to tell, or stricken by the taboos of decency, but because the ways of sex were obscure; it was elusive by nature; its energy and its mechanisms escaped observation, and its causal power was partly clandestine. By integrating it into the beginnings of a scientific discourse, the nineteenth century altered the scope of the confession; it tended no longer to be concerned solely with what the subject wished to hide, but with what was hidden from himself, being incapable of coming to light except gradually and through the labor of a confession in which the questioner and the questioned each had a part to play. The principle of a latency essential to sexuality made it possible to link the forcing of a difficult confession to a scientific practice. It had to be exacted, by force, since it involved something that tried to stay hidden.

4. *Through the method of interpretation.* If one had to confess, this was not merely because the person to whom one confessed had the power to forgive, console, and direct, but because the work of producing the truth was obliged to pass through this relationship if it was to be scientifically validated. The truth did not reside solely

in the subject who, by confessing, would reveal it wholly formed. It was constituted in two stages: present but incomplete, blind to itself, in the one who spoke, it could only reach completion in the one who assimilated and recorded it. It was the latter's function to verify this obscure truth: the revelation of confession had to be coupled with the decipherment of what it said. The one who listened was not simply the forgiving master, the judge who condemned or acquitted; he was the master of truth. His was a hermeneutic function. With regard to the confession, his power was not only to demand it before it was made, or decide what was to follow after it, but also to constitute a discourse of truth on the basis of its decipherment. By no longer making the confession a test, but rather a sign, and by making sexuality something to be interpreted, the nineteenth century gave itself the possibility of causing the procedures of confession to operate within the regular formation of a scientific discourse.

5. *Through the medicalization of the effects of confession.* The obtaining of the confession and its effects were recodified as therapeutic operations. Which meant first of all that the sexual domain was no longer accounted for simply by the notions of error or sin, excess or transgression, but was placed under the rule of the normal and the pathological (which, for that matter, were the transposition of the former categories); a characteristic sexual morbidity was defined for the first time; sex appeared as an extremely unstable pathological field: a surface of repercussion for other ailments, but also the focus of a specific nosography, that of instincts, tendencies, images, pleasure, and conduct. This implied furthermore that sex would derive its meaning and its necessity from medical interventions: it would be required by the doctor, necessary for diagnosis, and effective by nature in the cure. Spoken in time, to the proper party, and by the person who was both the bearer of it and the one responsible for it, the truth healed.

Let us consider things in broad historical perspective: breaking with the traditions of the *ars erotica*, our society has equipped itself with a *scientia sexualis*. To be more precise, it has pursued the task of producing true discourses concerning sex, and this by adapting—not without difficulty—the ancient procedure of confession to the rules of scientific discourse. Paradoxically, the *scientia sexualis* that emerged in the nineteenth century kept as its nucleus the singular ritual of obligatory and exhaustive confession, which in the Christian West was the first technique for producing the truth of sex. Beginning in the sixteenth century, this rite gradually detached itself from the sacrament of penance, and via the guidance of souls and the direction of conscience—the *ars atrium*—emigrated toward pedagogy, relationships between adults and children, family relations, medicine, and psychiatry. In any case, nearly one hundred and fifty years have gone into the making of a complex machinery for producing true discourses on sex: deployment that spans a wide segment of history in that it connects the ancient injunction of confession to clinical listening methods. It is this deployment that enables something called "sexuality" to embody the truth of sex and its pleasures.

"Sexuality": the correlative of that slowly developed discursive practice which constitutes the *scientia sexualis*. The essential features of this sexuality are not the expression of a representation that is more or less distorted by ideology, or of a misunderstanding caused by taboos; they correspond to the functional requirements of a discourse that must produce its truth. Situated at the point of intersection of a technique of confession and a scientific discursivity, where certain major mechanisms had to be found for adapting them to one another (the listening technique, the postulate of causality, the principle of latency, the rule of interpretation, the imperative of medicalization), sexuality was defined as being "by nature": a domain susceptible to pathological processes, and hence one calling for therapeutic or normalizing interventions; a field of meanings to decipher; the site of processes concealed by specific mechanisms; a focus of indefinite causal relations; and an obscure speech (*parole*) that had to be ferreted out and listened to. The "economy" of discourses—their intrinsic technology, the necessities of their operation, the tactics they employ, the effects of power which underlie them and which they transmit—this, and not a system of representations, is what determines the essential features of what they have to say. The history of sexuality—that is, the history of what functioned in the nineteenth century as a specific field of truth—must first be written from the view- point of a history of discourses.

Let us put forward a general working hypothesis. The society that emerged in the nineteenth century—bourgeois, capitalist, or industrial society, call it what you will—did not confront sex with a fundamental refusal of recognition. On the contrary, it put into operation an entire machinery for producing true discourses concerning it. Not only did it speak of sex and compel everyone to do so; it also set out to formulate the uniform truth of sex. As if it suspected sex of harboring a fundamental secret. As if it needed this production of truth. As if it was essential that sex be inscribed not only in an economy of pleasure but in an ordered system of knowledge. Thus sex gradually became an object of great suspicion; the general and disquieting meaning that pervades our conduct and our existence, in spite of ourselves; the point of weakness where evil portents reach through to us; the fragment of darkness that we each carry within us: a general signification, a universal secret an omnipresent cause, a fear that never ends. And so, in this "question" of sex (in both senses: as inter-rogation and problematization, and as the need for confession and inte-gration into a field of rationality), two processes emerge, the one always conditioning the other: we demand that sex speak the truth (but, since it is the secret and is oblivious to its own nature, we reserve for ourselves the function of telling the truth of its truth, revealed and deciphered at last), and we demand that it tell us our truth, or rather, the deeply buried truth of that truth about ourselves which we think we possess in our immediate consciousness. We tell it its truth by deciphering what it tells us about that truth; it tells us our own by delivering up that part of it that escaped us. From this interplay there has evolved, over several centuries, a knowledge of the subject; a knowledge not so much of his form, but of that which divides him, determines him perhaps, but above all causes him to be ignorant of himself. As unlikely as this may seem, it should not surprise us when we think of the long history of the Christian and juridical confession, of the shifts and transformations this form of knowledge-power, so important in the West, has undergone: the project of a science of the subject has gravitated, in ever narrowing circles, around the question of sex. Causality in the subject, the unconscious of the sub-ject, the truth of the subject in the other who knows, the knowledge he holds unbeknown to him, all this found an opportunity to deploy itself in the discourse of sex. Not, however, by reason of some natural property inherent in sex itself, but by virtue of the tactics of power immanent in this discourse.

Scientia sexualis versus *ars erotica*, no doubt. But it should be noted that the *ars erotica* did not disappear altogether from Western civilization; nor has it always been absent from the movement by which one sought to produce a science of sexuality. In the Christian confession, but especially in the direction and examination of conscience, in the search for spiritual union and the love of God, there was a whole series of methods that had much in common with an erotic art: guidance by the master along a path of initiation, the intensification of experiences extending down to their physical components, the optimization of effects by the discourse that accompanied them. The phenomena of possession and ecstasy, which were quite frequent in the Catholicism of the Counter Reformation, were undoubtedly effects that had got outside the control of the erotic technique immanent in this subtle science of the flesh. And we must ask whether, since the nineteenth century, the *scientia sexualis*—*under* the guise of its decent positivism—has not functioned, at least to a certain extent, as an *ars erotica*. Perhaps this production of truth, intimidated though it was by the scientific model, multiplied, intensified, and even created its own intrinsic pleasures. It is often said that we have been incapable of imagining any new pleasures. We have at least invented a different kind of pleasure: pleasure in the truth of pleasure, the pleasure of knowing that truth, of discovering and exposing it, the fascination of seeing it and telling it, of captivating and capturing others by it, of confiding it in secret, of luring it out in the open—the specific pleasure of the true discourse on pleasure.

The most important elements of an erotic art linked to our knowledge about sexuality are not to be sought in the ideal, promised to us by medicine, of a healthy sexuality, nor in the humanist dream of a complete and flourishing sexuality, and certainly not in the lyricism of orgasm and the good feelings of bio-energy (these are but aspects of its normalizing utilization), but in this multiplication and intensification of pleasures connected to the production of the truth about sex. The learned volumes, written and read; the consultations and examinations; the anguish of answering questions and the delights of having one's words interpreted; all the stories told to oneself and to others, so much curiosity, so many confidences offered in the face of scandal, sustained—but not without trembling a little—by the obligation of truth; the profusion of secret fantasies and the dearly paid right to whisper them to whoever is able to hear them; in short, the formidable "pleasure of analysis" (in the widest sense of the latter term) which the West has cleverly been fostering for several centuries: all this constitutes something like the errant fragments of an erotic art that is secretly transmitted by confession and the science of sex. Must we conclude that our *scientia sexualis* is but an extraordinarily subtle form of *ars erotica*, and that it is the Western, sublimated version of that seemingly lost tradition? Or must we suppose that all these pleasures are only the by-products of a sexual science, a bonus that compensates for its many stresses and strains?

In any case, the hypothesis of a power of repression exerted by our society on sex for economic reasons appears to me quite inadequate if we are to explain this whole series of reinforcements and intensifications that our preliminary inquiry has discovered: a proliferation of discourses, carefully tailored to the requirements of power; the solidification of the sexual mosaic and the construction of devices capable not only of isolating it but of stimulating and provoking it, of forming it into focuses of attention, discourse, and pleasure; the mandatory production of confessions and the subsequent establishment of a system of legitimate knowledge and of an economy of manifold pleasures. We are dealing not nearly so much with a negative mechanism of exclusion as with the operation of a subtle network of discourses, special knowledges, pleasures, and powers. At issue is not a movement bent on pushing rude sex back into some obscure and inaccessible region, but on the contrary, a process that spreads it over the surface of things and bodies, arouses it, draws it out and bids it speak, implants it in reality and enjoins it to tell the truth: an entire glittering sexual array, reflected in a myriad of discourses, the obstination of powers, and the interplay of knowledge and pleasure.

All this is an illusion, it will be said, a hasty impression behind which a more discerning gaze will surely discover the same great machinery of repression. Beyond these few phosphorescences, are we not sure to find once more the somber law that always says no? The answer will have to come out of a historical inquiry. An inquiry concerning the manner in which a knowledge of sex has been forming over the last three centuries; the manner in which the discourses that take it as their object have multiplied, and the reasons for which we have come to attach a nearly fabulous price to the truth they claimed to produce. Perhaps these historical analyses will end by dissipating what this cursory survey seems to suggest. But the postulate I started out with, and would like to hold to as long as possible, is that these deployments of power and knowledge, of truth and pleasures, so unlike those of repression, are not necessarily secondary and derivative; and further, that repression is not in any case fundamental and overriding. We need to take these mechanisms seriously, therefore, and reverse the direction of our analysis: rather than assuming a generally acknowledged repression, and an ignorance measured against what we are supposed to know, we must begin with these positive mechanisms, insofar as they produce knowledge, multiply discourse, induce pleasure, and generate power; we must investigate the conditions of their emergence and operation, and try to discover how the related facts of interdiction or concealment are distributed with respect to them. In short, we must define the strategies of power that are immanent in this will to knowledge. As far as sexuality is concerned, we shall attempt to constitute the "political economy" of a will to knowledge.

Notes

1. Cf., for example, Dèsirè Boumeville, *Iconographie photographique de la Salpêtrière* (1878–1881), pp. 110 ff. The unpublished documents dealing with the lessons of Charcot, which can still be found at the Salpêtrière, are again more explicit

on this point than the published texts. The interplay of incitement and elision is clearly evident in them. A handwritten note gives an account of the session of November 25, 1877. The subject exhibits hysterical spasms; Charcot suspends an attack by placing first his hand, then the end of a baton, on the woman's ovaries. He withdraws the baton, and there is a fresh attack, which he accelerates by administering inhalations of amyl nitrate. The afflicted woman then cries out for the sex baton in words that are devoid of any metaphor: "G. is taken away and her delirium continues."

2. Greek law had already coupled torture and confession, at least where slaves were concerned, and Imperial Roman law had widened the practice.

17

GRAND NATIONAL NARRATIVES AND THE PROJECT OF TRUTH COMMISSIONS

A Comparative Analysis

Molly Andrews

Perhaps the 20th century will be best remembered by the harrowing phrase 'Never forget.' In the post-Holocaust age, committing the unthinkable to memory has become a moral obligation. Renate Siebert, reflecting on her position as a German living in a post-fascist Germany, articulates some of the most critical questions of our age:

> What is our relationship with the past . . . which is a heavy burden on our consciousness, and which shadows our historical and social memory? Who are we, as individuals, in relation to this past? Do we have choices in the face of what the past forces upon us? What strategies do we have to face the past? to remember? to forget? (Siebert, 1992: 165)

The questions Siebert raises invite many answers, and many layers of answers, and indicate, too, both the potential and the challenge confronting truth commissions in documenting national memory. Indeed, the report of one of the most famous truth commissions, that of Argentina, was entitled

Molly Andrews, "Grand National Narratives and the Project of Truth Commissions: A Comparative Analysis," *Media Culture Society* 25, no. 1 (January 2003): 45–65. DOI: 10.1177/0163443703025001633. Copyright © 2003 by SAGE Publications. Reprinted by Permission of SAGE Publications, Ltd.

Nunca más (Never again). Truth commissions are one way in which citizens of a country help to determine what shall be included and what shall be left out in the story a nation tells itself about a traumatic past.

Ethically, we have a responsibility to remember, 'to keep memory alive, not to forget – the Jewish "zakhor"' (Siebert, 1992: 166). But never forget what? Keep which memory alive? Nations are, among other things, communities of shared memory and shared forgetting (Renan, 1882/1990). Truth commissions are one way of mediating memories—consisting of both the remembered and the forgotten—and thereby weaving the nation's post-traumatic identity. Citizens of a nation come together in a communal activity of telling and listening to stories of one another; and through such a process the stories of individuals become transformed into threads of a new national narrative. In *Country of My Skull*, Antjie Krog's account of her experiences observing South Africa's Truth and Reconciliation Commission, she writes 'by a thousand stories I was scorched a new skin' (1998: 279).

Woods (1999) describes national or public memory as performative; memory is not something we have, but something we do. South Africa's Truth and Reconciliation Commission (TRC) represents one dramatic illustration of the 'doing of memory'; for two years, private memory was performed publicly in town halls across the country, and re-performed for the rest of the country on nightly news and in the daily paper.[1] 'In the cities and in many smaller towns, in improvised courtrooms fashioned out of town halls and community centres and churches, the drama of Apartheid and the struggle against it was played out' (Krog, 1998: vii). In this article, I will argue that truth commissions act as conduits for collective memory; as individual stories are selected as being somehow representative, these stories come to frame the national experience. Truth commissions are not, however, mere conduits for stories; rather they wield an important influence on which stories are told and how they are to be interpreted. Thus they both produce and are produced by grand national narratives, and must be understood in the particular context(s) in which they emerge and the particular goals, either implicit or explicit, which guide their work.

Truth Commissions and Stories

When a society suffers an 'administrative massacre' 'its members will often seek to reconstruct its institutions on the basis of a shared understanding of what went wrong. [They do this through a variety of means.] But mostly, they tell stories. The "telling and retelling" of a people's central stories constitute its collective identity' (Osiel, 1997: 76). Thus, in the words of Jose Zalaquett of Chile's Rettig Commission, truth commissions write into being a new 'collective memory' (cited in Wilson, 1996: 14). But which stories are to be included in this new national narrative? What is the relationship between the experiences of individuals and the fate of a nation?

In the case of South Africa, more than 21,000 victims of apartheid have given testimony before the Truth and Reconciliation Commission. In makeshift courtrooms across the country, in the presence of an officially sanctioned body of listeners, headed by Archbishop Desmond Tutu, person after person has recounted the horrors they endured in the apartheid years. Telling and listening to stories is a key component of the journey to reconciliation, for it is in this exchange that individuals can begin to make sense of their experiences, to understand if not to condone why things happened in the way in which they did. But documenting such stories is only part of the work of truth commissions. As Charles Villa-Vicencio, Research Director of the TRC, comments:

> Reconciliation is facilitated, *inter alia*, by telling one another stories, as a basis for getting to know the other—for understanding the nature of their suffering and their aspirations. It has to do with uncovering the 'motives and perspectives,' something which the mandate of the Commission requires it to make known. Story-telling is a central part of the Commission. And yet, it will take a damn side more than that to heal the nation. Healing depends to a significant extent on how we respond to those stories. (Villa-Vicencio, 1998: 13)

But as painful and unique as each individual story is, it is in their collectivity that their indictment against apartheid is most powerful, not only because of the strength of numbers, but because of the transformation from individual into collective narrative. The relationship between individual and collective memory is symbiotic: not only do 'private accounts become woven together into a larger narrative about the period as a whole' (Osiel, 1997: 276), but the country, in the officially sanctioned body of the truth commission, helps scarred individuals to rebuild their lives. As the Chair of one of the TRC hearings told George Oliphant, the brother of an activist who had been killed:

> We are enormously grateful to all of you who come to give testimony here to expose your pain to the public. We hope so very much that in that process a healing will begin to happen because the nation acknowledges that something did happen to you. (TRC unpublished transcripts vol. 6, Case GO\1094, p. 400)

Another observer describes the relationship between the healing of individuals and the healing of the country: 'as victims put their own lives together, they also pull the whole country together' (Human Rights Program, 1997: 26).

The 20th century has seen a sharp rise in the number of truth commissions globally; Hayner (1995) has identified 15 between 1974 and 1994 alone. In this article, I shall compare the truth commissions of South Africa and East Germany, exploring how the very different sets of circumstances leading to their creation also helped to define their purposes and to influence, if not determine, their outcomes. Any comparison between East Germany and South Africa must, however, begin by noting the obvious: the difference in the scope of the battle in the two countries. Although repression was systematic and pervasive in East Germany, the price for falling out of line with the regime was most often an extended prison term. As Hayner notes:

> The repression under the East German system was different from the extensive violence seen in other regions [which have had truth commissions]. . . . Although there certainly was physical repression against dissidents, many of those who expressed opposition to the system suffered less violent consequences: they were barred from universities, prohibited from working in their chosen profession, or continually harassed by authorities, for example. (Hayner, 2001: 61)

It is possible that the very differences between the circumstances of East German activists and those of South Africa ultimately contributed to the nature of the truth commission adopted by each country, although this is beyond the scope of the current argument.

Collective Memory and Contested Terrain

Irwin-Zarecka comments that 'in its common usage the expression "collective memory" suggests a consensus' (1994: 67). This consensus, however, is only 'an ideal that memory workers aspire to and willingly struggle for' (1994: 67). In fact, the force of collective memory can best be understood by examining the 'dynamics of conflict' (1994: 67) which it embodies. Memory, both individual and collective, is a contested terrain; claims about the past are very often met with counter-claims. Sturken uses the term 'cultural memory' to refer to:

> . . . a field of cultural negotiation through which different stories
> vie for a place in history . . . a field of contested meanings in which

[people] interact with cultural elements to produce concepts of the nation, particularly in events of trauma, where both the structures and the fractures of a culture are exposed. (1997: 1–3)

Sturken argues that such cultural negotiation occurs in myriad settings, and that cultural memory is 'produced through objects, images, and representations' (1997: 9). Truth commissions function as such a setting, and are virtually unique in their capacity to expose 'the structures and fractures of a culture': through the different voices that are heard, truth commissions illuminate the conflictual nature of collective memory.

But, because of the shifts in the balance of power—the hallmark of truth commissions—the precise nature of the 'dynamics of collective memory' can, at times, be difficult to articulate. Concepts such as 'counter-memory' (Foucault, 1977)—calling attention to the 'residual or resistant strains [of memory] that withstand official versions of historical continuity' (Davis and Starn, 1989: 2)—and 'oppositional memory work' (Irwin-Zarecka, 1994: 83) are inadequate to describe the complexity of relations between a community's rememberers. In the context of South Africa, is 'oppositional memory' or 'counter-memory' to be found with de Klerk or Mandela? As it is the work of truth commissions to establish a new 'official history,' it is not clear who or what is to be considered 'the outsider,' precisely because such commissions are the products of societies in transition. As Wilson remarks, 'the main subtextual statement [of truth commissions] is how previous victims of the state are now having their story documented in an official state setting, demonstrating how the balance of power has shifted away from the perpetrators to the victims' (1996: 16). Whereas national identities are usually forged by 'othering' those who live across some imaginary border, truth commissions offer nations the opportunity to construct an identity in which it is the former national self which is the primary focus of the 'othering.' This is the case of South Africa, where the new national identity is premised upon two key sites of othering: (1) 'other' South Africans, and (2) the 'old South Africa' (clearly the two are not entirely unrelated). Regarding the second of these, Wilson comments 'the new South African identity is constructed upon a discontinuous historicity' (Wilson, 1996: 18), with the TRC being the representative benchmark between the old and the new. As such, the commission is involved in the fundamental nation-building task of creating a 'new official version of the nation's history' (Wilson, 1996: 18), a topic to which I shall return. This contrasts with East Germany, where the primary site of otherness has been West Germans and the western part of the now unified Germany, the boundaries demarcating us and them being both more important and more complex because of the shifting status of the East Germany nation.

The conflict of memory articulated in truth commissions is primarily of an interpretative nature—much of what is 'revealed' in the course of testimony is uncontested. Indeed, its ultimate utility is questioned by people such as Nigerian poet and Nobel Laureate Wole Soyinka, who questions the power of such 'revelations' to heal:

> Will the South African doctrine work, ultimately? Will society be truly purified as a result of this open articulation of what is known? For even while we speak of 'revelation,' it is only revelation in concrete particulars, the ascription of faces to deeds, admission by individual personae of roles within known criminalities, affirmation by the already identified of what they had formerly denied. Nothing, in reality, is new. The difference is that knowledge is being shared, collectively, and entered formally into the archives of that nation . . . [but] will it truly heal society? (1999: 33)

The power of truth commissions lies not so much in discovering truth—in the form of new facts—as in acknowledging it. Moreover, once the facts of the past have been established (for instance the fate of loved ones, etc.) the challenge of deciphering meaning behind such facts still remains. The courtroom contest between the tales of victim and victimizer is not, then, primarily factual, but interpretive. But, ironically, the political context in which the events described at truth commissions originally occurred is often implicitly accorded less importance than the subsequent political context of the recounting. The case of East Germany is particularly illustrative in this regard.

East Germany: The Enquete Kommission

There were five primary mechanisms through which a unified Germany attempted to 'work through' the (East German) communist past: (1) criminal investigations into the crimes committed by particular individuals, ranging from border guards all the way up to Erich Honecker. Hundreds of border guards and other officials have been convicted, most of whom received parole or suspended sentences (Kamali, 2001: 105); (2) the screening of individuals for connections with a Stasi past, resulting in approximately 50,000 people in both the public and private sectors being dismissed from their positions after testing 'Stasi-positive' (McAdams, cited in Yoder, 1999); (3) restitution of property, as dictated in the unification treaty demanding 'return instead of compensation' for land confiscated under the totalitarian regime; (4) the passage of the Act Concerning the Records of the State Security Service of the Former German Democratic Republic ('the Stasi Records Act') granting individuals the right to see files collected on them by the East German Secret Police; and, finally (5) the establishment of a truth commission. This article will deal primarily with the last of these—the creation, functioning and ultimate performance of the truth commission—but will also draw on primary data collected immediately after the opening of the Stasi files as evidence for some of the arguments.

In March 1992, two and a half years after the 'bloodless revolution' of East Germany, the German Bundestag founded the *Enquete Kommission Aufarbeitung von Geschichte und Folgen der SED-Diktator in Deutschland*—the Study Commission for the Assessment of History and Consequences of the Socialist Unity Party (SED) Dictatorship in Germany—whose goal it was to produce 'a judgment of Communism and its methods' (Kamali, 2001: 117) and to 'improve the preconditions for scholarly inquiry into the SBZ/GDR past' (Weber, 1997: 203). (Yoder comments 'The choice of the term "dictatorship" in this *Enquete Kommission*'s title to describe the GDR suggested to many the bias of the commission. It is not possible to say that a consensus exists in the former GDR that the regime was a dictatorship' [1999: 70].) Although all truth commissions are in some sense comprised of memories and counter-memories, or contesting versions of the same events, Maier comments that one of the key problems with the truth commission of East Germany was its 'failure to make contestation central.' Rather, he states, the Enquete hearings were:

> . . . touchingly didactic . . . [but] only the contestation of truth, the simultaneous unfolding of rival perspectives, can assure an adequate history. . . . At a minimum, rulers and ruled, those advantaged and disadvantaged, government and opposition, sometimes oppressors and victims, offer their own narratives. (1997: 326–7)

But what is aired in a truth commission depends very much on the purpose behind it being established in the first place. Unlike the 'bottom-up' approach of South Africa's truth commission, which explicitly set out to engage a large portion of the population and which permeated South African media, the East German commission was never intended as a means of collective catharsis. The 'project' of the commission was not so much to heal a broken nation, as with South Africa, but rather one of setting the record straight. Its intended audience was never the people of East Germany—indeed, many still are not aware that such a commission ever existed—but rather the Bundestag. The Enquete Kommission was intended as a scholarly investigation into the history of the GDR, and as such it solicited expert academic opinion (Weber, 1997: 205). There were 148 reports commissioned on 95 questions. In addition to these special reports, 'The author of each report was asked to present the problematical dimensions of the issue on the basis of the latest research and the archival material that had recently become accessible. Special emphasis was placed on suggestions for further research' (Weber, 1997: 205). It is not surprising, then, that 'the hearings had the atmosphere of a political science or sociology congress, rather than a people's tribunal' (Yoder, 1999: 72). In addition to these 'special reports,' the commission collected 759 academic papers on all aspects of the East German regime, which it published in a 15-volume compilation; all in all, the commission accumulated over 15,000 pages of testimony and expertise (McAdams, 2001: 90).

The original Enquete Kommission was in operation for two years (from May 1992 to May 1994), and was made up of 16 Members of Parliament and 11 outside 'experts.' While 10 of the 16 commissioners were from the East, they were all from the 'dissident milieu of the former GDR' (Yoder, 1999: 73); the rest of the commissioners, and all the outside experts, were West German. The composition of the truth commission led many to suspect its motives; for them 'the past was filtered and evaluated through western eyes and easterners were again subjects rather than participants in the corrective justice process' (Yoder, 1999: 73). This of course contrasts with South Africa's TRC; Richard Goldstone, South African Constitutional Court Judge, like many, believes that 'the TRC was morally justified because it was created by South Africa's first democratically elected legislature—a legislature that represents the victims of apartheid' (cited in Kamali, 2001: 126)—a view shared by many, if not most, South Africans, as well as by the international community.

The East German truth commission, then, focused its work on establishing didactic public history; this mission, in turn, created space for only certain kinds of tales to be told about daily life in the GDR. The commissioners, as noted above, shared a perspective that was highly critical of the GDR. Of the 327 witnesses who told their stories to the commission, many were 'the unsung victims of SED rule' (McAdams, 2001: 91). (This statistic itself speaks volumes. The Enquete Kommission listened to the testimonies of 327 persons (out of a population of 16 million); by comparison, the TRC heard evidence from 22,000 people, out of a population of 41 million.)

The final report of the first Enquete Kommission recommended that more research must be done into the GDR's past. In May 1995, the second Enquete Kommission was established by the Bundestag, this time with a more explicit agenda regarding the kinds of stories it was seeking to document. Its purpose, as described by Rainer Eppelman (the Chair of both the first and second commissions, and himself a former dissident of the GDR), was to investigate 'the thousands of people . . . who did not permit themselves to succumb to the criminality or immorality . . . of the SED dictatorship, who complained, stood firm, and achieved some kind of protest' (as quoted in Yoder, 1999: 73–4). It is not the case, then, that there was no attention given to stories 'from below' (i.e. personalized accounts of life under state communism) but rather that such interest was selective. As McAdams comments:

> When this perspective could be equated with the hardships of citizens who had been directly victimized by the SED's policies, the commission had no difficulty addressing the subject. Over two years of proceedings the body's [the second Enquete Kommission] deputies heard testimony from scores of individuals—teachers, journalists, artists, students, and pastors—who faced formidable odds in leading fulfilled lives under authoritarian rule, and, in many cases, made substantial sacrifices to remain true to their convictions. (McAdams, 2001: 111)

Indeed, as evidence of the utility of these kinds of stories for embracing a new national identity (and discarding the old), the final report of the second Enquete Kommission speaks of the importance of the stories of the victims of Communism, especially at a time 'when memories of the horrors of the fallen dictatorship are weakening in the face of an undifferentiated "GDR nostalgia'[2] (cited in McAdams, 2001: 111).

The effect of this weighting, as Yoder describes it, was that:

> . . . exploring the past and assigning blame invariably took on a right-wrong, and in many ways, west-east dimension. For some, the entire GDR past, the society's whole set of experiences, and in some ways the individual's sense of identity were all cast in doubt and, in the extreme, interpreted as being of no value. (1999: 75)

One can only understand this if one considers the context in which the commission was established, that is, the unifying of the two Germanys. As Weber comments, 'It was the goal of the Commission of Inquiry . . . to help cement a democratic consciousness and to foster a common political culture for the whole of Germany' (1997: 203). Its purpose, then, was not only to document the GDR past, but to establish an interpretation of that past. In bringing together certain kinds of stories about the past, it sought to establish a national memory, and thus a national identity, which was part and parcel of the new Germany.

The Enquete Kommission was unusual in two ways. First, while most other truth commissions have focused their investigations on a relatively limited period of time—Chile, Uganda and South Africa being exceptional in the length of the period covered (16 years, 24 years and 33 years respectively)—the GDR commission covered the full 40 years of the country's existence. Second, the truth commission was intended to document the events of a country which, even at the time of the commission's establishment, no longer existed. One can only really appreciate the project of the commission if these factors, particularly the latter, are borne in mind. As one commentator described it: 'In Germany, the offending regime is no longer in power. The new regime has instigated a process of settling accounts with a discontinuous past' (Geoffrey Hawthorne, cited in Human Rights Program, 1997: 71).

East Germany: The Stasi Files

Much has already been written on the unique decision on the part of a unified Germany to make the Stasi files available to the former citizens of the GDR. As historian Timothy Garton Ash comments: 'There has been nothing like it, anywhere, ever' (1997: 19). Joachim Gauck, East German Protestant clergyman who chaired the Gauck Authority, custodian of the Stasi archives, outlines what he sees to be the significance of this act.

> Thanks to this law, we are not walking in the fog: we can eliminate
> the doubts and restore the faith in democracy to the segment
> of society that had come to think this country could not be
> democratically ruled. . . . Just imagine what would have happened
> if the files had been kept secret: not only would it have been
> impossible to create a climate of trust, but the files could have been
> used to threaten and blackmail people. (cited in Kritz, 1995: 609)

How did the stories which emerged from this process contribute to creating a national memory of the GDR past? To appreciate the significance of the opening of the files, it is important to note the utter pervasiveness of the Stasi in East German life. The Stasi kept records on the lives of approximately 6 million East Germans out of a population of 16 million (Yoder, 1999: 63), although its ultimate goal was 'the perfection of an espionage network that would cover every citizen in the GDR' (Darnton, 1991: 125); 97,000 full-time employees, and an additional 170,000 informants, 'unofficial collaborators.' (The precise number of unofficial employees has been difficult to ascertain, for obvious reasons. One account cited by Yoder estimates the figure as high as 2 million [1999: 63]). Of the official, full-time employees, 1052 were surveillance specialists who tapped telephones, 2100 steamed open letters and 5000 followed suspects. Thus, the Stasi earned its internal slogan 'We Are Everywhere.' As a result of all this activity, when the leaders of the citizens' groups stormed the Stasi headquarters across East Germany in late 1989 and early 1990, what they found was approximately 110 miles of files.

Interestingly, these files contain a relatively high level of accuracy (though Vera Wollenberger, whose husband reported her dissident activities to the Stasi, describes the files as 'a dangerous mixture of fact and fiction' [Miller, 1999: 13]). One reason which explains this is that 'information deemed significant was generally confirmed from a number of informers, whose identities often remained unknown to one another' (Miller, 1999: 17). The Stasi prided itself in being interested in 'correct information.' Accordingly, it often sent spies to spy on its own spies. It is perhaps not surprising, then, that there seems to be a general consensus among those who have consulted their files that, at some level, what is reported as having occurred did in fact happen. The inaccuracy of the files is not in the facts that they contain, but rather in the interpretation of those facts (for a discussion of this see Andrews, 1998). Garton Ash describes the experience of reading his Stasi file, and comparing it to his diary, which covered the same time period.

> The Stasi's observation report, my diary entry: two versions of one day in a life. The 'object' described with the cold outward eye of the secret policeman and my own subjective, allusive, emotional self-description. But what a gift to memory is a Stasi file. Far better than Proust's Madeleine. (1997: 10)

This reviewing of the files of the Stasi has made possible open (and sometimes public) encounters between victims and perpetrators (*tater-opfer*—victim-victimizer—talks), which, in contrast to the proceedings of the Enquete Kommission, did whenever possible receive much media coverage.

I travelled to East Berlin in February 1992, one month after the opening of these files, and spent six months there speaking with people about how the transition to the new Germany had transformed their daily lives. Perhaps because of the timing of my visit, the subject that appeared to be the most absorbing for the people I encountered was how to deal with the revelations made by the opening of the files. For many with whom I spoke, this question had profound implications. In an interview with

East German dissident Werner Fischer, he described one *tater/opfer* event in which he had participated with a former friend, who, he learned, had been reporting to the Stasi on him. Following the meeting, the friend joked with him about what a charismatic media duo they made, and suggested they consider it as an alternative career. For Fischer and others, the question emerges: can one, and should one, seek to repair relationships which have been marked by deceit? What are the costs and benefits to be weighed, not only personally but politically? If this is a desirable goal, what is the best way to go about trying to achieve it?

The unusual situation of East Germany has produced interesting and sometimes surprising alliances between 'victims' and 'victimizers.' For instance, in the days when the East German state still existed, the relationship between the spies and the spied-upon, was one of 'us' and 'them.' However, since unification—what Gunter Grass describes as 'the unity that knows no mercy' (cited in Wolf, 1997: 206)—many in East Germany feel that what was promised as a partnership was in fact a takeover. As a consequence, East Germans who were once adversaries now find themselves attached by a peculiar bond, living with a kind of siege mentality.

Werner Fischer was one person with whom I spoke about this strange bed-fellowship. In the days of East Germany, Fischer had been one of the key figures of the underground opposition. Because of his anti-state activities, he spent much time in and out of prison, finally being exiled to Britain at the end of the 1980s. After the changes of 1989, he was appointed to lead the disbandment of the Stasi, something he regarded as one of life's great ironies. Speaking in 1992, he describes the transformed environment to me:

> Today I am sitting in a pub with my former interrogator and ask him how it was at that time . . . what went on in his head while he was interrogating me daily for 12 hours . . . what he told his wife in the evening he had been doing all day when I was taken back to my cell. . . . Many Stasi people try to establish a feigned or real relationship to former opposition members by being chummy and by asking 'Well, tell me now, did you want things to be as they are now? We really were on your side, we admired what you were doing and thought what you were writing was quite reasonable, but, you know the GDR legislation.' . . . They always hide behind the law and insist that that is how it was and that they could not act in any other way.

Similar stories were repeated to me time and again during my stay. For instance, in the midst of an interview with Gerd and Ulrilke Poppe, leading East German dissidents, the telephone rang. The caller had informed upon them for the Stasi, in what were commonly referred to as 'former times.' Now this same person was phoning to talk about what he saw as the bond between himself and them: they were all East Germans, after all. Perhaps now that things had turned out the way in which they did, could the Poppes not understand why he had done what he had done? They were appalled but not surprised by this sentiment. It is not uncommon for those who once informed upon friends, colleagues, even spouses, now to cling to the present circumstances as a form of justification for their past behaviour; the damage which it wreaked in the lives of others, while perhaps unfortunate, was a necessary and relatively small price to pay for holding at bay the onslaught of the voracious West. Importantly, this shared citizenship of a country which is no longer helps to frame the way in which stories of the past are both told and received.

Despite the fact the Enquete Kommission sought to establish a clear moral boundary between 'good pasts' and 'bad pasts,' in fact close investigation of the Stasi files reveals the fragility of such boundaries. What Vaclav Havel said of Czechoslovaka can also be said of East Germany: 'everyone in his or her own way is both a victim and a supporter of the [old communist] system' (quoted in Kamali, 2001: 131). Fulbook contrasts what she calls the 'Checkpoint Charlie theory of GDR history,' complete with villains and heroes, and the 'Octopus theory of GDR history' which 'emphasizes the ways in which an all-pervasive state extended its tentacles into nearly every corner of society' (1997: 190). While Fulbook comments that 'the easiest history to narrate is one in which one can easily identify with the Goodies and Baddies . . . [and] the easiest history to sell is one that explores in loving detail the vicissitudes of the Baddies . . . and depicts the heroic resistance of those who dared to rise up and challenge injustice' (1997: 180) the past is never so simple, and East Germany is no exception. We shall examine this further in the following section.

Moral Narratives, Nation-Building and Nation Dismantling

Osiel (1997) has explored the idea of truth commissions as modern morality plays, where characters function allegorically: the forces of good and evil are clearly separated, and those who have done wrong must come forward and be made responsible for the suffering they have inflicted on others. Victims often look to truth commissions to provide 'a grand metanarrative of liberal redemption, recounting of an epic of collective destruction and rebirth' (1997: 275). While Osiel's metaphor is in some ways appealing, a close examination of the truth commissions of East Germany and South Africa reveals a level of complexity that challenges its applicability.

Indeed, Osiel himself discusses the limitations of the morality-play model for some truth commissions, stating 'when complicity in such crimes is widespread throughout a society, because of diffuse support of connivance enjoyed by immediate perpetrators, the simple bipolarity of the morality play is inadequate' (1997: 286). In our conversation together, Werner Fischer highlights the relevance of Osiel's comment to the East German situation:

> I refuse to accept a polarization of victim/victimizer. . . . I am not able to draw a clear line. I am very cautious with this categorization. Do I know in how far I, as a so-called victim, who was in prison and so on, contributed in a certain way to a stabilization of the system? Because the Stasi strengthened this apparatus, could only strengthen it by constant referral to the opposition. That is how the system legitimized itself. In that respect I belong to the criminals, who ensured that the Stasi found more and more reasons to expand. Who can judge this?

While Fischer admits to using the language of victim and victimizer occasionally, he regards this polarity with caution, even aversion. While such a dualistic model is in many ways attractive—as a linguistic shorthand, and more importantly, as a mechanism by which to exculpate oneself—it oversimplifies and thereby obscures the reality which characterized everyday life in East Germany. Fischer comments on the investment of many in a model of moral polarity:

> People are only too eager to point a finger at the other person, to the guilty one 'that was him, the Stasi' in order to disguise their own shame of not having been able to—even only in a very minute way—show resistance. This simply must happen, but at present does not, that people ask themselves, 'how far have I contributed to make this system function, if only by my silence?' This is an exceedingly difficult process.

The internationally renowned East German writer, Christa Wolf, who was herself accused of Stasi collaboration in her youth, comments upon the difficulties of personal reckoning, exacerbated by the context of Western triumphalism:

I know how hard it is to work yourself out of feelings of injury,
hurt, helpless rage, depression, and paralyzing guilt and soberly to
confront the events or phases in your life when you would prefer to
have been braver, more intelligent, more honest . . . the people I am
talking about are 'ordinary' people. (1997: 301)

Despite the difficulty of the circumstances, she comments 'you really
must reach the point at which you can account to yourself for your life,
regardless of how difficult other people may make it for you, and regardless of how much guiltier other people may be' (1997: 241). In the context of daily life under the East German dictatorship, guilt and heroism
are not absolutes, though many may persist in the discourse of good and
evil in framing their stories of former times.

If one questions the use of the dichotomous descriptors of victim and
victimizer, as Fischer explicitly does and Wolf does by implication, is there
not a risk of imposing chaos on the moral order? Surely, at some level, it
is important to be able to distinguish between opposing moral forces. In
the words of Wolfgang Ullmann, one of the founders of the East German
truth commission, some people were spies and others were spied upon;
this is clear and the distinction is important. Ullmann's concern is that
the relativism suggested by those like Fischer provides a shelter for those
who should be made answerable for their actions: if all are guilty, none
are guilty.

In my interview with Stasi employee Jorg Seidel, he stresses the point
that people like him were motivated in their work 'by the same ideas' as
the country's dissidents. He rejects the terms victim and victimizer 'because you have to see the background.' He suggests that his willingness
to participate in research such as mine is proof of his ideological bond
with dissident activists: 'I believe if I wouldn't have had these ideas, I
wouldn't sit here in this very room. I will say we are thinking of a human
who is really in the centre of the interests of the society.' He concludes
by comparing himself with Jens Reich, one of the key opposition figures
and co-founder of the anti-state group Neus Forum, which spearheaded
many of the changes in the autumn of 1989. Reich, Seidel comments, is
someone whose ideals he 'almost fully' shares. In a subsequent interview
with Jens Reich, I relate this comment; not surprisingly, it is greeted with
disdain. Yet Reich himself is someone who rejects any stark construction
that obscures the complex reality which characterized East German life.

How different is the East German situation from that of South Africa? Did the level of violence in the latter create more stark contrasts—
goodies and baddies? Does Osiel's morality play have more applicability
in describing the central figures in the South African truth commission

proceedings, where presumably the boundaries between victim and perpetrator were not nearly so opaque as they were in East Germany? Before
addressing this, I would like to call attention to the original purpose behind the creation of the TRC.

It is instructive here to examine a passage from the Preamble of the
Promotion of National Unity and Reconciliation Act, which among
other things established the TRC.

> This Constitution provides a historic bridge between the past of
> a deeply divided society characterized by strife, conflict, untold
> suffering and injustice, and a future founded on the recognition
> of human rights, democracy and peaceful co-existence and
> development opportunities for all South Africa, irrespective
> of colour, race, class, belief or sex. . . . The pursuit of national
> unity, the well-being of all South African citizens and peace
> require reconciliation between people of South Africa and the
> reconstruction of society. . . . The adoption of this Constitution lays
> the secure foundation for the people of South Africa to transcend
> the divisions and strife of the past, which generated gross violations
> of human rights, the transgression of humanitarian principles in
> violent conflicts and a legacy of hatred, fear, guilt and revenge.
> (quoted in Ntsebeza, 1998: 4)

First and foremost, the truth commission of South Africa was intended as a
bridge from the past to the future, a key lynchpin in healing the wounds of a
deeply divided nation. In the Foreword to the final report of the TRC, Desmond Tutu appeals to fellow South Africans to use the report not to attack
others, but rather as an instrument that can contribute to 'the process that
will lead to national unity through truth and reconciliation' (Tutu, 1998: 4).
The importance to the nation of looking forward is echoed by Nelson Mandela, in the handover ceremony of the Truth and Reconciliation report in
October 1998, when he comments upon the country's 'hope and confidence
in the future' and refers to the report as 'the property of our nation [which]
should be a call to all of us to celebrate and to strengthen what we have done
as a nation' (BBC Online Network, *www.monitor.bbc.co.uk*).

The transcripts of the proceedings of the TRC are peppered with the
phrase 'the new South Africa,' and the thousands of pages are awash with
sentiments like the following:

> We hope that as we listen to those who are not statistics but human
> beings of flesh and blood, that you and I will be filled with a new
> commitment, a new resolve that our country will be a country

where violations of this kind will not happen, that the context will be inhospitable for those who seek to treat others as if they were nothing. (TRC, 1998: vol. 5, p. 411)

Victims of horrendous crimes are thanked for having given their testimony, as their special contribution to building this new country, and the entire endeavour is seen as an important aspect of the overriding goal to achieve national unity and reconciliation. While there are many in South Africa who support this nation-building function of the TRC, there are some who regard it as part of a specifically ANC vision. As one spokesperson for the far right Freedom Front phrased it:

> The ANC wants to build one nation out of a large variety of people's [sic] and tribes. . . . We . . . oppose the concept of one-nation; we don't believe in it, one nation does not exist in this multiracial country. . . . The TRC not only seeks to give the people a common memory; they want to rewrite history. . . . We will not accept their version of history. (quoted in Christie, 2000: 109)

The Freedom Front are not alone in their cynicism about nation-building, and indeed the project has been the target of some controversy within South Africa. As one observer describes it: 'what the ANC meant by national liberation as their goal, while appearing inclusive of all groups, is not shared by all groups' (Christie, 2000: 113). While most countries have some degree of diversity within their populations, South Africa is perhaps unusual in that there are approximately 160 different ethnic groups (Christie, 2000: 116); perhaps not surprisingly, then 'there are multiple visions, perspectives and solutions to what constitutes South Africa and in turn these have consequences for what it means to be engaged in a nation-building project (Christie, 2000: 98). In contrast to the Enquete Kommission, which it could be argued was involved in constructing a narrative around a once again unified Germany—although, of course, historically there has never been a Germany that was comprised of the GDR and the FRG and, for this reason, many reject the phrase 'reunification,' preferring 'unification'—the TRC was building a grand narrative of a country which never existed. As Christie comments, 'South Africa has never really been a nation in the classical sense of what constitutes nationhood. . . . A South African nation has yet to be born' (2000: 106). The role of the TRC was but one component of many engaged in this task of giving birth to the nation.

> Not only is it [the TRC] seeking to examine and acknowledge aversion [sic] of South Africa's past which lays claim to a more

> objective truth, it is seeking to institutionalize that memory to
> reconcile different groups in society. A common memory in theory
> is one of the first steps toward a more unified nation and nation-
> building. (Christie, 2000: 117)

While the TRC is trying to construct a grand national narrative of its past,
it is doing so with the purpose of reconciling a painfully fragmented society.
Some feel that the perpetrators of crimes have not been dealt with harshly
enough (for instance in being granted amnesty for their actions), others
feel that the TRC has acted as a witch-hunt. (Christie reports a study in
which roughly 46 percent of the white South Africans surveyed thought
that the TRC was 'an ANC inspired witch-hunt to discredit its enemies'
[2000: 115]). In reality, as still others have argued, 'the TRC was a compromise and should be seen in that light' (Christie, 2000: 114). While the
commission made no attempt to disguise its clear moral vision, during the
proceedings the commissioners emphasized time and again that wrongs
were perpetrated on both sides of the struggle. Moreover, unlike the case
of East Germany, where many felt that the Enquete Kommission was yet
another form of 'victor's justice' and that the history of the GDR was written by its strongest critics (from both East and West), 'there was no clear
victor in South Africa after the collapse of apartheid' (Kamali, 2001: 121).
As Desmond Tutu commented, '[n]obody was in a position to enforce so-
called "victor's justice" . . . without some amnesty provisions, our reasonably peaceful transition from repression to democracy would instead have
become a bloodbath' (cited in Kamali, 2001: 121).
    Andre Du Toit comments:

> If truth commissions address fundamental moral questions—of
> justice and truth, violence and violation, accountability and
> reparation—they do so not at the level of theoretical reflection or by
> means of established institutions but as eminently political projects.
> Conversely, the politics of truth commissions is informed by
> distinctively moral notions and objectives to a degree that is unusual
> in modern and secular societies. (du Toit, 2000: 122)

The goal of the TRC is to advance national reconciliation, but this political end is encased in the spirit of *ubuntu*, a concept which Desmond
Tutu explains as follows:

> I am human only because you are human. If I undermine your
> humanity, I dehumanize myself. You must do what you can to
> maintain this great harmony, which is perpetually undermined

by resentment, anger, desire for vengeance. That's why African jurisprudence is restorative rather than retributive. (Tutu, 1996: 53)

The spirit of *ubuntu* is expressed by Ms Cynthia Ngewu, whose son was murdered by the police. She explains:

> What we are hoping for when we embrace the notion of reconciliation is that we restore the humanity to those who were perpetrators. We do not want to return evil by another evil.
> We simply want to ensure that the perpetrators are returned to humanity . . . all South Africans should be committed to the idea of re-accepting these people back into the community. We do not want to return the evil that perpetrators committed to the nation. We want to demonstrate humaneness towards them, so that they in turn may restore their own humanity. (TRC, 1998: vol. 5, p. 367)

A similar sentiment, from a very different perspective, is voiced by Mr. Kimpani Peter Mogoai, an 'askari':

> As I regard myself today as a disgrace to my mother, my family and my relatives . . . and the nation as such . . . it is with my deepest remorse that I ask for forgiveness and hopefully wish to be reconciled with everybody once more and be part of a better and brighter future of South Africa. (TRC, 1998: vol. 5, p. 391)

It is not only for the sake of the individual (both perpetrator and victim) that it is important to recognize dignity in all persons; it is crucial in building the new nation. Unfortunately, the sentiment expressed here—acknowledging responsibility for past misdeeds—is not very typical. As Christie comments, 'the white population in general have had difficulty coming to terms with the past. There is a state of denial in most quarters and a refusal by most to accept any kind of responsibility for the past' (2000: 114). Christie then cites a study carried out by the Centre for the Study of Violence and Reconciliation which showed that 'a majority of white South Africans . . . were unconvinced they had any role in apartheid abuses, and more than 40% of them thought that apartheid was a good idea, but with poor implementation' (2000: 114).

The importance of the principle of restoring dignity to all South Africans is apparent throughout the transcripts of the TRC, and seems for many to be a core component of the new nation. As one of the commissioners summarizes this position at the end of one of the hearings:

> Ultimately . . . you give people the chance to change. You open
> a door for someone to move from a dark past to a new and
> enlightened present and future. . . . All of us need to change, all of
> us are wounded people, all of us are traumatised people, all of us are
> people who need to forgive and who also need to be forgiven. And
> for all of us then to move together into what is a wonderful prospect
> . . . and look at the wonderful contribution that all of the wonderful
> people can make to this new South Africa. (TRC proceedings,
> Johannesburg, Case GO/0135, p. 10)

Conclusion

Truth commissions are conduits for collective memory, and that memory, like all memory, is constantly changing. The 'national narratives' about a country's traumatic past which emerge from the proceedings of truth commissions document stories of the past, and these stories are in turn firmly situated in the circumstances of the present. Terms such as victim and victimizer thus reflect not only the moral dimensions of the *ancien régime*, but also the realities of the present, the latter wielding a powerful influence in distinguishing and categorizing that which is memorable. As 'the struggle for possession and interpretation of memory is rooted in the conflict and interplay among social, political, and cultural interests and values in the present' (Thelen, 1989: 1127), in truth commissions we witness the dynamics of the making of collective memory, with all of the tensions and ambiguities that this entails.

In South Africa and East Germany, truth commissions were established which had as a key focus bringing together, or reconciling, a fragmented populace. In South Africa, this project of reconciliation is a key component of a larger, and somewhat controversial, project of nation-building, bringing together the 'rainbow people of the new South Africa.' It is based on principles which recognize the dignity of all South Africans—victims and perpetrators alike. South Africa is, as one author phrased it, a nation still to be born, and the TRC is a vital component in the success of this endeavour. In its work, the commission is guided by a vision which must include all of its divergent groups, if it is to work at all.

In East Germany, the truth commission functioned primarily as a means of establishing a shared history for all of the newly united Germany. The cost of doing this, however, was the silencing of the stories of the majority of East Germans, for whom state socialism was not the focus of resistance but merely a fact of daily life. In East Germany, the contestation of memory was more in evidence in the open talks between victims and victimizers, although here the public nature of these meetings tended to mitigate against any genuine possibility for dialogue.

Villa-Vicencio and Verwoerd refer to the close link between process and product of the TRC, adding:

> The commission sought, however imperfectly, to implement and manage an inclusive, accessible, and transparent process in order to facilitate a pluralistic public account, generated by diverse individuals 'telling their own stories.' . . . The alternative would have been a more typical, 'elitist' commission of experts attempting to produce an authoritative version of the truth. (2000: 289)

These observers have perhaps captured the key difference between the commissions of East Germany and South Africa; the former saw its mission to compile an authoritative account of the 40 years of state socialism. The TRC, in contrast, offered a many-sided truth, seeking to include all South Africans in the renewal of their country.

If truth commissions are a 'method of remembrance, a way of developing shared memories' (Christie, 2000: 187), they are also eminently political projects. Truth commissions are a vital means of establishing a link between a nation's traumatic past and its future, and they must be examined within this 'bridging' function. Ultimately, the truth or truths that they uncover are those that help to establish the new grand national narrative, embodying a journey out of darkness into light.

Notes

The East German data reported in this article was collected as an Associate Research Fellow at the Centre for Socialization and Human Development of the Max Planck Institute in Berlin.

1. Yazir Henry writes poignantly of the personal cost which testifying before the truth commission can exact from the individual, summarizing his own experience by saying: 'It took me almost a complete year to recover psychologically from my testimony and the form it took publicly after having testified' (forthcoming: 5).
2. For a rich and nuanced discussion of this nostalgia, see Berdahl (1999). For a discussion of the effects of a decade of unification on East German identity, see Andrews (forthcoming).

References

Andrews, M. (1998) 'One Hundred Miles of Lives: The Stasi Files as a People's History of East Germany,' *Oral History* 26(1): 24–31.

Andrews, M. (forthcoming) 'Continuity and Discontinuity of East German Identity

Following the Fall of the Berlin Wall,' in P. Gready (ed.) *Cultures of Political Transition*. London: Pluto Press.

Ash, T. G. (1997) *The File: A Personal History*. New York: Harper Collins.

Berdahl, D. (1999) '"(N)Ostalgie" for the Present: Memory, Longing, and East German Things,' *Ethnos* 64(2): 192–211.

Boraine, A., and J. Levy (eds). (1995) *The Healing of a Nation*. Cape Town: Justice in Transition.

Christie, Kenneth. (2000) *The South African Truth Commission*. London: Palgrave.

Darnton, R. (1991) *Berlin Journal 1989–1990* New York: W.W. Norton.

Davis, N. Z., and R. Starn (1989) 'Introduction,' Special Issue on Memory and Counter-memory, *Representations* 26: 1–6.

De Brito, A. B., C. Gonzalez-Enriques, and P. Aguilar (eds). (2001) *The Politics of Memory: Transitional Justice in Democratizing Societies*. Oxford: Oxford University Press.

Du Toit, André. (2000) 'The Moral Foundations of the South African TRC: Truth as Acknowledgement and Justice as Recognition,' in R. Rotberg and D. Thompson (eds) *Truth v. Justice: The Morality of Truth Commissions*. Princeton, NJ: Princeton University Press.

Foucault, M. (1977) *Language, Counter-memory, Practice: Selected Essays and Interviews*. Oxford: Blackwell.

Fulbook, Mary. (1997) 'Reckoning with the Past: Heroes, Victims, and Villains in the History of the German Democratic Republic,' in Reinhard Alter and Peter Monteath (eds) *Rewriting the German Past: History and Identity in the New Germany*. New Jersey: Humanities Press.

Halbwachs, M. (1950/1980) *The Collective Memory*. New York: Harper and Row.

Hayner, P. (1995) 'Fifteen Truth Commissions—1974–1994: A Comparative Study,' in N. Kritz (ed.) *Transitional Justice: How Emerging Democracies Reckon with Former Regimes*, vol. 1. Washington, DC: United States Institute of Peace Press.

Hayner, P. (2001) *Unspeakable Truths: Confronting State Terror and Atrocity* London: Routledge.

Henry, Yazir. (forthcoming) 'Reconciling Reconciliation: A Personal and Public Journey of Testifying before the South African Truth and Reconciliation Commission,' in P. Gready (ed.) *Cultures of Political Transition*. London: Pluto Press.

Human Rights Program. (1997) *Truth Commissions: A Comparative Assessment*. Cambridge, MA: Harvard Law School and World Peace Foundation.

Irwin-Zarecka, I. (1994) *Frames of Remembrance: The Dynamics of Collective Memory*. New Brunswick, NJ: Transaction Publishers.

Kamali, Maryam. (2001) 'Accountability for Human Rights Violations: A Comparison of Transitional Justice in East Germany and South Africa,' *Columbia Journal of Transnational Law* 40(1): 89–142.

Kritz, Neil (ed). (1995) *Transitional Justice: How Emerging Democracies Reckon with Former Regimes, vol. II, Country Studies*. Washington, DC: United States Institute of Peace.

Krog, A. (1998) *Country of my Skull*. Johannesburg: Random House.

Maier, C. (1997) *Dissolution: The Crisis of Communism and the End of East Germany*. Princeton, NJ: Princeton University Press.

McAdams, A. J. (2001) *Judging the Past in Unified Germany*. Cambridge: Cambridge University Press.

Miller, Barbara. (1999) *Narratives of Guilt and Compliance in Unified Germany: Stasi Informers and their Impact on Society*. London: Routledge.

Minow, M. (1998) *Between Vengeance and Forgiveness: Facing History after Genocide and Mass Violence*. Boston, MA: Beacon Press.

Ntsebeza, D. B. (1998) 'The South African Truth and Reconciliation Commission: Its Process and Actions: Victims, Perpetrators and Findings,' unpublished paper presented at 'Burying the Past: Justice, Forgiveness and Reconciliation in the Politics of South Africa, Guatemala, East Germany and Northern Ireland,' Oxford University.

Renan, E. (1882/1990) 'What is a Nation?,' in H. Bhabha (ed.) *Nation and Narration*. London: Routledge.

Osiel, M. (1997) *Mass Atrocity, Collective Memory and the Law*. New Brunswick, NJ: Transaction Publishers.

Siebert, R. (1992) 'Don't Forget: Fragments of a Negative Tradition,' in L. Passerini (ed.), *Memory and Totalitarianism*. Oxford: Oxford University Press.

Soyinka, Wole. (1999) *The Burden of Memory: The Muse of Forgiveness*. Oxford: Oxford University Press.

Sturken, M. (1997) *Tangled Memories: The Vietnam War, the Aids Epidemic, and the Politics of Remembering*. Berkeley, CA: University of California Press.

Thelen, D. (1989) 'Memory and American History,' *Journal of American History* 75: 1117–29.

TRC (Truth and Reconciliation Commission) (1998) *Truth and Reconciliation Commission of South Africa Report*, vol. 5. Cape Town: Truth and Reconciliation Commission.

Tutu, Desmond. (1996) 'Healing a Nation,' *Index on Censorship*, Special Issue: Wounded Nations, Broken Lives: Truth Commissions and War Tribunals 5: 38–53.

Tutu, Desmond. (1998) 'Chairperson's Foreword,' in *Truth and Reconciliation Commission of South Africa Report*. Cape Town: Truth and Reconciliation Commission.

Villa-Vicencio, Charles. (1998) 'The South African Truth and Reconciliation Commission, Some Guiding Principles: Justice, Amnesty and Reconciliation,' unpublished paper presented at 'Burying the Past: Justice, Forgiveness and Reconciliation in the Politics of South Africa, Guatemala, East Germany and Northern Ireland,' Oxford University.

Villa-Vicencio, Charles, and Wilhelm Verwoerd. (2000) 'Constructing a Report: Writing up the "Truth,"' in R. Rotberg and D. Thompson (eds) *Truth v. Justice: The Morality of Truth Commissions*. Princeton, NJ: Princeton University Press.

Weber, Hermann. (1997) 'Rewriting the History of the German Democratic Republic: The Work of the Commission of Inquiry,' in Reinhard Alter and Peter Monteath (eds) *Rewriting the German Past: History and Identity in the New Germany*. New Jersey: Humanities Press.

Weschler, L. (1990) *A Miracle, a Universe: Settling Accounts with Torturers*. New York: Pantheon Books.

Wilson, R. (1996) 'The Sizwe Will not go Away: The Truth and Reconciliation Commission, Human Rights and Nation-building in South Africa,' *African Studies* 55(2): 1–20.

Wilson, R. (2001) *The Politics of Truth and Reconciliation in South Africa: Legitimizing the Post-apartheid State*. Cambridge: Cambridge University Press.

Wolf, C. (1997) *Parting from Phantoms: Selected Writings, 1990–1994*. Chicago, IL: University of Chicago Press.

Woods, N. (1999) *Vectors of Memory: Legacies of Trauma in Postwar Europe*. Oxford: Berg.

Yoder, Jennifer. (1999) 'Truth without Reconciliation: An Appraisal of the Enquete Commission on the SED Dictatorship in Germany,' *German Politics* 8(3): 59–80.

Part IIIB
Narratives from Below

This section provides the counterpoint to the previous one. If narratives can be imposed from above, as it were, if they can be a form of social control, then they can also emerge from below, as a form of resistance. People can use narratives to challenge domination or stigmatization and to defy prescribed identities and labels. They can use them to oppose efforts to impose ideologically invested forms of speech or to silence them altogether. As Carol Rambo Ronai and Rebecca Cross explain, "narrative resistance is a response to discursive constraint" (1998: 105). It is "an active speech behavior which serves to decenter the authority of specific individuals or society to dictate identity" (Ronai and Cross 1998: 105–6). By decentering authority, narratives of resistance (or counter-narratives) make sense only in relation to something else—namely, to whatever they are resisting. The narrative of resistance highlights the constraint, the authority structure, and the dominant belief. In short, the narrative of resistance points out power.

If accommodating to narratives from above requires nothing more than adopting a narrative form and content developed by others, narratives from below require far more imagination. If a person's story does not fit a standard form, that person must look elsewhere for resources to piece together a different kind of story. Where do they look? Patricia Ewick and Susan Silbey, whose work we include in this section, ask the question differently: "How are openings for resistance—the revelation of the taken for granted—created in situations where the probability of greater power lies with others?" (2003: 1329). But power, as Michel Foucault (1982: 788) has argued, does not "exist universally in a concentrated or diffused form." Power is exercised incompletely; systems of rules have loopholes and domination has cracks. Those familiar with the routine exercise of power learn to see the openings where oppositional discourse can arise and circulate.

Narratives from below are, then, a type of self-invention, both individual and collective. Narratives of resistance are how women and men, alone and in groups, create new identities and revise old identities. Slave narratives, one of the purest examples of narrative resistance, insistently recast enslaved persons as dignified, capable of deep intimate ties, and suffering but powerful rather than the dependent, childlike image of them propounded by many slaveholders (Davis and Gates 1985). Narratives of resistance are among the means women and men use to free themselves from their families of origin, from the conventions of gender, from the critical judgments of bosses and teachers and social workers and courts.

We should not imagine, however, that narratives from below operate without social constraint. In the first instance, narratives of resistance proceed in relation to an audience. There is always a question of who (including oneself) will be able—and willing—to hear. In the telling of a narrative, a "positioning" (Davies and Harré 1990: 43) takes place, whereby the narrative locates listeners as subjects. As particular images, metaphors, and storylines become relevant, audiences accept, reject, ignore, or improve upon the positions the narrative makes available to them. Concurrently, narratives of resistance also highlight the position of the teller. A narrative about the power of white people, for example, will be a tale of resistance if told by a black person, but something quite different if told by a white person, especially a white male.

In the second instance, narratives from below draw on available narrative forms. Slave narratives, for example, speak in the voice of an individual and his or her experience, but they also form a genre in which each narrative imitates elements of other narratives. Twelve-step groups share scripts for talking about addictions of various types in which the individual speaks for him or herself, taking responsibility for one's actions, but often in language supplied by others. Even nations, in constructing their own histories, hone stories of rebels and heroes and institution builders from the model stories told by other nations. If narratives from above are plagued by questions of sincerity, narratives from below are plagued by questions of originality.

This section begins with an excerpt from Ewick and Silbey's article, "Narrating Social Structure: Stories of Resistance to Legal Authority." They identify narratives of resistance as those that "described an opportunity to avoid the consequences of relative disadvantage." In focusing on how narrators draw on social-structural features to tell narratives of resistance, Ewick and Silbey's approach provides a conceptual bridge between narratives that emerge from below and those imposed from above. The difference comes as narrators reverse conventional features of social structures, appropriating rules and roles, as well as the time and space of the more powerful. As the patterned narrative strategies become part of the stock of common yet tacit knowledge, the acts of resistance they portray become more than momentary, individual encounters with institutional authority. They become, at least potentially, a means for upending that authority.

The excerpt from Francesca Polletta's research on civil rights activism in the United States continues this theme, while focusing on a collective rather than an individual narrative. The student sit-ins of the 1960s were repeatedly characterized as spontaneous events, with the urge coming on "like a fever," according to one account. The notion that acts of resistance arose in the moment, without planning, while incorrect and misleading, nevertheless became central to defining a new identity of the student activist willing to take risks. As a narrative strategy, spontaneity appealed to young participants disillusioned with bureaucratic attempts to organize. The open-endedness of spontaneity allowed activists to fill in their own meanings. However, the same qualities posed a challenge for the fledgling Student Non-Violent Coordinating Committee (SNCC). The organization's efforts to develop political strategies (such as voter registration) had to contend with the widely held image of spontaneous activism. Polletta's analysis serves as a reminder that resistance operates on both individual and collective levels (see also Richardson 1990).

In "Lifechangers and Lifesavers," Leslie Irvine examines narratives told by people at the bottom rung of society. This chapter from her book *My Dog Always Eats First* focuses on homeless people's narratives of how companion animals transformed them and even saved their lives. The narrators are addicts and alcoholics, many with long histories of living on the street. Faced with having to choose between a pet and addiction, these narrators chose their animals. For one teller, the choice to honor a commitment to an animal meant life, rather than death by suicide. These are stories of redemption, a common narrative theme (see McAdams 2006). They differ from most redemption stories in using animals as the means for changing the course of one's life.

References

Cordell, Gina, and Carol Rambo Ronai. 1999. "Identity Management among Overweight Women: Narrative Resistance to Stigma." In *Interpreting Weight: The Social Management of Fatness and Thinness*. Edited by J. Sobal and D. Maurer. New York: Aldine de Gruyter.

Davies, Bronwyn, and Rom Harré. 1990. "Positioning: The Discursive Production of Selves." *Journal for the Theory of Social Behaviour* 20(1): 43–63.

———. 1999. "Positioning and Personhood." In *Positioning Theory*. Edited by R. Harré and L. van Langenhove. Oxford UK: Blackwell.

Davis, Charles, and Henry Louis Gates. 1985. *The Slave's Narrative*. New York: Oxford University Press.

Foucault, Michel. 1982. "The Subject and Power." *Critical Inquiry* 8(4): 777–95.

McAdams, Dan P. 2006. *The Redemptive Self: Stories Americans Live By.* New York: Oxford University Press.

Richardson, Laurel. 1990. "Narrative and Sociology." *Journal of Contemporary Ethnography* 19(1): 116–35.

Ronai, Carol Rambo, and Rabecca Cross. 1998. "Dancing with Identity: Narrative Resistance Strategies of Male and Female Stripteasers." *Deviant Behavior* 19(2): 99-119.

Stryker, Susan. 1994. "My Words to Victor Frankenstein above the Village of Chamounix: Performing Transgender Rage." *GLQ* 1(3): 237–54.

Further Reading

Berger, Ronald J. 2010. *Hoop Dreams on Wheels: Disability and the Competitive Wheelchair Athlete.* New York: Routledge.

Berger, Ronald J., and Richard Quinney. 2005. *Storytelling Sociology: Narrative as Social Inquiry.* Boulder CO: Lynne Rienner Publishers.

Edin, Kathryn, and Maria Kefalas. 2011. *Promises I Can Keep: Why Poor Women put Motherhood before Marriage.* Berkeley: University of California Press.

Gimlin, Debra. 2007. "Constructions of Ageing and Narrative Resistance in a Commercial Slimming Group." *Ageing & Society* 27(3): 407–24.

Mitchell, Richard G. 2002. *Dancing at Armageddon: Survivalism and Chaos in Modern Times.* Chicago: University of Chicago Press.

18

NARRATING SOCIAL STRUCTURE

Stories of Resistance to Legal Authority

Patricia Ewick and Susan Silbey

To identify stories of resistance, we examined whether the narrative described an opportunity to avoid the consequences of relative disadvantage. In our analysis, we were particularly interested in identifying the means through which resistance was achieved. As we argued above, resistance does not so much rely on failures of power as appropriate the resources of the more powerful. We theorized that resistance is premised upon a recognition of those very same aspects of social structure that more often support taken for granted authority and power. Thus, we analyzed the stories we were told to see whether the description of resistance displayed an appreciation of structural opportunities present in the transaction. Since legal power is structured bureaucratically, we expected to find resistance appropriating these same structural features—often employing several simultaneously, as the examples below illustrate.

From our analysis of the stories people told us, we identify a number of ways in which the storytellers draw upon social structure in these stories. The ways in which social structure is invoked as a strategy of resistance include a manipulation of social roles, exploitation of hierarchy, responses to rationalized rules and regulations, and responses to the disciplining of social interactions along dimensions of time and space. Heuristically, we identify these reversals of conventional features of structural relations in the narratives as masquerade (playing with roles), rule literalness (playing with rules), disrupting hierarchy (playing with stratification), foot-dragging (playing with time), and colonizing space. In what follows we examine these various tactics of resistance and offer illustrative stories from our data. Although we present these various tactics as analytic categories, in the actual stories related to us in the course of the interview more than one tactic is often described. Similarly, a given act might reasonably be interpreted as an example of more than one type.

Masquerade

The sociologically informed view that social action is based on roles includes two insights. First, it expresses the idea that a person's behavior (as well as his or her obligations, privileges, entitlements, and power) accords with expectations associated with the person's social position. At the same time, this view encompasses an equally relevant insight: because roles are not synonymous with the person, they can be manipulated to influence transactions. The manipulation of roles might involve some degree of deception. In these instances, persons engage in literal *masquerade* insofar as they pretend to be something or someone they are not. They assume whatever role would lead to a more desired outcome. What is worth noting in regard to such commonplace deceptions is that people do not typically assume roles that carry greater social status or power but often enact the position of someone who is needier or less powerful, thus making a different sort of claim on power. For instance, a common form of informal resistance among subordinate workers involves "playing dumb," or presenting oneself as a less experienced, less knowledgeable worker in order to avoid work. Ironically, they feign a lack of the very knowledge that is necessary for the deceit in the first place (Prasad and Prasad 1998; Hodson 1995a, p. 144). In the more varied contexts in which persons encounter the law, the range of roles to be manipulated or assumed increases considerably beyond what is available in the workplace. Jesus Cortez, an elderly Hispanic man living in a rundown and dangerous area of Newark, told us that his calls to the police for help with neighborhood vandals were repeatedly ignored. Finally, he decided to change his voice to sound like that of a woman when calling. When he mimicked a woman, he told us, he got a "quick response."

Michelle Stewart reported lying about her age to a hospital in order to receive emergency room treatment. Because she was only 17 at the time, the first hospital she visited would not treat her without her parents' permission. Although she had been living independently for two years, having had no contact with her abusive parents, she realized that in the hospital's understanding of its legal obligations she was a dependent minor. Since she could not change her family situation in order to conform to hospital rules, she went to a different hospital and changed her age, matter-of-factly telling them she was 18.

In these two instances, Jesus Cortez and Michelle Stewart acted on an understanding of organizational behavior, an understanding acquired through experience and learning. These and other respondents presented themselves as whatever they needed to be—whether a (presumably) more vulnerable woman, an adult without family to help or support her, a naive litigant, or a maid, as we will illustrate below—in order to instigate organizational action.

Often, however, the manipulation of roles as a form of resistance is not deceptive but, rather, selective. People may not so much assume a false role as selectively invoke or present themselves in a role to which they can lay legitimate claim, though perhaps more appropriately in another setting. A person's ability to invoke any particular role, for purposes of resistance or conformity, draws upon their store of cultural and social capital, their experience and knowledge of alternative roles, and the likelihood that the performance will be accepted as genuine. One of our respondents, a 45-year-old African-American woman we call Millie Simpson, told us how she deflected the consequences of court-ordered punishment, imposed for failing to report an automobile accident and for possession of an unregistered vehicle. When she was required by the court to do 30 hours of community service, Millie used her well-rehearsed role of churchgoer and veteran volunteer to offer service at the church she already attended and provided service for many more than 30 hours a month. In this way Millie Simpson prudently invoked a role that defined the situation in a way that escaped the unwanted claims of power (criminal punishment for a court decision that was subsequently overturned, as it turns out, after she completed the mandated community service [Ewick and Silbey 1992]).

The choice of what role to invoke in a situation, of course, is not simply a matter of freely picking from a catalog of possibilities. Some role possibilities are not sanctioned, and the legitimacy and viability of role performances are not equally dispersed among populations. Middle-aged females of any race are more likely to successfully masquerade as church-goers and volunteers than are young, unemployed men. Moreover, the behavior associated with some roles may also be the privileged knowledge of particular classes. Nonetheless, although the cultural capital and probabilities associated with varying roles are unequally distributed, people do have at their disposal an array of roles on which they strategically draw in their efforts to mobilize and shape the direction of power in social transactions. Hoodfar (1991), for example, reports that some lower-middle-class Egyptian women have returned to wearing a veil in order to continue working in the public sphere without censure. Many of the women with whom she spoke reported that they wear a veil in order to avoid criticisms by family members and neighbors for working outside the home and moving about in public. Ironically, then, these Egyptian women rely on a traditional symbol of female subordination in order to achieve a level of autonomy and financial security.

In another story we collected, Aida Marks, a 55-year-old African-American woman, expressed her understanding of the sources and organization of institutionalized authority and how it might be duped to her benefit. Marks relied upon a feature of racial and gender employment subordination—African-American women's employment as housekeepers for white middle-class and upper-class families—to secure service from the telephone company when calls for repair went unanswered. Unable to get results through the normal channels, Marks called the president of the telephone company. Although such officers are insulated from consumer complaints by layers of bureaucratic hierarchy, Aida Marks was able to cut through the organizational barriers by invoking a role that legitimated such access.

> Interviewer: How did you finally get service?
>
> Marks: I start at the top because the people in the middle want to move to the top and the ones at the bottom can't help you, they're in the same situation you're in. So I always, that's how I got to meet Robert A— [the president of the phone company], I called over there first and I told them I was his maid.

By claiming to be the corporate president's housekeeper, she was immediately put through to him, voiced her complaints about her inadequate telephone service, and was very soon visited by an expert team of repair persons. Marks drew on her racially marked speech and her knowledge of the back doors of formal organizations to manipulate a conventional expectation that African-American women serve as domestic workers for white elites, thus circumventing her lack of power in her legitimate consumer role.

Rule Literalness

Where masquerade is based on a recognition that social interaction is based on roles, *rule literalness* is based on an appreciation that all transactions are governed by rules. Because rules commit organizations to lines of predictable action, rules create both opportunities to resist and means of resistance. They can be counted on but also displaced. The incompleteness and openings in any rule system provide opportunities that resisters can exploit (Beckert 1999). This might involve finding a lacuna within a network of rules, a space that, by virtue of not being governed or defined, becomes momentarily free of control. Or, it might involve subverting the purpose of the rule by rigidly observing it. *Rule literalness* is based on the understanding that most transactions, while governed by rules, can run smoothly only if rules are systematically overlooked, bent, stretched, and otherwise ignored. Even within highly rationalized settings such as bureaucracies, rules must be applied with significant discretion and restraint for effective functioning. Recognizing this, persons create disturbances by willfully refusing to participate in these routine violations. Sometimes people elevate a rule to a general principle (Simmel 1950) and apply it in unanticipated circumstances to the disadvantage of more powerful others. By its very conformity to the explicit language of a rule, this form of resistance challenges and disrupts power by holding it accountable to its own rationality, subverting the purpose of a rule by rigidly observing it.

When he was arrested on a Saturday for driving without insurance, Michael Chapin was compelled to put up $500 in cash as bail to guarantee his return to court for a hearing on Monday. In court, Chapin provided the evidence that there had been an error in the police insurance record and that indeed he had been insured at the time of his arrest. The charges were dismissed. At that point, he demanded that the court return the $500 in cash.

> Then they try to write me a check for my money back and I wouldn't accept it. I made a big stink. I said I want my cash back. I gave you cash, I want cash back. . . . I said I don't care what you have to do. I don't care if you have to print the money up. I want cash money. You didn't trust me for a check, I don't trust you either. I made them open the safe. [The judge] came back to see what I was yelling at the clerk, telling her I want my money.

In this case, Chapin appropriated the court's rules requiring that payments be in cash only and used them against the court. He could demand that cash refund from the court, which normally sent refund checks, because the court claimed to deal equally with all parties. By insisting that he be treated according to the court's own criterion for cash transactions, Chapin challenged its usually unquestioned prerogative.

Precisely because such practices are not defined or identified by the "laws of the place" (De Certeau 1984), they do not disobey those laws. By remaining scrupulously within the rules, a challenge may be indecipherable (within the rules) and remain invulnerable to control. More important, the moral claim of a challenge remains unsullied by counterclaims of deviance. Because stories of resistance make justice claims, this moral positioning of the storyteller is sometimes more important than any material benefit.

Much informal resistance thus consists not so much of transgression as of hyperconformity to rules. Some respondents acknowledge the power of literalness by writing their own rules, relying on the power of the informal, implied contract to relieve themselves of otherwise asserted obligations. George Kofie claimed that he did not pay medical bills when hospitals insisted on double-billing him. With a knowing wink, he told us how he manages this.

> When I go to the emergency room, I have a hospital bill, and a separate doctor bill. . . . I pay the hospital. Then I get a bill from some outside source for the treatment that I received in the hospital. This happens every time you go. And I've never been able to get any response from these people who send the bill. . . . I send letters telling them to explain to me the medical attention, then I will pay the bill. I don't get responses, then I don't pay it. [Int.: You don't pay the doctor bill?] I don't pay. I pay the hospital bill. . . . If the doctor is working in the hospital, why do I need to [pay him]? I go to the hospital and I pay the emergency room bill. Why do I pay twice? I don't pay unless I get the proper response. . . . When I go to my doctor's office, I don't get a bill from the hospital.

Rule literalness, or technical obedience, constitutes one of the most common ways in which persons manage their encounters with others who make compelling demands: ordinary citizens, legal agents, or organizations. It echoes the often repeated criticism of bureaucracy gone awry. Bradley Spears offered an analysis of how bureaucracies become unresponsive, and how hierarchy, which we will discuss further just below, and structure underwrite power. Describing a state office, he told us,

> If you don't dot an *i*, you jeopardize your complaint. . . . I'd like to reorganize their hiring practices, or training practices, so that the people who deal with the public are able to make decisions, are able to make judgment calls. I think they have no discretionary power, so consequently, if the dot on the *i* is upside down, they reject it. I think sometimes, there has to be some discretion used.

Disrupting Hierarchy

We were told stories about a third and familiar means of resistance: willfully ignoring hierarchy and with it the lines of authority, respect, and duty that are attached. Transactions among persons of different degrees of power and authority rely on a silent but mutual recognition of those differences. Because hierarchical deference so often goes without saying, ignoring these structural differences is disruptive precisely because it requires power to articulate itself. By demanding power to own up to itself, it calls what is more conventionally a bluff. In one form of disruption of hierarchy, another person's authority is appropriated and used against them.

Having, over the years, been subjected to numerous forms of harassment and humiliation at the hands of the local police, one woman described her response in one such instance.

> I was riding down Hadden Avenue one day and the cop pulled up in back of me. All of a sudden, [the cop] turned on his lights and siren noise. Scared the mess out of me. I almost hit a parked car. And the only thing he did it for was to pass the light. Then he turned everything off and was cruising on down the road, you know? And I very nicely cruised on down the road and pulled him over and told him exactly what I thought about it. [Int.: What did he say?] I didn't appreciate it. He laughed. I told him you wouldn't be laughing if I turned his badge number in . . . because they are supposed to observe all speed laws just like we are if they are not on call.

Michelle Stewart provided a similar example of inverting the lines of authority and responsibility that define common relationships. She told us that as a teenager she had feared her mother's reckless driving when her mother had been drinking. After futilely pleading with her mother not to drive, Michelle directed her parent to the local police station.

> I went with my mother one time when she was really drunk, like when I was fourteen. She was an alcoholic. She was always drinking and driving and crashing her car and everything. And I would get pissed off when she would come to pick up my friends and she'd be like that. She endangered us. So, I brought her into the police department. I called her on her bluff. She told me she wasn't drunk and I called her on it. She goes, I'm not drunk, let's go get a Breathalyzer. So I went there with her, and she was obviously drunk and driving a child, me.

Michael Chapin told us another story, this time not about something that happened, but about something he wished had happened. His story revealed, however, the same insight about how making lines of authority explicit exposes the sources of power too often overlooked. Not wanting to remain passive in the face of what he believed was blatant union corruption, Chapin plotted to invert the relationship between the carpenters' union to which he belonged and its members.

> My latest crazy idea was to picket the local. Get a hundred guys
> with signs. Call up the TV station, call up the newspapers and go
> down there and put them into shame. Shame them into doing
> something right. To change what's going on down there.

Had he arranged the picketing against the union local as he imagined he might, Chapin would have challenged the union's fiduciary relationship to the workers. More important, he would have made explicit the way in which union and management interests were aligned rather than contested, creating the corruption he was complaining about.

In these ways, asymmetrical lines of authority are reversed: a citizen stops a police officer, or a child usurps a parent's authority by reporting her mother's drunk driving to the police, or a union member envisions picketing his own local. In each instance, a person forces someone occupying a higher social position to make explicit the prerogatives of that status and to demand rather than simply to expect deference. The resistant acts impose costs by requiring those who would likely exercise greater power to use additional resources to reestablish authority (Parsons 1966).

In a second form of disrupting hierarchy, persons described the way in which they refused to acknowledge a line of authority or chain of command. One of the most common forms of resistance entails "leapfrogging" over layers of bureaucratic hierarchy. By reporting problems to those higher in the organization, people are also able to escalate the significance of their complaint, converting it from an individual into an organizational problem. Aida Marks incorporated this tactic in her story of her masquerade as a maid.

Sophia Silva told us her favorite story about her experience as a frustrated consumer.

> When my children were young, my washer kept overflowing and
> I was doing washes by the dozen, so I kept calling the repair place.
> They came and they kept fixing motors in it. This was costing us,
> and we were a young couple. Anyway, nothing was happening and
> I called, I think it was the General Electric number, and I called the

company and I got the president of the company. And the secretary said, "I'm sorry, he's not available." And I said, "Well, I am going to call him until he is." So she said, "Hold on a minute." And he came on, and said how can I help you? I started to cry, I was so nervous. And he said, "Now you sit down and you tell me the whole story." And I told him the whole story. That I have all these bills in front of me and I have this machine that does not work and nothing has been done. He said, "Don't you worry ma'am, it'll be taken care of." And five minutes later after we hung up, I got a call from a service company . . . out on Route 22, or something, and they came up and they fixed it. I mean, I don't mind paying for things, but. . . . This is my favorite story.

By going "to the top," respondents achieve three objectives. First, there is a high probability of having the concrete demands met. When superordinates are informed, the problem is usually remedied quickly. Many respondents discussed the routes they follow to get to the top. Gretchen Zinn cautioned, however, that this is a difficult climb. "I think you have to start through the regular channels though, or else they're going to send you back to that."

Second, by going to the top, respondents let higher-ups—the supposedly competent and responsible members of the organization—know about what is going on among their subordinates. Because it is often undesired information, the person who leapfrogs through bureaucratic hierarchy not only disturbs the official sequence of movement and action, she also introduces unwelcome information, or "institutional noise." David Majors, another union member, told us that the higher-ups in any organization or management "don't want any problems." Nonetheless, each level in the organization has its attention focused on those below as well as on those above (Emerson 1983). Respondents use this feature of organizational hierarchy as a wedge for their claims. Telling us about the state bureau of social services, David Majors commented,

On many occasions . . . I was forced to deal with their supervisors, and I usually got satisfaction out of them. Only because, you know, they don't want any problems. . . . If I couldn't get the answer that I wanted to hear, and knew that should be forthcoming . . . [if] they were just putting it on the back of the table, and saying, you know, "I got all this work in front of me, I'm not going to do it," all you had to do was talk to their supervisor, and they're going to do it. Because that supervisor doesn't want to hear any grief from upstairs. Because if I don't get satisfaction out of him, I'm going elsewhere.

By reporting problems to those higher in the organization, respondents are able to call forth higher authority to retaliate (for them) against those who have been obstructing the attempts at redress.

Third, going to the top of an organization allows respondents to experience a measure of agency and freedom that the bureaucratic processes of large organizations normally stifle. It is no doubt this satisfaction that accounts for the fact that one of Sophia Silva's "favorite stories" concerned the washing machine repair. The satisfaction of being heard is often enough for people to pursue this strategy even in situations they define as futile.

> I don't necessarily think that it [letter writing and calling officials] has any value. For example, when we just went through the Persian Gulf War, I called different legislators in our state. I called each one of them and got myself, my opinion heard. (Gretchen Zinn)

> I think on a couple of occasions [I sent] copies of the letter to the governor's office. Knowing the system, having access to the books and whatnot, it's pretty easy to find out what the chain of command is and to write. Not that it gets you anywhere. (Bradley Spears)

> I go to whoever his superior is. I write a letter, not knowing, you know, if the letter would do any good or not. But I put it down in writing, my grievances. (Sophia Silva)

Other respondents also talked about letter-writing campaigns and barrages of registered packages directed to the homes of corporate executives. Although legal resources, such as consumer protection laws, are widely available, most consumers understand that mobilizing these laws is unreasonably demanding for most of the small, daily transactions in which they feel cheated, misled, or ignored. Instead, citizens forgo the law and find ways of directly negotiating their disputes. These often involve some form of leapfrogging in which people rely on the shape of the organizational hierarchy and patterns of accountability to enhance their claims.

Foot-Dragging or Taking Time

Modern rationalization of social action converts time into units (minutes, days, weeks, or years) as a foundation for organizing complex social relations. Rather than understanding time as passing in an indivisible, continuous stream, one sees it as a set of distinct elements that can be abstracted, partitioned, calculated, and mapped onto social interactions as a mechanism of regulation and control. Shaped by temporal rhythms that are often inconsistent with subjective experiences of time, the more disciplined and formally distributed interactions within modern organizations are often experienced not merely as an interruption but as a confiscation of private life. One of the most common forms of resistance to the discontinuities and incongruities of contemporary time reckoning is *foot-dragging*, or *taking time*. Note that we did not use the more familiar construction "taking *one's* time." As a form of resistance, the time taken in foot-dragging is not that of the resister. It is time that belongs to one's employer, one's creditor, to anyone who defines and controls behavior in terms of time. In this regard, foot-dragging is a modem form of resistance that depends on, even as it defies, the rationalization of time.

Thus, when people cannot resolve disagreements with those whose profit depends on time rationalization, they sometimes accept defeat by complying but at a pace and in a manner that exacts its own price. As one woman involved in a credit-card dispute said, in these circumstances "I try to get a little of my own back," however she can. Although the motive may be to avoid what is perceived to be an unfair charge, the response is to comply in a way that disarms retribution. Rita Michaels said that a hospital unfairly charged her for being a subject in one of their medical experiments because they had not told her of the cost when they solicited her participation. Because the hospital was not charging interest on the statement, she took time in paying the hill.

> It was $250. And he sent me a bill for that, and I questioned it. And he told me what it was for. Every month I'd get a bill. It would say if you don't pay this bill, we're going to send you to a collection agency. I paid it ten dollars a month. I could've paid it all off in one shot, but I should have been told about [the costs up front]. . . .
> I did it to be a pest, you know. You can't take me to court if I'm making at least an effort to pay.

Anticipating problems, some people use time to avoid or minimize what they believe is their victimization. When asked if she had ever had problems with rental housing, such as having her security deposit withheld, Sima Rah responded:

> [Laughter.] No. I laugh because we don't give the owner a chance to withhold our security. If we know we have to move, we don't pay that month's rent, which is our security. Because we know these landlords. They won't give your security back.

Recognizing the value of time, people report "taking" it in compensation for losses that cannot be redeemed in other ways. Although Nell Pearson could not get full compensation from the insurance company for her losses in a car accident, when the opportunity arose she managed to make the insurance company lawyer "spend" the money she should have received. When he called her to negotiate a lower settlement, she used her knowledge of lawyers' billing practices (where labor is reckoned to the minute) and kept him on the phone for as long as would likely equal the difference in what the insurance company offered and she wanted.

> They turned it over to their insurance company, and I got a call from the insurance company's lawyer, wanting to settle the night before the small claims hearing. And we were haggling over $50. I had already decided that he probably wasn't going to pay me the $50 but I would get $50 of his time on the telephone. So, after about a half an hour, he was screaming. . . . And he said, "I'm just going to have to see you in small claims." I knew he didn't want to go. It was too small an amount of money. So I said, "That's okay, you don't have to do it, I've gotten my $50 out of you," and he said, "Is that what you were doing?" And I said, "Yeah. I know what lawyers are worth." And he said, "You've got your $50."

In this way, foot-dragging is a means of exercising some control within situations in which little opportunity for control exists. As these examples illustrate, foot-dragging is less of a refusal (to pay, or act, or work) than it is an assertion of some level of autonomy in the course of complying.

Colonizing Space, Camping Out

Modern power can be defined in terms of a set of distinctive spatial as well as temporal practices. In large part, these practices involve the enclosure of space and the containment of individuals within enclaves such as those factories, schools, hospitals, barracks, and, more recently, shopping malls. The typically unarticulated norms regarding the occupation of these spaces (who will be where, for what purpose, and for how long) present abundant opportunities for disrupting power (Rofel 1992; Shields 1989).

It is also true that law not only regulates but occupies space, most importantly by privileging writing and inscription. By converting human transactions into written documents such as files, cases, transcripts, or police reports, relationships and situations are concretized, objectified, transformed into static objects. These written documents freeze thoughts, words, and transactions, imparting to them a greater fixity and truth value within the epistemological sphere of the law. Unable to penetrate the legal texts, many persons and groups remain unrecognizable in a world of paper, precedent, and archive. Even those who are able to enter the law's text often cannot control where they are placed or deployed. Having entered law's textualized realm, they are easily confined by it. Through inscription, words and transactions are given an existence apart from their authors.

In their dealings with bureaucracies, including legal bureaucracies, people often report, for instance, being transformed into "a case," which is then filed away and forgotten. In many of the stories we heard, the privileging of texts and other forms of inscription were recognized as a central ordering principle of law (cf. Smith 1987, 1990). For example, Aida Marks told us a story in which she displayed her appreciation of the power of documents to organize social relations, enabling some and disempowering others. After her son Ronald had been shot, he was brought to a hospital that Marks believed provided substandard care to nonwhite patients. On the advice of a family doctor, she tried unsuccessfully to arrange for Ronald's transfer to another hospital. When she failed to persuade the hospital doctors and administrators to transfer Ronald, the medical records hanging on the end of his bed presented an opportunity to move him. Knowing that these records are the only official recognition of a patient's existence, Marks was able to make her son "disappear" from the hospital along with the papers.

> I went up there at eight o'clock in the morning after Dr. Abraham told me to get him out of there. I had that big bag from Avon with me and this silly old nurse up there . . . , she gave me all of Ronald's records [to look at how he was doing]. So I pushed them down into my bag. . . . They didn't care whether he went, I don't think. They couldn't find those records. They was havin' fits.

After the "silly old nurse" mistakenly handed her Ronald's medical records, Aida Marks seized the opportunity to do what she could not do through direct means—transfer Ronald to a better hospital. Recognizing her relative powerlessness in the situation, Marks did not directly contest or question the authority of the doctors, nurses, or hospital administrators. Yet even without openly defying the professionals, she successfully disabled them by depriving them of their forms of privileged communication. Perhaps most revealing of her understanding of the role of textualization in the formal institutional world of the hospital was her observation that the nurses and doctors ultimately didn't care whether

Ronald went, but they cared deeply whether the papers went. They were, she said, "having fits" about that, not about Ronald.

With regard to practices in physical geographical space, Martha Lee described how she would respond to a good friend who did not return an expensive tool he borrowed. She could cry, she suggested, or "camp out on their front porch until they gave it back to me. I don't think I would sue my friend." Thus, to Martha Lee, intentionally and obstinately being "out of place," occupying her neighbor's front porch, represents a more efficient and legitimate means of seeking compensation than those provided by law.

Sophia Silva described how she had learned this tactic of colonizing space, how she used it to get service in a department store when she was being ignored, and how she subsequently taught the strategy to a young mother having difficulty getting service at Sears.

> I was in Sears one day, and this young girl was there with all these children around her. . . . She had bought a vacuum cleaner like a week before and it did not work, and they were telling her to mail it back [to the manufacturer]. . . . And she was distraught. I said to her, "Don't you move." I said, "You stay there, you'll have to stay two or three hours until they give you a new one." And I kept coming back to check, and they did give her a new one.

Finally, Joan Walsh told us that she learned the usefulness of colonizing space by observing other parents who were "pushy advocates" for their kids. Sensitive about being a member of the "working-class in a snooty suburb," and about the fact that her son had some special learning needs, Walsh decided to occupy the guidance counselor's office at her son's high school because the counselor was not providing the paperwork her son needed for his college applications.

> My son wasn't getting any place [trying to obtain a copy of his transcript]. So, one morning, I got up and I dressed nicely. Not jeans, but I got dressed nicely. And, I went to school with him at 7:30 in the morning and I went to the guidance waiting room and I sat in the chair and I said I'm going to sit here until I talk to him. And when he walked in and realized I was sitting with my son—because he recognized my son—he was very friendly. . . . So I got results. . . . But I feel that if I hadn't done that he'd probably, he may have missed out on the only school he wanted to go to, because they weren't sensitive to his needs. So I don't like to have to interfere like that but I learned back in elementary school when other mothers used to do it, and

> I used to be the type who didn't say much and sat back, that other
> parents were getting what their kids needed for them. . . . So I had to
> change my way and I had to start speaking up.

The spaces occupied are not only physical places or discursive texts. Odette Hurley described how her neighbors got together to occupy the police telephone lines in order to get help with some dog packs running around the town. Although she had called each time she had seen the dogs, the police never responded. "And finally when all the neighbors kind of formed together and started timing their calls, and we'd just call one right after another and kept calling and calling until they finally came and cleaned them up."

Here, as with other forms of resistance, the shape and form of defiance described in the stories derived from an appropriation of the structural resources of spatialization against which it was poised. Frustrated or defrauded consumers, taxpayers, and counseling clients challenge the rationalized processes that transform their grievances and problems into manageable cases by insisting on being physically present. Unarticulated understandings about such matters as how long one stays in a department store or how hospitals authorize medical procedures are the grounds upon which such resistances operate. By recognizing and using these conventional expectations, previously ignored claims, requests, or pleas for help are heard.

References

Beckert, Jens. 1999. "Agency, Entrepreneurs, and Institutional Change: The Role of Strategic Choice and Institutionalized Practices in Organizations." *Organization Studies* 20:777–99.

De Certeau, Michel. 1984. *The Practice of Everyday Life*, translated by Steven Rendall. Berkeley and Los Angeles: University of California Press.

Emerson, Robert. 1983. "Holistic Effects in Social Control Decisionmaking." *Law and Society Review* 17 (3): 425–56.

Ewick, Patricia, and Susan S. Silbey. 1992. "Conformity, Contestation, and Resistance: An Account of Legal Consciousness." *New England Review* 26 (3): 731–49.

Hodson, Randy. 1995a. "Cohesion or Conflict? Race, Solidarity, and Resistance in the Workplace." *Research in the Sociology of Work* 5:135–59.

Hoodfar, Homa. 1991. "Return to the Veil: Personal Strategy and Public Participation in Egypt." Pp. 102–24 in *Working Women: International Perspectives on Labor and Gender Ideology*, edited by Nanneke Reddift and M. Thea Sinclair. New York: Routledge.

Parsons, Talcott. 1966. "On the Concept of Power." Pp. 79–107 in *Varieties of Political Theory*, edited by David Easton. New York: Free Press.

Prasad, Anshuman, and Pushkala Prasad. 1998. "Everyday Struggles at the

Workplace: The Nature and Implications of Routine Resistance in Contemporary Organizations" *Research in the Sociology of Organizations* 15:225–57.

Rofel, L. 1992. "Rethinking Modernity: Space and Factory Discipline in China." *Cultural Anthropology* 7:93–114.

Shields, Rob. 1989. "Social Spatialization and the Built Environment: The West Edmonton Mall." *Society and Space* 7:147–64.

Simmel, Georg. 1950. "On Superordination and Subordination." Pp. 181–89 in *The Sociology of Georg Simmel*, edited and translated by Kurt H. Wolff. New York: Free Press.

Smith, Dorothy E. 1987. *The Everyday World as Problematic: A Feminist Sociology.* Boston: Northeastern University Press.

———. 1990. *Texts, Facts, and Femininity: Exploring the Relations of Ruling.* New York: Routledge.

19

"IT WAS LIKE A FEVER . . ."

Narrative and Identity in Social Protest

Francesca Polletta

On February 1, 1960, four Black students sat-in at a segregated lunch counter in Greensboro, North Carolina and touched off a wave of similar demonstrations around the South. Two months later, Harvard graduate student Michael Walzer returned from a tour of Southern colleges to report that "every student" he met had given the same account of the first day of protest on his or her campus. "It was like a fever. Everyone wanted to go" (Walzer 1960:111).

Metaphors of wildfire, fever, and contagion were common in early accounts of the sit-ins. The *New Republic* reported in April 1960: "No outside organization masterminded the recent uprisings. . . . In almost every instance, they were planned and carried out by students, without outside advice or even contact between schools except by way of press and radio news" (Fuller 1960:13). The *Nation* in May: "Up to this point, the student demonstrations have been spontaneous" (Wakefield 1960:404). *Harper's* in June quoted an NAACP branch president: "How can I correlate anything when I don't know where and when it's going to happen" (Lomax 1960:47). Paul Wehr (1960), one of the first academic observers of the sit-ins, was surprised by the "absence of any effective liaison" among sit-in groups on eight campuses (quoted in Oberschall 1989:35).

Francesca Polletta, "It Was Like a Fever . . .": Narrative and Identity in Social Protest." *Social Problems* vol. 45, no. 2 (May 1998): 137–59, by permission of Oxford University Press

Martin Oppenheimer, in another early study, dismissed prior organizational links as explanation for the spread of the sit-ins, arguing that "the sit-ins caught on in the manner of a grass fire, moving from the center outward" (1989:40; see also Carson 1981; Matthews and Prothro 1966; Piven and Cloward 1977; Zinn 1964). A grass fire indeed: by the end of February, demonstrations had spread to thirty cities in seven states; by the end of March to fifty-four cities in nine states. By mid-April, fifty thousand people had taken part in the sit-ins (Carson 1981; Chafe 1980).

Twenty years later Aldon Morris persuasively challenged the alleged spontaneity of the student sit-ins. As part of a broader assault on sociologists' neglect of the activist traditions and networks that precede social protest, Morris revealed that the Greensboro sit-inners were members of an NAACP Youth Council and had close ties with people who had conducted sit-ins in Durham in the late 1950s. Their discussions of nonviolence and direct action were pursued in an organizational context of skilled strategists. After the sit-in began, a network of ministers, NAACP officials, and other activists swung into action, contacting colleagues to spread the news, training students in sit-in techniques, and persuading adults to support the protests. The church was the linchpin of student activism, Morris argued, supplying leaders and guidance, training and inspiration. "To understand the sit-in movement, one must abandon the assumption that it was a college phenomenon. . . . The sit-ins spread across the South in a short period because [adult] activists, working through local movement centers, planned, coordinated, and sustained them," he concluded (1984:200, 202).

Subsequent chroniclers have taken Morris's lead in detailing the extensive adult networks that preceded the sit-ins (Blumberg 1984; Chafe 1980; Powledge 1991). Why then did Walzer's interviewees say they had been "like a fever"? Why, in interviews with reporters, statements to Congress, letters to friends, articles and editorials in campus newspapers and in the *Student Voice*—organ of the brand new Student Nonviolent Coordinating Committee—did sit-inners describe the protests as sudden, impulsive, and unplanned? Certainly, there were good strategic reasons for conveying that image to the American public. Spontaneity deflected charges of communist influence, and were likelier to garner public support for a "homegrown" protest. But students also referred to the spontaneity of the sit-ins in less public statements, in articles and letters in campus newspapers, and in communications with each other. One would imagine that the chief aim in these communications would be to make sense of unfolding events and to inspire and mobilize fellow students. Why then emphasize the *absence* of planning, represent the sit-ins as driven not by concerted student action, but by a zeitgeist over which students had no control? Would not the latter undermine the sense of collective efficacy essential to successful mobilization (Benford 1993a; Gamson 1992, 1995; Klandermans 1988, 1997; McAdam 1982; Piven and Cloward 1979)?

My examination of students' descriptions of the sit-ins as they were occurring suggests that "spontaneous" did not mean "unplanned." In the stories that students told and retold about the sit-ins, spontaneity denoted independence from adult leadership, urgency, local initiative, and action by moral imperative rather than bureaucratic planning. Narratives of the sit-ins, told by many tellers, in more and less public settings, and in which spontaneity was a central theme, described student activists and potential activists to themselves and, in the process, helped to create the collective identity on behalf of which students took high-risk action. Sit-in stories—and their narrative form was crucial—also motivated action by their *failure* to specify the mechanics of mobilization. Their *ambiguity* about agents and agency, not their clarity, successfully engaged listeners.

Sit-In Narratives

The narrative form of students' representations of the sit-ins is striking. They told stories, and similar stories, over and over again. A piece published in the Shaw College campus newspaper in May 1960 opened:

> It was night time Tuesday, Feb. 9. Radio and television commentators had announced that 'it' was not expected to happen in Raleigh. Wednesday morning, Feb. 10, 10:30—BOOM!—'it' hit with an unawareness that rocked the capital city from its usual sedateness to a state of glaring frenzy.[1]

The same month, from a letter sent by the just-formed Student Nonviolent Coordinating Committee to Congressmen:

> The sit-ins began February 1st in Greensboro N.C. when four freshmen at Negro North Carolina A and T sat down at a variety store lunch counter after purchasing several items in other departments of the store. They were refused service. Their action was a spontaneous rebellion against the accumulated indignities suffered by Negro Americans since Reconstruction days. "Why must we be continually under tension and indignity when we want to eat, or find a lodging place, or use a rest room?" they asked. Their action has led others to ask the same question—and to do something about

it. Since February, the sit-ins have spread to almost 100 cities in every Southern state.[2]

One can imagine other ways of representing the sit-ins. Writers or speakers might have first described the current state and scale of the sit-ins in snapshot rather than chronological form (for example, "there are students currently sitting-in in fifty cities"). They might have begun by questioning or advocating the future course of the demonstrations ("we must build on the sit-in movement to fight for more radical changes," "after the sit-ins, what next?"), or by appealing directly to fellow students' commitment ("your fellow students are putting their lives on the line. Where are you?"). Instead, they recounted events in chronological order from "the beginning," with the moral of the story conveyed by the events themselves. Newspaper accounts are more likely to recount events in narrative form than are speeches or personal letters, and I cite more of the former than the latter. But newspaper stories typically do not display the degree of suspense, moral as well as temporal directionality, and ambiguity around causality that the sit-in narratives did. Interestingly, the very first campus newspaper accounts of the Greensboro sit-in, which appeared in the Agricultural and Technical College *Register*, used much more conventionally journalistic and editorial formats. The difference between these and subsequent accounts suggest that the narrative representation of the sit-ins took some time to develop.[3]

Students' narratives of the sit-ins exhibited each of the elements that Miller (1990) sees as characteristic of the form: plot ("an initial situation, a sequence leading to a change or reversal of that situation, and a revelation made possible by the reversal of the situation" [75]); personification ("a protagonist, an antagonist, and a witness who learns" [75]); and repetition of a complex word. With respect to plot, the sit-ins reversed a situation of student apathy and a movement dominated by adult gradualism; they created a new, student-led, action-oriented movement. The revelations generated by the reversal were multiple. To the country, they showed the level of Black discontent, to mainstream civil rights organizations, they showed the inadequacy of a moderate agenda, to students themselves, they showed the potency of students' collective agency. "Saint Paul College students have been joltingly awakened to the fact that we must do our part as thinking Negro Americans, and take a definite stand in the fight for equal rights," a student writer ended his account. "Because of [the sit-ins] Baltimore will never be the same," another concluded. "When, in the future we look back on the 60's may it be remembered as the years in which the American Youth forced the nation to dedicate itself to turning the American Dream into a Reality."[4]

The successful plot makes the familiar unfamiliar or, as Roman Jakobson puts it, "the ordinary strange" (quoted in Bruner 1991:13). We read because we sense that the story we know will transpire differently on this occasion. The sit-in narrative made the quotidian act of sitting down at a lunch counter and ordering a cup of coffee—what should have been a nonpolitical act—a dangerous and unpredictable epic. In conversations with North Carolinian students, Michael Walzer observed that they "told one story after another about . . . minor but to them terribly important incidents in the buses, in stores, on the job. The stories usually ended with some version of 'I ran out of that store. I almost cried . . .'" (Walzer 1960). The sit-in narrative thus transformed a too-common story of humiliation into one of triumph. In several accounts, the adventure was funny as well as exciting. Editors of a college newspaper wrote, "Here were two harmless young people sauntering through a store . . . stalking them in true dragnetness were no less than half a dozen police officers, while customers and managers hovered in corners as if the invasion from Mars had come!" A Knoxville College writer composed an "Ode To A Lunch Counter": "Little lunch counter with your many stools / And your nervous pacing manager fools / How do you feel amid this confusion and strife? / Do you object to a change inevitable in life?"[5]

Students who did not participate in the demonstrations constructed narratives in which the sit-ins were a subplot of their own larger story. For example, a White high-school student wrote to sit-inners of his experience in a race relations-themed summer camp:

> And now it is September. For many of us we will return to homes and schools which will irritate us even more after knowing and living what we have learned and what we have lived. But we do seem to agree that we cannot behave quite the way we did before we came to this camp. We have talked so much about what the sit-in movement means to us. It would be almost impossible to know how much it means to you. To us it is an affirmation of so many things. Of the courage of our young people. Of the miracle of spontaneity. Of the faith in people who will do something about what they believe.[6]

Conversations about the sit-ins, about "the miracle of spontaneity" were thus integrated into campers' own story of enlightenment. Swarthmore College editors wrote in the same vein, "Because our minds are knit into a web, the agitation of a few will tremble in all dimensions. Students cannot control, they can only communicate, in a Tokyo snake dance demonstration, a Nashville sit-in, or a chorus behind their printed word."[7]

Personification was a second key feature of the sit-in narrative. The witness role that Miller (1990) refers to was fulfilled by at least four players: the sit-inners themselves who realized their own capacity for transformative action; adult movement leaders; the national public; and potential student activists who would recognize their potential selves in the sit-in story. Dramatis personae expressed a set of appropriate emotions. Sit-inners were "weary" of oppression and the slow pace of change, "tired" of waiting for the "American dream to materialize." They were "apprehensive" about the repercussions of their actions, plagued by "butterflies." Yet, they were "all so very happy that we were (and are) able to do this to help our city, state and nation," and "maintain[ed] high enthusiasm." None of the stories represented the sit-inners as angry, cynical, or calculating. SNCC's Jane Stembridge wrote to a sit-inner that she had "read and re-read" his story "with the deepest pain, joy, laughter, and chills. . . . You have written a story of Life," she observed. "We can write fact after fact about the movement, and never touch the real elements."[8] Narrative made "real" the movement in a way that nonnarrative "facts" could not.

Miller's (1990) third narrative feature, repetition of a complex word, occurs in the repeated reference to the spontaneity of the sit-ins. Again, in these communications aimed at mobilizing fellow students as well as understanding what had happened, why would students draw attention to—indeed, celebrate—the unplanned character of the protest? There were good strategic reasons for representing the sit-ins that way. Spontaneity offered some defense against charges that the demonstrations were led by "outside agitators"—read, communists. The students' image as eager, impatient, and fearless also may have allayed potential financial supporters' fears of communist inspiration, and gave older leaders a valuable bargaining chip in their threat of disruption.[9] But an exclusively instrumental account is belied by the fact that students represented the sit-ins as spontaneous in communications with each other as well as in more public settings.

It is unlikely that if asked, they would have denied the involvement of specific adults and organizations in helping to plan the sit-ins. Referring to the spontaneity of campus mobilization was not at odds with the existence of planning networks. For example, one group of sit-inners described their action as "the result of spontaneous combustion," then went on to chronicle the planning that had preceded it. They emphasized, however—and this seems to be the point of using the term "spontaneous combustion"—that "there was no organizational tie-in of any kind, either local or national." But they also acknowledged "in order to make the story complete" that members of the sit-organizing group had previously received a "Letter to Christian Students" from the National

Student Christian Federation urging them to seek ways to participate.[10] This insistence on spontaneity in spite of evidence and acknowledgment of planning suggests that the term meant something other than that the sit-ins were unplanned. Closer examination of student sit-in narratives suggests three meanings.

First, the sit-ins' spontaneity signaled a decisive break, both with students' prior apathy, and with adults' moderation. Howard University's newspaper, *The Hilltop*, ran a story titled "Students Picket in Spontaneous Move" which opened: "A group of 130 Howard students did much recently to destroy the myth of student 'apathy.'" Editors of a new campus journal wrote: "No longer may students be called the 'Silent Generation.' Dissatisfied with a passively immoral society, they are increasingly involved in the world they want to change." "Our impatience with the token efforts of responsible adult leaders, was manifest in the spontaneous protest demonstrations which, after February 1, spread rapidly across the entire South," SNCC's chair Marion Barry told Platform committees at the Democratic and Republican national conventions.[11] The sit-ins were thus represented as signaling the death of an old movement and the birth of a new. Commending the formation of a new Black periodical, SNCC wrote to its editors, "There is no longer a way to rationalize gradualism. It did die on February 1, 1960, in Woolworth's of Greensboro. It will die again and again when every individual rises to his responsibility. . . . We hope for [the continuation of the *Atlanta Inquirer*] and its effectiveness as a death blow to apathy, fear, and gradualism." A piece published in the *Student Voice* referred to the student sit-ins as giving "birth" to a "freedom child." "The Baltimore Sitdowner," read a flyer for that city's movement, "was born on a bitter, cold night in March."[12]

A second prominent theme in the sit-in narrative, one again evoked by the term spontaneity, represented the demonstrations as motivated by a moral imperative rather than a strategic plan, a directive to lay one's body on the line that did not admit of negotiation. "Despite fears, the sit-ins will continue for a long time," one story concluded. "Many more tears will be shed, and perhaps many of my friends will be hurt. They feel that they must go on." A piece in the *Student Voice* opened, "It is really strange—to do things alone. Sometimes we have no alternative," then described student Henry Thomas's frustrated efforts to mobilize students in St. Augustine, Florida. "I decided to make another try at it," Thomas was quoted. "Still thinking of the opposition I would have, I decided to carry out my plans regardless if there was no one but me—I did it alone." "Hank Thomas road a train South"—now the editor's voice. "He had to do this thing now. People on the train talked, said go slow, said don't try too hard, said no to Henry . . . but the train did not stop till it got home and Hank was on it." The story combined agency and zeitgeist: Hank acted on his own and yet was just a passenger on a freedom train.[13] Seven of the thirteen students interviewed by sociologist James Laue in 1962 attributed the start and spread of the sit-ins to the "tenor of the times," or called them "inevitable." "Your relationship with the movement is just like a love affair," said one. "You can't explain it. All you know is it's something you have to do" (quoted in Laue 1989:62, 78).

Howard University's Lawrence Henry related the story of that campus's sit-ins: "Who started it? No one started it. What united us was the American principle of freedom and equality and the fact that we want to be free." Jane Stembridge told members of the National Student Association, "The fact that the protest broke out overnight and spread with fantastic speed said simply this: the Negro, despite the thoughts of too many Whites, is NOT content. . . . And *nobody* could escape this." For students at Penn State, the sit-ins were "symbolic of a new era in race relations and of a new Negro—one who is unwilling to wait until the sweet by-and-by." "We had been ready to do something like this for a long time"; "We have been planning it all our lives"; "We're living in a jet age and we're tired of moving at an ox-cart pace"; "Sure we've been influenced by outsiders, outsiders like Thoreau and Gandhi. But our biggest influence has been inside—all those years of second-class citizenship"; "We have 'taken it' since the day we were born"; "After 95 years of discussions, delays, postponements, procrastination, denials, and second-class citizenship, the Negro of today wants his full citizenship in his day"— formulations like these peppered the sit-in narratives. Editors of Shaw University's newspaper wrote, "[T]he students say—and it is reasonable to believe them—that they are tired of waiting for the humane aspects of the American dream to materialize."[14]

Students of Philander Smith College in Little Rock, Arkansas wrote, "The spirit reached the boiling point at 11:00 a.m., March 10, 1960. It was on this day that the students of Philander Smith College cast their lots into the New Student Movement." On this rendering, protest was an expression of centuries of frustration. SNCC's letter to Congressmen said of the sit-inners: "Their action was a spontaneous rebellion against the accumulated indignities suffered by Negro Americans since Reconstruction days." Third, then, the sit-ins were represented as driven by an imperative over which individuals had no control, as expression of a world historical force. "This situation was inevitable," a speaker told Howard University students. "Negroes are in the process of discovering a new self-image; and they are no longer willing to accept the injustices done to them." The "current wave of demonstrations is the spontaneous ground swell of the profound determination of young Negroes to be first-class citizens" wrote students at Vanderbilt University. From SNCC: "We know now that we must inexorably win the battle against injustice."[15]

Descriptions of the student protest "burst[ing]," "breaking," "exploding," "sweeping," "surging," "unleashed," "rip[ping] through the city like an epidemic," of students "fired" by the "spark of the sit-ins," of "released waves of damned-up energy," of a "chain reaction" were common and suggested again an unstoppable moral impetus. Attacks on desegregated accommodations were just one manifestation of a protest that could expand in myriad ways. "It was not the coffee that caused an unbelievable wave of demonstrations to arise spontaneously and, within weeks, to cover the entire South. It was, as the Atlanta students wrote, 'an Appeal for Human rights.'"[16]

If the twentieth century American "standard story" is one in which significant actions occur as consequences of the deliberations and impulses of independent, conscious, and self-motivated actors (Tilly 1998), then students' representations of the sit-ins as spontaneous challenged that rationale for action, along with its connotations of adult gradualism and amoral instrumentalism. Students narratively constructed what was happening in order to make sense of it, but also to signal its significance. In the process, they created a new collective identity of student activist. "The sit-ins," SNCC Chair Charles McDew said in October 1960, "have inspired us to build a new image of ourselves in our own minds" (McDew 1967). That identity supplied the selective incentives that made "high risk activism" (McAdam 1986) attractive.

Narratives of the sit-ins also motivated by their very failure to convey a single meaning. References to the sit-ins' spontaneity simultaneously explained and failed to explain the sit-ins in a way that called for the story's retelling—and reenactment. To clarify, I return to the third feature of Miller's (1990) characterization of narrative. Again, the complex word at the heart of all narratives is not only polyvalent but finally indeterminate, Miller argues; its core meaning is unfixable. The impossibility of a conclusive meaning calls for more stories that recapitulate the dilemma, but differently. All stories both explain and fail to explain, Miller goes on, but the dynamic is clearest in stories of humankind's origins. The point at which man separates himself from beasts is unknowable, since "whatever is chosen as the moment of origination always presupposes some earlier moment when man first appeared" (72). The question cannot be answered logically, and the alternative is a mythical narrative whose illogical premises will nevertheless require that it be retold. Thus Sophocles' *Oedipus the King* depicts a man who both has and has not broken the incest taboo—that which separates humans from all other species—and is punished (punishes himself) for that which he did not know. The enigma is revealed but unresolved; hence the need for more stories—for Shakespeare's *Hamlet*, for Faulkner's *Absalom, Absalom*. "What cannot be expressed logically, one is tempted to say, we then tell stories about," Miller concludes (74).

The question of origins is just as unanswerable in the case of social movements. When does protest begin? In this case, did it begin when the first students were arrested? Did it begin with the Montgomery bus boycott? With *Brown v. Board*? Did it begin with the first slave rebellion? With the first song sung, or African tradition preserved, or Christian ritual reinterpreted in what James Scott (1990) calls an "infrapolitics of dissent" stretching back to Africans' enslavement in this country? The question of origins is historical but also personal. When does collective action begin? When can I call myself an activist? The sit-in narrative posed those questions and resolved them in a way that called for their re-asking. The students acted, and yet it was a force that made students act, an impetus that acted through the students.

The word "spontaneity" means both voluntary and instinctual (involuntary)—contradictory meanings contained in the same (complex) word. In the sit-in narratives, spontaneity functioned as a kind of narrative ellipsis in which the movement's "beginning" occurred; "IT HAPPENED," and the non-narratable shift from observer to participant took place. This ellipsis or ambiguity strengthened the engagement of the listener/hearer in one of two ways. Either, following Iser (1972) and Leitch (1986), its underspecification of the mechanisms of participation forced listeners/ hearers to fill in the missing links, to become co-authors of the story. Or, following Miller (1990), the story could not establish, could not fix the motivation for participation and so required its retelling. And since the story was a true one, retelling required reenactment of the events already described. Either way, ambiguity was crucial to narrativity, to readers' engagement and identification with the story.

A concept of narrative thus captures the action-compelling character of the discourse around the sit-ins better than does the concept of frames by virtue of narrative's combination of familiarity and undecidability, convention and novelty, and truth (representing reality) and fiction (constituting reality). It was not the sit-in narratives' clarity about the antagonists, protagonists, stakes, and mechanics of struggle that made them so compelling but rather their containment of ambiguity, risk, and mystery within a familiar discursive form.

Institutionalizing Spontaneity

How compelling were the sit-in narratives? In addition to the number of students who joined the sit-ins (70,000 by September 1961 [Oberschall

1989]), the challenges created for SNCC as a fledgling organization by the sit-in narratives suggests their potency. Spontaneity, emblematic of students' independence and their unique contribution to the movement, became organizational commitments which both animated and constrained strategic action. Students called for coordination but were resistant to direction, wanted the movement to speak to the nation but were wary of leaders, wanted to expand the scope of protest but distrusted adult advice. Southern Regional Council official Margaret Long advised SNCC workers on their fundraising activities: "I wonder if it is really true, as this brochure says, that you 'seek to be a coordinating agency.' I see a great deal of uprising and brave and impeccable and successful marches on the Bastille, but I don't see any coordinated movement by you or anybody else. And I don't know that there should be."[17] SNCC leaders apparently took Long's advice, for in funding appeals, newsletters, and speeches, they represented the group as extension of the spontaneity of the sit-ins, and of the values of moral imperative, local autonomy, and radicalism that spontaneity connoted. A narrative of the sit-ins warranted SNCC as a kind of "anti-organization," as observers would later call it, an organization that sought not so much to guide the struggle as to go where people were "moving"; that was less interested in executing a well-planned agenda than in enacting in its own operation the society it envisaged, and that privileged direct and moral action over political maneuvering.[18]

The strength of the sit-in narrative, and its equation of student protest with moral—as opposed to political—action, is also suggested by the internal conflict SNCC faced the following year in moving from direct action (sit-ins and freedom rides) to voter registration. Proponents of voter registration within SNCC were careful to emphasize that "the only group that could do a complete voter registration program southwide was a student group,"[19] thus asserting SNCC's distinctive identity as a *student* organization. But they still met with fierce resistance (Carson 1981; Zinn 1964). Detractors were wary of the federal administration's support for a voter registration campaign and worried about cooptation. They also saw electoral politics as "immoral," and as antithetical to the moral protest that had animated SNCC's activism thus far (Stoper 1989).

An organizational split was averted only through the intervention of advisor Ella Baker, who persuaded the group to form direct action and voter registration wings, an arrangement abandoned as some direct action proponents left the organization and others shifted to voter registration. SNCC workers were also discovering, as one put it later, that "voter registration *was* direct action" (Charles Jones quoted in Stoper 1989:197). Accompanying Black people to southern courthouses to register provoked the same violence and disruption as had the sit-ins and served equally well to dramatize to the nation the denial of African-Americans' constitutional rights. Marches and demonstrations to protest the harassment of civil rights workers drew new members to local movement organizations; "Freedom Days" where people went to the courthouse en masse built solidarity; and public facilities testing through direct action did both (Carson 1981; Payne 1995).

Yet SNCC workers never fully integrated direct action with political organizing, a failure evident in field reports that allude to conflicts between residents' desires to test public accommodations and SNCC directives to focus on electoral mobilization.[20] Organizers' commitment to "letting the people decide" the direction and methods of struggle sat uncomfortably with their persistent suspicion of direct action as not properly *political*. In 1963, for example, SNCC workers framed the choice between voter registration and direct action as whether "the emphasis should be political or religious, spontaneous or rigidly political."[21] The formulation is revealing. "Spontaneous" had come to refer to action not oriented to electoral politics, action motivated by religious commitment rather than strategic calculation, and action orchestrated by local groups rather than national committee. Its meaning went far beyond an absence of planning, but remained locked within a set of dualities: spontaneous versus political; political versus moral; moral versus instrumental. Since even proponents of direct action accepted these dualities, they were ill-equipped to challenge direct action's relegation to the sphere of the personally satisfying but politically ineffectual. The problem thus lay in the power of the canonical narrative to shape strategic options. In this movement, like in others, the conventional storyline that has people acting out their moral commitments in emotional and impulsive protest overwhelmed one in which people acted emotionally, morally, *and* in politically instrumental ways.[22]

Notes

Research was supported by a grant from the Columbia University Humanities and Social Sciences Council. Thanks to Marc Steinberg, Gregory Polletta, two anonymous reviewers, the editorial staff of *Social Problems*, members of the City University of New York Graduate Center Sociology Colloquium, and of the Great Barrington Theory Group for their comments on previous drafts. Thanks also to Linda Catalano and Joyce Robbins for research assistance, and to the many archivists who helped to locate and search campus newspapers, especially Ms. Kathy Jenkins of Howard University's Moorland-Spingarn Research Center, Ms. Tanya Moye of Atlanta University's Robert W. Woodruff Library, and Ms. Ledell B. Smith of Southern University. Direct correspondence to Francesca Polletta, Department of Sociology, Columbia University, 510 Fayerweather Hall, New York, New York 10027; e-mail: fap8@columbia.edu

1. "Drama of the Sitdown." *Shaw Journal*, March-April 1960.

2. "Newsletter to Congressmen." August 1960, SNCC microfilm reel 1 #291-2.

3. The latter used an explicitly persuasive mode—"you as students can believe me when I tell you this will benefit every one of us who sit at the Woolworth counter"—and emphasized not transformation but continuity: "The waitress ignored us and kept serving the White customers. However, this is no great surprise to me because I have been exposed to segregation at lunch counters for 15 years and the situation is predominately unchanged" (*Register* February 5, 1960).

4. Saint Paul's College (Virginia) *Student Journal*, May 1960; "The Sitdowns Came in 1960, But They Remain for 1961" by George Collins, SNCC microfilm reel 44 #98; Joan Burt to Dear Editor, *Hilltop*, May 31, 1960.

5. "Column from Cambridge Correspondent." SNCC microfilm reel 62 #130 (ellipses in original); "Ode to Lunch Counter" by Robert Booker, *Aurora*, June 1960.

6. Sidney Simon to Dear Friend, September 8, 1960, SNCC microfilm reel 4 #1230.

7. *Albatross* (Swarthmore College).

8. Marion S. Barry to Congressman Byron L. Johnson, August 22, 1960, SNCC microfilm reel 1 #285; "Sitdown Protest in Pictorial Retrospect," *Shaw Journal*, May 1960; Edward King to Dear Friend, September 12, 1960, SNCC microfilm reel 4 #920; NT, Henry Thomas report, ND (July 1960), SNCC microfilm reel 5 #170; Fuller, 1960:16; "Civic Interest Group Progress Report," October 13, 1960, SNCC microfilm reel 4 #1279; Jane Stembridge to Henry James Thomas, July 20, 1960, SNCC microfilm reel 5 #174.

9. NAACP head Roy Wilkins announced a nationwide economic boycott as the sit-ins spread, explaining, "We have always used persuasion through various means of political and economic pressure, but now we're going to use it much more intensively than in the past because the membership has become restless over the slow pace of the civil rights proceedings" (Bennett 1960). Lewis Killian argues that the need to deflect red-baiting charges led the organizations assisting the sit-inners in Tallahassee, Florida, to deny their own involvement (1984:782).

10. "A Report on the Student Direct Action Movement at Penn State as of March 31, 1960," SNCC microfilm reel 44 #22.

11. *Hilltop*, March 7, 1960; "The New Freedom," SNCC microfilm reel 4 #108; "Statement submitted by SNCC to the Platform Committee of the National Democratic Convention," July 7, 1960, SNCC microfilm reel 1 #243–248.

12. The Student Nonviolent Coordinating Committee to Mr. Bill Strong, July 31, 1960, SNCC microfilm reel 1 #207; Bob Moses, "A Freedom Child," ND (July 1960), SNCC microfilm reel 4 #939; "Inside the Sitdowner," ND, SNCC microfilm reel 44 #100.

13. Stephen Henderson "A White Student Sits-In," *Social Progress*, February 1961; Jane Stembridge to Henry Thomas, July 20, 1960, SNCC microfilm reel 5 #174; SNCC newsletter entry, 1960, SNCC microfilm reel 5 #190.

14. "Call for Unity in Struggle for Freedom," *Hilltop*, March 7, 1960; Speech to NSA by Jane Stembridge, SNCC microfilm reel 44 #1280-1283; "A Report on the Student Direct Action Movement at Penn State as of March 31, 1960," SNCC microfilm reel 44 #22; Fuller 1960:13; Walzer 1960; Dykeman and Stokely 1960:10, "Justifiable Recalcitrance," *Shaw Journal*, March-April 1960; Letter to the editor, *Aurora*, April 1 960; "Sitdown Protest in Pictorial Retrospect," *Shaw Journal*, May 1960.

15. "Up Against the Obstacles." NA, ND, SNCC microfilm reel 4 #980; "Newsletter to Congressmen," August 1960, SNCC microfilm reel 1 #291-2; "Author Says Sit-Ins Were Inevitable," *Hilltop*, April 29, 1960; "This is Important," ND, SNCC microfilm reel 44 #113; Edward B. King to Dear Friend, September 20, 1960, SNCC microfilm reel 4 #920.

16. Jane Stembridge to Lillian Lipsen, August 18, 1960, SNCC microfilm reel 4 #207; Sample Fund-Raising Letter for Student Nonviolent Coordinating Committee, SNCC microfilm reel 3 #785; Bennett 1960:35; "An Appeal for Dignity," *Student Voice*, November 1960, reprinted in Carson 1990:23; "Across the Editor's Desk," *Student Voice*, November 1960, reprinted in Carson 1990:22; *Student Voice*, special supplementary issue, November 1960, reprinted in Carson 1990:20; "Drama of the Sitdown," *Shaw Journal*, March-April 1960; "Students Continue Woolworth Picket," *Hilltop*, April 8, 1960; "Dear Congressmen, from the Student Nonviolent Coordinating Committee," August 12, 1960, SNCC microfilm reel 12.

17. Letter to Julian Bond from Margaret Long; Heirich to Jane Stembridge, SNCC microfilm reel 4 #122.

18. *Student Voice*, April and May 1961, reprinted in Carson 1990:2.

19. SNCC Minutes, July 14–16, 1961, SNCC microfilm reel 3 #792-5.

20. See, for example, Meridian Report, November 23, 1964, SNCC microfilm reel 66 #1259-1230; Field Report: Perry County, Alabama, Jan. 16–25, 1965, SNCC microfilm reel 37 #123; Overall Report, Southwest Georgia, February 1965, SNCC microfilm reel 37 #839b-843.

21. Summary of Selma Workshop, December 13–16, 1963, SNCC microfilm reel 9 #382-389. Among White new leftists, the skepticism was even greater. In 1961, Tom Hayden of Students for a Democratic Society praised SNCC's "new emphasis on the vote" as "signal[ing] the decline of the short-sighted view that 'discrimination' can be isolated from related social problems." "The moral clarity of the movement has not always been accompanied by precise political vision," he went on, "and sometimes not even by a real political consciousness." Another SDS leader concluded in 1962 that, "The focus of action on Negro campuses in the non-violent protest movement has been largely 'non-political.'" (To SDS, From Hayden Re: Race and Politics Conference, ND [1961], SNCC microfilm reel 9 #1142; "For Dixie with Love and Squalor," by Robb Burlage, ND [1962], SNCC microfilm reel 9.)

22. Rosenthal and Schwartz (1989) note that a tendency to associate spontaneity with expressive, even irrational action is common in sociological accounts of collective action.

References

Benford, Robert
    1993a   "'You could be the hundredth monkey': Collective action frames and vocabularies of motive within the nuclear disarmament movement." *Sociological Quarterly* 34:195–216.
Bennett, Lerone, Jr.
    1960   "What sit-downs mean to America." *Ebony* 15:35–43.
Blumberg, Rhoda L.
    1984   *Civil Rights: The 1960's Freedom Struggle*. Boston, Massachusetts: Twayne.
Bruner, Jerome
    1991   "The narrative construction of reality." *Critical Inquiry* 18:1–21.

Carson, Clayborne
    1981   *In Struggle: SNCC and the Black Awakening of the 1960s*. Cambridge,
              Massachusetts: Harvard University Press.
Carson, Clayborne, ed.
    1990   *The Student Voice*. Westport, Conn.: Meckler.
Chafe, William H.
    1980   *Civilities and Civil Rights: Greensboro, North Carolina, and the Black
              Struggle for Freedom*. New York: Oxford University Press.
Dykeman, Wilma, and James Stokely
    1960   "Sit down chillun, sit down!" *Progressive* (June 24):8–13.
Fuller, Helen
    1960   "'We are all so very happy.'" *New Republic* (April 25):13–16.
Gamson, William A.
    1992   *Talking Politics*. New York: Cambridge University Press.
    1995   "Constructing social protest." In *Social Movement and Culture*, eds. Hank
              Johnston and Bert Klandermans, 85–106. Minneapolis: University of
              Minnesota Press.
Iser, Wolfgang
    1972   "The reading process: A phenomenological approach." *New Literary
              History* 3: 279–299.
Killian, Lewis M.
    1984   "Organization, rationality and spontaneity in the civil rights movement."
              American Sociological Review 49:770–783.
Klandermans, Bert
    1988   "The formation and mobilization of consensus." *International Social
              Movement Research* 1:173–197.
    1997   *The Social Psychology of Protest*. Oxford, U.K. and Cambridge,
              Massachusetts: Blackwell.
Laue, James H.
    1989   *Direct Action and Desegregation, 1960–1962*. Brooklyn, New York: Carlson.
Leitch, Thomas M.
    1986   *What Stories Are: Narrative Theory and Interpretation*. University Park:
              Pennsylvania State University Press.
Lomax, Louis E.
    1960   "The Negro revolt against 'the Negro leaders.'" *Harper's* (June):41–48.
Matthews, Donald, and James Prothro
    1966   *Negroes and the New Southern Politics*. New York: Harcourt, Brace, and
              World.
McAdam, Doug
    1982   *Political Process and the Development of Black Insurgency*. Chicago:
              University of Chicago Press.
    1986   "Recruitment to high risk activism: The case of Freedom Summer."
              American Journal of Sociology 92:64–90.
McDew, Charles
    1967   "Spiritual and moral aspects of the student nonviolent struggle in the
              South." In *The New Student Left*, eds. Mitchell Cohen and Dennis Hale,
              51–57. Boston, Massachusetts: Beacon.
Miller, J. Hillis
    1990   "Narrative." In *Critical Terms for Literary Study*, eds. Frank Lentricchia
              and Thomas McLaughlin, 66–79. Illinois: University of Chicago Press.

Morris, Aldon
    1984   *The Origins of the Civil Rights Movement: Black Communities Organizing for Change*. New York: Free Press.
Oberschall, Anthony
    1989   "The 1960 sit-ins: Protest diffusion and movement take-off." *Research in Social Movements, Conflict and Change* 11:31–53.
Payne, Charles
    1995   *I've Got the Light of Freedom: The Organizing Tradition and the Mississippi Freedom Struggle*. Berkeley: University of California Press.
Piven, Frances Fox, and Richard Cloward
    1977   *Poor People's Movements*. New York: Vintage.
Powledge, Fred
    1991   *Free At Last? The Civil Rights Movement and the People Who Made It*. New York: Harper Collins.
Rosenthal, Naomi, and Michael Schwartz
    1989   "Spontaneity and democracy in social movements." *International Social Movement Research* 2:33–59.
Scott, James
    1990   *Domination and the Arts of Resistance: Hidden Transcripts*. New Haven: Yale University Press.
Stoper, Emily
    1989   *The Student Nonviolent Coordinating Committee: The Growth of Radicalism in a Civil Rights Organization*. Brooklyn, New York: Carlson.
Tilly, Charles
    1998   "The trouble with stories." In *Teaching for the 21st Century: The Handbook for Understanding and Rebuilding the Social World of Higher Education*, eds. Ronald Aminzade and Bernice Pescosolido. Thousand Oaks, California: Pine Forge Press.
Wakefield, Dan
    1960   "Eye of the storm." *The Nation* (May) 190:396–405.
Walzer, Michael
    1960   "A cup of coffee and a seat." *Dissent* (Spring) 7: 111–120.
Wehr, Paul
    1960   "The sit-down protests." M.A. Thesis, Department of Sociology and Anthropology, University of North Carolina.
Zinn, Howard
    1964   *SNCC: The New Abolitionists*. Boston, Massachusetts: Beacon.

Collections

Student Nonviolent Coordinating Committee Papers Microfilm, 1959–1972. 1982. Sanford, N.C.: Microfilming Corporation of America.

Legal Citations

Brown v. Board of Education, 347 U.S. 483 (1954).

20

LIFECHANGERS AND LIFESAVERS

Leslie Irvine

In chapter 2, I introduced Boucher, who helped estblish VET SOS after more than twenty years of homelessness. Pali found joy in caring for other creatures also living on the streets, such as stray dogs, feral cats, and injured pigeons. Pali explained, "Being able to take care of animals and heal whatever was wrong was the only feeling I ever had in my life that was a good, whole feeling."[1] Along the way, she befriended a dog she called Charlie. But during Pali's frequent trips to jail for "stupid things, like trespassing," Charlie would end up impounded in the San Francisco Animal Care and Control facility. "One time," Pali recalled, "when they brought Charlie in, she had bitten somebody, and they put her to sleep. It was the first time in my life I realized that I wasn't just affecting myself by going out and being loaded, that I was directly responsible for the pain of somebody else." Pali began visiting the San Francisco Society for the Prevention of Cruelty to Animals. She had no intentions of adopting a dog, but she fell in love with Leadbelly, a constantly baying coonhound scheduled for euthanasia. "Somehow, I got the money, faked an address and adopted him," she said. They lived on the streets together, and as she recalled, "Every second of every day I was trying to keep that dog safe." She worried about how her drug use and drinking would cause her to lose Leadbelly as she had lost Charlie. "I was in and out of jail all the time," she said. "I narrowly dodged the bullet of losing my dog so many times that it just stressed me out too much, man. I had to make some changes."

Pali had missed some court dates and consequently had a warrant out

Leslie Irvine, "Lifechangers and Lifesavers," in *My Dog Always Eats First: Homeless People and Their Animals* (Boulder CO: Lynne Rienner Publishers, 2013), 133–55. Reprinted with permission of Lynne Rienner Publishers.

for her arrest. A friend agreed to take Leadbelly if she were arrested—a prescient arrangement, as it turned out, for Pali soon spent six months in jail. Upon her release, she checked into a detox center, and visited Leadbelly on the weekends. He was "my life and my joy," she said. "I couldn't lose him because of old habits." Clean and sober after a year in rehab, she found subsidized housing that allowed dogs.

Pali had to say goodbye to Leadbelly in 2001, but she stayed sober because "he helped me learn how to take care of myself by taking care of him." She began Rocket Dog Rescue in his honor. "Leadbelly was a gift sent to me," she claimed, "and every step of the way it was my responsibility to follow through. Now, I want to devote my life to animals."

———————

In this chapter, I examine narratives that construct animals as redemptive figures who keep people alive or turn their lives around. In general, redemption stories take the following plotline: "My life took the wrong course. I almost lost hope, but things turned out for the best." They depict a moral arc with redemption entering somewhere between losing hope and having things turn out for the best. Redemption can enter stories in various forms and combinations of forms. It can enter through religion, in the path from sin to salvation. It can enter through serious illness or injury, and it can enter because of separation through divorce or death. In the stories analyzed in this chapter, redemption takes animal form.

The theme of redemption exemplifies how historically and culturally specific models of stories combine with subjective experience in personal narratives. The concept of redemption has roots in the Hebrew Bible and related social and legal customs, but it found its fullest expression in Christian theology, through the atoning crucifixion and resurrection of Jesus Christ. Scholars point out that the redemption theme resonates with uniquely American ideals (McAdams 2006b; see also Bellah et al. 1985). For example, the Puritans viewed their "city on a hill" as a model community that would redeem the religious persecution they had endured (see Erikson 1966; Wills 1990). Later, the popular (and to some, laughable) Horatio Alger stories took variations on the redemptive plotline of hard work, crisis, struggle, and eventual success. Stories of redemption from adversity often appear in popular culture. For example, Dan McAdams found the theme of redemption in over half of the feature stories in *People* magazine over an eight-month period (2006b:20–22). Redemption also constitutes a significant element in self-help discourse. Groups based on the "twelve step" rhetoric of Alcoholics Anonymous offer a particular formula for redemption stories whereby personal growth comes out of addiction and "dysfunctional" relationships, thereby redeeming the hardship and abuse (Irvine 1999).

Before I offer examples of how animals fill the redemptive role, I want to point out that, with one exception, the tellers of these stories had made it off the street when I met them. In the preceding chapters, I have emphasized how the circumstances of homelessness shaped particular forms of narrative. Here, I include the stories of formerly homeless people for the same reason; getting off the street—or even the promise of doing so—creates an opening for redemption stories. Circumstances allowed these interviewees to tell a particular kind of story that I did not hear from those who were still on the street. I will let the examples make my point.

Constructing Animals as Lifechangers

Donna's Story

I met Donna in San Francisco at an event called Project Homeless Connect (PHC), which provides "one-stop shopping" for homeless people in over 200 US cities. By collaborating with businesses, nonprofits, and government organizations, PHC offers everything from haircuts and dental work to legal assistance and veterinary care. The events feature music and food, and even "parking areas" for the shopping carts that often hold the life possessions of many homeless people. VET SOS regularly holds clinics at PHC events. In late spring of 2010, I interviewed pet owners at the event in Bayview Park, in the southeastern corner of the city. A 2011 article in the *New Yorker* described the predominantly African American Bayview–Hunter's Point area as "the poorest and most violent neighborhood in San Francisco" (Tough 2011:25), but a festival atmosphere filled Bayview Park that day. When we arrived well before the official start of the event, clients had already begun to line up with their animals.

Dr. Strubel had pointed Donna out and told me that I really needed to hear her story. Donna did not have an animal with her that day. Nevertheless, she waited in line to sign up for a veterinary examination. She then walked out of the crowd and I lost sight of her. When she returned to check on the progress of the list, I introduced myself. She explained that she had brought her friend Emily, the rescuer of the spray-painted dog whom I introduced in chapter 5. Emily's dog, Hobo, needed a checkup, and because Donna had a car, she had provided transportation. Hobo did not like other dogs, so the three of them sat away from the crowd, across the street from the park. Emily stayed with Hobo while

Donna periodically checked on Hobo's position on the examination list. Meanwhile, I talked with Emily about her relationship with Hobo. As our interview ended, she told me, "You know, you really should interview Donna." Clearly, I had to hear this story.

After Hobo's examination, Donna and I sat on the sidewalk leaning against a brick building with our legs stretched out in the sun. At fifty-three, Donna was petite and almost elfin-looking, with long, light brown hair and deep-set brown eyes that held my gaze intently. Her weather-worn skin and missing teeth spoke to a life of hardship. She explained that she was now living upstairs in her mother's Bernal Heights home, but had lived on the streets for nearly forty years. At age fifteen, she had begun drinking and using heroin. She said she had set out not only to follow her older sister's lead, but also to surpass her by becoming "a bigger dope fiend." Donna left home so that her mother would not have to see her hooked on heroin. She soon added crack to her repertoire, and supported her habit through prostitution. I asked what she felt the first time she sold her body. "I was scared," she recalled. "But I had to have that drug. I didn't care."

After leaving home, Donna's life consisted of homelessness, prostitution, drug addiction, and abusive relationships. She hitchhiked across the country numerous times, buying drugs and turning tricks at truck stops from Illinois to Washington. She recounted the time a john pushed her out of a moving tractor-trailer cab after refusing to pay for her services, and recalled, somewhat proudly, that she had "tucked and rolled" when she hit the ground. Eventually, she "got the virus," meaning HIV, from either "the sex or the needles." Her son, who was twenty-one at the time of this interview, fortunately "came out negative" when she gave birth to him. "I would never, ever shove a needle in my arm anymore," she told me. I asked her how she quit. She paused while tears sprang up in her eyes. She said softly, "Athena." She paused again, then looked at me and said, "She was the love of my life."

Athena, a German Shepherd/Labrador Retriever mix, was Donna's companion for ten years. I asked if she had a picture of her dog on the phone she held in her hand. She did not, but it mattered very little, because she gave me a detailed description that reminded me of J. R. Ackerley's portrayal of his beloved German Shepherd, Tulip.[2] After describing Tulip's often troublesome temperament, Ackerley wrote, "It is necessary to add that she is beautiful" (1965:8). He continued:

> Her ears are tall and pointed, like the ears of Anubis. How she manages to hold them constantly erect, as though starched, I do not know, for with their fine covering mouse-gray fur they are

soft and flimsy; when she stands with her back to the sun it shines through the delicate tissue, so that they glow shell-pink as though incandescent . . . dark markings symmetrically divide up her face into zones of pale pastel colors, like a mosaic, or a stained-glass window . . . her sable tunic is of the texture of satin . . . no tailor could have shaped it more elegantly. (1965:8–9)

Reading this, I felt as though I had never really seen a dog, such was Ackerley's focus and admiration. Likewise, Donna described Athena's thick black-and-sable coat, her amber eyes rimmed in black, with the dark brows over them that make the dogs so marked especially expressive. In his book *Merle's Door*, Ted Kerasote reports, "The Hidatsa, a Native American tribe of the northern Great Plains, believe that these sorts of dogs, whom they call 'Four Eyes,' are especially gentle and have magical powers" (2007:3). This certainly seems to fit Athena, at least in Donna's description of her.

Athena and Donna came together through Pali, long a common denominator between homeless people and homeless animals in San Francisco. About a decade ago, Donna lived with an abusive boyfriend in a garbage-strewn underpass encampment. Worn out from addiction and hard living, the pair pitched a tent in her mother's backyard. Pali and Donna had known each other on the street, and, as Donna recalled, "Pali said, 'You need a dog in your life.'" Pali had rescued three-year-old Athena from death row in a shelter. Although it might not seem that a homeless drug addict in an abusive relationship would make the best guardian for a dog, the match saved two lives. As Donna explained, "Athena did everything for me. She got me out of an abusive relationship. It was either the dog, or him, and I chose the dog. He used to take my money. My shoes. Everything. The guy used to beat me up and Pali told me it was either the man or the dog, so I chose Athena. I got the dog. Got rid of the man."

With the boyfriend out of the picture, Donna moved from the yard into her mother's house, to her own space in what she called "the upstairs." But Pali had said, "You have to be clean to have the dog." Donna's mother agreed, so she faced a decision. "I realized Athena meant everything to me," she told me. "I said to myself, 'My dog comes first in my life. Would I rather use drugs, or feed my dog?' And I fell in love with Athena, so I gave up the needle. Gave up the pipe. I gave up liquor. Everything."

This intrigued me greatly, to say the least. I had heard and read horrendous accounts of alcohol withdrawal. I knew that similar misery accompanied withdrawal from heroin. I had heard about the cramping, nausea, and the feeling of "itchy blood." I could not imagine adding crack

cocaine into the mix and withdrawing from all three at once. I wanted to
know how Donna had done it. She said, matter-of-factly, "Cold turkey."

"You went cold turkey?" I repeated, just to make sure I had heard
right.

"Cold turkey," she said again.

"By yourself?" I asked. "You went through withdrawal?"

"Yup. I went through withdrawal, and from there, I went to the methadone clinic. Got on methadone. Athena went with me, and everybody
loved her, too. Athena was everything. Okay? Athena was everything.
Everywhere I went, Athena followed. She knew the pet stores. She sat
down at the coffee shop. Everything."

Donna also credited Athena with improving her HIV status. Once
clean, Donna began taking care of herself, and she felt better. She went
for a blood test and the results gave her proof. "She helped get my HIV
level down. Yeah. Having Athena got my T-cells going up. When Athena
came into my life, everything was beautiful."

Donna has never worked at any job other than being a prostitute, and
her HIV, combined with dyslexia uncovered in middle age, prevents her
from working now. Considered fully disabled, she receives monthly SSI
checks. Athena had died over a year prior to the interview, from cancer, at
age thirteen. A local pet supply store had held a memorial service for her.
VET SOS arranged for cremation, and Donna has kept the ashes because
she wants them mixed and distributed with hers when she dies. "We
made it so that when I die, I'm going to be with her," she said, explaining
how, having journeyed together in this world, they would meet again at
the final destination.

Donna says she is in no hurry to reach that destination, however. Pali
found her another dog, and a cat, too. She showed me the pictures of
both on her cell phone. "I hope I don't die," she told me. "I got to take
care of Buddy, my new dog. I will start AIDS medication Tuesday because I want to live for my dog." As if to make sure we both heard clearly,
she repeated herself, saying again, "I'm going to take the HIV medicine
because it's going to make me live for my dog." Donna quickly added that
she loves the cat, too. "They mean everything in my life," she said. But she
considers the dog special because she believes Athena chose him. As she
explained, "After Athena died a year ago, Pali asked me to help another
dog. So Athena sent Buddy. They have the same temperament. Everything Athena had, Buddy has. They're afraid of the same things. They
like the same things." Donna had to stay in the hospital recently and she
thought only of getting home to her dog and cat. "It killed me," she said.
"Every day, I asked the doctor, 'When can I go home so I can be with my
pets?' Just to have them in my life means everything."

Tommy's Story

I met Tommy at the Mercer Clinic in Sacramento. He had brought his young black-and-tan dog, Monty, for a checkup and nail trim. Tommy sat in a folding chair and I sat cross-legged on the ground next to him. The sun shone brightly and warmed us after what had started as a chilly morning. Tommy and I speculated about Monty's bloodlines, and we decided on a mix of Rottweiler and some kind of terrier. It really was anyone's guess. Monty weighed about thirty pounds. Monty let me pet him and he took the treat I offered, but he was much more interested in checking out all the other dogs passing by than in getting to know me. He wagged his tail, sniffed the air, and ventured out to the end of his leash before returning to check in with Tommy. He panted and did a little dance with his front paws. Then he repeated the routine all over again. As we watched Monty, I asked Tommy about his ten years of homelessness. At first, he shrugged and said he had been "down on his luck." As David Snow and Leon Anderson point out, this explanation both "exempts the homeless from responsibility for their plight, and it leaves open the possibility of a better future" (1993:204). After all, bad luck can happen to anyone and thus, as a causal account of homelessness, it salvages one's sense of self-worth. But as Tommy continued his story, he clearly saw less-random forces at work. "I was a bad kid for many years," he told me. "I stole and I did drugs. Fighting. Stabbings. Shootings. Years of abuse." He had done time in jail.

When we met, Tommy had been living in his van outside of Sacramento for several months. The van did not run, but friends allowed him to park it on their property. Someone had abandoned Monty as a puppy at the church Tommy was attending. After no one came for Monty, the church staff suggested that he would make a good companion for Tommy. "I took him home," he said, using the language of the houseless but not homeless to describe his van, "and he's been the best thing for me." I asked him to tell me more. Tommy explained that he was suffering from debilitating depression, and added, "Monty helps with that."

"How so?" I asked.

"He makes me come out and walk with other people. He gets me socializing with other people. And he's like my best friend because, being homeless, you don't really have friends unless you're drinking and doing drugs and all. You just walk the streets and just try to find what you can on the streets. He gives me energy because he can make me get out and walk. He's just adorable to other people. They just come up, and it makes me feel better because I have mental illness also, where I don't like to be around people. And he just, he's just a joy to be with. He's good when people come up to our camp or something. He'll bark and let me know that somebody's there."

In this brief statement, Tommy assigned Monty most of the roles outlined in the preceding chapters. He depicted Monty as his best friend, social facilitator, and protector. He credited him with providing emotional support and promoting physical health. As his story continued, however, Tommy invoked an account of dog-as-lifesaver that I came very close to missing.

Now approaching forty, Tommy had been working in the construction trades for many years until he witnessed a fatal accident on a construction site. He saw his boss and another man die when they both fell from a great height. "I haven't worked since then," he told me. "It really screwed me up." A few months before I met him, Tommy had started receiving SSI payments after a long struggle to qualify as disabled. As he explained, "Seven years, I was fighting for my SSI. It took seven years to get that."

"No kidding?"

"Till they finally figured out that I'm not mentally stable," Tommy said. "They wouldn't take me for the physical. Three times, I had to go before the judge."

Now, he and Monty were getting by on a modest monthly check. Tommy was on a waiting list for a low-income apartment. He said he was doing well now, thanks largely to Monty's companionship and what he called his "psych pills."

I had begun to think of the interview with Tommy as unremarkable, providing more of the same kind of information I already had. Then, as we wrapped up, Tommy mentioned that he would soon start treatment for hepatitis C, a consequence of years of drug abuse and drinking. I had almost turned off the recorder when he said, "Monty also got me off alcohol and got me off drugs. Now I'm sober and I'm healthy." Clearly, the story was not over yet. Doctors refer to these moments as "doorknob conversations." After an uneventful office visit, with a hand already on the doorknob, the patient says, "I forgot to mention this, but . . ." or "It's probably nothing, but . . ." I asked Tommy how Monty had helped him stop drinking and using drugs. He explained that he had gotten sober by necessity in jail. After his release, he started attending the church where Monty had turned up as a stray. Tommy felt he was beginning to get his life back on track, but Monty provided the motivation he needed: "When I got out of jail, I told myself that I would never drink again or smoke again, and I told that to Monty, and every time I want to go to get a drink, he just looks at me, almost shaking that head, saying, 'You know what you just went through the last thirty-five years!'"

In both of these stories, Donna and Tommy tell a narrative that constructs the dog as redeeming them from the clutches of addiction. For now, I will postpone the discussion of how this narrative works. First, I want to present narratives that, while of the same sort, delve even deeper into human frailty. Whereas Donna and Tommy credit their dogs with *changing* their lives, the following section examines stories that construct animals as *saving* people's lives.

Constructing Animals as Lifesavers

Trish's Story

I met Trish on a cold December day in Boulder. She stood on the median at the exit of a busy shopping center with her Jack Russell terrier bundled up in a dog bed beside her. She was "flying a sign" that read, "Sober. Doing the best I can. Please help." I had finished some shopping and noticed her with the dog on my way out. The flow of traffic prevented me from stopping, but I circled the block, returned, and parked nearby. I went into the nearby restaurant and bought a large cup of hot tea. I brought it over to Trish and introduced myself. She expressed interest in my project and was eager to talk. In fact, she said she would enjoy the company.

Trish told me that her dog, Pixel, came from a pet store where she had done the feeding and cleaning nearly a decade ago. As a puppy, Pixel had contracted parvovirus and Trish attributed his survival to her care. Although Pixel recovered, the store owner thought he could no longer sell him, and offered the dog to Trish. She could hardly afford to feed herself, much less a dog, she said, but she took him anyway and the two had been inseparable ever since. On the day we met, Trish had bundled Pixel up in two jackets and brought his bed along so that he would stay warm. She said she sometimes tried to leave him in the mobile home in which they now lived, the first "home" with four walls that they had ever shared. But she explained that, after being with her around the clock for years, curling up next to her in cars and under bridges, Pixel had separation anxiety without her. "It's funny," she said, "because we have a place now, and he won't stay. He won't. He would rather be out here, cold and with me, than being there by himself."

Trish told me that she had been homeless "off and on" for over ten years. For her, *not* being homeless meant sleeping in a car or in the back of the pet store. When she was much younger, she had left home to follow the Grateful Dead, and she eventually landed in Boulder. By then, she had a heroin habit. When she could not get high, she drank to dull the cravings. "I didn't really like to drink," she explained, "but if I was sick from not having opiates, I had to drink because I couldn't walk, you know, or eat or do anything." When I met Trish, she had been clean and sober for two years. She had found an addiction rehabilitation facility that covered the costs of her treatment through a well-timed state program. "It was awesome," she said. "I just happened to call when the government was doing this study. They were paying for people's treatment, and then they wanted to follow them for six months. So, I went there and got sober." She found a friend to care for Pixel, "someone with a house," while she went through what she described as a "severe detox." Trish explained that when she was released from rehab, "I wanted to get off the streets but I had to find a job and try to do all those things I couldn't do before because I was messed up, which was really, really weird. It had been so long since I had to have a schedule. I loved it, though. I was like, 'I can do this.'" She supported herself by working various jobs that paid under the table, mostly cleaning houses. "It took about six months," she said, "and I got us off the streets. We lived out of my car." That work, however, had recently dropped off. "As it got colder, I started losing jobs," she said, "not by anything that I was doing, but I don't know, maybe they're afraid of the economy, afraid of whatever and they're trying to hold on to their money. The holidays are coming, and this and that."

Trish had had to sell the car and, when we met in midwinter, she and Pixel were sleeping in an abandoned mobile home. Although it was condemned, the trailer-park manager nevertheless charged her a "lot fee" of three hundred dollars a month. Without a job, she had to come up with the rent. She calculated that she needed to earn forty dollars a day. "Earning" meant panhandling, for Trish could not easily get work because of a felony on her record for possession of heroin. "I had that charge fifteen years ago," she explained.

"It was a felony then. Now it's a misdemeanor, apparently. But back then, twenty dollars' worth of heroin was a felony, so I have that on my record. I am having a hard time getting a job even at Burger King or McDonald's. Everybody does background checks now, so if I don't want to be homeless again, here I am." She brandished the cardboard sign to illustrate her point. Through it all, Pixel had kept her going, she said, even during her darkest times. She added that Pixel even kept her alive.

"It was something to lose, you know? Yeah. I was [on the streets]. I hated it. I was totally at rock bottom. I just wanted to die. But I couldn't, because he needed me. I didn't want to be out here anymore. I couldn't see the light at all anymore. And I'd asked for help so many times and I couldn't get it, so at some point, I was just, like, 'I'm done. I can't do this anymore.' But I couldn't give up because I had something else to take care of besides myself. So he kept me alive."

I asked, "You mean you might have committed suicide if it weren't for him?"

"Yeah," she replied. "I don't know if I actually could have gone through with it. I just wanted it over. I just didn't want to be here anymore. I never really thought about, 'I'm going to get a gun, or a knife, or a razor blade,' but I was losing all motivation. But, you know, I still needed to feed him and keep him warm at night. I didn't care about myself, but I had to care about him, you know? He got me through a really tough spot. If I would've had to be without him out there before, I don't think I would have made it, at all."

In the two years since that "tough spot," Trish believes that Pixel has helped her stay sober. "He definitely helps keep me on the straight and narrow," she told me. She claims that Pixel "hates the smell of alcohol," and has kept her away from "bad elements, or groups of people, because of the alcohol, the drugs, and all that." She claims that the dog will nip the heels of people who approach smelling of alcohol. Using the construction of discernment familiar from protector narratives, Trish said, "He's an awesome judge of character. He just knows." She looked down at Pixel and added, "Right, buddy?" The little dog never took his eyes off her.

Rudy's Story

Like Trish, Rudy credits his dogs, a pair of Dachshunds, with keeping him alive. He had his eight-year-old male with him when we met at the Mercer Clinic. We sat in the shade on folding chairs while he waited for his dog's turn to have a routine examination and vaccinations. Rudy declined to talk to me at first, because he said he did not consider himself homeless. Nevertheless, he soon seemed to realize that talking with me would pass the time. Reticent even then, he repeatedly said that he did not have much to say. But what he did say revealed his image of a powerful bond he felt with his dogs.

Rudy prided himself on never having slept on the street, but he had slept in nearly every kind of habitation imaginable. Now in his sixties, he was staying in the homes of family members around Sacramento. Like Tommy, he had worked in construction for most of his life. He had lost a finger and part of his thumb along the way, but he kept working until cancer forced him to stop. He held up crossed fingers and smiled as he said, "But right now, it's in remission." He explained that his SSI check of almost nine hundred dollars a month more than covered his expenses because, "Unlike most of the people around here who get Social Security, I don't spend it on drugs." Perhaps because Rudy saw himself as resourceful enough to have avoided sleeping on the street, he seemed to want to distance himself from the "truly" homeless people all around us (see Snow and Anderson 1993).

I asked Rudy how he spent his time, and he smiled and pointed to the dog. "I take him out about twenty times a day," he said. "Walk, walk, walk. I take him to the park. I got a female, too, that's ball nuts. She could play ball all day long. I talk to them. Pet them. He sleeps in my bed. They both do. One's up by my head. Other one's down by my feet. Other than that, I don't do much else. I take good care of my dogs. If I didn't have my dogs, I'd be unhappy."

Rudy explained that he had come close to losing his dogs not long ago. He had shared an apartment with a roommate, whom he described as "someone I thought was my friend." But Rudy had gone to jail for sixty days on what he called a "trumped-up" drug charge. While in jail, Rudy's landlord evicted him and the roommate sold everything—except the dogs.

"Why not the dogs, too?" I asked.

"Couldn't find nobody to buy 'em, I guess," he said, and added, "It's a good thing, too, 'cause they're keeping me alive."

I asked, "How are they doing that?"

The man of few words struggled to answer. After a pause, he said. "I can't really say. Just their aura, I guess you would call it."

"Their what?" I asked.

He looked at his dog, smiled, and looked back at me, sheepishly. "Love," he said. "It's unconditional. It's like mine for them." I could tell he felt embarrassed speaking this way. Just to ease the awkwardness I said, "So they just care for you no matter what?"

"Yeah," he said softly, stroking his dog's smooth copper coat and avoiding my eyes. The dog looked up at him adoringly. "Just like I do with them. I just love 'em. Just like they was real people."

Denise's Story

Lest it seem that people construct only dogs as having the power to transform or even save lives, other stories placed cats in the lifesaver role. I met Denise and her cat, Ivy, at a VET SOS clinic in Dolores Park. White, middle-aged Denise defied the stereotype of the homeless person. Slender and nicely dressed, she had white teeth and clean, neatly styled hair. Ivy, a tiny, black-and-white cat, sat sphinx-like in a carrier, with her white paws tucked neatly underneath her. I put my finger near the carrier's door for her to sniff. She leaned forward to check it out and, proclaiming me safe but uninteresting, turned her head just enough to look past me into the middle distance, as if to say, "Ho hum." Denise and I sought some shade from the afternoon sun. We found it on a nearby cement staircase, where we sat down to talk.

I asked Denise how she became homeless, and she explained that she had been self-employed as a graphic artist, but severe depression caused her to miss deadlines. Major clients lost faith in her, and the accounts gradually dwindled away. She fell behind on rent, and her landlord evicted her. She tried to find a place to live before she had to move out of the apartment, but that did not happen. When time ran out, she put her belongings in storage. She and Ivy had lived in her car for over eight months when we met. "Half of the car is taken up by her stuff," Denise said, "because there's a big carrier, which she sleeps in, and then her litter box, and her bowls, so she essentially has the whole back seat and then I'm in the front seat." Denise said she felt like she was living in a "glass display case." She was parking in her former neighborhood because it was safe. But because living in a car was illegal, she was trying to avoid trouble by obeying the area's parking laws. "My time is taken up just moving the car," she told me. "I have to keep moving it. I can't park more than two hours." Even when she could find a place, the traffic and lights kept her awake. "I get very little sleep," she said. "So I'm very sleep deprived." She admitted to shutting herself in her storage locker just to rest in dark, quiet privacy for a while. Sometimes she would bring Ivy with her, but other times she would let the cat sunbathe in her favorite spot on the rear ledge of the backseat. Although Ivy enjoyed this, it was putting Denise at risk. Her quandary echoed the concerns about "humaniacs" voiced by Linda in chapter 3. As Denise said, "I'm really afraid that somebody is going to come along and go, 'Oh, no! Animal cruelty. A cat's locked in the car,' and report my vehicle. So I don't want to do anything that draws attention to the car at all, which means I don't want people to see her."

At the time of the interview, a friend was allowing Denise to shower at his apartment twice a week while he was at work. She would take her cat with her and claimed that Ivy "seems to know that we're going someplace else where she can run around. So she chirps, and her tail's up, and she purrs, and it's incredible to me. And it helps lift my spirits."

The eviction had made it very difficult for Denise to find another apartment, as it had for other people. In addition, Denise's situation did not qualify her for most of the housing programs available to the homeless. She never imagined she would live in her car for over eight months.

As she explained, "I have a caseworker working very aggressively to find me housing, but in my particular situation, I kind of slip through the cracks. I don't fit into the demographic profile of the different housing prospects that are available. I'm not the right age. I'm not the right ethnicity. I'm childless. If I had children, there would be some housing."

Having Ivy initially made finding housing even more difficult. When I asked if she had considered finding Ivy another home, she shook her head side-to-side emphatically. Denise had adopted Ivy as a kitten from the SPCA five years prior to the interview. Ivy had come from an abusive situation, she said. She went on to explain: "She was a bit distant when I first adopted her, and then she grew to know me, but she's very frightened still of any new people, new situations. So I've kept her pretty protected, and that's why, when I became homeless, I didn't want to give her up, even though I know I had a lot of housing opportunities if I didn't have my cat."

Although Denise felt that she was protecting Ivy and doing the best thing for her, she explained to me that people often told her she had no right to keep a cat in her circumstances. When I asked her how she responded, she said: "I have a history with depression up to suicide ideation, and Ivy, I refer to her as my suicide barrier. And I don't say that in any light way. I would say most days, she's the reason why I keep going, because I made a commitment to take care of her when I adopted her. So she needs me, and I need her. She is the only source of daily, steady affection and companionship that I have. The only one. I can't imagine being without her, wanting to go on at all, without her."

By portraying Ivy as a "suicide barrier," Denise's account gives the cat significant influence on her construction of self. Fortunately, she would not have to decide between keeping Ivy and finding housing. Her doctor had provided documentation certifying Ivy as her necessary companion. The document qualifies Ivy as a "reasonable accommodation" to a disability, and landlords cannot refuse to rent to Denise because of Ivy, even if they usually do not allow pets. Meanwhile, Denise takes solace from how Ivy has adapted to their situation:

> I don't know what I would have done if eight months ago I'd known that I was still going to be homeless, how I would have done it differently. Because I actually do live each day thinking, "This has got to be the last day. I know I'm going to get a break tomorrow," and it hasn't come. So I actually have to sort of not really think about my situation too much because I become—go into a state of despair. And it amazes me how she endures this. She knows where all her stuff is. She's got her bed, she's got her little cushion to

lounge on. She's got her little sun deck. She knows where the food is. This is her place. That helps me keep going.

Redemption in Personal Narratives

Psychologist Dan McAdams, who has studied narrative and identity for decades, has examined the role of redemption in life stories (2004, 2006a, 2006b, 2008). He identifies the typical teller of a redemption story as an adult in midlife, concerned with what Erik Erikson (1950) called "generativity." I cannot do justice here to the theory of human development in which Erikson defined the term, but I can summarize generativity as an interest in leaving a positive legacy and making the world a better place. Following Erikson, McAdams argues that "generativity is the central psychological and moral challenge adults face, especially in their 30s, 40s, and 50s" (2006b:11). To understand generativity, it can help to place it against what Erikson posed as the contrasting potential outcome of the same life stage: stagnation, the feeling of being stuck or making no contribution.

In his research, McAdams most often hears redemption stories from American adults who score highly on psychological measures of generativity. Redemption stories resonate with midlife beliefs, values, and goals, but their roots extend back to childhood, reflecting a particular set of circumstances and experiences. McAdams found that generative adults often began life with some advantage or privilege. This could take the form of economic privilege, but it could also manifest itself as a talent or skill, a special destiny, or even the sense of being deeply loved. Whatever the case, such children gain a sense of being special. In addition, while growing up, the suffering of others makes an impression on them, and they consequently develop a robust sense of empathy. By adolescence, they have a strong commitment to religious, political, or ethical beliefs, which motivates them to want to take action, to help, and to make things better. In adulthood, generativity manifests itself as a desire to produce good things and see them grow and continue. This includes the family; generative adults make warm, involved, albeit disciplined parents. Their sense of commitment extends outside the family to the community and beyond. Generative adults engage in prosocial activities, such as volunteering or civic leadership. Overall, their experiences give them the skills and resources to engage in struggle and to triumph over the adversity that comes their way. The stories they tell of their lives essentially say, "I bear fruit; I give back; I offer a unique contribution. I will make a happy ending, even in a threatening world" (McAdams 2008:20).

According to McAdams, generative adults tend to tell redemption sto-

ries because of the combination of early advantage and moral commitment. The teller feels endowed with an essentially good self, guided by
upstanding principles. This prompts him or her to see positive outcomes
even from negative events. In this formulation, without the right predis-
posing factors in one's background, his or her orientation, and thus the
stories, would take another tack. The redemption stories told by homeless
pet owners challenge these assumptions because the tellers are *nongenerative* adults, not seemingly predisposed to tell redemption stories. Their
backgrounds do not include privilege or a sense of a special purpose, but
rather addiction, prostitution, violence, poverty, jail, disabling mental
illness, and HIV. They did not grow up feeling secure and loved. While
their generative peers-in-the-making developed moral commitments
through religion or politics, these tellers focused on staying high, staying
out of jail, or staying alive. Nevertheless, they envisioned brighter futures
emerging out of their struggles. The construction of their stories around
their pets highlights the symbolic power of animals.

Animals as Vehicles for Redemption Stories

As mentioned, redemption can enter a story in several ways, including the narrator's perseverance, the help of friends or benefactors, good
fortune, or divine intervention. As an analytic tool, McAdams has outlined six "languages" of redemption, or "sets of images and ideas that
people routinely draw upon when they try to make sense of the moves in
their lives from negativity and suffering, on one hand, to positivity and
enhancement, on the other" (2006b:41). These languages include *atonement* (or salvation), borrowed from religious sources, and *emancipation*,
which yields a narrative of freedom from oppression. They also include
the language of *upward mobility*, in the familiar form of the rags-to-riches
story, and the language of *recovery*, which applies to stories of healing
the mind or body. In addition, the list includes the language of *enlightenment*, in which knowledge brings the teller out of ignorance, and the
language of *development*, which draws from sources in self-fulfillment and
self-help discourses. People mix and match these languages in telling the
stories that depict their lives as moving from suffering to a more positive
outcome, if not to triumph.

In the stories recounted in this chapter, animals provide the medium
for redemption. One of Donna's statements captures this well. She said,
"When Athena came into my life, everything was beautiful." The other
stories contain variations on this theme: "My life is better because this
animal is in it." The redemptive power of animals works in the narratives in
three related ways. First, animals' dependence draws on and encourages

the guardian's sense of responsibility. In other chapters, I discussed the importance of caregiving and responsibility and their relationship to the moral identity. Here, I add that providing for an animal's needs can offer a direction or a structure for one's life. Rudy talked about his dog wanting to "walk, walk, walk." Donna said that she had to take care of her new dog, Buddy. In some narratives, the decision to provide care constitutes a turning point. Donna, for example, had to decide between her dog and her abusive boyfriend, with the drugs and other baggage that came with him. In other stories, caregiving and responsibility constitute a reason to keep going. Trish realized that Pixel gave her "something to lose." Denise described wanting to fulfill her obligations to Ivy by protecting her.

Second, the perceived unconditional love from animals also makes them especially well suited for incorporation into redemption stories by producing a sense of mattering—a reward for caring, in a sense. Donna, Trish, and Rudy described caring for their animals and consequently feeling cared for by them. Tommy, too, said Monty was both "the best thing" for him and "a joy to be with." Denise's story depicts the nexus of caring for and feeling cared for particularly well. Her commitment motivated her decision to live in her car rather than enter housing without Ivy. In turn, she described Ivy as providing "daily, steady affection."

To the best of my knowledge, only one other scholar acknowledges the construction of animals as a "suicide barrier," to use Denise's term. In Amy Fitzgerald's (2007) research on domestic violence, some of the battered women she interviewed described animals as their "lifeline." Although neither Denise nor any of those who mentioned suicide discussed having had this experience, Fitzgerald's research supports the argument about the importance of the nexus of caring and feeling cared for. She found two related ways that "pets kept [women] from 'leaving' the abusive situation through suicide." In some cases, women stayed alive to provide care for their animals. In others, animals "provided the women with the emotional and social support they needed to stay alive" (2007:372). In many cases, animals moderated suicidality in both ways. They gave women a sense of responsibility *and* they provided emotional support.

A third factor that makes animals appropriate for redemption stories involves our imagination of animals as simultaneously innocent and incorruptible. They embody ideal, hyper-positive identities to which the tellers can aspire. They stand as silent witnesses to human behavior, and the tellers, through the practice of "speaking for," make use of this capacity by casting animals as principled advisers. This appears strongly in the story told by Tommy and, to some extent, in that told by Trish. For example, Tommy described promising Monty that he would not drink or do drugs, and the dog "reminded" him to keep his promise. When he described Monty as looking up at him and saying, "You know what you just went through the last thirty-five years," Tommy "spoke for" his dog. In doing so, Tommy constructed Monty's identity for me. But more important, he also constructed the dog's identity for *himself*. He gave Monty the attributes of an older brother or a knowing uncle, someone wise to Tommy's ways, who pointed out that the past was not worth repeating. When Tommy "spoke for" Monty in this particular way, he added a twist to the concept. In most instances of "speaking for," the socially more competent party—in this case, the human caretaker—has the power to define the identity of the less competent actor, the dog. Guardians often create rather simple-minded, albeit lovable, identities for animals, especially for dogs (see Sanders 1993, 1999). In contrast, Tommy constructed a nearly heroic identity for Monty, which surpassed his own, in a moral sense, by always having Tommy's best interests in mind. Monty "reminded" Tommy that he must continue on the straight and narrow path by staying clean and sober. For Trish, Pixel's morally superior character comes through in his ability to read people and keep her away from bad "elements," thus helping her stay clean and sober. Both dogs allow for the telling of a redemption story by making sure the narrative's positive course does not take a negative turn. Constructed as silent witnesses, animals keep the tellers from lapsing into risky behavior. Their uprightness and discernment provide the equivalent of the moral compass that generative adults would have acquired growing up.

These three factors allow animals to serve as both the mode of atonement and the medium of salvation in redemption stories. The animal's dependence offers immediate ways to express care, allowing for the manifestation of a "good" self. The fulfillment of the associated responsibilities requires a sacrifice, which, in these stories, involves giving up drugs and alcohol or deciding to live in a car. The perceived unconditional love the animal provides, and the accompanying sense of mattering, reward the sacrifice. And the construction of the animal as the provider of this love, while simultaneously innocent of the adversity in the teller's past and yet wise to it, adds an implicitly Christ-like element to the narrative. Moreover, animals' acceptance of their human companions, despite their histories, imparts additional Christ-likeness.

Animals and the Languages of Redemption

Narratives that construct animals as their redemptive hope draw on several existing languages of redemption. Some contain distinct elements of atonement and salvation, with the teller moving from sin to forgiveness. Narratives incorporating addiction and alcoholism show influences of the language of recovery, in which the teller moves from sickness to health.[3] The narratives recounted here also employ the redemptive language of development, suggesting personal growth and lessons learned in the struggle. More important, however, the stories depicted here suggest the need to expand the list of redemption languages. In particular, the narratives constructed around animals make sense of the tellers' moves from negative to positive, from instability to relative security, through fulfilling responsibilities to an "other." Consequently, I maintain that *commitment* belongs among the languages of redemption. Although a form of commitment appears in McAdams's work, it refers to a moral steadfastness across the life-span, associated once again with the precursors of generativity (2004; McAdams et al. 1997). In contrast, I use the term to denote commitment in the context of a relationship. It encompasses the virtues of friendship, love, and compassion to narrate a redemptive move from self-interest to interdependence, even selflessness.

The culture's imaginations of animals as innocents, knowing advisers, and providers of unconditional love give even nongenerative narrators access to redemption stories. The benefits these stories hold for these particular tellers represent a unique strength of the language of commitment. Redemption, in general, casts identity in a positive light, portraying the possessor as deserving forgiveness and salvation. In stories that emphasize commitment, however, accounts of the activities associated with caring for and about an "other" help to construct a distinctly *moral* identity. Stories of commitment thus bestow a sense of self-worth—essential for everyone, but especially difficult to accomplish when resources for establishing personal significance are scarce. For homeless people and others on the margins of society, the language of commitment can "salvage the self" from reminders of a stigmatized status.

The Power and Limitations of Redemption Stories

The main power of redemption stories comes through the sense of hope they convey. The tellers talk optimistically, if cautiously, about their futures. Because they have overcome significant obstacles, they express confidence in their ability to cope with the difficulties that come their way. This is not to say that they envision the future as entirely one of sweetness and light. Rather, these tellers have specific or focused goals. Tommy wants to stay clean. Donna wants to stay alive to care for her new dog and cat. Ivy helps Denise look forward to finding housing. In sum, they have reasons for optimism. Ample research documents the benefits of optimism for emotional and physical well-being (see Bennett 2011 and McAdams et al. 2001 for reviews). Overall, optimism offers a demonstrably healthier way to face the world than pessimism. In their roles as the vehicles for redemption, animals help provide this sense of hope.

Another strong point of the redemptive self involves what it reveals about relationships among the homeless. The commitment that provides the language for these redemption stories contrasts with claims about the supposed isolation and disaffiliation of the homeless, a topic I return to in the next chapter. At the broader societal level, the importance of commitment in these narratives also contrasts with enduring claims about American individualism. Redemption stories often employ a highly individualistic vocabulary, through which the person faces his or her struggles alone. In contrast, the language of commitment conveys a sense of interdependence, where the "real me" exists, and can even thrive, because of a desire to ensure a good life for the other. This counters some of the individualism that often characterizes stories of triumph over adversity.

As in the narratives discussed in previous chapters, the redemption story casts a positive moral light on the teller's sense of self. It portrays a self that merits redemption. But unlike the other narratives, redemption stories show how the skills involved in caring for animals can translate into those required for getting off the street. I do not argue that every drug-addicted or alcoholic homeless person should have a pet. But in some cases, at least, a commitment to an animal can turn things around.

One limitation of the redemptive self is that it is not available to everyone. The redemption story is a strategy for the construction of a particular kind of identity. In the perspective I have taken in this book, I have emphasized how positionality shapes one's narrative. Consequently, it is important to reiterate that, with the exception of Denise, the tellers of these redemption stories lived more or less stably. They had made it off the street, albeit some to a "houseless but not homeless" situation. They did not live in circumstances most of us would want to emulate, but they had nevertheless attained a certain quality of life they had not experienced before, or for a long time. Even Denise believed her worst days were behind her. The tellers have survived addiction, abuse, alcoholism, depression, thoughts of suicide, and the hardships of street life. Telling a story about rising above adversity comes more easily for them now than it would have years ago. Although anyone, in any circumstance, can construct a story in which things work out for the best, it is easiest to do so when the reality of one's situation supports this conclusion. Unfortunately, that is not the case for many of those I interviewed for this book.

Finally, constructing redemption stories around animals may lead the tellers to downplay their part in their own struggles. In other words, by crediting their animals with providing the catalyst for overcoming adversity, the tellers of redemption stories may inadvertently obscure the reality that they did the "heavy lifting" of going through withdrawal, staying sober, or staying alive. Moreover, my research did not delve into the impact of these animal-centered narratives over time, but I do wonder what will happen to the sense of hope and moral steadfastness of the narrators in the absence of their animal heroes. Donna's story of Athena suggests that animals' influence endures even after their death. If this holds true for others, then we can understand relationships with animals as a symbolic force of culture that shapes an enduring redemptive self.

Notes

An earlier version of this chapter appears in an issue of the *Journal of Contemporary Ethnography* as "Animals as Lifechangers and Lifesavers: Pets in the Redemption Narratives of Homeless People," *jce.sagepub.com/content/early/2012/08/21/0891241612456550*.

1. Quotes from Pali are from interviews by Lord Martine (2002) and Sally Stephens (2006).
2. Ackerley calls Tulip an "Alsatian," as was the custom in Britain. After World War I, German Shepherds were renamed Alsatians out of fear that anti-German sentiment would make the dogs unpopular. The Kennel Club of the United Kingdom maintained that designation until 1977, when dogs could be registered either as Alsatians or as German Shepherds. In 2010, the General Committee of the Kennel Club agreed that "Alsatian" would cease to be the Kennel Club's formal name for the breed.
3. Similarly, Teresa Gowan (2010) found frequent use of "sin" and "sickness" discourses among the homeless, although in accounts of the path *to* the street instead of *away* from it.

References

Ackerley, J. R. 1965. *My Dog Tulip*. New York: New York Review Books.

Bellah, Robert N., Richard Madsen, William M. Sullivan, Ann Swidler, and Steven M. Tipton. 1985. *Habits of the Heart*. New York: Harper and Row.

Bennett, Oliver. 2011. "Cultures of Optimism." *Cultural Sociology* 5:301–20.

Erikson, Erik. 1950. *Childhood and Society*. New York: Norton.

Erikson, Kai. 1966. *Wayward Puritans: A Study in the Sociology of Deviance*. New York: Wiley.

Fitzgerald, Amy J. 2007. "'They Gave Me a Reason to Live': The Protective Effects of Companion Animals on the Suicidality of Abused Women." *Humanity & Society* 31:355–78.

Gowan, Teresa. 2010. *Hobos, Hustlers, and Backsliders: Homeless in San Francisco*. Minneapolis: University of Minnesota Press.

Irvine, Leslie. 1999. *Codependent Forevermore: The Invention of Self in a Twelve Step Group*. Chicago: University of Chicago Press.

Kerasote, Ted. 2007. *Merle's Door: Lessons from a Freethinking Dog*. New York: Harcourt.

Martine, Lord. 2002. "Saving Dogs Helped Her Save Herself." *San Francisco*

Chronicle, November 29, p. WB-5. *www.sfgate.com/cgi-bin/article.cgi?f=/ c/a/2002/11/29/WB241239.DTL.*

McAdams, Dan P. 2008. "American Identity: The Redemptive Self." *General Psychologist* 43: 20–27.

———. 2006a. *The Redemptive Self: Stories Americans Live By*. New York: Oxford University Press.

———. 2006b. "The Redemptive Self: Generativity and the Stories Americans Live By." *Research in Human Development* 3:81–100.

———. 2004. "The Redemptive Self: Narrative Identity in America Today." Pp. 95–115 in *The Self and Memory*, edited by D. Beike, J. Lampinen, and D. Behrend. New York: Psychology Press.

McAdams, Dan P., Ann Diamond, Ed de St. Aubin, and Elizabeth Mansfield. 1997. "Stories of Commitment: The Psychosocial Construction of Generative Lives." *Journal of Personality and Social Psychology* 72:678–94.

McAdams, Dan P., Jeffery Reynolds, Martha Lewis, Allison H. Patten, Phillip H. Bowman. 2001. "When Bad Things Turn Good and Good Things Turn Bad: Sequences of Redemption and Contamination in Life Narrative and their Relation to Psychosocial Adaptation in Midlife Adults and in Students." *Personality and Social Psychology Bulletin* 27:474–85.

Sanders, Clinton R. 1993. "Understanding Dogs: Caretakers' Attributions of Mindedness in Canine-Human Relationships." *Journal of Contemporary Ethnography* 22:205–26.

———. 1999. *Understanding Dogs: Living and Working with Canine Companions*. Philadelphia: Temple University Press.

Snow, David A., and Leon Anderson. 1993. *Down on Their Luck: A Study of Homeless Street People*. Berkeley: University of California Press.

Stephens, Sally. 2006. "For the Love of a Dog." *The Woofer Times*, January, p. 1. *www .rocketdogrescue.org/pdfs/woofertimes06.pdf*. Accessed 3/2/12

Tough, Paul. 2011. "The Poverty Clinic." *New Yorker*, March 21, 25–32.

Wills, Gary. 1990. *Under God: Religion and American Politics*. New York: Simon & Schuster.